P9-EGN-632

THE FREEDOMS WE LOST

THE FREEDOMS WE LOST

CONSENT AND RESISTANCE IN REVOLUTIONARY AMERICA

Barbara Clark Smith

THE NEW PRESS

NEW YORK
LONDON

Published in the United States by The New Press, New York, 2010
Distributed by Perseus Distribution

ISBN 978-1-59558-180-8

The New Press was established in 1990 as a not-for-profit alternative to the large,
commercial publishing houses currently dominating the book publishing industry.
The New Press operates in the public interest rather than for private gain, and
is committed to publishing, in innovative ways, works of educational, cultural,
and community value that are often deemed insufficiently profitable.

Composition by NK Graphics
This book was set in Janson

Printed in the United States of America

Book Club Edition

For Dan,
Hattie, and Hal

Contents

Preface

Colonial Americans were less free than we are, and in countless ways. Their political theories accepted lack of freedom as normal and often desirable. Their society promoted and protected the enslavement of African, African American, and Indian women, men, and children; encouraged the free poor to submit themselves to years of legal servitude; bound propertyless youth to long apprenticeships; and expected women of every social class to enter the potentially lifelong bonds of marriage, in which they would enjoy few rights either to property, the earnings of their labors, or a public voice of their own.[1] When it came to making decisions about the policies of government or framing legislation for their society, even those free, white men who were blessed with some property, skills, and independence were seen as having limited competence at best. One cliché of British North American politics ran like this: "A cobbler in his Stall can easily tell whether the Nation is well or ill governed."[2] But the people who said that tended to be gentlemen, and they often praised the cobbler in order to emphasize their own, superior capacities by contrast. (If even the cobbler could tell, then educated members of the political elite were surely qualified to criticize government policies.) Besides, that was the relatively generous position on cobblers, held by Englishmen of the "Real Whig" tradition and adopted by colonists for its usefulness in opposing high-handed governors appointed by authorities an ocean away. There was another saying about cobblers that was also familiar in British North America and that showed less respect for the humble artisan's po-

litical judgment. Certain men should govern and think about government, but tradesmen should keep their minds on their labors. Thus, "a
cobbler should stick to his last."[3] Political writers who said that reminded
the lesser people that government stood above their ken; and, when they
put the phrase in Latin ("Ne sutor ultra crepidam"), writers made clear
that even the *discussion* of political competence, let alone the discussion of
public policy, belonged in the hands of the educated, privileged, undoubtedly well-shod few.

Cobblers did pretty well in British North America, as did tradesmen
with finer skills and the great many farmers who owned at least a bit of
land. Compared to Europe, American society offered opportunities. One
immigrant spoke of Pennsylvania as the "best poor man's country," and
indeed contemporaries associated the continental colonies not with poverty
but prosperity.[4] In their eyes, it was a society striking for the numbers
of the "middling" sort of people and for the ease of middling acquisition. Nonetheless, the common man's comfort and opportunity did not
routinely or easily translate into substantial political say. For the most part,
in most places, the powers of provincial government resided in the hands
of a narrow elite: in Southern colonies, a planter aristocracy; elsewhere, a
mix of prosperous landholders, well-to-do merchants, traders, and professional men.

From stem to stern, top to bottom, these people accepted many aspects
of social and political inequality and claimed that such inequality had
been established by God. How different the America of the twenty-first
century, the century we are now entering, shaped and illumined by ideals
of equality, humanity, diversity, and participation. How different, indeed,
the nineteenth century, when slavery was attacked and marriage modified; when African Americans and women reached for a political voice; and
when propertyless free white men in most states of the nation acquired the
vote. When the workingmen of Philadelphia organized to promote their
own interests in 1828, it was a signal advance for cobblers and their kind.
Above all, by the nineteenth century, America had discarded monarchy in
preference for government of, by, and for the people. Who could question that this was radical change, or that it was a new and meaningful
birth of freedom?

It is far from my intention to dispute the idea that people gained freedoms during the Revolutionary era and the years and transformations
that followed. I would not be so foolish as to suggest that we should
wax nostalgic about colonial times, or yearn for the opportunity implied
by white families' access to "open" or "free" land, bought at the cost of

dispossession of Native American peoples. Nor does it seem to me that knowing later generations would dismantle some social and political inequalities makes inessential the colonial era's powerful commitment to those inequalities. Undeniably, in early America, a relative few enjoyed riches, a fair number enjoyed middling status, and many suffered from structures of inequality that allowed small and large tyrannies along lines of class, gender, age, and race. Early America was no golden age.

This book proposes something far more modest and (so I hope) far more reasonable. I want to suggest that there existed in colonial America elements of liberty, forms of participation in public affairs, that later generations would not experience. Put differently, I want to raise the possibility that some (not all) colonial Americans were not so much *less* free than succeeding generations, as *differently* free. Their understanding of liberty is not adequately measured by nineteenth-century ideas and institutions, nor by later centuries' unalloyed celebration of the Revolution and its aftermath. What happens if we view colonial Americans without being certain that the freedom they lacked was more important than the freedom they had? What if we suspend the certainty that being subject to the British crown was necessarily (in every way and for everyone) *less* than being a citizen of the U.S. state? To do that is to question the belief that what is delivered or at least promised under the aegis of the American state, on the American continent, can be neatly identified with human freedom, *tout court*. The promises of citizenship are not to be despised, and, as I will reflect in an epilogue to this book, the rights of citizenship are not so secure or universally enjoyed, even in U.S. society, as to be taken for granted or belittled. Nonetheless, without diminishing the rights of citizens of the United States, I want to explore the freedoms of subjects in colonial America. Those freedoms included participatory forms that, however wanting by some standards, many people who lived two and a half centuries ago dearly prized. My goal is to understand that sort of freedom and the sort of Revolution that British subjects in America waged—in part, at least—through its exercise and on its behalf.

.   .   .

This book makes a number of arguments that I want to summarize here. The first chapter surveys what I call the "common ground" of colonial political life—the sites at which, and the forms by which, relatively ordinary or common male colonists were accustomed to play a part. By "ordinary" and "common," I mean to designate free, white men, many of whom owned sufficient property to vote for a delegate to their provincial legislature, but who did not aspire to serve as a representative or other provincial figure themselves. To call them "ordinary" is not to suggest that they had no privileges over others, or that they composed a majority of the population, or that their situation represents the situation of those outside their ranks. Rather, I mean to emphasize their location in relationship to provincial political institutions: these were men who, however free and capable of consenting to government, would themselves be ruled rather than rulers in colonial societies. In social terms, they were common rather than genteel; they were the cobblers, rather than the men who pronounced upon the political abilities of cobblers. The political forms proper to such men included the vote and other forms of participation as well. Indeed, chapter 1 contends that the "common ground" embraced a surprising range of occasions on which ordinary men's status was sufficient and ordinary men's knowledge was enough to establish significant political agency. Recovering those occasions involves recovering types of freedom that many British subjects of the eighteenth century assumed themselves to possess. That project takes us beyond the vote, that act of consent which later generations would put at the center of political life, to emphasize political participation outside the electoral moment.

Chapter 2 turns from political forms to the historical and social experience that shaped ordinary colonists' use of those forms. For to know that many men enjoyed liberties, that they had opportunities to participate, is not yet to know how and why they treasured those liberties and used those opportunities. When they acted to make their ideals felt in their society, what beliefs and commitments moved them? We know that many colonists shared a wariness about the dangers of what they often called "oppression," and that their perception of British policies as oppressive would rally them to resist in the years after the French and Indian War. Chapter 2 offers an essential background to understanding that resistance movement. It surveys specific social institutions that shaped many colonists' ideas of what was right and fair, including such institutions as household, neighborhood, and congregation. These institutions deeply informed men's understanding of transactions that took place in the market, the law, and the empire. This is to say that many people viewed broad matters of economic, legal, and imperial import through the lens of their experiences in relationships closer to home. In particular, I will suggest, experiences and ideals of "neighboring" colored their perceptions. In the British and Protestant traditions of the era, neighboring represented the antithesis of oppression, and concrete practices of neighborhood life could provide an antidote to or at least a bulwark against it. Chapter 2 shows that, to a striking extent, in the face of would-be oppressors, colonists made recourse to the claims of neighborhood standards and networks of neighborhood obligation. Those standards and networks were central to many colonists' capacity for and practice of *being* "the people."

In chapter 3 I turn to the resistance movement that Americans formed in response to British policies of the mid-1760s and 1770s. Calling themselves "Sons of Liberty" or—what became the most popular term—"Patriots," many colonists mobilized against what they saw as British oppression. In that mobilization, I argue, the political forms of the common ground and the social values of neighboring both played a significant role. That role has rarely been fully recognized, in part because historians have paid more attention to the reasons and resources of elite Patriots than of ordinary ones. Moreover, we have been quicker to identify—and identify with—the Revolutionaries' declarations of independence than their claims of neighboring, or mutual *interdependence*. Viewing the resistance as it unfolded on the common ground, however, offers a new perspective on the Patriot cause. In popular crowd actions and boycotts of trade, ordinary colonists expressed the understanding that Patriots—significantly called *"friends* to their country"—were those who put aside self-interest and self-regard to join with their neighbors in common cause.

Indeed, the Patriot movement represented a coalition that joined colonists across lines of region, belief, interest, and social class. In forming that coalition, colonists of the ordinary sort worked to establish a broad public jurisdiction over political, economic, and social actions, requiring that all those who aspired to be recognized as "Patriots" renounce aspirations to oppress, that they establish themselves thereby as neighbors and brethren to one another. Chapter 3 shows that the ideal of neighboring— unquestionably within the compass of ordinary people and ordinary knowledge—rendered the Patriot movement hospitable to the participation of many men outside the ranks of the elite, and even to the participation of some women. Such colonists claimed a capacity to determine the direction and boundaries of the resistance movement. For their part, elite Patriots distinguished themselves from more conservative members of their social class by their willingness to accept their lesser neighbors' claims. When they renounced subjecthood to George III, in other words, many Americans understood themselves to remain subject to and members within a larger society.

Chapter 4 traces both the persistence and the unraveling of the coalition between elite and ordinary Patriots during the years 1776 to 1780. During these years, the common cause continued to depend profoundly on the participation of ordinary men and on their standards of Patriotism. We see this most particularly in popular agitation for sharing the burdens of the war, for equitable pricing and supply of goods, and against the influence of Loyalists within American societies. In these contests, many continued to measure Patriotism by the standards and values of neighboring. Yet public debates about popular political activity and the related issue of social and financial policy began to divide the movement. Like other historians before me, I see a change in the nature of the Revolution around the year 1780. By then, a good many leading Patriots sought to discredit and discourage popular participation, whether by voters or by participants in crowds and committees. Many of the Patriot elite became less hospitable to ordinary men's participation, as they became more concerned with winning the support of moneyed men. These pages take us through the decline of the original Patriot coalition and to the brink of a new coalition, one that would recast the meaning of Patriotism and the purposes of the Revolution.

Finally, the book's closing chapter takes stock of these changes. I explore disputes in the 1780s that explicitly challenged commitments once central to the common cause. By the end of the decade, Americans lived under a new constitutional order. They discovered that forms of participation once proper to subjects of Britain might appear inappropriate—even impermissible—to citizens of the United States.

Acknowledgments

This book originated just this side of "time immemorial." More than most, these acknowledgments will surely be inadequate as expressions of my indebtedness and gratitude to others. Still, I will do my best.

I owe a tremendous amount to supervisors at the National Museum of American History, Smithsonian Institution, who generously provided me with research time, especially Roger Kennedy, Brent Glass, Gary Kulik, Jim Gardner, Anne Golovin, Susan Myers, Harry Rubenstein, and the late Rodris Roth. I would also like to thank the wonderful librarians at the National Museum, including Chris Cottrill, Rhoda Ratner, James Roan, and Stephanie Thomas. Thanks also to a museum intern, Kelly Ruppel, who caught errors in an early draft. I am grateful in a profound way to curators and other museum professionals who provide an essential community at the Smithsonian. I have been sustained by their intellectual companionship for many years; I continue to be inspired by their dedication to collaboration and public service.

Outside the museum, I want to thank participants in the Fall Line Early Americanists group, who read some chapter drafts and provided valuable feedback. Especial thanks to Woody Holton and Marion Winship, who generously read outside the group as well. At the University of Virginia, Professors Peter S. Onuf and Charles W. McCurdy took time to answer my questions. Reference librarians in the Humanities and Social Sciences at Alderman Library and in Special Collections, University of Virginia, have been unfailingly helpful.

I am also grateful for the institutional support of the John Carter Brown Library in Providence, Rhode Island, and the American Council of Learned Societies.

I have a particular intellectual debt to a number of high school history teachers, with whom I have explored the American Revolution at a variety of workshops over the years. I particularly want to thank participants at the New-York Historical Society's 2003 Summer Institute and the Boston People and Places Program. These teachers kept me on point by asking probing questions not about historiographical disputes but about more important topics, such as human freedom. Drawing on their experience in classrooms, they also helped to confirm my distinctly nonacademic suspicion that people who fill authoritative roles sometimes follow—and nearly always negotiate with—those whom they apparently lead.

Many people have read or listened to ideas in this book and responded with valuable insights and questions. I particularly want to thank Hattie Bluestone, Herbert Tico Braun, Peter Dimock, Susan Mackinnon, Janet Ray, Jamie Ross, Howard Singerman, Jeff Schneider, Henry Bluestone Smith, Al Young, Rosemarie Zagarri, and Michael Zuckerman. My gratitude to Linda Bierer as well. Aaron Wunch helped me with many puzzling questions, and Daniel Bluestone read, commented, but mostly encouraged. I have been lucky to have the benefit of encouraging editors, including Deb Chasman at the *Boston Review* and the patient Marc Favreau at The New Press.

Not least, profound thanks to Professor Edmund S. Morgan, who years ago encouraged my interest in the complexities of American freedom.

·   ·   ·

This book incorporates arguments I have made in earlier publications: "Social Visions of the American Resistance Movement," in *The Transforming Hand of Revolution: Reconsidering the American Revolution as a Social Movement*, ed. Ronald Hoffman and Peter J. Albert (Charlottesville: University of Virginia Press, 1996), 27–57; "The Freedoms We Lost," *Boston Review*, February/March 2004; "Beyond the Vote: The Limits of Deference in Colonial Politics," *Early American Studies: An Interdisciplinary Journal* 3, no. 2 (Fall 2005): 341–62.

1

The Common Ground of Colonial Politics

In 1768, the Reverend George Micklejohn of North Carolina described what happened when colonists voted for representatives to their provincial legislatures: "We not only yield our consent before-hand to whatever laws they may judge it expedient to enact, but may justly be said to have had a principle share in enacting them ourselves, inasmuch as they are framed by their wisdom, and established by their authority, whom we have appointed for that very purpose."[1] In Micklejohn's account, the consent that took place through elections was essential to colonial governments' claims of rule—and their expectations that the people would obey the law, pay what taxes were levied, and abide by decisions of the court system that carried their statutes into execution. Equally important (and here was the reverend's main point), Micklejohn claimed that consent through legislative elections was *sufficient*. Having chosen representatives, or "appointed" them to pass laws, the people had had their say. Now they should recognize that the law had binding force.

This logic would make sense to later Americans, for the act of consenting through the vote would be central to their political lives. Our government can claim to be "by the people" precisely because the electorate has chosen representatives to make and execute the law for us. Yet modern Americans' focus on the ballot box—on what Micklejohn called "before-hand" occasions of consent—can make it difficult for us to understand the freedoms that mattered to many colonists in eighteenth-century British North America. For voting was not the only form of

political participation in that era, and Micklejohn's view of political obligation was not the only one. When we consider the farmers, tradesmen,
and shopkeepers of colonial America as voters, we grasp only one element of their political identities.

Indeed, Micklejohn spoke before the governor of the colony and some
1,400 assembled militiamen, a group that had gathered precisely because
hundreds of North Carolina farmers disputed the notion that they were
obliged to submit to decisions of the legislature. They did not feel obligated to pay taxes levied by their representatives or to allow the court of
law in their county to bring suspected criminals to trial. Some of these
farmers, too, had had the opportunity to vote for representatives to the
North Carolina legislative assembly. Yet they apparently believed that they
had not thereby consented "before-hand" to its acts; or else that such consent was insufficient to make the law binding; or perhaps that, having
given consent before, they might go on to withdraw their consent after-
ward. These farmers were unusual in the extent of their disaffection from
provincial government, but not in many of their basic tenets and assumptions. Their position won sympathy from many New Englanders who
read about it in the press, for example, and from time to time colonists in
every province acted according to the same principles, as if obedience to
the law were in some respects, or on some occasions, optional rather than
mandatory.[2] Throughout the colonies, people responded to the official
summons of authorities selectively; they routinely evaded or mitigated
various laws, not infrequently challenged courts, and openly disobeyed
magistrates who sought to inform them of what the law required. Put differently, many colonists sometimes claimed a right to consent after their
representatives created legislation. They were accustomed not only to
being *represented* "before-hand," but also to being *present* in the execution
of the law that had been passed.

This chapter explores popular representation and the popular presence in colonial British America. It surveys an arena that I call the "common ground" of colonial politics, defined as the institutions in which, and
the terms on which, those common men who qualified as political agents
were accustomed to act. In these institutions, ordinary status was acknowledged to be sufficient and ordinary knowledge acknowledged to be
enough. On this ground, colonists acted in at least three ways. First, they
were subjects of the king, mere commoners who (alongside their social
inferiors) filled a role as spectators of the drama of state.[3] Second, they
acted as Micklejohn described them, as voters in provincial affairs who
selected legislators to play an increasingly significant consenting and gov-

erning role. Finally, they constituted a presence "after the fact," in processes of executing the law. Through these varied political forms, common men made their notions of fairness and right felt within their society.

The People as Subjects

The men who lived in the American colonies were subjects, not citizens. They lived in a system that located power and authority at the top. Thus, "Rulers are Gods," said the Reverend Ebenezer Pemberton in 1710, and if other colonists in Massachusetts Bay might have dissented, the clergyman probably pleased some of his audience, which included the royal governor, lieutenant governor, council, and lower house of the provincial legislature.[4] In colonies less known for piety, officials less concerned with religion similarly tied secular power to God's will. In 1741, South Carolina Chief Justice Benjamin Whitaker explained why colonists should obey the commands of government and the provisions of the law. "Let every man in a private Station . . . 'be subject to the higher Powers because there is no power but of God.'" These were the sentiments of Christian monarchy, which focused power in the being of the king and the symbol of the crown.[5]

The model for this idea was the English monarch, and it had to be admitted that, in normal times at least, God indeed determined the English succession by blessing specific kings and queens with specific offspring in specific birth order. Monarchs were the Almighty's vice-regents on earth, even if some of them ruled poorly or conducted themselves vilely. Indeed, the idea that authority came from God might not excuse monarchs' misdeeds but rather limit their transgressions. Being God's vice-regent was a responsibility—how onerous only rulers themselves were likely to know—and English theorists and parliamentary leaders used that fact to recall monarchs to their duty. When, as happened rather often under the reign of the Stuarts, the king adopted a policy that parliamentary leaders considered oppressive, they responded by endorsing his divinity and attacking his plans. After all, God's vice-regent could not wish to be oppressive of the people. Surely, then, designing courtiers or ministers had misinformed the king or hidden their own ambitions behind his name, so that true loyalty to the monarch required subjects to oppose these new and oppressive policies. By this logic, the association between rulers and God's will was not always permissive but sometimes prescriptive: rulers *should* be gods, or approximate them at least. It was a high standard of behavior. A good ruler would be merciful and just, rule in kindness to his people, and do God's will. The Stuarts were not the only ones who might have difficulty measuring up to that.[6]

Whether or not they were successful at acting like gods, rulers put effort into appearing godlike, or at least dignified, authoritative, and impressive. Not televised in their subjects' living rooms or even represented by likenesses in the press, rulers of the early modern era might appear to their subjects in two significant ways. First, their images were cast on coins, conferring value on the money and receiving it back in turn. Second, monarchs themselves circulated. They appeared in person on a variety of public occasions, formal presentations, celebrations, and anniversaries. Elizabeth I was particularly fond of doing this. She "progressed" her realm, from one to another urban center, providing her subjects with a glittering and dramatic pageantry. In January of 1559, for example, she traveled through London, bedecked in gold cloth and jewelry and carried on an open litter attended by one thousand horsemen. Here was the dramatic power of artistic representation deployed to create charismatic effect. Other actors, too, took the stage on such occasions, as local lords, gentlemen, and officials of varying ranks recognized and responded to the queen's majesty in heavily ritualized interactions. Large numbers of spectators of different social classes had the opportunity to watch the proceedings, as their social superiors symbolically laid claim to status at the center of power.[7] Subjects enjoyed the opportunity to observe the majesty of the crown, to recognize and acknowledge the monarch and subordinate officials. Cobblers who lined the streets or stood at nearby windows were able to tell that they were being splendidly governed. Although monarchs could not be everywhere, in provincial towns local officials enacted similar ceremonies, celebrating monarchy and grandeur in the absence of the king or queen. Even those who were unable to attend such events could read in cheap published ballads, broadsides, and chapbooks detailed accounts of processions, coronations, and other ceremonies.[8]

Colonists lacked the opportunity to view monarchs in the New World, but they made the most of occasions when they could view the lesser figures that they had. All the colonies were ruled by a governor, and though a couple of these were elected, most were appointed by a proprietary lord or the king himself. These governors generally arrived in capital cities armed with papers stamped with the royal seal and with written instructions that expressed the will of the Crown, establishing their status as vice-regents of God's vice-regent. When they arrived in colonial capitals they expected due ceremony, so that towns such as Annapolis, New York,

Boston, and Philadelphia were the scene of processions from time to time. In 1758, for example, Francis Bernard landed in Trenton, New Jersey, to take up the government, and the inhabitants provided a proper reception: "His Excellency was received at this antient Seat of Government with great Demonstration of Joy, and having received the Compliments of numbers of Gentlemen of Distinction, the Evening was concluded with Bonfires, Illuminations, ringing of Bells, &c." Elements of the festivities were reserved for the elite of the city, but processions to "the large Meeting-House," where the governor's commission was read, and to "the House of Mr. Shaw," provided the populace at large the opportunity to observe the new governor and local worthies. The mass of people could approve the occasion by attending bonfires in the streets or setting lights in their windows as demonstrations of joy. Custom decreed that the Jersey governor travel to Burlington and Perth Amboy for public ceremonies as well.[9] Two years later, Bernard traveled overland to become governor of Massachusetts, and inhabitants along his route took the occasion to show their respects. "The people had conceived a favourable opinion of him, and evidenced it by publick marks of respect, as he traveled through the province, and upon his arrival at the seat of government." Transitions in government needed to be publicly marked by processions of the few and the great, and the processions needed to be observed by the many and the small.[10]

On these and similar occasions, colonial governors and other high officials were expected to make efforts to be dignified and charismatic. The first governor of Massachusetts, John Winthrop, encouraged the colony's legislative and judicial leaders to exert conscious efforts to make a proper entrance: "Magistrates shall appear more solemnly in public, with attendance, apparel, and open notice of their entrance into court." When well done, it would excite admiration. "The Superior Court met yesterday and made a Good Figure," wrote a merchant approvingly. Again, those who missed the exciting spectacle might read about it in the press. Governors in particular should live, dress, and act like king's vice-regents. The governor's house in Williamsburg, Virginia, was impressive, and the North Carolina legislature agreed to spend thousands of pounds sterling to create a "palace" for the governor's residence in the town of New Bern. In Connecticut, Governor Gurden Saltonstall acknowledged that some people considered him "too strict, severe, and lordly," but noted that his office entitled him "to deserve submission and accordingly to expect it."[11] Indeed, it disrupted right order when rulers and officials failed to set themselves apart and above, or when ordinary people failed to recognize their superiority. In York County, Pennsylvania, a man named William Hatton was found guilty of contempt of court when he insulted justices of the county by "calling them Coopers, hogg trough makers, Pedlars, Cobblers, tailors, weavers, & saying they are not fitting to sit where they doe sit."[12] Hatton's case testifies to the expectation that magistrates should be more august than such lowly tradesmen, as well as to their willingness to use the force of law to punish aspersions on their dignity. Kings, governors, judges and magistrates were supposed to be superiors. There were occasions when a qualified voter himself stood above the lesser members of his society; nonetheless, in the face of the king and his officials, voters and nonvoters alike served as audience for the great pageantry of state.

The People as Voters

On the face of it, such a system left little for the people to do but serve and submit, for rulers were exalted far above the ordinary people. Citizens have a dignity; subjects were, after all, subjected.[13] This mode of thinking logically had an impact on ideas about government, as those that informed the plans of proprietors and lords who shaped New World colonies. Thus, having seized New Netherlands from the Dutch in 1666, the Duke of York appointed a governor and a council to rule his province; he required nothing of the rest of the people in the settlement "but obedience and submission to the Lawes" those authorities would proclaim.[14] Some years later, William Penn planned his colony of Pennsylvania to afford greater participation for the common people. He began with first principles of Whig political philosophy. "It has been the judgment of the wisest men and practice of the most famous governments in all ages, as well as that it is most natural, reasonable, and prudent in itself, that the people of any country should be consenting to the laws they are to be governed by."[15] Yet consent did not necessarily amount to very much; Penn, too, imagined ruling chiefly through and with his appointed councilors. His Second Frame of Government—the plan that first took effect in the colony— gave legislative initiative to the governor and council. Only once these gentlemen had agreed among themselves on desirable policies would they refer the matter to the "freemen of the province," who might concur with their leaders' policies through the medium of representatives elected from each county. The representatives' prerogatives were narrowly hedged: they would spend eight days conferring, send proposals for changes back to the governor and council, then on the ninth day either accept or reject the bills the council and governor proposed.[16] This arrangement barely approximated the situation that Rev. Micklejohn described, in which ordinary freemen "had a principle share" in legislation. Here, the people's power to consent boiled down to the right of freemen to vote for representatives, who in turn had little power beyond saying yes or no to policies devised by their superiors.

The Proprietors of Carolina similarly envisioned elected representatives who would be "mere witnesses" to the actions of their betters. In early New Jersey, proprietor Sir George Carteret declared that the governor and his council would decide what measures to introduce into the assembly for the representatives' consideration. And English officials of the 1670s and 1680s, seeking to consolidate control over their growing empire, hoped to govern all the North American colonies with legislation that took shape only at the top. The British Lords of Trade ruled Ireland under a law called Poynings' Act, which reserved initiative over legislative bills to themselves and provided for the Irish parliament to assent or withhold assent. Royal governors in both Virginia and Jamaica received instructions to secure legislative enactment of several bills that had already been drawn up in England. In future, moreover, governors were to draft bills in collaboration with their councils, secure approval from the Privy Council in London, and only then submit the bills to the provincial assembly. The House of Burgesses in Williamsburg seemed amenable to the limited initiative powers they would enjoy under the new arrangement, but Jamaican legislators strongly protested being reduced to the position of Irishmen. Their opposition scuttled English plans to extend the practice to other royal colonies.[17] Despite that, it remained an underlying principle of much political thinking: men at the top would formulate policy, after which the lesser sort would respond.

In this perspective, consent properly remained to the people after the informed and knowledgeable people had established the law, formed the policy, debated and considered the bill. After all, the right to legislate came from above. As William Penn told a correspondent, King James II's patent to him provided "that I and my heirs, with the assent of the freemen or their deputies, from time to time may make laws" in his colony.[18] Likewise, other proprietors of New World provinces derived their power to make laws from royal grants. Surely they might consult the people's representatives. Yet the role of the people's representatives was reactive; they were to respond after the policy had been established. Such was the role of assemblymen because such was the power appropriate to the merely common people. As Penn put it, assemblymen should under no circumstances act as "debator[s], or judges, or complainers." And this was because assemblymen were commoners, capable of telling whether they were well governed perhaps, but in no way governors themselves. They could offer a "negative voyce" to the plans of their superiors; yet theirs was "not a debateing, mending, altering, but an accepting or rejecting pow'r."[19] Such power does not seem so very different from the popular role at official processions: as when the executive progressed, so when the executive proposed policy, the common people might recognize what they saw and tell whether they were well governed.

To the distress of proprietors and governors, matters were by no means as simple as that. Although many colonies were founded in an era when power was seen to flow from above, there were other ideas abroad in the seventeenth and eighteenth centuries. As early as 1604, a committee of the House of Commons prepared a statement to inform King James I of their own role in relationship to his government. They believed that their body was essential to the passage of laws and, most particularly, to initiating laws that levied taxes and raised revenues from the people. Chosen by voters in the counties and boroughs of the realm, members of the House were entitled and obliged to petition the monarch for redress of their constituents' grievances. They might provide good counsel, offering "public information as to the civil estate and government" in different parts of the realm. Although they were undoubtedly lesser than the king, the Commons acted on their own source of authority. The Commons spoke with "the voice of the people," and in some affairs of life—"in things of their knowledge"—the voice of the people "is said to be as the voice of God."[20] That saying also came in learned language: vox populi, vox Dei, and the premise it expressed allowed even commoners sometimes to have their influence on the government of England.

Indeed, when the Stuarts ignored the advice of Parliament and denied its authority, the people of England removed them from power. Strictly speaking, James II was the last English monarch who could properly style himself God's vice-regent. His successors, beginning with William and Mary, needed to accept that God spoke through the people as well as the monarch, and that the nation accordingly required a constitution that balanced those powers. A balanced constitution gave an important role to the people's representatives in the legislature.

These members of Parliament were common in the strict sense, neither royal nor noble. But those distinctions—royalty, nobility, commonalty—were wholly insufficient to describe society either in England or its Atlantic colonies: the category of commonalty had always embraced families of widely varying fortunes. John Logan, an English authority on social rank and its public recognition, noted that people's social aspirations and resulting practice had long supplemented the distinctions between nobles and commoners. "Although by the Civil Law there be no Gentlemen of Title under Knights, but all the rest went under the name of People; yet with us there are in this rank which have names of Preheminence, whereby they are in Degree above the rest, as Esquires and Gentlemen, all of which have Ensigns of Coats of Arms and thereby are distinguished from the meaner People."[21] Riding in expensive carriages decorated with family ensigns of coats of arms, esquires and gentlemen distinguished themselves in the language of political and social hierarchy. Logan cited another authority on the quality of gentlemen and esquires: "*Bartoll's Tract de Ensignes* calleth them Noble; but yet of weak Nobility; for it hath no further Prerogative in it, than it makes them differ from the baser sort of People." No further prerogative—which was to say, gentlemen and esquires possessed no automatic political privilege or position by virtue of their status, as did peers, who enjoyed the distinction of sitting in the House of Lords and being tried for crimes only by one another. But if no political position necessarily came with the status of gentleman, it was increasingly true in practice that only somewhat minor local positions would come without that status. The gentry class, with ensigns painted on their carriage doors and incised on their silver teapots, took on various trappings of nobility.[22] And though English law did not worry much about the niceties that distinguished gentlemen and esquires from one another, the distinction of these men of "preheminence" from the baser sort was essential, at least to them. In the House of Commons, members wielded more power as they came less to resemble the bulk of "the common people" of the realm.

The rise of the English Parliament found a parallel in the North American colonies, where assemblies also gradually gained power and stature. All the colonies did develop representative legislative bodies, called variously "the commons house," "the House of Burgesses," or just "the assembly." In these institutions, the representatives of the people increasingly took on an initiating function. In clashes with governors and sometimes with governors' councils, colonial assemblies modeled themselves on the House of Commons in England and gradually asserted a variety of rights and privileges. They sought the right to be "debators and complainers," including the right to deliberate, to speak their sentiments on the floor of the House without fear of legal retribution, even if those words might offend governors or proprietors. In the course of the eighteenth century, assemblies acquired these and other prerogatives of their own—most crucially, the sole right to initiate money bills. Controlling the purse strings, including the governor's salary, was often tantamount to controlling policy; at the least it conveyed the ability to frustrate many of the best-laid plans of Privy Counsellors and the monarch's vice-regents.[23] In the colonies, too, then, power shifted toward common men, and voters might congratulate themselves that their delegates now had greater voice.

As in England, moreover, as they became more elite, representatives became less representative. In a world neatly divided between rulers and people, the representatives' gain in initiative power created some logical ambiguity about their status. Were they rulers, who might "judge, debate, or complain," or were they people, who might only acquiesce to power? Their social status certainly set them above the majority. By 1750, the combined wealth of members of the English House of Commons surpassed that of the Lords; in British North America, the economic stature of representatives varied somewhat from province to province.[24] Yet every American society likewise developed elites. The Southern gentry was known for its impressive adaption of aristocratic forms, but great families acquired substantial fortunes and power in every colony. Men with mercantile wealth in New England, proprietors of great estates along the Hudson Valley, proprietors in the colony of New Jersey, landholders in the Connecticut River Valley called "River Gods"—all dominated their societies in both social and political terms. In South Carolina, a man had to fulfill a higher property requirement to serve in the assembly than merely to vote for a representative.[25] In other colonies, too, though it might be called "the commons house," the assembly comprised men who were distinctly superior to the average. English Quaker Thomas Rudyard had worried that some delegates to the Pennsylvania legislature would be small men, "having only 50, 100, or 200 acres," who, being "of such parts Education abilityes &c. as theyl probably be—may produce Clamour Insolence Ambition, if not worse; such person[s] being unmete for councill and Govermt."[26] At times there were clamor, insolence, and ambition in the Pennsylvania government, but even members of the lower house in the colony tended to be men of property, education, and pretensions to gentility. In Massachusetts one royal governor complained that most assemblymen there could boast only "small fortune and mean education." And a Maryland governor similarly disparaged burgesses there as "the lowest Persons at least Men of small fortunes no Soul and very mean Capacities."[27] Yet this was a top-down view that exaggerated the case. True, residency requirements in most colonies meant that some deputies from relatively new and undeveloped constituencies would be less exalted than some might desire; but middling men who made it to the legislature would generally qualify as "backbenchers" at best, remaining outside the circles of substantive power. The representatives were generally established men, and legislative leaders were more established than most. Governors' criticisms aside, by most standards most deputies to the lower house ranked as well-to-do and socially "preheminent."[28] Many delegates could boast impressive educations, either at colonial colleges or at English institutions "at home." By the mid-eighteenth century, moreover, a growing number were the sons of men who had themselves served in office; political leadership was growing more exclusive, more continuous, less reflective of colonial societies as a whole. If their wealth and social standing would have impressed few in England, provincial legislators might still preside at home. They were the sort of people who were accustomed to debate and complain.

There was a rationale behind this idea, not that riches might reflect an individual's ability, but that property (especially in land) would tie his interest to the interest of the larger community. Beyond that, the enjoyment of property allowed men to develop ability. Rudyard wrote as if England had conducted a careful experiment: "The more Considerable and Valluable (in terra firma, &c.) our representatives have bin, with the greater honour & safety to the nation and its reputation also have they carried on & managed Affaires."[29] More succinctly: the richer, especially in landed estate, the better. Members of the House of Commons must be commoners, but not of the common sort. Riches might allow for ability, providing the blessings of education and the breadth of a cosmopolitan outlook. Learning was necessary, because statecraft was difficult, policy making complex. The ruler required "Time to be spent in Reading and Study in order to furnish him with Knowledge in State Affairs, that he might serve the Publick the better."[30] William Douglass of Boston seconded that view in 1749: "A Man of Reading, Observation, and daily conversant with Affairs of Police and Commerce, is certainly better qualified for a Legislator, than a Retailer of Rum and small Beer called a Tavern-keeper."[31] What qualified the legislator was book learning, but also a wider scope of cosmopolitan attainments, experience in the world's affairs. This view sharply limited the possible candidates for office, for access to such knowledge was limited. Literacy was widespread among white men at least, but only the lucky few received substantial education. Men with classical learning and contacts with the wider cosmopolitan world had first claim on political as well as social leadership. Against this claim, some political analysts promoted the idea that a good representative must not differ too greatly from his constituents; ultimately, a delegate should have the same interest as the voters. Nonetheless, no one argued that representatives with less learning, fewer achievements, or more narrow outlook should be preferred. The key was to find a loyal superior, not an average man. The trouble with the cobbler was that he was confined to "his stall," plying his trade and serving his customers within the narrow bounds of parochial experience. Nor was a cobbler likely to pick up cosmopolitan ideas from elite customers. Leading men did not typically inform their inferiors about policy or expect to discuss current affairs with them. If the educated wrote pamphlets about political matters, they generally addressed an audience of their peers. There were some exceptions, particularly in the heterogeneous middle colonies, when a writer would sometimes address the voters in a partisan style. Most, however, continued to assume that a substantial line separated the concerns of ordinary men from the affairs of government. When a philosopher such as Bernard Mandeville spoke of "the Art of Governing," he meant to indicate that local and common knowledge about ordinary affairs was insufficient to understand matters of state. Men needed particular or specialized knowledge to govern; it was outside the ordinary, and the merely common men were thus excluded from much of the conversation. *Ne sutor ultra crepidam.*[32]

In practice, the delegates to colonial houses of assembly combined two statuses: they were both ruled and rulers. They were common men, at one with their constituents. In countless communications with the governor they spoke for "the people," and they generally wrote as if "the government" included only the executive and the upper house or council. At the same time, or a moment later, they were better and wiser, especially chosen and entrusted for rule. They were "servants of the people" who were nonetheless most people's social superiors. They had it both ways. In the logic of the era, they held power because they were the common men; they had substantial power because they were not.[33]

The language of the day acknowledged the ongoing difficulty over the actual status of representatives: awkwardly, there was a specific term needed to designate "the people" as a body outside the lower house of the legislature. The phrase "the people out-of-doors" came into use as a way of acknowledging while also denying the claims of the House of Commons to constitute "the people" of England. In like manner, in the colonies writers sometimes specified that the people "without doors"—outside the legislature—had ideas and sentiments that might differ from those of their representatives within. Only rarely, however, were such ideas considered helpful to ongoing government decision-making. Local constituents might certainly petition their legislature for an alteration in law, and the representative's job surely involved promoting local interests at the provincial capital. Yet the job did not necessarily involve following constituent instructions about how to vote on any particular issue. When a Massachusetts governor suggested that voters send instructions to their delegates, House members reacted with outrage. Moreover, legislators routinely limited public access to information about their actions. The Massachusetts Assembly imprisoned printer Daniel Fowle on a charge of contempt, for publishing a pamphlet that reported how various legislators had voted when an excise bill came to the floor. New York legislators also acted in high-handed ways. In 1747, when the governor opposed publication of a remonstrance they had adopted, the House invoked "the undoubted Right of the People of this Colony, to know the Proceedings of their Representatives." Twice in the next few decades, however, the House prosecuted printers for publications that attributed the sufferings of inhabitants to legislative policy.[34] In other colonies, too, the people's representatives enforced limits on the press; in 1758, for example, the Pennsylvania Assembly indicted William Moore for publishing an attack on the legislature, then indicted William Smith for reprinting the same article in a German-language newspaper. Both men faced imprisonment for their "false, scandalous Libel," or for "breach of privilege"—a phrase that claimed the privileges of Parliament for the provincial legislature. Though the cobbler might be able to judge if he was well governed, he should not necessarily know how different legislators had voted or be able to read criticisms of the House in the public press.[35] Representatives acted as rulers when they emphasized their distinction and defended their prerogatives.[36]

Indeed, by voting for a representative in this system—at most once a year in New England, as rarely as once every seven years in Virginia— voters could be construed as consenting only with some difficulty or only in part. Only by particular construction could voting for candidates constitute consenting to laws they would go on to make in the company of council and governor. So we are wise to be skeptical of Reverend Micklejohn: only in a restricted sense had the voters of North Carolina given their consent to acts of government "before-hand," or had a "principle share" in making laws.

But it is time to modify this picture of powerlessness and deference. We need to move away from a focus on what voters lacked to consider the powers they had. So far I have written in the same terms as many eighteenth-century writers did: as if voters stood at the bottom of the pyramid, forming the broad base of the political nation. When we put "before-hand" consent in the center, as Micklejohn did, then we constrict our world to rulers and voters. Yet in fact voters stood far from the bottom of their society; if they tallied the majority of adult white men, they represented a minority of the population in every colony. Pennsylvania lawyer James Wilson described the justly exclusive nature of the vote in the early 1770s. Property holding was a key requisite to the franchise, he wrote, because the voter needed to be "capable of exercising his will," voicing his own genuine sentiment rather than yielding to the pressure of a social or economic superior. The voting public should thus exclude everyone who was "servile" and beholding to a great man for position or livelihood, for surely that great man would control his decision-making at the hustings. In Britain, Wilson noted, the great many who lacked property were all excluded from the vote. As a result, those who qualified as the "independent Commons of England" could be assured that their votes for members of the lower house of Parliament would not be "adulterated" by the votes of others, whose dependence on landlords or other powerful men constrained their thoughts and actions. "Thus is the freedom of elections secured from the *servility*, the *ignorance*, and the *corruption* of the electors."[37]

Everywhere in the colonies, the "servile and dependent" described by James Wilson outnumbered the so-called independent colonists. In Carolina and in some Virginia counties, indeed, the majority of the population consisted of enslaved Africans and African Americans in the mid-eighteenth century, and *their* consent to government rule was considered distinctly inessential. Everywhere most of the population was too young for a voice in choosing a legislator, and one-half of the population was the wrong gender to vote. Among white men, some lacked the vote because they were sons living at home on their fathers' farms. These could expect to accumulate and inherit property of their own in due time, to come into political as well as economic and social independence. Yet others were laborers, transients, or servants. Their futures were less certain, but a fair number never expected or acquired the right to vote for a representative or in local affairs. We might conclude, first, that the consent enacted by the vote, however important to some, was even less substantial than has already appeared. In other words, if there are doubts about how far legislative delegates represented "the voters," there are equal doubts about how far the voters represented "the people." We might note, second, that voters themselves were more substantial than they first appear in the context of some contemporary political theory. Voters might be supposed to be ignorant about provincial and imperial affairs, but they were (by definition) not "servile" or "dependent," and surely they knew and treasured that distinction. What separated them from the men they elected might not seem so great, compared to what separated voters and rulers alike from lesser men, women, and the legally unfree. They were surely accustomed to make judgments and decisions closer to home.

Equally important, if not lacking in stature and power when viewed closer to home, ordinary voters were also not entirely lacking in knowledge. The other side of the cobbler's isolation in daily life, his distance from learned and cosmopolitan knowledge, was his immersion in the parochial. And although a gentleman might measure his status precisely by his transcendence of the merely local, to the bulk of free colonists this knowledge proved generally sufficient. It made up the ground on which they knew their own minds, experienced their own competence, and made their judgments of right and wrong. It was a ground of substantial political possibility.[38] Here are some examples of local knowledge: in Boston, from the 1690s into the 1750s, the knowledge that, statute law notwithstanding, it was the renters of residential property, not landlords, who were generally responsible for paying the province tax on dwelling houses.[39] In Charles County, Maryland, in the year 1663, the knowledge that "in his hows" Arthur Turner mistreated his apprentice.[40] In New York City, the knowledge that the best water for brewing tea came from the pump on Chatham Street.[41] In Hartford, Connecticut, in the 1760s, the knowledge that a man named Cuff held a generally recognized status of "black Governor."[42]

Local knowledge did not respect social status; it was not necessarily specific to elite or non-elite. John Hancock, the single largest landlord in Boston, knew as well as his tenants who would pay the province tax. (They also knew if he was more or less likely than other landlords in town to forgive late or short payment of rent.) Equally important, local knowledge was something that people had, information available to them, not by virtue of special learning or contacts outside, but by contacts inside. It was a function of residency in a community, understood as the business of those in the locality. An English visitor to Philadelphia described the city's inhabitants: "The people must either talk of their neighbors, of whom they know every particular of what they both do and say, or else of marketing."[43] What was true in the colonies' largest city was undoubtedly true in many smaller localities: "every particular" of one's neighbors' affairs absorbed a good deal of attention. Equally, local ways had authority. In one Connecticut town, when a new trader introduced lower prices on goods merely to attract customers, established merchants objected that competitive pricing was an innovation. They denounced the interloper as "an intire Stranger to the knowledge of any Thing which belongs to the gentleman, or merchant." Merely a "transient," the new trader should "conform to the known, just, and reputable Rules of Trade, practised in this Place."[44] What was "practised in this Place" carried authority.

There were two other sorts of knowledge that deserve attention, for these too made themselves powerfully felt in ordinary people's lives. First was specialized knowledge, typified by the skills and mysteries passed by the institution of apprenticeship, which guarded entry to many trades. Though English guilds did not put down roots in the colonies, the knowledge and very identity of artisanship still passed from tradesman to apprentice. The "misteries" of trade encompassed not only specific skills and techniques but also expectations about the length of the workday, standards of work and workplace conditions, and the appropriate relationships among apprentices, journeymen, and masters of the trade.[45] Most apparent in the lives of those formally trained through apprenticeships, specialized knowledge was also the province of the many informally trained in their own and their neighboring households. The vast majority of colonists grew up on farms, where they learned to read the seasons and work the soil from fathers and a wider network of neighbors and kin. "A man cannot be busied in the arts of husbandry (they consist of so great variety) without many things coming under his observation."[46] Similarly, much of the knowledge peculiar to women passed from generation to generation within household and neighborhood, including the many arts of housewifery, from dairying and gardening to cooking, spinning, needlework, and ordinary healing. Women also passed on to women the vital skills of midwifery, which "no man can be a judge of."[47] Even the so-called unskilled and semi-skilled trades had their substantial know-how. Such specialized knowledge was in some aspects local in character, for it might vary from place to place; growing tobacco was not the same as growing rice or wheat or peas.[48] By contrast, the specialized skills and knowledge of sailors created a community of widely diverse people across the Atlantic world. The elite had their professions—medicine, divinity, the law—distinguished from ordinary people's learning by their heavy reliance on knowledge from books. But theirs was by no means the only sort of specialized authority.[49]

Finally, there circulated in the world of ordinary, white colonists a good deal of *common* knowledge. What "everyone knew"—truths from the Bible; the history of Oliver Cromwell; the liberties secured by Magna Carta and the more recent Glorious Revolution against James; the dangers of

Jacobin plots; the tyranny of popes. By any number of measures, of course, a fair amount of ordinary knowledge might be inaccurate.[50] Popular or common knowledge of the law, as we shall see, may not have tallied with the knowledge held by lawyers trained at the Inns of Court. Moreover, many people in isolated communities felt the lack of information from metropolitan centers. They attended court days and frequented taverns in part out of hunger for knowledge from the outside, brought by travelers and, increasingly, by published broadsheets and newspapers. For all that, taverns were also a source of knowledge from the inside of a given neighborhood, a site for local conversation, local news and gossip, and local opinion. Over and against those who saw all important learning as taking place in metropolitan centers, accessible to a relative few, there was an alternative source of authority. After all, "in things of their knowledge," the saying went, the common people might speak with "the voice of God."[51]

If they sometimes spoke at the ballot box, the people also spoke in another venue. Every colony provided other key sites for "the people"—sometimes interpreted as the voters, sometimes interpreted as a population beyond voters alone—to consent and dissent. Many colonists believed it essential to English liberty that laws be subject to popular scrutiny and consent *after* their passage by the legislature. It remained to be seen whether a law would have "binding influence," whether, that is, it would garner the necessary consent on the ground. To a degree that would strike later Americans as unworkable, people did overrule their representatives and dispute the validity of laws.[52]

Whig theorists of the day not only recognized but celebrated the space for "the people's" participation after "the law" was passed by the government. What gave "Security" to "English-Men's Lives," wrote Sir John Somer, was not merely the guarantee that they "would be subject only to the laws made by their own Consent in their general Assemblies." It was also the guarantee that those laws would "be put in Execution chiefly by themselves, their Officers and Assistants."[53] Pennsylvania jurist James Logan explained English liberty in similar terms. Other nations, he said, "confined and limited" the power of justice to "the Hands of but a few." France, Spain, and sometimes Italy were the examples that English and colonial writers usually had in mind when making such comparisons. Superior to these tyrannical systems, "an English Constitution supposes all the Powers of Government, like Life in the Body, to be in some Measure diffused through the whole Community of Freeholders and Freemen." *All* the powers of government—not merely the power of deliberating policy in order to legislate, but equally the power to execute the law. The people—a group that sometimes meant qualified voters, sometimes others as well—could lay claim to a right to participate and consent in another arena.[54]

We can call this arena law enforcement, so long as we rid ourselves of present-day assumptions. We think of political decision-making as taking place in the passage of a bill into law, enforcement as a means of carrying out intentions already established and expressed. Some colonial Americans tended toward a similar view. Yet a great many understood execution of the law as a key site of participation and consent, a place for substantive rather than instrumental action. The execution of the law involved more than "Officers of the Crown," and more than men "Concerned in Aid of the Magistrate in Courts of Judicature." It also involved "the Execution of the Laws without Doors."[55]

The People as Executors of the Law

"To relieve the Oppressed, to guard the Innocent, to preserve the Order of Society, and the Dignity of Government" constituted the "Duty of every Individual of the Community."[56] In some colonies, that duty extended to the selection of officers charged with enforcing the laws. In New England, town meetings elected a variety of such officials, called constables or tithingmen, to oversee behavior and execute laws. A minister might thus charge the voters themselves with responsibility.

> Without you, all that our rulers in civil and sacred orders can do will not avail. Though our legislature enact never so many good laws for the regulation of the morals of the people, unless you do your part, and improve the power and liberty you are invested with, in your several towns, to make choice of such for your grand jurors, tithingmen, etc. as are men fearing God, men of truth and fidelity, men of wisdom equal to the trust committed to them, and have the interest of religion at heart—who will carefully inspect the manners of the people, and bring the transgressors to open shame and punishment, I say, unless you are careful and conscientious in this, all our laws for the reforming of the manners and morals of a corrupt people are insufficient and our lawmakers labor in vain.[57]

This was a situation of some voter discretion, as was apparent in the gap between laws and their application. Towns in Massachusetts repeatedly elected legislators who passed laws regulating taverns, then chose selectmen who failed to enforce the regulations. Outside New England, where county courts rather than voters appointed sheriffs, constables, and similar officials, we might expect less flouting of the law, surer enforcement of policies decided by the government. Here, too, elite lawmakers repeatedly sought to establish that taverns existed for the use of strangers and travelers, not for the entertainment of locals. Laws limited the number of taverns, specified who could attend them, limited the length of time patrons might linger there, and regulated the alcohol consumed and behaviors indulged there. Yet voters and nonvoters alike disregarded these laws, and in specific instances the local elite ignored the law in favor of either their own preferences or a broader local opinion. South Carolina could not get officials to punish either tavern haunters or the negligent tavern keepers who failed to curb disorders: "No proper and sufficient Notice has been taken of them, either by the Magistrates, Church-Wardens, Constables, or other Officers,"[58] complained one justice. Taverns remained too numerous, perennially run by the wrong sort of people, and patronized by the wrong customers, who habitually behaved badly and stayed too long. Even where magistrates and other officers were not elected, they might defer to local standards when it came to enforcing the tavern law.

Moreover, other acts of assembly also made themselves felt selectively. A 1723 law requiring that planters limit their tobacco crop in order to enhance the price was executed "very sparingly in the Northern Neck," according to wealthy planter William Byrd.[59] Similarly, in Maryland, the various county courts departed from statute law in customary, predictable ways. The law was specific about the punishment for runaway servants, but in practice the penalty varied substantially from county to county.[60] This variation reflected the discretion and power of the local elite, and it reflected their vulnerability and accountability to local ground. It seemed to at least one frustrated royal official that Boston town meeting felt it had the right to decide which provincial laws applied to them.[61]

Once elected or appointed, officials depended on popular support to apprehend wrongdoers. Authorities issued proclamations, magistrates signed warrants and writs, and in extreme cases they called for militiamen to gather. But by all reports, in practice as well as in theory the public proved unreliable in its response. The people might cooperate with authorities or they might not, depending on a host of variables from the personal to the political. Non-cooperation took a multitude of forms. For example, the Royal Navy was a notably dreaded institution that satisfied few colonists' conception of the liberty that Englishmen should enjoy. As a result, deserters from British vessels were likely to find a haven in city or countryside, or at least to meet colonials who, when later questioned by officials, would prove forgetful of a fugitive's appearance and whereabouts. On other occasions, officials met with outright opposition in their efforts to carry out the law.[62] One magistrate in Albany County, New York, sought to bring a gang of counterfeiters to justice, only to find himself hamstrung by widespread non-cooperation and even violence against his property. John Munro was forced to throw up his hands: "What can a Justice do when the whole Country combinds against him?"[63] Well, he could berate the sheriff and his deputies and bemoan his situation. The people's role was not merely apprehension of the criminal in this system, but apprehension of crime itself. Here we see the matter clearly: what might seem the *absence* of a professional colonial police was the *presence* of British liberty.[64]

It was up to ordinary people to identify or apprehend crime in another sense as well: governors appointed attorneys general in various colonies to prosecute some cases in the name of the king, but many crimes came to court by means of private prosecution on the part of self-described victims. In Connecticut, many cases of theft, defamation, and even assault were prosecuted by the victim, if at all.[65] The governor of Bermuda analyzed criminal offenses in three categories: crimes against God, such as blasphemy; crimes against the king, such as treason; and crimes against "ourselves," ranging from murder through burglary, larceny, perjury, oppression, slander, dishonesty in weights and measures, and more.[66] Both of the latter categories encompassed crimes that a later system would employ public prosecutors to pursue on behalf of "the people." In eighteenth-century proceedings, by contrast, the prosecutor was "Rex" or "Regina"; as a result, it was substantially less incumbent on colonists to conflate the cause of the government with the cause of "the people."

Private prosecution clearly left space for the victim's discretion, and some preferred arrangements outside the overview of justices, outside the logic of legal authorities. Having admitted such space for settlements, colonial authorities employed various means to bring the transactions of the population under the jurisdiction of the law. From time to time, executives issued proclamations calling for specific acts of enforcement, and in sermons and other speeches, authorities encouraged colonists to bring their knowledge of their neighbors' behavior to the attention of officers of the state. One Massachusetts law made it a crime for a victim to "smother" a theft—that is, hush up the matter once the stolen goods had been privately recovered—unless the thief turned out to be a member of the immediate family. Even the law, in this case, recognized that the family as an institution might dispense (or dispense with) justice. Yet many laws provided incentive to bring wrongdoers to law, awarding one-third or one-half of the fine levied on the convicted to the informer in the case.[67]

Once under jurisdiction of the law, the disposition of events nonetheless remained vulnerable to the ordinary knowledge of ordinary men. English writer Henry Care put it succinctly in his seventeenth-century account of "the Free-Born Subject's Inheritance": "This Birthright of English-men shines most conspicuously in two things: 1. Parliaments 2. Juries."[68] In both of these institutions, the theory ran, the will of the king met the will of the people.

The juries that Care prized were of two sorts, each of them essential to the workings of justice in the criminal law. First was the grand jury, a body composed of fifteen or more men qualified to vote in provincial elections, called together in their various counties to bring the disorders and misbehaviors of the people to the jurisdiction of the courts. It was true that local justices of the peace might handle some misbehaviors on their own knowledge, dealing out summary justice. In cases of petty debt or minor transgressions, judges might awe and rule without a jury. Moreover, grand juries were not the sole means of bringing significant crimes to trial. Suspects could be prosecuted based on "information" from the king or his officers, "without any finding or presentment by the Verdict of Twelve men," but by "discretion" alone.[69] It was certainly easier for an appointed official to bypass the grand jury in difficult or controversial cases.[70] Yet even a conservative jurist, Thomas Hutchinson of Massachusetts, acknowledged danger in such proceedings. Englishmen should be "very tender how these are indulged," he warned, "as 'tis a Hardship on the Subject" for petit trials to take place without grand jury indictment, "and I think there is no Case, in which a Man shall be tried for life on an Information."[71] By broad consensus, then, grand juries were generally needed to bring a suspected felon to trial, and the great bulk of criminal matters in the colonies passed under the jurisdiction of a grand jury.

Jury gatherings provided the occasion for official pomp and public display. They opened with an address from the chief justice in charge, who might briefly describe categories of criminal law, explain the significance of the execution of law for the maintenance of the king's peace, and sometimes draw attention to recent outrages or issues of concern to the government. Grand jurors were to hear charges against various suspects, interview witnesses, and decide whether to find "a true bill"—saying the accused was guilty and should go on to petit trial—or "ignoramus"—literally, "we do not know," hence that the accused could not be indicted. At least twelve of the jury had to find a true bill to present a defendant to further trial. There was some disagreement over the nature of this decision. Some authorities urged the examination be rather cursory, since an entire second trial would follow; yet Whig writers argued forcefully that if grand jurors were not convinced of a defendant's guilt, they should return a bill of ignoramus. It was essential to the system of justice, said one, that twenty-four men must find a defendant guilty. This first trial, held in private, could spare the innocent from the next and more public stage of proceedings, the petit or "petty" trial.

The responsibility of the grand jury included not only identifying malefactors but discerning problems of public order, a task that fell to everyone in the society in principle but that was "particularly incumbent" on grand jurymen.[72] English practice licensed grand juries to present public dangers or nuisances to the court and suggest legislative or executive remedies. Thus, though it involved no crime and suggested no criminal ran at large in the county, the "unnecessary multiplication of licensed houses"—that is, taverns—was a frequent problem that might engage the grand jury. This and other "things neglected or things damaging"—the sorry condition of the county jail, the unmet needs of the poor—lay within the "discretionary Power" of the grand jury to notice and bring to the court's attention. The latitude provided to grand juries might encourage their members to bring local affairs under the jurisdiction of the central state and its law.[73]

The grand jury's discretion to speak to public problems, and especially to present specific grievances to authorities above them, meant that the institution in some respects resembled a representative body, often assembled on the county level. In seventeenth-century New York, the Duke of York considered that the people needed no elected assembly; they could seek redress for grievances when the grand jury gathered once every year, and the jury members were (in his opinion) pretty much the same men who would be chosen as representatives anyway. Events paradoxically proved the duke right: in 1681 the provincial grand jury proved sufficiently representative to present the need for an assembly, since the inhabitants were otherwise "wholly shut out and deprived of any share, vote, or interest in the government."[74] The grand jury explicitly denied its own adequacy as a representative body, even as it proved representative enough to express its view to the governor and proprietor. In Maryland, grand jurymen presented written grievances to circuit judges, who in turn were expected to communicate the matter to governor and council.[75] Like deputies who promoted private bills for their towns or counties, moreover, members of the grand jury were to look after the well-being of their districts.[76]

Like assemblies, too, grand juries were properly composed of members of the colonial elite: grand jurymen were not to be average voters but "persons of Note," who "ought always to be the principal of the County for Character and Estate." South Carolina set high property standards for participation in the grand jury; everywhere else, all freemen were eligible to serve, but in practice members of these panels seem to have generally ranked among the relatively well-to-do.[77]

Grand jurymen needed these traits of rulers because their task was twofold. First, they must speak the popular voice in the face of executive power. New York jurist Robert Livingston flattered the grand jury of that province by explaining that their elite status made them well qualified to serve. As members of the "better sort," they were "less liable to temptations, less fearful of the frowns of power," hence better able to resist the pressure of the government to bring its power against the innocent. Second, members of the grand jury might need to withstand popular opinion in order to enforce the law. The better sort "may reasonable [sic] be supposed of more improved capacities than those of an inferior station."[78] They might need to disagree with what most people in their neighborhoods believed. One chief justice said: "Popular Applause and the Approbation of the Multitude can never sanctify Iniquity, or alter the Nature of Things. We are not at all Times to be guided by their Voice. The People in all Ages and Countries have been sometimes deceived."[79] From that point of view, the grand juryman should "represent" his locality much as a delegate to the provincial assembly ought to do, being wiser and better informed, willing to depart from the common view. To help them withstand popular opinion, grand juries deliberated in private. If privacy offered the accused some protection against unwarranted damage to reputation, at the same time, like the privacy of the provincial legislature, the privacy of the grand jury provided space for the formulation of unpopular decisions. Secrecy about deliberations was essential, for "People out of Doors will influence your Conduct if they know the Business you are engaged on."[80]

In Connecticut, grand jurymen were elected by freeholders at town meetings, two from each town, but in most places they were selected by an appointed official—usually the sheriff—who was himself obliged to the governor or the county court for his position.[81] Selected "by the King's proper Officer," and not by the voters, most grand jury members could represent only in a geographical sense. Jurors gathered "from all the several Parts of the County to represent the State of it." They might overlook a great deal, leaving out of court matters they deemed satisfactorily settled by other means. They were in a position to judge which disorders were of the scale or the sort that might be brought to the state's jurisdiction. They should use discretion. "You are summoned from all Parts of the Province, and the Law supposes, that you best know the Crimes, Offences, Disorders, and Grievances, that are committed or suffer'd in the several Places and Districts from whence you come."[82] "Does not the grand jury (tho' chose by the Sheriff) represent the county?"[83] Well, only in a manner of speaking: grand jurymen represented not a group of constituents, but local knowledge.

Indeed, in both theory and practice, a vital qualification for membership in a jury of any sort was geographical, a qualification of inhabitancy. Jurors needed to come from the vicinage of the crime and be "neighbours" of the parties. English writer John Somers said jurors should be "Companions" of the accused, "known to him, and he to them, or at least his Neighbours or Dwellers near about the place where the Crime is supposed to have been committed, to whom something of the Fact must probably be known."[84] Chief justices specifically charged grand jurymen with bringing their own personal knowledge to the attention of the court. Jurymen's knowledge of local events was sufficient basis on which to act; they might bring suspects to trial even if no one complained of a crime and no witness appeared to swear that one had even occurred. Intimate knowledge of the locality was equally valuable in determining cases brought by third parties. Which witnesses to believe, which accounts of the parties' transactions were most plausible—jurors were expected to make such decisions not merely on the impression and information received at court, but on the grounds of prior knowledge. The ideal juror would be impartial, not prejudiced toward one side or the other, but he would also be informed, able to draw on a personal history of specific local relationships. Many justices stressed the need for grand jurymen to privilege local knowledge. Grand jurymen, said Logan, should be those "standing fairest to be acquainted with, and most likely to be affected by any Disorders among the Subjects."[85]

Writers who imagined grand juries to be representative, then, imagined them as representing the world of neighborhood life. These bodies might count as representative, in other words, only if what mattered most was their shared membership in the deep horizontal grouping of their communities—if only mutuality and interdependence were recognized as salient. And where, as must have often been the case, their mutuality with their neighbors proved less salient than their differences from them—that is, whether they proved representative or not—jurymen could sometimes make their own notions of right and fairness felt by action or inaction, by their knowledge or ignorance. If it did not rise to the significance of sitting in the provincial assembly or require men of such exalted stature, serving on a grand jury was yet a recognized form of political participation. It was, says historian Gwenda Morgan, the largest element of political participation in the lives of many Virginia planters.[86]

In this system, the right to grand jury proceedings belonged both to the accused and to the people as a whole. Grand juries protected individuals from being bothered by law, filtering frivolous from well-grounded accusations and, since they proceeded in secrecy, shielding people's reputations at the early stages of proceedings against them. Equally important, the people in general had a stake in maintaining the powers of grand juries, for these bodies had figured largely in late seventeenth-century contests between king and people, prerogative and liberty. Every subject had a stake in preventing the king and his agents from oppressing people "under the colour of law." After all, merely being accused could create substantial damage, and the grand jury sought to remove the threat of such damage from the hands of the king. "The true the Original and Intention of Grand-Juries" was to have men of their neighborhood—not courts of inquisition or mere informers—responsible for "looking into the Behaviour of the People."

Like other colonial political theorists, James Logan concurred that service on a grand jury was political participation: "For as these [freeholders and freemen] by Birthright, are vested with the inherent Privileges of choosing their own Representatives, to appear for them in Legislation . . . so likewise in Regard to the executive Powers, it is presumed expedient that every Man shall think himself obliged like a Watchman, to be ever intent on the public Peace, and the Preservation of good Order, in the District wherein he dwells; and accordingly to be capable of rendering an Account of the Conduct of those in his Vicinage."[87] Logan's complicated locution here suggests some indecision over whether voting and serving as grand juryman were strictly parallel acts. Was voting a "Privilege," while serving "like a Watchman" an obligation? Generally speaking, both public acts were sometimes styled obligations—in Carolina a qualified voter might be legally fined for nonappearance on election day—and both acts could be seen as privileges (or rights) as well. Equally important, Logan seemed uncertain whether jury service was more closely akin to voting or to filling a public office. Despite the difficulties, Logan nonetheless articulated a critical commonality: when they participated either as voters or as grand jurymen, colonists were enjoying precious aspects of British liberty.

The extent of that liberty was subject to debate. From the point of view of many among America's elite, this was what was right with courts of law: namely, their capacity to impose notions of fairness determined at the top (by the provincial or metropolitan elite) and at the center (in colonial capitals or London). Courts were agencies of rule that could inflict fines, distrain property, arrest persons and sentence them to punishment on the streets and in the gallows. Those coercive powers might back up local authorities or overrule them, sustain popular notions of justice or correct them.

It was judges—justices and magistrates—who represented the provincial government, British power, and arguably the law itself on these occasions. Appointed to power, men qualified for the bench by possessing sufficient substance and repute to carry so great a responsibility. Thus, in Virginia the "gentlemen justices" were large landholders who controlled church vestries, the militia, and other county institutions. In New England they were substantial property owners from prominent families and often held other offices—deputy to the lower house, councillor in the upper house, militia officer, church deacon. Where judges were not so exalted, upper-class colonists worried about their capacity to represent the law, lest magistrates and justices carry insufficient status to awe and rule. For the courtroom to embody the vertical relations of colonial society, litigants and defendants must be brought face-to-face with judges who were "worshipful" in character and appearance.[88] In New York, Chief Justice James DeLancey explained, "The appointment of the Judges and Officers is Part of the King's Prerogative, or more properly of his Office."[89] Thus, judges, as another authority phrased it, "represent the king's person, they are his officers, and act in his stead."[90] In Newark, New Jersey, Judge Sanford declared his authority on the bench by wearing not only a "hatt and wigg" but a sword.[91] Hats on top of wigs removed the justices from "the uncovered ranks of society."[92] Justices, said one Virginian, should be "members of that estate of Men which be Called Worshipful."[93] They were indeed powerful: justices in Virginia enjoyed "singular authority" over men's property and persons.[94] It was their task to "bring law" from the center—whether London or a provincial capital— to the various parts of the realm. It followed that jurymen needed to represent the people. Only then could the courtroom be an arena where elite and common people, governors and governed, the king's prerogative and the liberty of the subject came into relationship.

Although the grand jury acknowledged the significance of local knowledge, it was the petit jury that more firmly embodied that power. Petit jurymen were apt to be ordinary voters, men who could lay few claims to broad horizons or to an exceptional ability to withstand the popular voice. Even Carolina set a low property requirement for playing this role, and other colonies qualified all voters. In Barbados and parts of the South, the great gentry considered themselves above serving on a petit jury. Maryland law required the sheriff to choose among the "best and understanding freeholders" for grand jury, but petit jurors must only qualify as "good and lawful men."[95] In principle, indeed, petit jurymen were understood to be interchangeable with the accused. Under the jury system, "all men of the like condition, and quality, presumed to be sensible of each others infirmity, should mutually be Judges each of others lives, and alternately tast[e] of Subjection and Rule."[96] Equally, jurors should be interchangeable with the generality of men who attended court as spectators, witnesses, and parties. Sheriffs could tap any qualified man in the area if needed to fill out the jury to the number of twelve.

Defendants in criminal cases might arguably want men of the neighborhood to comprise the pool of potential jurors, for the accused were likely to know more about such men than they could know about strangers. With a "better knowledge" of would-be jurymen, an accused person might know "to except against, or to approve of them" as members of the panel.[97] Yet again, the system protected the people as a whole. By authorizing local men with local knowledge to apply the law, this jury system provided space for the people's notions of justice—or at least prevented the king's notions of justice from running rampant.

Like grand jurors before them, petit jurymen were understood to have greater local knowledge than the gentleman justice had. They would know the witnesses, hence whether it was probable that they had been where they said they'd been, heard what they said they'd heard, seen what they said they'd seen. They would know whether local relationships might lead someone to misrepresent the truth, whether long-standing alliances or grudges might come into play in different witnesses' accounts of events. If judges were to have superior and broader knowledge of the world, jurors were to have specific and local knowledge. Here was a second source of authority, then, needed to complete the law. Jurors from the vicinage of the crime "may also the more likely know somewhat themselves of the party, of the matter, of the credit of the witnesses, and all circumstances" at stake in the case before them. They should be impartial: "not to be of the Kindred or Alliance of any of the Parties; not prejudiced or predisposed" but yet knowledgeable about local events. If disputes arose about where the jury should come from—as when crimes involved parties from different vicinages—the jurymen "shall come from whence the matter is like best to be known." In the courtroom, two sources of authority came face-to-face: the authority of legal learning and the authority of local knowledge.[98]

So petit jury trials were more broadly public, in a twofold sense of being open to spectators, on the one hand, and engaging less uncommon commoners as jurors, on the other. When a defendant requested a jury trial, he was said to "put himself upon God and his country." Judges, one writer wryly insisted, were not to imagine themselves as indicated by either of these terms. The "country" was a phrase that referred to neither bench nor bar, but solely to the jury. In this moment, on this occasion, the jury were the people.[99] Here again, a man did not have to mount as high as his provincial house of representatives to play that role.

The jury did more than sort through conflicting testimony to conclude what was likely to have happened. Eighteenth-century juries routinely decided law as well as fact, judging whether specific actions qualified as a greater or lesser offense or, indeed, whether those actions constituted an illegality at all. The distinction between the "facts" of a case and the pertinent "law" is a fine and possibly unsustainable matter, since the simplest statement of events contains assumptions and definitions framed by the law.[100] Yet seventeenth- and eighteenth-century writers felt it vital to maintain a line between the two, then to assert that juries were competent authorities over both elements: juries could judge what had happened and also its significance, its amenability to categories and conditions of statute and common law. They were to rule on events and also provide the authoritative interpretation of them.[101]

In critical respects, this power enjoyed by juries ran counter to logic: if, in the ideal case, jurymen knew their neighbors and justices knew the law, it would make sense to allow judges to decide whether laws might have been violated by the facts of a jury's finding. Few disputed that judges should have superior knowledge of the law, defined either as statutes passed by the provincial legislature or as the common law, the precedents established at the King's Bench in England. Yet though a judge might inform the jury of the law's dictates, he had little power to overrule them if they ignored his information. The jury should make decisions "in their own sense, and as they apprehend or understand it themselves, and no otherwise, though the judge differ with them." The logic of this position might render a judge nearly superfluous. "Upon the whole, one may see that a judge ought not to meddle at all with the jury: if he differ not with them, it is needless and troublesome; if he differ, they are not to mind him; take it which way one will."[102] Why should a judge speak in the courtroom at all? "According to our Constitution," wrote a minister in Massachusetts, "even Jurors may be said to be Judges."[103]

On what philosophical grounds could local knowledge and common judgment trump the expertise acquired at the Inns of Court or from the admittedly difficult pages of Coke and Blackburn? Some thought it absurd: judges should overrule incorrect jury decisions. "The court"—which is to say the justices and magistrates—had the power to grant a new trial when the jury gave a verdict against evidence in civil cases. "Jurys are to try Causes with the Assistance of a Judge," stressed one authority. But even advocates for judicial expertise had a hard time giving leeway to judges without obviating the powers of juries altogether. "I confess I wish for a Power in the Court to set aside Verdicts," said Robert Auchmuty of the Massachusetts Superior Court, "but not for an unlimited one." After all, it would render juries meaningless if the only verdicts that held were those "agreeable to the Mind of the Court." Auchmuty's colleague Edmund Trowbridge put it this way: "Jurors [are] to take law from the Court," and if a jury was to convict someone against the advice of the judges, the condemned might expect a reprieve until the king's pardon might be sought.[104] These were conservative men, and other men saw less to fear in popular decisions at court. The less conservative insisted that juries were not instruments of a law or justice already fixed and established; rather, juries brought their own knowledge of justice to the court. Henry Care certainly muddied the waters when he suggested that jurors should judge: "The office and power of these Juries is Judicial. They only are the Judges, from whose sentence the Indicted are to expect Life or Death."[105] Even conservative jurist Jonathan Blenman of Barbados, responding to a published account of the famous Zenger case, noted that he agreed that the jury should find law as well as fact, "when they are complicated"—that is, when law and fact were clearly entangled with one another. It was, Blenman noted wryly, "almost the only Point in which I can have the Honour of agreeing" with Zenger's defense.[106]

The structure of the confrontation between judge and jury was not unfamiliar. We have seen that, in provincial governments, members of the lower house of assembly, armed with constituent instructions or their possibility, faced up to or faced down the governor, armed with royal instructions or their possibility. This scene was replicated when jurymen, informed by local knowledge, faced a judge informed by knowledge of Coke's, copies of statutes, and law reports. Perhaps it was this essential similarity that prompted Care to write his list of elements of British liberty: "1. Parliaments 2. Juries." Both institutions stood charged with speaking the voice of the people.

Yet if this was the thinking of authorities and experts, how far did it describe courtroom practice in colonial America? It is easy to overstate the independence of the jury; Whig writers often argued against the stream, or at least against the reality that judges, so learned, socially superior, and wealthy, frequently directed juries, who frequently deferred. In important cases, moreover, sheriffs might pick prospective jurors with care, ensuring a panel prone to the conclusions the authorities desired. Handpicked by those in authority, a grand jury might be "Chosen on purpose to find the Presentment," as one indicted New Yorker complained in print and others doubtless complained as well.[107] In the eighteenth-century Chesapeake, sheriffs were members of the gentry class and chose only some of the local yeomanry, from families they considered worthy and respectable, to serve on juries.[108] Elite influence over jury selection may well have had a paradoxical effect: rendering the actual makeup of juries less representative of the free population as a whole, allowing or encouraging acceptance of the prerogatives of jurors to find law as well as fact.[109]

In practice, it seems safe to say, writers' insistence on the sufficiency of local knowledge, of a jury "unlearned in law," contended with the realities of social power. Writings directed at "the jury-man" undermined their own case when they cited legal authorities to convince readers of the sufficiency of local knowledge. Had local knowledge been universally understood to be sufficient for juries to decide both fact and law, in other words, no theorist would have had to reassure prospective jurors of their prerogatives. "The people" on the jury might be as deferential as "the people" casting ballots on election day. Judges would not have bothered with robes, wigs, and other expensive tokens of stature if such things did not impress. "Greater things confound and astonish us, and things above us dazzle our eyes."[110] Advocates for jury powers acknowledged that juries often failed to exert their rights. Many wrote lamentations about what they saw as decline, suggesting that juries used to stand up to judges but now were apt to meekly follow. This common view of the declining independence of juries may or may not have been accurate as history; in practical terms, it was an effort to embolden jurors of the present day, an admission of juries' tendency to follow the lead of judges. In practice, the opposition or contest between king and people might often prove a gracious and cooperative meeting of the minds. Besides, there was another theory, expressed by Thomas Hutchinson: "We . . . who are to execute the Law, are not to enquire into the Reason and Policy of it, or whether it is Constitutional or not;—whether one Part of the Community are oppressed, and whether another Part oppress; We . . . are to enquire what is Law, and see that the Laws are inforced."[111]

Still, juries were not so compliant as many justices or prosecutors wished. Grand juries would not indict in countless cases brought before them by their superiors. In New Jersey, the proprietors believed that juries were local kin groups, therefore biased; the popular belief was that the board's patronage gave them control of bench and bar.[112] There were frequent denunciations of juries that did nothing, or that did the wrong thing. The foreman of one New York jury informed the provincial attorney that, despite the experts' clear statement to the contrary, "the Defendant had not transgressed any Law."[113] When two servants stole their masters' possessions, a Maryland jury decided to convict them only of a misdemeanor rather than a felony. "We do not find it valluable to Reach the law of Fellony Conserninge the goods that John Whit and Sarah Tayler Did Cary away from Capt Thomas Brodnox," declared one Maryland jury. Whit and Taylor's misfortunes as servants of Brodnox, apparent in other proceedings of the court, may have influenced jurors to a certain sympathy.[114] Such undervaluations of goods, calculated to mitigate the crime, were reportedly common among juries. In these and similar cases, the courtroom became an arena for negotiation over the law. The courtroom was understood in these terms by many. According to John Adams, the jury system introduced into "the executive branch . . . a mixture of popular power," for jurors spoke with the "Voice of the People."[115]

How clearly everyone understood that role appeared not only in the decisions of some juries but also in popular literature of the day. One satirical pamphlet suggests colonists' widespread familiarity with the courtroom as a scene of competing policies. "The Trial of Sir Richard Rum," of "Anonymous" authorship and heavily beholden to an English pamphlet of similar name, was first issued from an American press in 1724. Twenty-four editions reputedly followed, printed by both New England and Middle Colony presses. In several respects this pamphlet represented the transfer of what one scholar has called England's "small, merry" cultural tradition to American shores.[116] There were no Latin phrases, no authorities cited, nothing of the high learning that graced the bulk of political publications in "Sir Richard Rum." Rather, the pamphlet displayed affection for the broadly humorous, satiric presentation of rustic "types," placed in a setting of rural conviviality. It followed in the footsteps of earlier "low ballads" that were deplored by elite and learned readers and that circulated among the population at least from the late seventeenth century. In Sir Richard's trial, witnesses held forth on injuries he had inflicted and benefits he had bestowed. Humorous characters came to stage, and together they embodied the various social and legal roles understood to negotiate in the courtroom: Justice Worthy presided, but it was jurymen, such as "Tosspot" who—full of specific local knowledge of the character of the defendant—listened to the evidence on both sides and decided to acquit him. The anonymous writer set his dispute over social policy in the courtroom, expecting his readers to know that setting as a possible site of competing social ideals. Amenable to being read aloud, "Sir Richard Rum" cast its readers in a role with which they were likely to be familiar: the role of listeners and observers at court. Rhetorically, the vernacular speeches of different characters approximated oral culture, making the pamphlet accessible to wide numbers of semiliterate readers and listeners.[117]

Like good Whigs, the judges in the case of Sir Richard Rum spoke not at all in the case. The jury, in turn, decided guilt or innocence wholly without reference to specific legislation or common law, but merely consulted their own notions of what was beneficial. In "Sir Richard Rum," popular ideas of what was good prevailed over the strictures of elite moralists, clerical and secular, who disapproved of the lower classes' consumption of rum. Readers, who acted as spectators at this trial, presumably adjourned to celebrate the verdict at a nearby tavern themselves. Even the cobbler in the tavern could tell whether Sir Richard was guilty of a crime.

If we can easily underestimate the accepted and vital place of local knowledge in the colonial courtroom, it is because we work to bar prior, local knowledge from the proceedings of criminal justice. "Whatever it is the law is after," says the anthropologist Clifford Geertz, "it is not the whole story."[118] The law, in other words, necessarily simplifies the messy interactions of life, selecting elements to be deemed pertinent, definitive of legal outcome. In the eighteenth century, the role of the jury was to bring more of the "story" into account, making more—or sometimes merely different—factors of a case count in these determinations. In the eighteenth century, the jury trial was a means by which locally significant elements of the story made it into consideration in the criminal courtroom.[119]

So, when a "Chymist" of Philadelphia named Dr. Evan Jones came to trial for the death of an apprentice, witnesses made clear the events to spectators and jury alike. Yet, noted one observer, "for several Months before the Tryal came on, there was hardly any Person in Philadelphia, who could be ignorant of the Affair in all its horrid Circumstances."[120] Despite such widespread familiarity with the event, no one proposed that justice might be better served by trying the case in Lancaster. To suggest a change of venue to a more neutral site would have been to value ignorance or equate it with impartiality. But a substantially different sense of justice informed the colonial process than informs ours today: a later age would prize informed and opinionated voters but uninformed jury members; the eighteenth century preferred something approaching the reverse.[121]

Among the ideas that empowered juries, here were two. First was the belief that law was inherently reasonable, that it embodied reason in the form of statutes and judicial decisions alike. The law, wrote James Parker, "is nothing but improved and refined reason."[122] Such a claim frequently bolstered admonitions that people should abide by the law; it was only reasonable to do so. Turning the logic on its head, the reasonable nature of law could suggest that nearly anyone could understand it—and that they did not have to enforce or abide by it when obviously unreasonable. "Virtue and Vice, Good and Evil, are for the most Part very distinguishable, and I am persuaded there is no one of common Understanding, but feels either Pain or Pleasure, Uneasiness or Satisfaction, as he is conscious of having done one or the other."[123] When a New York provincial attorney challenged a jury's right to be "Judges of Law," the defense insisted that jurymen's judicial discretion was essential to the English project of preventing tyranny. "Paenal Laws are strictly to be taken and interpreted, and not allowed to the ruin of the Subject, to extend, or be interpreted beyond the plain and strict sense of the words."[124] Surely jurymen, however common, might be able to discern the "plain and strict sense" of the law.[125] Much like the parliamentarians who informed the Stuarts that measures oppressive could not be the will of the king, jurors might easily deduce that measures unreasonable could not be the will of the law.

The oath taken by jurymen seemed to argue for independent judgment as well. Jurymen had not sworn to do whatever the judge told them, but rather to enforce "the laws of this jurisdiction"—a remark that left open the possibility that jury members were as likely to be knowledgeable on those laws as the judge was. Moreover, jurors were "sworn to condemn or acquit according to their consciences," and conscience was taken as an attribute of virtually all mankind, however humble. Over and against the book learning brought to the courtroom by judges, the consciences of jurymen might disagree.[126]

Two other elements affected transactions in the criminal courtroom in the eighteenth century. Theorists wrote largely about judges and jurymen, but in fact there were other actors in criminal courtrooms of the eighteenth century. The absence of lawyers from the imagined setting of "Sir Richard Rum" may have reflected their relatively recent and often disruptive arrival in the processes of law. Certainly the drama had been simpler without them. In the seventeenth century, an attorney was someone who spoke or acted for another party at court; the role took no specialized training, and it was not unusual for a woman to play the part. In the eighteenth century, law became Anglicized, or more like the English system at home, as greater numbers of ambitious colonists took training in England at Inns of Court or read the law in formal apprenticeship in an established lawyer's chambers. Learned advocates began to push out amateurs, the group John Adams disparaged as "pettifoggers." As they did so, they tended to reduce law to special forms of pleadings, to make it increasingly obscure and expensive. By 1750, there were the beginnings of a professional bar in every colony.[127]

How did lawyers change the balance of power in courtrooms, the nature of interactions or popular understanding of the law? Testimony on the matter is mixed. Reuben Searcy complained about what might be considered the excessive lawyerly skills of the North Carolina attorney general, Robert Jones Jr., claiming that "by the great volubility of speech and the superiority that he by his wiles insinuations and chincanerie as aforesaid has insinuated himself into, [Jones] very frequently works on the passions of weak juries to blind their conception of Justice in order to gain his point." As a result of this behavior, "men flock daily to him to comence very trivial and frivolous lawsuits which tends to the great disadvantage and prejudice of our inhabitants." Searcy concluded by suggesting that Jones be stricken from the Granville bar for overawing juries' ideas of justice.[128] Like Jones, other councillors at law might "for their fees strive only to baffle Witnesses and stifle Truth"—a shocking idea.[129] At the same time, as lawyers influenced juries, they also had an impact on the role of magistrates. In Virginia, one historian suggests, especially in the years after 1750, magistrates enjoyed less singular authority. Well-read and well-trained lawyers put pressure on country justices in particular to professionalize law, making it efficient and predictable and limiting judges' discretion.[130] Other scholars have suggested that the rise of lawyers empowered jurors to a greater degree, for contending lawyers in a case offered alternative but still authoritative and learned versions of legal reasoning to the jury.[131]

Moreover, there were other players at court, and these were the spectators, the public who stood within the courthouse, mingled in the yard outside, or refreshed themselves at the taverns nearby. "Every male person can attend such a court and every one is permitted to takes notes," reported a German observer at a military court martial in Cambridge, Massachusetts. "The courtroom is packed, and not even the humblest is refused admittance."[132] The public administration of the law had a clear didactic function. In the semiliterate society of eighteenth-century Virginia, historian Rhys Isaac writes, court day "served not only to make the community a witness to important decisions and transactions but also to teach men the very nature and forms of government."[133] Everywhere court day informed people of the law, and it provided the occasion for the populace to recognize authority in the persons of magistrates and in their ritualized language, dress, and gesture. Most adult males in eighteenth-century Connecticut ended up at court at one time or another, as litigant, juror, observer, or witness. The same probably held true in other colonies too, and since even free women occasionally appeared as litigants, witnesses, or defendants, a substantial portion of society might at one time or another be present at court.[134]

Of course, spectators were by no means intended to feel themselves the equals of "the Court," and judges' silk gowns and lawyers' wigs reminded them as much. Rules of decorum required that spectators show deference toward the gentlemen justices. Architects of courthouses embodied relations of power in their designs, sometimes underscoring judges' prominence by seating them above, placing lawyers within the bar and with their backs to the public, and providing spaces outside the courthouse to be allocated to less substantial spectators.[135] Yet these efforts to constrain the popular presence reflect the fact that the proceedings might depend precisely on the quality of spectators' engagement and reception. The public exerted a force in the courtroom, and no player remained untouched by it. Judges' social standing could insulate them from "the humours of the populace," but they reached their decisions knowing that courtroom events might be widely broadcast through the county. Good lawyers concentrated on swaying judge and jury, but it would not hurt to bring "tears to the eyes" of onlookers too.[136] Finally, what made it plausible to cast jurymen as an extension of "the people" was in no small measure that they remained face-to-face with their peers and inferiors. While public attendance at court provided the colonial elite with a critical opportunity to preside, it also provided the occasion for more ordinary colonists to exercise political discretion. If spectators did not recognize that this was justice, these were their superiors, then the majesty of the law became a mockery. Even in court, in the face of the gentlemen justices, there was the possibility of withholding one's confidence, allegiance, and respect from (their version of) the law. If the courtroom was a drama, it is worth remembering what the early nineteenth century would call the "sovereignty" of the audience—its capacity to influence and even enter into events on stage, its status as ultimate arbiter of the play.[137] Magistrates' social superiority and coercive powers restrained dissent. Nonetheless, it remains that spectators increased the courtroom's vulnerability to a public voice.

To maintain that vulnerability, it was essential that trial by petit jury be a public event. When a group of counterfeiters came to trial in Boston in 1768, "the concourse of people [was] the largest ever known at any trial in that city." Since the courthouse could not accommodate the crowd, court adjourned and reassembled at "one of the largest meeting houses in town."[138] Rather than exclude members of the public, in other words, the court relocated, responding to a broadly recognized public right to attend. The popular audience was necessary to magistrates who intended to awe and rule. People learned the law at court, and they learned of its substantial powers and considerable reach by attending. At the same time, even conservative jurists acknowledged that "trial by jury," secured to English men and women by Magna Carta, implied a necessary and proper vulnerability to public view. Friends of public order might sometimes lament the popularity of court day. "Many Persons in places where Courts are held, and in other Places also, that really have no Business at them, will notwithstanding leave their Business, and spend their Time unprofitably" in observing the proceedings of law and discussing them at the public house. Yet the same writer acknowledged the importance of the public presence, noting that it would influence the decisions of jurymen. "The Eyes of Men are upon you," he told the jury, "and you may be sure will be so."[139]

Indeed, as in the theater, so in the courtroom, the public exerted a force, and no player remained untouched by it. Judges donned their robes, lawyers honed their oratory, and jurors reached their verdict—all partially in reference to "the humours of the populace" that watched the proceedings. The public presence meant that courtroom events would become widely known in the neighborhood. Jurymen knew their decision would be condemned or praised at the tavern and in neighborhood households. It made more plausible the jury's "democraticall" character that jurors remained face-to-face with their peers and inferiors in the gallery. I have already noted the fluid line between bystanders and jurors. One legal expert proposed that jurymen be permitted to wear hats in order to distinguish them from the rest of the men who thronged the courtroom. But though distinction seemed important to some, apparently jurymen's similarity to the rest of the men in the courtroom took priority. By the law and in practice any bystander was liable to be tapped by the sheriff to serve on the jury. It was vital that authorities support the perception of widespread competence and responsibility. Thus, the presence of spectators put pressure on a jury, and everyone present, to accord with strong popular belief. After all, if *grand* jurymen needed to be private in order to withstand the influence of their inferiors' opinions, then the men of lesser stature who sat on the petit jury might logically require isolation as well. Some writers cautioned that the good juror should not "cater to the stalls" in making his decisions, but rather withstand popular opinion to announce the judgment of his conscience. Of course, not every juror was all that good.

Nor was the verdict of the petty jury necessarily the last word that "the people" might have on the matter. The popular role in execution of the law extended beyond the courtroom. Some convicted criminals, especially those with some economic means and social stature, paid their debt to society by paying a fine. Poorer people faced public and physical punishments, ranging from whippings or brandings in the pillory and exposure in the stocks, to the final punishment of hanging. These public punishments took place in the marketplace, near the meetinghouse, by the county courthouse in Virginia, on the "common" of a town. Stocks and pillory were a standard part of the landscape. Maryland law was typical in requiring that the various towns and counties maintain these.[140]

Punishment involved an expectation of public shaming along with fatigue and physical pain.[141] On January 11, 1733, a counterfeiter of money named Watt was punished on market day in Philadelphia, by being whipped, pilloried, and "cropt." "He behaved so as to touch the Compassion of the Mob, and they did not fling (as was expected) neither Snow-balls nor any Thing else."[142] Even the procession from the court or jail to place of punishment was an occasion for popular participation. Two itinerant clergymen complained when they were arrested for unlicensed preaching in New York City, for they had been treated as "Exemplary Criminals," the sort of transgressors "to be carried about in Triumph to be insulted over." Presumably, the meaner sorts of lawbreakers—accused pickpockets, prostitutes, or rioters, say—*were* appropriately paraded "in Triumph," with dual intent: making miscreants vulnerable to insult by bystanders, and making bystanders vulnerable to the example of wrongdoers brought to shameful punishment.[143]

Indeed, the people "out of doors" or even "the Mob" were expected to complete the sentence handed down from the bench. In these circumstances, too, "the people"—or some of them—had the right and the capacity to make their own judgment felt. They might mitigate or support the sentence of the court, add to the culprit's pain, fatigue, and abasement, or, on the contrary, express sympathy with the victim. In cases such as Watt's, the criminal might play to public viewers, so as to ease his reintegration into the community. In other cases, miscreants ran afoul of the popular sentiment.

At the extreme, popular participation in punishment could involve outright armed opposition to the dictates of the court. Indeed, what made punishments so dramatic was their combination of order and the potential for its disruption. This was most clear at the many cases of the ultimate punishment: executions. "Executions are intended to draw spectators," wrote Dr. Johnson in 1783.[144] Ninety years earlier, in Bucks County, Pennsylvania, one spectator was disappointed when a hanging was poorly attended: there were simply "too few there to make the affair enjoyable."[145] Whether or not they were enjoyable, executions were always occasions of information. Authorities scripted and staged punishments hoping to teach onlookers a lesson. It was a lesson of order—the dignity of magistrates, the awesomeness of the law, the power of the government, the ruthlessness of authority. The purpose of punishment, wrote Dr. Benjamin Rush, was "to instill terror in onlookers."

But ruthlessness asserted had also to be denied. Executions and other punishments had to be widely recognized as justice. Like other acts of rule, executions employed solemn ritual and a large public gathering to dramatic effect. Ministers read sermons, and the prisoner him- or herself might address the crowd. The audience would be extended by printed versions of executions, sometimes including woodcuts, virtually always including accounts of the criminal's wayward youth, inattention to social duties, entanglement with bad companions, and degeneracy into serious crime. Stories of a criminal's demeanor en route to and on the gallows also spread by newspapers and by word of mouth.[146]

It heightened the terror of executions that they remained uncertain, often until the last moment. Official reprieves and pardons were not uncommon, and some such acts of mercy were purposely announced only when the convicted stood on the scaffold and the spectators had assembled. Late in the seventeenth century, the governor of Maryland pardoned a man condemned to hang for the crime of witchcraft, provided that he be kept in ignorance of the pardon until the very rope was around his neck.[147] There was a lesson in such a pardon, for the criminal and the onlookers alike. In 1730, Pennsylvania's governor pardoned two young men sentenced to hang for burglary just as they stood on the gallows, citing public sympathy for the "tender youth" of one and the "supposed Innocence" of the other. No doubt he was gratified to learn that the "common People" gathered to see the executions "were unanimous in their loud Acclamations of God bless the Governor for his Mercy."[148]

By the same token, even execution took popular cooperation. At a minimum, it took a cartman to hire his team and his labor, a carpenter to build the scaffold, a hangman to do the job. The governor of Bermuda regretted that cooperation with legal punishment suffered from bad repute in his colony: "Every man flies from the office of a whipper more than from the crime which causeth the whippinge." It was particularly hard to get someone to serve as hangman.[149] Moreover, if the prerogative power could summarily set aside the decision of the court, so could the common power wielded by ordinary people.

At times they went so far as to deliver from punishment those whom popular opinion deemed unjustly convicted, sentenced too harshly, or otherwise ill-used. In Hadley, Massachusetts, for example, a dozen men armed with clubs and cudgels set upon a corporal in the colonial militia when he tried to execute a sentence on a man delinquent in his duty.[150] In 1702, unknown persons prevented capital punishment in New York City by cutting down the gallows. Sixty years later in the same city, two felons sentenced to hang enjoyed a temporary reprieve because "the sheriff cannot find any person to act as hangman," and officials feared "an Attempt . . . to rescue" the condemned.[151] Only the presence of British troops finally allowed the execution to proceed. In Boston, a crowd rescued a British soldier sentenced to "ride the stang," a "sort of Wooden Horse," on the common.[152] Bostonians similarly prevented the sheriff from whipping a "French Boy" at the pillory in 1770.[153] A stock breaking in Farmington, Connecticut, seems to have been an interracial affair, involving Samuel Adams, Hue Negro, and Abell Negro.[154] In seaports, crowds violently resisted when naval officials tried to impress colonial seamen. Seamen in Newport, Rhode Island, observed the king's birthday one year by rioting against a press crew from the naval ship *Maidstone*, seizing and burning the ship's barge, and abusing a lieutenant who opposed them. In rural areas, proprietary disputes and attendant conflicts over land titles led to violence, and crowds in New Jersey, for example, prevented arrests, broke open jails, and freed those accused of "treason" and lesser crimes. On these occasions, a local "public" deprived the state of its pound of flesh.[155] In both England and the colonies, the possibility of rescues, even from the scene of final punishment, led authorities to take possibilities of nonconsent into account. Rescues presumed that local and popular notions of justice might take precedence over notions expressed in statutes or from the bench. If the executive had power to give pardon to the convicted, in other words, a united populace might have the power—and the liberty—to give rescue.[156]

Although historians generally call such crowds "extra-legal," in fact the eighteenth century would never have admitted that idea. The law claimed jurisdiction over crowds, presuming that such popular actions lay well with the law's purview. Many people considered specific crowds to be criminal, and officials sought to have their members indicted and tried, with some success. "Riots," after all, were *illegal*, as were "Rescous," listed among the offenses falling under the jurisdiction of a magistrate: "a Resistance against a lawful Authority, and by Violence taking away a Prisoner, or procuring his Escape."[157] (For that matter, the less heinous "refusal to assist constable" was also a crime.) By the same token, and equally important to the logic of the period, crowds were necessary to the law, their possibility implicit in the expectation that people might participate in executive as well as legislative aspects of their government. Put differently, the law of the eighteenth century was not fully "extra"-crowd. For the law presupposed that moments of public gathering would be part of its execution. The law made sense to many people only in light of the claims of crowds to jurisdiction over aspects of its execution. To call crowds extra-legal is to suggest that the law was sufficient in the absence of the crowd, which was precisely what crowd members and their apologists disputed.[158]

Historians' indecision over what to call these actions reflects a historical reality. Should we term them "crowds," which emphasizes that they were often focused and orderly, or "mobs," which emphasizes that they were often coercive in character and disreputable in social makeup? In fact, popular gatherings were potentially legal, and potentially illegal— potentially crowds, potentially mobs—it depended on what they did and of whom they were composed. Equally, it depended on what authorities did, how the institutions of the law, as they operated after the fact, would find them.[159] Let me be clear: there were riots and rescues, criminal and often discreditable acts, undertaken to secure private benefit or indulge private grudges, acts with no pretension to public significance and acts with so feeble pretensions to fairness that even superficial scrutiny would lead most observers to conclude that they were simply crimes. But there were also, and not infrequently, crowd actions that laid claim to lawful status; that were open to good-faith doubt about their legality, and about their amenability to courts of common law.[160]

Such actions posed an alternative understanding of legality, one that—on specific occasions—replaced the voice of rulers (or representatives) with the voice of the people.[161] The entire legal system depended on the existence of a common ground of political participation on which riots took place. Indeed, law was not self-validating in the colonial era. In a sense, laws were virtually always incomplete, always pending, always and repeatedly in need of confirmation by "the people." Many ordinary Americans were accustomed to thinking about law as unbinding unless and until it was executed on the common ground. By itself, the courtroom was ultimately insufficient to the execution of the law. Even when sentence had been handed down from the bench, there often remained the possibility of further revision. Justice needed to be confirmed or disallowed. Once again, the court's determination of justice came under the jurisdiction of the society's two centers of power, the monarch and the people.[162] A balanced constitution provided that local knowledge and local peculiarities would make themselves felt in the process of law. All parties, surely, knew that there would be arenas for the discretion of grand juries, petit juries, and the broader public that might gather at trial or at punishment.

The effects of that understanding can be seen in the striking case of New Yorker James Wilkes, accused of killing Under Sheriff John Christie in 1756. According to authoritative accounts, Christie had arrived at Wilkes's house carrying a writ and intending to arrest Wilkes, found the front door open, and walked in. Reportedly there was some exchange of words, but shortly Wilkes seized a knife, attacked Christie, and killed him. Not surprisingly, Wilkes was indicted, tried, convicted, and sentenced to hang for murder. More surprisingly, the governor gave Wilkes a reprieve and then a pardon. The avowed reason for this move was simple. The murderer, the governor explained, "strongly believed a common Error generally prevailing among the Lower Class of Mankind in this part of the world." And this was the error: "That after warning the Officer to desist and bidding him stand off at his Peril, it was lawful to oppose him by any means to prevent the arrest."[163] Wilkes claimed the right to consent, or withhold his consent, in the face of a judge's writ and a king's officer.

Authorities understandably took the occasion to impress upon the public the erroneous nature of their view. The *New-York Mercury* sought to correct popular misconceptions in their region by citing "Sundry Authorities" that had been read at the trial. There was the case of "one Mackelly, who killed a Serjeant of London, reported in the 9th Part of Sir Edward Coke's Reports," and which had led to resolves "by all the Judges of England, and Barons of the Exchequer, who met together by the King's Command." Those resolves estabished that men were not to resist arrest in this manner. "It is to be hoped," the *Mercury* concluded, "that the unhappy Condition of the Prisoner now under Sentence of Death, will be an Example and a Warning in preventing such Rashness for the future." Here the *Mercury* published the position of authorities with didactic intent; the paper apparently never reported on the reprieve and the pardon, and never mentioned the popular interpretation of the law that was essential to Wilkes's defense.[164]

Yet after all the explanations and admonitions, the authorities in New York deferred to popular misconceptions. Though the court found him guilty, the governor let Wilkes off. Government thereby acknowledged that, in the last analysis, even "the lower class of Mankind" had a place in defining what was just and, indeed, what was legal. We see in the Wilkes case the failure of the law, formed in statute and case, to contain people's lives or constrict their thinking. It is permissible to cast this as popular ignorance but more accurate to name it recalcitrance, the hardheaded preference of some colonists for their own version of what was lawful. The "lower class of Mankind" were not so misinformed as to believe that they held *fewer* rights against arrest than the government recognized. Together, this verdict and this pardon made clear that the workings of the law might sometimes be modified by the giving or withholding of "after the fact" consent. Over and against the professionalizing efforts of magistrates and lawyers, even in the face of the jurymen who indicted and convicted Wilkes, people debarred from jury duty asserted a different power.

What allowed them to do so was, in one sense, structural. When government was not "We the People," when it did not therefore preempt the role of "the public," then there existed political space for someone else to play that role. Houses of assembly, voters, jurors, printers of newspapers, and their writers and readers—all might at times experience themselves as such. So might crowds that acted as spectators at occasions of public rule such as court days and punishments. People were capable of acting as "the people." Equally, many ordinary Americans' capacity to participate depended on their residence within the horizontal relationships of eighteenth-century America, within an everyday life characterized by its relative proximity to public time.[165]

In all this, "the people" offered a fiction of use to top and bottom, inside and out. We should recognize "popular sentiment" or "the public" for what they were: constructions that might serve to totalize, notions that flattened the social landscape, portraying themselves as embracing everyone outside the ranks of the elite, while in fact leaving out a good many actors and interests. Moreover, plausibly passing as "the people" or "the town" might be a complicated negotiation. In the view of political insiders, surely, far from every crowd qualified as "the public." Few gatherings composed wholly of African Americans, Native Americans, mere apprentices or laborers passed muster as legitimate expressions of "the public voice." When a gentleman denounced a crowd as composed of "Negroes and boys," it was precisely an effort to deny the group the capacity to occupy the role of "the public," "the people," "the town," or "the country." Men of low status were not adequately intimidated by such judgments, and even colonial women occasionally acted as a group to intrude their own moral sensibilities onto the public stage.[166] Yet, for the most part, when African Americans, European-American boys, or women took part, their participation depended on their indistinguishability, a capacity to blur into the midst of their betters. To this extent, the common ground felt the press of notions of competence applied in provincial political systems: crowds seemed more like "the town" as they approximated or assimilated to those who qualified as voters and jurors.

Nonetheless, in this realm, even those colonists entitled to vote or sit on juries achieved political identity not by virtue of their individuality or distinction but by virtue of their boundedness, their situation within a community. Other premises of competence here made themselves felt. Authority lay in ordinary knowledge and the common point of view. For their part, elite colonists, and the political insiders among them, acknowledged the existence of popular power and, with greater or lesser equanimity, recognized and observed members of the ranks beneath them, for a time, for a purpose, and in a not extra-ordinary transformation, occupied the public ground. In turn, more ordinary colonists surely considered elite opinion, weighing their chances of finding toleration or opposition from those who wielded legislative and courtroom law. That they sometimes defied such authorities meant that eighteenth-century government officials not only failed to command a police but also failed fully to command the law.

Indeed, what I have described as the vulnerability of the legal process to the possibility of strong public sentiment might also be understood as a difficulty in locating the law or adequately establishing its source in the colonial period. Legislatures enacted statutes, but no one believed that statutes comprised the totality of law or that legislators could pass whatever laws they wished. In the absence of a written constitution or the institution of judicial review, English and colonials alike held "a vague belief" that law was something prior to or more fundamental than legislation.[167] Moreover, the common law was unevenly but notably in force in the continental colonies, and it consisted of a slippery body of precepts that evolved as customary practice encountered judicial reasoning. The common law embraced custom, but it did not necessarily legitimate the particular customs of a given locality; lawyers aspired to authority precisely on the basis of their access to common law as a learned if not esoteric tradition.[168] Despite that, that law arose from practice as well as from parliaments meant it was not so neatly in lawyers' and jurists' pockets as they wished. Jurors might effectively decide whether the law applied, hence what in practice, not in statute, the law really was in the neighborhood in question.[169]

We return to the cobbler and his capacity to recognize whether he was well or ill governed. In light of these institutions of public participation, we need to reassess that capacity. Cato's adage located the cobbler "in his stall"—that is, in the marketplace or shop, in the midst of daily life. But cobblers might sometimes recognize authority as it paraded about the streets of leading towns, or as it sat on the bench in county court, or as it set men and women in the pillory or on the gallows. What was ordinary men's role at such moments, and in what sense might it be understood as one of political participation? Even when they merely observed processions, the cobblers played a vital part. In France, one scholar observes, kings might stage royal ceremonies and even public executions in order to "solicit opinion" from the people, to gain a sense of the popular sentiment.[170] English processions, too, had a participatory quality. Queen Anne's processions demonstrated an admirable accessibility to her people. They created a "ceremonial dialogue" between court and town; and, even when the commonalty had little to say, the people were still significantly present. Both Anne and Elizabeth were known to accept petitions while in progress, and many monarchs understood and used them as invitations to popular opinion.[171] We may call the popular role at such events "spectatorship," if we can shake the term's connotation of passivity and understand it instead as a particular proximity to public time.[172] Spectators on the streets who observed the theatrical forms of government also had the capacity to enter into the occasion. Everyone knew themselves to be in the presence of power, at the center of events and meaning; at the same time, they knew the possibility of disruption, reversal, or ridicule. When governors proclaimed or magistrates pronounced, these were acts of rule, giving both the elite and commonalty the obligation to attend. At the same time, they were acts of vulnerability, providing people with the opportunity to attend.[173]

Processions thus provided for unequal but mutual recognition, an occasion when power circulated. Like money, authority changed hands, which is how many felt its potency and could be reassured it existed at all. We need to remember that "to recognize" can mean to *convey* power, to *give* public status, to *provide* space and time within which someone (say, for example, a distinguished senator) can speak. Inherent in occasions of elite display was the need for audience, the fact of a relationship. There existed the possibility that unlearned, common people might nonetheless see through the emperor's new clothes. Such insight was not a mere abstraction (nor yet a children's tale).

It is important not to overstate the freedom in this: authorities expected recognition and assent from their inferiors, and they had at their disposal various sanctions should it not be forthcoming. If the monarch and magistrate set themselves on view, so too were cobblers visible to the agents of power. We are not yet in the nineteenth-century state, when the government's near-constant surveillence of the citizen became central to its form of rule. Still, individuals who decided to demonstrate their lack of respect to a magistrate, sheriff, or other worthy knew they risked consequences. Members of crowds sometimes took care about being seen, limiting their own visibility and distinguishability, blacking their faces.

The powers commonly exerted on such occasions were not the powers of citizen-individuals, but rather the liberties of subjects, collective and subordinate. "The people" might recognize whether they were well or ill governed, but if an individual or a small group dissented, they were apt to find themselves punished for contempt of court. Indeed, people enjoyed these liberties not by being individual and distinctive, above the herd, but by being indistinguishable—and by being many instead of few. This is to suggest new meaning to the frequent frustration of officials who, when they called for information against rioters, found no witness able to recognize and distinguish a single member of a mob. Being undistinguished, a liability that disqualified colonists from voting before the fact, might prove an asset on occasions of after-the-fact consent. This argument has two implications, not incompatible: (1) ordinary people were accustomed to being mere witnesses of power; and (2) witnessing could be far from insubstantial.

What we see is the existence of a particular political role in the eighteenth century, the experience of a different public, open to the participation of a fair number who could not vote, as well as to many who could. This political role is not adequately described by theories that cast political crowds under the auspices of elite notions of when it was appropriate to resist, or what oppression consisted of. Exercised most prominently at court days and public punishments and extended to occasions uninitiated by the elite, that role involved independent judgment, the right not to be convinced by elite notions of justice, and the ability to hold and express their own. Capacity to act within this public, on this ground, arose not from individual traits that set one person apart and above, but rather from embeddedness in neighborhood, community, and society. For many colonists, the presence of this public was essential to British liberty. It would surely prove essential to the American Revolution.

2

The Commitments
They Brought

We are still some distance from understanding the commitments that took eighteenth-century Americans into conflict with Britain in 1776. We have seen that there existed surprising space for ordinary, free men to consent to decisions of government in colonial societies: "before hand," in elections that chose representatives to houses of assembly, and after the fact, in institutions that executed the law. Yet to know that such political forms existed is not yet to understand why people valued and defended them. What made colonists in British North America cast ballots for legislators, dissent from judges, overrule juries, or rescue offenders from officers of the law? What prompted ordinary people to gather and step into public time?

To answer those questions, this chapter explores colonial Americans' ideas of fairness and right, on the one hand, and their fears of oppression and wrong, on the other. It looks at some of the various sources of their ideas: English history, law, Protestant belief, and practices of both neighborhood and market exchange within their societies.

It also surveys a number of occasions when colonists joined in concerted actions against what they saw as the threat of oppression in their lives. The debates that animated those conflicts addressed the fairness of economic exchange, the nature of property, and the proper and necessary limits of men's ambition. Although the details of people's conflicts were specific to place—different in urban centers than the countryside, different in the backcountry than the settled East—many disputes revealed common ideas about the nature of social good. They show that ordinary as well as elite and well-to-do colonists had profound concerns about their societies. This chapter seeks to understand those concerns.

We begin where so many colonists began.

England

If monarchs had been the only source of oppression, the English could have dispensed with them altogether, as they demonstrated in the seventeenth century. Twice Stuart kings ran afoul of the English people. Charles I decided to tax and rule without Parliament; James II decided to disregard its laws. Members of Parliament objected that this behavior was "arbitrary" and even "absolute." The Stuarts acted as if they did not need to consult, as if kingship might render the voices of the people's representatives sweepingly irrelevant. Charles lost his head, and James lost his throne.

Yet the English did not give up on monarchy. Kings and their laws continued to be useful, for there were other ambitious men within the empire, and their pursuit of wealth and position could also threaten the people's well-being and trespass on their liberties. So we start with this crucial fact: the oppressions that Englishmen knew and feared in the early modern era did not all come from overreaching government but sometimes represented the failure of government to restrain (they might say "regulate") the ambitions of individuals.

Indeed, it was on those grounds that political writers of varying opinions commonly lauded the value of civil government—"the most inestimable Blessing that Mankind enjoy." Englishmen should support the authority of government, advised one seventeenth-century writer; equally, they should insist that it operate "for the Happiness and Security of all." Thus, "if there be any particular Form of government amongst Men, where the Supreme Magistrate is not vested with enough Power to protect the People and promote their Prosperity—if there be any such Constitution as enables the Prince to injure and oppress the Subject; such Constitutions . . . are inconsistent with civil Society."[1] In this statement, reprinted in the colonies in the mid-eighteenth century, the threat of oppressive government appeared second to the danger of incapable government. This was not an endorsement of governments that "governed least," then, as some later thinkers would promote, but rather an endorsement of government that was both accountable and effective, mindful of its obligations to execute laws that protected lesser people from the excessive ambitions of the great or would-be great.[2]

Such insistence on the powers of law made sense to many people in early modern England, where extraordinary changes were transforming society. Ambitious men were plentiful on the ground, and they might sometimes be blamed for or credited with challenging received ways of ordering English society. The English had been accustomed to thinking of themselves as rooted, situated in geographical place and in a network of relationships with peers, superiors, and inferiors. People were born into families, of course, and into the wider ties of kinship, but also the overlapping categories of household, neighborhood, parish, shire, church, and kingdom. They inherited a relationship with their Creator and His Church, their sovereign and his government, and in these and other relationships they might hold expectations and also owe obligations. As there was no life that began without claims and obligations, so human existence was not widely or easily imagined outside relationships, in locations both geographical and social. In the year 1600, when 90 percent of the British population lived in countryside villages and small market towns, to know who you were was to speak of kin and place, of occupation and established affiliation.[3]

English men and women enjoyed essential liberties by virtue of such affiliation, by membership within a larger body. More than a way of thinking about people, in other words, this was also a way of thinking about liberties and rights. At the broadest level, the British appealed not to human rights but to British rights. (So that when they sang of freedom, it was in terms of a specific collective identity: "*Britons* never will be slaves," ran the eighteenth-century anthem; there was no telling about the French, and there would be only limited objection to the bondage of Africans for some years.) And although this was narrowness and parochialism, it also represented an impressive breadth of vision, as it embraced a large population, both expressing and resulting from a shared history of struggle in which specific Britons had won specific guarantees and recognitions from past monarchs, promises that arguably bound those rulers' descendants and successors. On a more local and mundane level, individuals might claim poor relief by virtue of belonging to the neighborhood or parish. A tradesman was "free" of a specific town, and free to practice the particular trade to which his apprenticeship entitled him. Location was not always and never only geographical, then; in *both* geographical and social terms, people were imagined to have a place. That place was undoubtedly a source of limitation, but it was also a source of security and entitlement.[4]

These conventional ways that the English imagined themselves and their society, never fully stable, came under considerable pressure by extraordinary developments in the early modern era.[5] One pressure was population growth; the size of the English population doubled in the sixteenth century and again in the seventeenth. There was sweeping social and economic change, as landowners promoted innovations sometimes described as agricultural "improvement." In the sixteenth century, many landlords turned farmland to pasture, raising sheep for the wool cloth industry. Some combined patches of common lands into larger farms; they eliminated common work on open fields, promoting the practice of a more productive agriculture. In so doing, they pushed many rural households off the land, out of long-standing customary ties with specific holdings, villages, and neighbors. This was economic disruption as well as social. Families accustomed to supplementing their means by harvesting from forests, wastelands, and common fields, or by grazing livestock on common lands, now needed to find new resources. This process—also called "enclosure" for the hedges or fences used to delineate new bounded fields and farms—continued in the following centuries. As it remade the English landscape, it remade English lives.[6]

In profound ways, the process of enclosure challenged the presumption that people were properly located in place and social station. The nation saw unprecedented levels of geographical mobility and the flow of population into urban centers, especially London. (That city grew to an amazing half million in population by 1700, a million by 1800, and with it grew manufactures and unprecedented commerce within the realm and with the growing New World colonies.) People moved to where they could better get a living, some to provincial towns, others to parts of the countryside where common use rights perisisted or where it was easier to obtain a small landholding. In some rural areas, the uprooted became unlanded wage earners in woolen manufactories or in households that produced cloth on output.

In social terms, England experienced a process of differentiation, the emergence of new social categories. The agricultural population of medieval England had been one of lords and peasants. Now there grew a class of yeomen farmers, households that held long-term leases on the landlords' farms and that conducted a newly competitive and productive agricultural practice engaged with the market. A far greater number of peasant families, separated from access to the land, became a population of laborers, forced to sell their labor on the market.[7] While the 1600s may be best known for their remarkable political contests between Parliament and king, these social changes—population growth, a shift to urban centers, geographic mobility, and the differentiation of social groups—continued in that century, then redoubled in the next.[8]

Urban growth also brought differentiation. Commentators of the day began speaking of more different "sorts" of people, new social identities that required new categories. Seventeenth-century writers increasingly identified a "middle sort" of English, a term that composed no single cohesive group but rather embraced households of different occupations, resources, and cultural aspirations. The middling ranged from prosperous skilled artisans to educated professionals, overseas merchants, and financiers. To describe the new social divisions, some writers categorized people by wealth, others by occupation, still others by cultural values.[9] There was no easy consensus, in other words, about how to tell who was who.

In the midst of these transformations, some people formed new religious communities. They joined in new congregations for a new reading of the Word. So-called Puritans sought to replace older ties with an internalized discipline, insisting on personal relationships with God; they also established a tight discipline of fellow believers. The Christian project—to negotiate and ultimately transcend the boundaries between self and neighbor, neighbor and stranger—necessarily evolved new forms of fellowship and practice.

Social theorists also advanced new ideas. It was clear that, for some, "agricultural improvements" brought opportunity. Some people acquired more, and they owned (or at least claimed) more right to the unhindered and unshared use of property. Those claims constituted new freedoms for individuals, a shedding of social duties and constraints. Accordingly, some writers challenged the idea that men's lives need be defined by inherited social obligations. Some celebrated a new and liberal individualism, a liberation for those who might abandon the obligation to consult their neighbors in many dealings. Landlords of the aristocracy and gentry classes, the stewards they hired to manage their estates, and the lawyers they paid to find ways and means promoted exclusive ideas of property. Arable land, pasture, timber, and other resources, once associated with the livelihood of a local community, might be captured for more private, productive, and profitable purposes.[10]

For their part, those who experienced these innovations as oppressive might appeal to the king's law, with its ability to bind even the powerful to a larger good. The process of enclosure did not cause conflict everywhere, but in many places agricultural improvers met with opposition from those who saw their households losing resources and families stripped of customary use rights. Many protested when rents and other fees were stretched (painfully, as on the rack, according to those who called the new exactions "rack rents"). Some communities mounted legal cases to challenge proposed changes to their tenure on the land; small-holders might associate together, pool their money, and take their case to court. In Cumbria, for example, tenants on Lord Percy's estates orga-nized into a "Strict and Solemn Combination and Confederacy" in 1723, promising "to stand by and Assist each other with Mutual Contributions and all other ways and means of Assistance." They successfully opposed the lord's imposition of "Exhorbitant unreasonable" fines for the tenants to keep their holdings. In such cases, the law sometimes provided protec-tions, slowing the process of expropriation when landlords deviated too far from the "customary" or the "reasonable."[11]

Opposition to enclosure also took place outside the courtroom.[12] There were symbolic warnings, as when enclosing landlords were hanged in ef-figy in Buckinghamshire in the 1570s and 1580s. There were seditious libels, anonymous threats, and the breaking or leveling of hedges. Sweep-ing eviction of established tenants provoked substantial disorders, "ris-ings" of the people, as at Galway in 1723–25. These sorts of actions expressed people's nonconsent to changes on the land. Rural people's abil-ity to "combine and confrate"—that is, to join in confraternity with one another—slowed the pace of change. Challenges by improving landlords prompted association and reinvigorated neighborhood ties, as the identity of neighbor in good standing became a source of leverage. In these dis-putes, claims of location and membership were doubly meaningful: peo-ple threatened with uprooting and loss insisted that landlords, too, were neighbors, social beings who, however superior, nonetheless were always already in relationship with others. And if landords were neighbors with obligations, tenants were neighbors with just expectations and liberties; they objected when landlords behaved in the high-handed manner of Stuart kings.[13]

There was another form of oppression that roused ordinary English people to engage in public action. Eliminating the access of petty house-holds to once common resources made many more dependent on daily hire in manufacture or in the field. Some observers welcomed this trans-formation. It was certainly in the interest of landholders and owners of manufactories, and it was arguably in the interest of "the nation," to di-minish the customary securities of the poor. From the point of view of some Britons, this was what was good about enclosure: it provided cheap labor in the realm's growing industries; it pressed people to work more unremittingly. It prompted the creation of wealth and its accumulation in the hands of some.[14]

Yet observers noted the growing presence of a population of laboring poor, who worked yet suffered. By the year 1700, one historian estimates, roughly half of the English population were dependent on the uncertainties of the wage. Many enjoyed little control over the market for their products or the price of materials or food.[15] Without access to other resources, the wage did not always suffice. Sometimes there were labor actions. Workers acted collectively to protest when masters imposed wages inadequate to maintaining what the workers considered a decent livelihood. In 1726, for example, a group of weavers in Bristol complained of the "unreasonableness of the Masters, in abating the old Prices at a Time when Provisions were dear." Calling themselves "Regulators" of wages, they decried the "arbitrary will" of employers who cut wages in the industry.[16] More commonly, poor people who suffered a disjunction between wage and food prices targeted the latter. The marketplaces where many Britons secured their daily bread increasingly became arenas for felt oppression and dramatic conflict.

Indeed, the most common popular disorder of the era was the food riot. Great merchants gradually integrated a national market in grain, so that staple foodstuffs might flow to city populations and to coastal towns for export. Dealers sometimes found greater profit in foreign markets or in supplying the British navy than in sales in the English countryside. Crowds responded by interrupting the export of grain, or seizing it from dealers, millers, and farmers who would not sell, or would sell only in bulk, or would sell at too high a price. At times the crowd paid in exchange a price they considered reasonable. By so doing, crowd members both acknowledged individual ownership of grain and placed a limit to it. In these food riots, the English poor across the countryside expressed a set of ideas and collective practices, "the moral economy of the English crowd."[17] Against those who transported foodstuffs, crowds acted as agents of location. They made claims that countered the logic of enclosures: as land became dissociated from the sustenance of a local population, crowds insisted that the most vital products of the land remained intrinsically and properly amenable to the needs of the people. Even the dislocated, in other words, unsuccessful at maintaining access to land on the grounds of being neighbors, might still invoke rights of access to grain on the grounds of being English.

In food riots, even poor English people might have an impact on execution of the law. Rioters drew on the fact that the term "oppression" was firmly associated, in common use and law alike, with dealers' misbehaviors in the marketplace. Statutes passed under the Tudors and Stuarts had outlawed as oppressive specific acts by individuals: technically, forestalling the market (buying before the market bell opened purchasing to the public); regrating (buying for resale at the same or nearby market); and monopolizing the supply of necessary goods into one's own hands in order to "oppress," or raise the price. Moreover, distribution of grain in particular was subject to oversight by officials of the king. Justices in their various counties were expected to act when shortages suggested hoarding.[18] At the end of the seventeenth century, when the philosopher John Locke wrote about property, he specified that everyone possessed an "equal right," or "a right in common . . . [to] provide for their subsistence," which entailed the "right to the surplusage" of someone else's goods in cases of need.[19] The eighteenth century saw debates among legal experts and policy makers about the matter, but regulatory statutes remained in place until the 1770s, and many localities enforced these laws until late in the century.[20]

The sheer number of food riots testifies to the energy and entrepreneurship of English dealers, the striking opportunities available in the market in this era, and the coercions experienced in that same market. Riots show us deep disagreement as well as persistent reiteration of moral economic norms. Paradoxically, the *absence* of riots might also evidence powerful support for the claims of the poor, either from elite jurists or middling interests. Although historians associate the "moral economy" with the poor, the middling also believed that economic life had an ethics. They, too, thought government was obligated to secure not only order, but *social* order, meaning safety, security, and sufficiency.[21] In the counties of the realm, the middle sort sat on juries of "honest and substantial" men, charged by justices in times of shortage to interview farmers, retailers, brewers, bakers, and dealers about the amounts of grain they had in store. Such juries might require neighbors to bring their surplus to market at "convenient and charitable prices."[22] The same logic that presumed the prerogatives of juries in other cases underscored the ability of the middling to judge the state of the market. "No man can be deceived in facts like famine, pestilence, fire; a jury are always competent judges of these natural necessities."[23] Grand juries sometimes initiated exemplary prosecutions of particular offenders in the provisions trade in order to set an example for others. Similarly, it was retailers, tradesmen, and manufacturers who, serving on the common council of eighteenth-century London, actively limited corn merchants there. Less dramatic than riots, occasions when members of a community managed to avert disorder were surely also numerous, and they depended on middling and even elite Englishmen acknowledging a collective responsibility.[24]

Moreover, if they did not see the world precisely as poor people saw it, various groups within the middle sort made moral judgments about the sort of dealings appropriate to their lives in a commercial society. Middling tradesmen and shopkeepers, professionals, merchants, financiers, and manufacturers all relied on the market, accumulated profits, and employed others in their households and their businesses. Many unquestionably admired the efficiency with which the market could move goods to where there was need for them. Yet some still disapproved when dealers removed grain and other necessaries altogether from the nexus of human need. Monopolists and engrossers impeded the free flow of goods, after all; and, unlike useful and legitimate traders and transporters, they could not claim they simply served consumers. Many middling English believed powerfully in commerce as it contributed to social well-being, or, as one historian sums it up, in "a just and profitable commerce."[25] They might also consistently approve of policies that capped the profits of middlemen in transactions vital to survival of the many.

Indeed, contemporaries pointed to clear parallels between the "oppressions" in the marketplace and the oppressions of which the Stuarts had been guilty. Kings who levied taxes, landlords who raised rents, and dealers who engrossed bread all annexed the property of others while denying them space for consent. So the gentry in Parliament had protested to King Charles: he was in an established relationship with them, and he needed to acknowledge as much. So peasants defending their tenure on the land addressed their landlords, and landless workers, conservative jurists, and many craftsmen, retailers, and manufacturers spoke to speculators who cornered the market on grain. The acts of the great, wealthy, or ambitious could not be arbitrary, the logic ran, and their claims of ownership could not be absolute. The English people had legitimate expectations of influencing the terms of many dealings that were crucial to their lives. They insisted that they possessed by right a certain property, a space for consent or withholding of consent.

Perhaps they could establish such space across the Atlantic.

British North America

Emigrants to the New World were certainly mobile. Those who ventured across the Atlantic could hardly think of themselves as located and settled Englishmen. They were not attached to geographic place or even necessarily to a social one, as many surely hoped to improve their fortunes when they reached American soil. No doubt they wanted distance from England—from kings, bishops, ambitious landlords, and more. Some may even have wanted distance from kin and neighbors as well. Yet many also desired a measure of connection and continuity. It was only human to want it both ways: to be English but from a distance, on one's own ground, in the most literal sense of the phrase.[26]

Indeed, colonists showed a striking propensity for establishing familiar institutions in the New World and for putting down roots. Studies of the many English who migrated from the countryside into London in these years have found that "migration appears to have intensified, rather than diminished, reciprocal ties with kin."[27] In the same manner, migration to North America often put a premium on social connections that could help people weather the challenges of a new environment. Some came not only with their households but with larger networks of relatives and neighbors. Puritans arrived in New England hoping to be "knit together" in religious community. Still others came to Pennsylvania and New Jersey as "Friends," intending to live in the light of that friendship. Even in the Southern colonies, where tobacco culture encouraged more dispersed patterns of settlement, households chose what proximity with others was compatible with plantation economy. And in early Maryland, people compensated for high mortality by creating new ties, serving as godparents for one another's children. Such acts reproduced practices of "neighbouring"—in New England they preferred "the Injoyment of neer-Neighbours"—as a part of life.[28] In the eighteenth century, when immigration into the colonies soared, social connections remained an important determinant in some newcomers' lives. They chose places to settle where there was economic opportunity, but also ethnic, linguistic, and religious ties with others. They did not duplicate Old World institutions, even when that was the intention, yet in adapting to the New World they drew on familiar social resources. The specific *ways* they lived as neighbors, Christians, and English men and women varied from place to place, in other words, as well as from time to time. Nonetheless, such identities remained salient in people's lives.[29]

On the level of provincial institutions, colonists insisted on representative assemblies in order to protect themselves against overreaching by rulers. They instituted the legal units known as shires and the office known as sheriff. Settlers in North Carolina, which adopted the system belatedly, agitated loudly for its institution: "There are a thousand inconveniences in this wide extended country for want of sheriffs and the people are strangely bent on having them established by law," wrote an official to the British Board of Trade.[30] Yet sheriffs were familiar figures in the lives of Britons, and Carolinians' desire for their establishment was not strange but typical. After all, people displaced from Britain by the conflicts we have surveyed were not likely to underestimate the ambitions of men or their penchant for oppressing others, even if they were neighbors, even if they were English. And although officers of the law could certainly become oppressive, they also played a vital role in the law as an institution sometimes amenable to those outside the ranks of rulers and well-to-do.[31]

What happened in the Chesapeake could serve as a cautionary tale. In the tobacco boom of the 1620s, ambitious Englishmen sought to control the labor of others. Far from the oversight of Old World authorities, Virginia's leading men found it possible to whittle down the freedoms of English laborers below those that workers enjoyed at home. To the extent that the Chesapeake colonies eventually became better countries for laboring English people, it was not because employers gave up on exploiting their workers but because they replaced English servants with African slaves, a population that could not easily claim the protections of the English king and the English law. One lesson of the Chesapeake experience was that too great a distance from protections of king's law might leave the English more vulnerable to exploitation. There was nothing inevitably freer about the New World, in other words, no guarantee that men of ambition would not oppress and take advantage in their aspirations for wealth and power.[32]

The knowledge that men might oppress led localities throughout the colonies to routinely institute legal regulations on trade in grain, flour, and bread. Every colonial port town would establish an assize on bread, regulating its weight, quality, and cost. (Some would maintain these into the nineteenth century.) The precise regulations and observation of them varied from place to place, but the port cities all would enact prices on various other goods (such as meat, bricks, or leather); services (such as sawing wood or grinding corn); and regulations on other trades (such as innkeepers and carters of goods), the practice of which had impact on the public well-being.[33] When grain dealers in New York bought directly from farmers and bypassed the city, aldermen considered the matter their business. When the people of Maryland feared there might be grain shortages, the governor duly issued proclamations forbidding dealers from exporting it.[34] Such regulations may have prevented disorders. The colonies did not experience food riots—or just a very few—but that was not because they had jettisoned the relevant law but because they lacked a large population of free, landless, wage-dependent poor. The great bulk of the population was rural, and a great many rural families enjoyed access to the land.[35] That fact made American societies less vulnerable to distress from great grain merchants. They could worry less about bread.[36]

The New World's distance from the Old even provided some protection from great landlords. Ambitious men in England wished to become great lords of the American soil, and various friends or creditors of the king received royal patents entitling them to vast estates. Yet to translate those patents into wealth required that they first attract tenants and settlers to work their land. Emigrant families understandably preferred tenure outside the holdings of great men, or else the security of long leases at minimal cost. The great proprietors could not rack rents when land was available on better terms nearby; for much of the seventeenth century, they could hardly collect rents at all. In every province, the result was a society in some respects very different from England, as a great many households became middling in their social standing and material status. To a greater degree than in England, the ambitions of middling households would shape colonial ideas of right and fairness, wrong and oppression. And a good many households found themselves in a position to pursue ambitions of their own.[37]

A word they often used for their ambitions was "a competence." Historian Daniel Vickers defines the meaning of that term for Northern farmers in the eighteenth century. A competence, says Vickers, was enough land and other resources to absorb the labor of the household, to produce enough to provide a life with some comforts above the level of subsistence. Organized around the household unit, the goal of a competence informed the work that took place under the direction and discretion of the head of household. For that (usually male) household head, in other words, the goal of a competence had value as an experience of nondependence. It was associated with a stage of life, when one was no longer a servant, an apprentice, or a youngster working for someone else. It expressed aversion to service as a mature and lifelong status. Men who sought a competence distinguished themselves from the plight of the landless, wage-dependent poor of England. A man with a competence was possessed of resources, enough to go on, an ability to hold his own.[38]

Yet while possession of a competency suggested an experience of nondependence, it was not truly an experience of *independence*, if by that we mean self-sufficiency or a construction of one's identity as somehow "self-made." The goal of a competency did not suggest or even allow independence from one's neighbors or the commercial market. As a result, it was plausible for urban craftsmen also to use the term "competence" to describe their own ambitions, though they acquired the very basics of daily life through exchange with agricultural producers. If tradesmen did not own land, they might own skills, tools, and relationships with both customers and fellows within the trade. These assets, too, represented a form of property, and such property might let a cobbler in his stall command his own labor so as to work for the well-being of his own rather than another household.[39]

On such grounds both the rural and the urban engaged in neighborhood exchange, trading, say, the cider from one household's orchard for the honey from another household's beehives, the fine linen shirt stitched by one household's skilled needlewoman for a measure of grain at another household's harvest. Such exchanges were routine and frequent; they involved different members of households—female and male, old and young. Often, too, they took place over the course of time, with two elements of a single transaction performed at different moments in the agricultural year. As a result, these dealings created networks of mutual obligation, so that, at any given moment, each household in a neighborhood was likely to be in debt to some of its neighbors and a creditor to others. Past dealings between households, and the expectation that the parties in question would continue to deal in the future, shaped these transactions. Each party had to walk away tolerably satisfied of its fundamental fairness in order to deal again. When there were disputes, the parties might appeal to a shared local authority, such as a clergyman or town official; they might refer the matter to "three disinterested men," presumed competent to assess the worth of local products and to evaluate claims and counterclaims. They might submit their case to a jury of their peers.[40]

Colonists also exchanged with more distant markets. From the outset, tobacco planters in the Chesapeake and cod fishermen in New England made their way by supplying the Atlantic market. Farm families in many parts of the colonies produced a surplus intended for overseas and regional markets, in order to secure in turn manufactures—a wide array of textiles, hardware, and ceramics—and exotic goods, such as sugars, coffee, spices, and tea. Farm households dealt with the wider market through the channel of a local storekeeper, who might provide book credit in return for payment in crops or other kind. To that extent, market relationships overlapped with local or neighborly relationships as well. Yet they ultimately involved people in dealings with strangers rather than neighbors. A growing class of storekeepers, overseas merchants, and dealers found fortunes or a least a living in commercial exchange. Farmers found outlets for a variety of products; in the Connecticut River Valley, for example, some households compensated for the declining productivity of the soil by shifting to cattle raising and timber harvest for export to the West Indies. Everywhere, the market offered attractive goods in return.[41] Many families wanted access to wider markets (and they reasonably preferred more channels of access to fewer); at the same time, they preferred to take part in market transactions for their own ends and on their own terms. They wanted a solid basis on which to take advantage of market opportunities but also avoid its coercions. I have suggested that they wanted to be English, but on their own ground; likewise, or similarly, they wanted to engage in the market, but from a place of some security rather than dependence.[42]

Finally, the idea of a competence expressed and provided a moral standard. One New England writer assumed that "men will be contented with a competent Quantitie of Land, and a comfortable Livelihood."[43] This idea presupposed limited acquisition and limited competition to be good and right; it provided space within which to conduct exchanges considered fair, to live in ways some considered Christian, to inhabit an identity known as "neighbour." The ideal of a competence helped mitigate conflicts between the practices of neighboring and the pursuit of a household's own particular interests. For that matter, maintaining one's status as a neighbor in good standing was a valuable resource for personal and household well-being. Neighbors might lay claim on others' assistance in times of difficulty, appeal for debts to be forgiven or at least payment to be postponed, and count on one another to be witnesses of character, supporters of reputation, and "evidences" of property boundaries and the history of dealings.[44] Equally, the practice of neighboring provided ground for unity over and against powerful men. This is to argue that concrete social institutions underlay the sense of location that allowed colonists to transform an abstraction (*"the people"*) into something concrete (the *presence of the people of this place in this moment*). Two identities were vital to that transformation: first was the colonists' identity as English and the concomitant claim that they possessed rightfully the liberties of Englishmen; second was an identity rooted in social institutions of American societies, having claims on the land and its resources, the place and its web of social connections. These identities proved critical in a number of eighteenth-century conflicts.

.   .   .

In the eighteenth century, the distance between England and its New World colonies grew smaller. The English renewed their focus on what might be gained through investment, trade, or careful administration of the colonies. Wars of the Old World spilled over into the new, and colonists repeatedly became entangled in British contests against the French and their Indian allies. Colonists also engaged in many new commercial transactions with British trading houses. In American port cities, a growing merchant class bridged ever greater distances. Merchants made it possible for colonial producers to reach markets in other provinces, the West Indies, and Europe. They brought new consumer goods into the colonies and transported them to stores in inland towns. Manufactures and exotic goods such as spices and tea became part of the lives of the middle sort as well as the well-to-do. A growing percentage of many men's dealings became commercial in nature, as they became links in extended chains of credit and debt.[45]

These changes widened men's horizons and encouraged new ambitions. In every province a burgeoning social elite became more prominent as a distinctive element of society. Many of them imported English fashions, adopted English standards of behavior, and modeled themselves on the provincial gentry of Britain. For those with aspirations to high political position or mercantile wealth, connections with Britain and the empire at large might loom more important than connections closer to home. In these years the Church of England gained a foothold in Puritan New England and grew in strength in other provinces. The law, too, became "Anglicized" in the first half of the eighteenth century, as growing numbers of lawyers and jurists, some trained in England, brought uniform procedure to courtroom pleadings and procedures.[46]

In the midst of these changes, colonists both embraced the new and tried to maintain the ground they had. The conflicts they experienced caused many of them to act and speak in defense of their ideals and commitments. Every dispute invariably had its purely local and distinctive elements; yet a brief look at a number of disputes offers us entry into the sorts of concerns that moved both urban and rural dwellers to take a public part. These cases generated popular actions and publications that expressed broad perceptions of the threat of oppression. In the following pages, we seek to overhear some colonists' arguments, follow their logic, and appreciate their commitments.

Boston, the most populous port city during the early eighteenth century, experienced substantial conflict during this time. "We are like to be involved under great difficulties and bondage by the Projecting Gentlemen of this Town," wrote one pamphleteer in 1714.[47] Not only "great difficulties" but "bondage"—this was apparently no small danger. The projecting gentlemen included some of Boston's leading merchants, ministers, and friends of the royal governor. Their attempts to make the town more orderly and hierarchical met with opposition from a loosely allied popular party that had the support of many town middling and poor.

Urban dwellers faced some of the problems of supply that beset British cities and rural areas where manufacturing households purchased their daily bread in the marketplace. In wars with the French, the British military's demand for grain and its offer of payments in pounds sterling disrupted established patterns of civilian supply. Colonists had occasion to mobilize to secure a sufficiency. Repeatedly, Boston town meeting urged its representatives to secure a law to ban export of grain in wartime, and town officials negotiated with grain dealers on behalf of the poor on several occasions. It was when official efforts failed that townspeople carried out food riots. In 1710 a crowd prevented Andrew Belcher's ship from leaving harbor (they hacked its rudder) in order to keep a cargo of grain in town. Another crowd forcibly opened a merchant's warehouse three years later. To prevent further turmoil, the town meeting established a public granary and appointed a keeper, who would buy grain on behalf of poor town consumers and distribute it at affordable rates. Townspeople would use their collective buying power to secure delivery of grain earmarked for local use. Adopted by other colonial cities as well, this method struck a compromise: it allowed merchants space to seek profits by dealing in grain, while committing public monies and moral imprimatur to supply the local poor. Boston thus endorsed some of the basic principles essential to many English of their day. Yet the city's fiercest disputes during these early decades of the eighteenth century reflect the distinctive tenor of colonial concerns. For if there was sufficient consensus on the matter of grain supplies, there was only contention when it came to the related issue of other modes of provisioning the town.[48]

Besides relying on merchants for import of grain, households in Boston also depended on members of that trade for other foodstuffs and necessities. Some goods came into town by water and were sold on the wharves and docks that belonged to private dealers. Merchants imported some provisions directly, subject to the expectation that their sales would privilege the needs of Boston households over maximal private profit. Law required that merchants notify inhabitants by town crier of three days' opportunity to purchase at retail before offering provisions at wholesale.[49] The other critical source of foodstuffs were country suppliers, members of farm households and sometimes middlemen and women, who carried produce and livestock across the neck that connected Boston to the rest of the province by way of Roxbury. It was over this trade that the town came into conflict. When they saw "difficulties" and "bondage," it involved proposed innovations in this element of city supply.[50]

Specifically, the gentlemen proposed plans for establishing town marketplaces to bring transactions under the eyes of town officials. They planned to concentrate country supply at three central places, while forbidding sales at any other place. Debates over establishing such markets filled town meetings from 1714 through 1718. The minister of Brattle Street Church, Benjamin Colman, put pen to paper to offer "Some Reasons and Arguments . . . for the Setting Up Markets in Boston." Other publications debated the matter, and dramatic conflict took place outside the press as well. The issues smoldered until the 1730s, when a group of "young merchants," allied with the royal governor, managed to pass some market plans. In the spring of 1734, the town narrowly voted to build three markets. Three wooden shelters duly opened in June.[51] Rules made daily supply of householders a priority by forbidding retailers to purchase for resale before 1 P.M. on any market day. Equally important, those who had opposed the market plan managed to prevent any regulations that would forbid selling outside the bounds of the market. At the insistence of the town meeting, hawkers might vend produce in the streets as usual. The system thus put in place elements promoted by each side in the dispute.

Yet the town suffered shortages in the next several years. In 1736 Boston signaled its abandonment of marketplaces by voting against motions to appoint clerks of the market and to ring the market bell every morning. The market structures stood idle. Even so, late in March 1736, nighttime mobs attacked two of the market buildings. The central market, recorded an observer, was "pull'd down and entirely demolished," while market posts in the North End were "sawn asunder." Some five to six hundred men all told were responsible for the destruction. By one report, some dressed as clergymen in an obvious insult to Benjamin Colman and his fellows in market schemes. The riots of 1736 effectively ended use of all three of the markets built two years earlier. It would be many years before reformers revived the project of limiting retailers to a market site.[52]

In most places, poor consumers benefited from and insisted on regulated markets and opposed innovative claims of dealers to "economic freedom." In English centers, as in other towns in British North America, regulated marketplaces and market days reflected moral economic presuppositions, a way of insisting that exchange of foodstuffs be vulnerable to public oversight. In Boston at least, some ordinary men seem to have valued a liberal sort of liberty, the individual right to truck and barter without government interference or oversight. If that contradicted these same classes' stance on grain supply, perhaps it reflected Americans' distinctive preferences.[53]

Yet just what was the oppression that seemed to threaten in these decades of dispute? It had a good deal to do with proposed changes in town government. The same interests proposed the two reforms. The two proposals were of a piece, both of them meant to increase inequality by concentrating decision making about the good of the town in fewer hands—and in hands less roughened by common labor. "A Dialogue Between a Boston Man and a Country Man," appearing in 1714, rehearsed a variety of objections to markets and to city government. Central among them was "the taking away the Ancient Rights, and undoubted Property of our Voting at Town Meetings, which we now enjoy."[54]

The "country man" in this dialogue supposedly presented the case for city incorporation. Surely, he argued, the aldermen and mayor of the city would be "men of considerable Substance." (In fact, an alderman would need an estate of £1,000 or more to qualify for office.) What did it matter, then, "if you lose your Priviledge of Voting, as long as you have Men in of good Estates, and undoubted Fidelity, for they take off trouble from you." In reply, the "Boston Man" expressed skepticism about the fidelity of many men of substance. The people of Boston should stand by their own common wisdom: "*If you would have your work done well, do it your self,*" ran the maxim. Moreover, the proposals for change in government had self-interest as a motive. The projecting gentlemen were simply "Coveteous . . . to have a fellow-feeling of every bodies Pocket in the whole Town, and of being like to the Great Fish, of being lords over the Small."[55]

A second anonymous publication agreed that the proposal was meant to serve the class aspirations of men who wanted to set themselves above their neighbors. It would multiply offices, "so that he that could not arrive to be a Counsellor, Treasurer or Secretary of State; might at least be distinguished, from his meaner Neighbours, by being made a Mayor, Alderman, Common Councilman, Recorder, Clerk, or Treasurer."[56] These positions would cost taxpayers money. Most important, the change would remove townsmen from decision making.

> Then Farwel to all Town-Meetings, and to the Management of the Town Affairs by the Freeholders, Collectively, Rich & Poor Men, then will no more be jumbled together in Town Offices, as they are in the Grave, no more Mobb Town-Meetings of Freeholders, (as some are pleased to call them:) No, no: Then the Rich will exert that right of Dominion, which they think they have exclusive of all others: Then the Town Affairs will be managed by a Representative Body of Men, who will do Honour to the Town; tho' 'tis to be feared, 'twill be a very Costly Honour to it; and then the Great Men will no more have the Dissatisfaction of seeing their Poorer Neighbours stand up for equal Privileges with them, in the highest Acts of Town Governments.[57]

As the pamphleteer portrayed it, great men's ambitions were posing a substantial threat to the well-being of middling sorts accustomed to a voice in town meeting. It seemed plausible to some Bostonians that such men wanted to engross political control into their own hands.

This description put some flesh on the bare-bones statement that the new proposals threatened "difficulties" and "bondage." As these anonymous pamphleteers depicted the issue, wealthy Bostonians hoped to increase their own political sway. They would dissociate themselves from their lesser neighbors. They would replace the town meeting with a merely "Representative" government in order to remove lesser men from the councils of decision-making. The proposal to abolish town-meeting government directly challenged many Bostonians' status and liberties as neighbors in good standing, participants in the life of the town.

The projecting gentlemen's second proposal, creating set marketplaces for sale of country produce within the town, reflected the same distaste for inadequate hierarchy and order. To many Boston inhabitants, it constituted the same sort of threat. There are two points to appreciate here: first, greater regulation of marketing by town meetings might sound innocent enough in isolation, until one considered that the same projecting gentlemen were intent on replacing the town meeting with a less open forum. Voters' rejection of market proposals must be understood as they surely understood it—in light of the pressure against their continued participation at town meetings. They were being asked to move jurisdiction over daily marketing from regulation by the people, as executors of the law, and into the hands of town government, just when wealthy men were trying to insulate that government from popular influence. Second, even viewed in isolation, the proposed change in marketing threatened town inhabitants' collective control. The controversy did not primarily pit advocates of regulation against advocates of free trade, in other words; there was something else at stake. For if set market days and places constituted traditional forms, the substance of the new proposals promised to bring the distinctly nontraditional value of "improvement" to the town.[58]

Indeed, just what the gentlemen were proposing was eminently clear in Benjamin Colman's pamphlet promoting the innovation. First, Colman explicitly recommended set marketplaces as an aid to controlling the behavior of the lower classes in town. Sellers from the country often got up to mischief once in the city: "As to the *Children and Servants* that are sent hither to sell things, they are in danger of idling and playing about the Town." Similarly, urban households who sent servants out to purchase risked unnecessary loss of those servants' time. What was more likely than that servants would merely loiter in the streets, meet with others of their class, and fall into gaming or other bad behavior? Servants were apt to return with excuses, "a lye in their mouth," pretending they had been unable to find victuals when they had not even looked for them. With marketplaces established about the city, Colman pointed out, masters and mistresses of servants could easily estimate the time needed for their hires to travel to and from the nearest place of sale. That would facilitate labor discipline.[59]

None of this suggested that the project would help the poor. Nor was Colman arguing on behalf of inhabitancy, promoting regulations that would ensure the access of townspeople great and small to foodstuffs. Instead, Colman stressed the importance of established marketplaces for impressing "strangers to the town," who were likely to be accustomed to European cities' more ordered institutions. Colman devoted a surprising number of pages to decrying what we might call the aesthetics of urban life. He expressed marked distaste for the "sauntering" men who brought in goods for sale, "loitering" in the city streets. Moreover, it was beneath the dignity of the town's "gentility" to wander about the streets in search of a chicken or a duck for dinner. Colman regretted the sight of "our very Gentry as well as Tradesmen travelling (as they are not ashamed now to do) to the Ends of the Town to get a little butter, or a few Eggs." The situation offended the minister's sense of class decorum. The gentry of Boston, by doing marketing themselves, "stoop . . . to that which becomes their maids." For Colman, established marketplaces and market hours offered an alternative, a system marked by "Convenience, Order and

Beauty." It was as if the primary matter at stake was social propriety rather than food supply.[60]

Eventually, Colman did address the meat-and-potatoes concerns of most townspeople in his pamphlet; eventually, he suggested, his proposed reforms would improve the supply of provisions to Boston. In time, he thought, the new markets would lower the prices of country products. Two sellers standing side by side would have to moderate their demands in deference to the presence and quality of one another's goods. "The poor might buy more for their money, and escape the fatal temptation to them of running upon Tick"—in other words, buying on credit.[61]

It is hard to imagine the poor or even the middling objecting to getting more for less. Yet in these remarks on supply, Colman described only the long-run promise of the town markets; in time, the markets might transform farmers' way of thinking about economic exchange and the role of surplus in their household lives. The short-run consequences looked rather different to many observers, however, who predicted that regulated markets would discourage suppliers. Whether or not farmers believed in the principles of free trade as a general matter, they opposed the particular regulations they anticipated Bostonians now adopting. Forced to stand side by side and compete, or pay fees, or secure a license, or merely appear at a set place at a set time, they would not come in at all.

The underlying difficulty of Boston consumers was that farmers did not rely on Bostonians in the same way that city dwellers depended on them. Country people produced far less surplus for sale in town than a steadier view of profit would have them produce. Many focused primarily on production for their own households and neighborhoods rather than for Boston. They brought provisions to townspeople only until they had earned enough to pay for the limited amounts of sugars, salt, and manufactured goods they desired. Under these circumstances, Colman believed, a marketplace would introduce elements of economic rationality into country people's lives. Once they realized they could count on a certain place of sale and conditions of competition, farmers would discover a desire to produce more foodstuffs for the city market. A competitive spirit would infect them. "Maids . . . as well as their mistresses at home would be ambitious to outdo their Neighbours, or at least not come behind them either in credit or profit." At a given market location, buyers could easily compare country people's products, with the result that farmers would soon learn that the best would sell soonest and highest. The competition of the markets would instill a more entrepreneurial cast of mind and lead farmers to adopt more commercial farming. The typical country man, assured of an outlet, would be encouraged to increase production for the city market. "This would set him upon using both his <u>brains</u> and his <u>hands</u> more than he generally does; and instead of a bare bringing about the <u>Year</u>, he wou'd with a little more care and labour make a great deal more <u>gain</u>."[62] Here Colman's concern for ordering the time of city servants and other urban householders was matched by an ambition to reorder the work and time of farmers in the hinterland. New opportunities would erode farmers' lamentable belief that "a bare bringing about the Year" was quite enough. Colman proposed to replace farmers' sense of sufficiency with a sense of possibility. He would instill an enterprising spirit in the apparently unenterprising, who, though they already marketed a surplus, yet produced for the purpose of getting by. A little more care and labor: he would induce them further into market production. He would help them look beyond a mere competency.

One additional element of Colman's proposal alarmed people in town. The minister suggested that some country suppliers might find it convenient to bring only samples to sell. Such a practice would be easier and more efficient. "Again, if the Farmer have quantities of Corn to sell, be it wheat or any other grain, have he some of the same sort better and some worse; how easy is it to take Samplers of it with him to the Market, and find Chaps, bargain and sell it all, and set the time of his delivery of it and for the receiving his money."[63] This account described a farmer selling wholesale to middlemen for resale or export, not retail to consumers of the town. The reverend also suggested a further modification: farmers might entrust their goods to the stores of city merchants rather than spending time to carry them back and forth on various market days. Why not bring in your goods once, then leave them for sale in a store? Both these proposals, mentioned only briefly in Colman's pamphlet, were sure to outrage consumers. In Britain and other American towns as well, the arrangement of selling by sample commonly provoked opposition, for it allowed transfers of provisions in private stores rather than open air. It made sales invisible to town inhabitants, whose ability to recognize what price was reasonable depended on knowledge of available supply. Nor did many consumers favor allowing town merchants, who already controlled the city's access to flour, to insert themselves as middlemen into the sale of country foodstuffs. This, surely, was what the "Boston man" meant when he worried that the merchants would manage to reach into "every bodies Pocket in the whole Town."[64]

There was thus little in Colman's pamphlet that portrayed market reforms as consonant with traditional English regulations that made profit seeking of dealers secondary to supply of the poor. True, Colman intended that these changes would increase the supply of foodstuffs to Boston, and that they might thereby ease the difficulties of all consumers. He may have been right that they would ultimately have done so. Yet he promoted values of competition and profit seeking. He aimed at inspiring distinctly nontraditional patterns of work both within and without the town. He believed that servants, town consumers, farmers with goods, hawkers—all might do better in a world of more consistent striving, competition, and efficiency. He sought some of the same transformation of social relationships as was taking place across the Atlantic.

To see as much is to begin to understand the bitter opposition to these reforms. For if market promoters were not in fact advocating traditional restrictions on free trade, then their opponents were not in fact opposing market regulation per se or advocating a principle of economic freedom in town marketing.[65] Boston's townspeople would surely have welcomed measures that effectively provided them more provisions at lower prices. Yet many Bostonians seem to have consulted their country acquaintances rather than economic theory. They realized that many of those country producers would simply not bring their goods into Boston, as a pamphleteer put it, "so long as Charlestown and Roxbury do stand" as alternative sites of sale.[66] Even Colman admitted that marketplaces would probably inhibit town supply at first. "We must be modest, humble, frugal, and every one content themselves with a little, a bare supply for the time."[67] Yet many townspeople knew what modesty and humility would be like; the wealthy would buy first and finest, and only then came the rest. "We shall all be gathering like Bees about the market, and ready to devour one another for their Leavings," wrote a pamphleteer. Greater competition among consumers would cause "Divisions and Animosities" in the town and endanger the fragile systems of cooperation, exchange, and mutuality that helped households keep their heads above water. The current system was more fair, judged by common notions of fairness: "The Market Men and Women pass along silently through the Town & spread themselves into the several Branches of it, offering and disposing of their Ware in a more just and equal Manner than a Market will admit of." Just and equal distribution of goods, from this perspective, was at the heart of the issue.[68]

Clearly, this was no appeal to traditional, paternalistic responsibilities of the great men to take care of town. On the contrary, critics of changing town government sought to prevent the wealthy from assuming greater political and economic control. What we see in Boston is a belief common to many among the middle sort in England and America alike: there was danger in trusting ambitious men's ideas of fairness. Once again, this perception did not amount to an over-simple opposition to commercial dealings, but it did view economic institutions as having proper and appropriate ends in the fulfillment of needs and the maintenance of society. In this case, that meant a preference for limits to competition and the invocation of social ties to keep exchange for foodstuffs in balance. It need not be government, in other words, that held would-be oppressors in line; it might be another public, come together closer to the common ground.

Indeed, in the face of an admitted reliance on country farmers, many city dwellers responded not by invoking market forces such as the profit motive or increased competition but by creating ties of mutuality. Colman noted that opponents of regulated markets preferred to keep up alternative relationships. "Some particular Persons or families may say . . . We have a sure Country friend who brings us all that we need, and we are not so much as at the trouble of going out of doors for it."[69] Such arrangements appeared to Colman an insignificant matter of convenience in daily supply. Yet what the clergyman dismissed as mere convenience— "a sure Country friend"—might represent to many householders a critical form of security. These town inhabitants preferred to deal with country suppliers they already knew and to secure the supply of foodstuffs in the context of relationships that resembled neighboring. Like other institutions of local exchange, those relationships were unquestionably economic, a matter of self-interest for both parties. At the same time they were ongoing social connections rather than anonymous market relationships. In a position of vulnerability, many Boston households preferred to rely on established relationships with known countrymen rather than engage in market competition. They recognized the countrymen's unwillingness to compete. Perhaps they regretted it, as Colman did, wishing that country people would show more entrepreneurial spirit and bring more goods to town in search of greater gain. Equally possible, town consumers may have valued countrymen's attachment to tenets other than profit maximizing. Surely it might seem safer to deal with men who shared the common idea that there were moral limits to accumulation and hence to ambition, who sought only a competence.

Many viewed with alarm the plan of merchants to intervene in those dealings, for there was little doubt about the extent of *their* ambitions. Like the food riot, the appeal to neighboring relationships was not a rejection of market transactions, sales and purchases; it was an embrace of some other sorts of transactions and a desire for space in which to enter the market on one's own terms. It was a way to deal with the market's power, its anonymity, its tendency to ignore whether a consumer was rich or poor, honest or false, its nonresponsiveness to considerations that human actors might take into account.

One final element of the Boston dispute shows us the benefits that ordinary colonists found in the tenets of neighboring, on the one hand, and the practice of associating in "combinations" among themselves, on the other. City and country dwellers alike relied on horizontal social connections to defend themselves from legal consequences of the crowd action. In the aftermath of the market destruction, Lieutenant Governor Spencer Phips publicly called on officials to prosecute the rioters and on all subjects to assist in their discovery. Spokesmen for the rioters replied with proclamations of their own. Someone posted a paper on the Town House door; someone scattered copies of two "prophane and seditious Letters" in the town.[70] The letters addressed Suffolk County sheriff Edward Winslow, whose duty it was to bring rioters to account. Rumor had it that Winslow meant to raise regiments of country people to march against the rioters. "Let alone your Drums and Guns," urged one anonymous writer, for the opponents of markets in the town "will oppose arms with arms." Should the sheriff "Commit any Man for that Night's Work," the jail would prove unable to hold him. More menacing still, one paper suggested that the governor himself stood in danger of his life. Over five hundred men had joined together "in Solemn League and Covenant." Members of the league agreed to stand by one another; they claimed they could "procure above Seven Hundred more of the same Mind." Governor Jonathan Belcher promptly called for discovery and prosecution of the authors of these papers, along with the rioters who had destroyed the market house. Yet no one offered information to authorities about the identity of the men responsible. Colman lamented that individuals suspected of taking part in the mob gained social respect rather than ignominy for their indiscretion, "their favourers being so many."[71] Combining and "confrating," or claiming that one would do so, served as a check on power. The value of neighborly ties appeared in this more purely political (if not martial) aspect of the dispute as well.

Efforts to reform town government and centralize marketing fell into abeyance for some decades, yet Boston remained riven by deep disagreements over accumulation and ambition. What divided people was not only interest but also outlook. Benjamin Colman had claimed to speak for no particular or private interest. "I have no private Interest separate from my Nei'bours to move me."[72] Nonetheless, the clergyman's view, shared with various enlightened, polished, and improving gentleman in town, separated him from many other inhabitants.

Rural people in the colonies did not face merchants controlling access to bread or engrossing the trade of the town. Yet men like Benjamin Colman had hopes of bringing their ideas of order to the countryside as well. In provincial legislatures, established elites increasingly served for longer tenures. In many places, a shortage of land put pressure on the supply of fertile land on which households might establish themselves in a competency. In the early decades of the eighteenth century, rural dwellers faced projecting gentlemen of their own.

The influx of new immigrants and natural increase within the colonies changed the balance of power between settlers and proprietors in many provinces. Having despaired of great revenues from rents, proprietary interests revived their holdings at law and began to collect quitrents on established farms. By midcentury, Lord Baltimore and the Penn family were reaping annual incomes on a par with those of England's great landed men. Lord Fairfax, who claimed over 5 million acres in Virginia, and Lord Carteret, who owned half the land of Carolina, aspired to the same. Proprietors with standing claims to land were joined by new speculators, men with skills at lawyering or surveying, capital to invest, or just friends in high places.[73] Households moving into eastern Connecticut in the 1710s and 1720s, for example, found land there claimed by two contending parties, one a recent governor, the other a speculator who had reportedly "engrosst so much land" as to qualify as "lord" of the colony. Conflicting claims of the two parties caused uncertainty and conflict among settlers, tenants, and clients seeking to establish tenure by settling, clearing, and planting farms. Before matters were resolved, settlers had both appealed to provincial government for solutions and resisted that government's authority. Connecticut men had prevented judges from proceeding and intimidated grand juries; "a great number of men and horses" in Colchester had blocked surveyors from their work of laying out tracts for legal title; and there had occurred a "most lamentable and very heinous mutiny . . . by sundrey ill minded persons who with violence broke the gaol."[74]

In other parts of the continent, too, the pressure for land caused conflict as it provided new leverage to men with great estates. Manors established along the Hudson River in New York attracted growing numbers of tenants. Tenancy grew in other provinces as well, as increased land values put ownership beyond the reach of many. In every province, change on the landscape was observable, as a few well-to-do families built imposing Georgian houses that proclaimed their mounting wealth and superior status. Colonists could see the progress of inequality around them.[75]

Like Boston townspeople, farmers in many parts of the continent defended their own interests by insisting there be limits to the acquisitiveness of ambitious men. In northern New Jersey, disputes over land and other resources were particularly bitter and long lasting, for great men there challenged the tenure of households on lands they already worked, occupied, and arguably "owned."[76] Some sixty-nine men ranked as "proprietors" of East Jersey in the early part of the century, having inherited or bought a share in royal patents of the colony.[77] Profit making, improving men, many of them aspired to landed estates with the goal of living as enlightened and virtuous gentlemen. They sought to "remake the countryside" by reestablishing their land title, collecting quitrents, making land sales, or setting up tenants to further improve their holdings. In the late 1730s and early 1740s, hundreds of thousands of acres became contested at law. In Newark township alone, proprietors pressed freeholders on thirteen thousand acres to buy the lands they lived on over again, or take a short-term lease on the property. Proprietors initiated suits of ejectment, and they claimed sole ownership of timber and mineral wealth on great tracts as well. The proprietors deployed learned lawyers, judges appointed by their associates in government, and the ability to maintain suits at law against households that, though they had improved their farms and hoped to make a good living from them, often had insufficient cash for court fees and lacked the specialized knowledge needed to plead without hiring lawyers themselves.[78] The following decades saw persistent opposition on the part of freeholders, tenants, and squatters in the area. In countless cases, juries prevented dispossessions, and households mounted their own legal cases as well. When proprietors tried to move title cases to a chancery court, Jersey inhabitants refused to recognize such courts' authority. Yet courts with local juries and appointed judges failed to resolve these disputes. When officials moved to distrain and dispossess, crowds blocked sheriffs from taking men's property in payment of rents and fines. As notable as the disorders themselves were the associations that farmers created to defend their interests. Various areas of the province elected committees—the Elizabeth Town Associates, New Purchasers' committee, and others—to coordinate their cases. Great Tract settlers "had two Great Meetings, in order to Agree to Stand by one another in Defense of their Possessions against the said Proprietors" in the spring of 1746. Farmers thus "associated . . . & entered into a Combination . . . to Obstruct the Course of Legal Proceedings."[79]

In this conflict over resources, the parties often expressed divergent cultural ideals. As important as tangled legal issues and complex local events was a stark difference in outlook that set men apart. On behalf of the Newark rioters, a man named Griffin Jenkins published a *Brief Vindication of the Purchassors Against the Propritors, in a Christian Manner* in 1746. The pamphlet reflected the impact of recent religious awakenings in the Middle Colonies, and it drew on evangelical ideas to impugn the proprietors' ambitions. Indeed, it dealt with those ambitions rather more than the legal principles under contest in the courts. Jenkins prefaced his discussion of land conflict in Newark township with four pages of "religious songs," hoping to "soften the heart" of adversaries who might read his argument. He summoned the parties to reconciliation on the ground of presumed common beliefs and shared sensibilities. There was authority in the Bible to adjudicate their differences, and Jenkins reminded the proprietors that "every godly Man" would give them clear advice: "Be strictly Just in all thy Dealing with Man, and think not thy self discharged from the Duty of Righteousness toward they Neighbour by an extraordinary measure of pretended Zeal and Piety toward God." Such duties toward neighbors were best discharged within the circle of face-to-face relationships, using institutions of mediation and mutual consent. The proprietors should "unwillingly undertake a Suit of Law, and most willingly make an End of it, chuse rather to buy Quietness with some Loss, than Gain much by Strife and Contention; for going to law is one of those lawful Things, which is very difficultly manag'd without Sin, 'tis rare if a Man wrongs not his Soul by righting his Estate." New Jersey's disputants should resolve their differences outside the courtroom, then, in relationships framed by law in the broadest sense. Equally important, in that sort of adjudication the logic and legality of land titles would not be the sole question at issue. Jenkins made a case for the property rights of smallholders who had improved the land, and he expressed skepticism of the claims of the "so-called Proprietors." Yet he also devoted great attention to questions of motive, conscience, and neighborliness—matters that arguably had nothing to do with the actual merits of the case. Thus, "Covetousness was the begining [sic] of this misrule and mistake that has happened among us," Jenkins assserted. Where small farmers were merely in pursuit of a modest and reasonable living, proprietors had less defensible motives. "And I think it is a plain Cause to all Men, that it was <u>Covetousness</u> brought in these Proprietors, as you call them, into the Plantations of these poor People." Here was an altogether different logic than the one that lawyers would present. Jenkins reasoned as if improvements were not self-evidently good and as if the desire for gain required justification. "If there was not some desireable Entertainment for the Flesh you would never seek these Improvements," he admonished the proprietors. Jenkins's *Vindication* highlights a particular mode of thinking about property, material wealth, and accumulation. It contrasted ordinary farmers' legitimate aspirations for a competent living for their households with the avarice of great men who had plenty but wanted more.[80]

Equally, it represented the conviction that courtroom law, in cases that were civil or criminal, represented but one determination of society. Such law might be revised, as the people might appeal to other authorities or constitute one themselves. No doubt evangelicals rejected the authorities of the secular world more sweepingly than many other believers, and the New Jersey court system enjoyed distinctly less legitimacy in the eyes of most people than court systems in other provinces. Nonetheless, it is worth underscoring that this was a division of the era: in other colonies, too, groups of people sometimes overruled debt decisions. Neighbors might refuse to bid on a neighbor's estate, seized for debt and now placed at auction. They might rescue property taken in distraint. In so doing, they appealed to "the tribunal of the people."

In *Vindication*, Jenkins impugned the proprietors: "You cannot properly say that you have observed that great Commandment of our Saviour, that is by loving thy Brother as thy self, or else methinks you could not have that Heart, to put one of thy fellow Creatures into Prison, for cutting Wood on his own Land, for that shows plain that there was no Love at all." One exasperated spokesman for the proprietary interest replied that Jenkins wrote as if the freeholders themselves were without sin. Indeed, some of the "poor people" who now held and worked these tracts may have loved their neighbors, and some men with secure and uncontested land titles apparently blocked ejectments and rescued arrested rioters simply because "they thought Their neighbors wronged."[81] Nonetheless, these were not peasants defending a regime of common use rights, as in parts of England, but yeomen pursuing ambitions of their own. Many New Jersey farmers specialized in grain production for export to markets in Boston and the West Indies. When they contested proprietary claims to sole use of timber or mineral deposits, they were claiming resources that they themselves hoped to exploit. They had their own aspirations for security, even comforts and conveniences, perhaps more. They no doubt hoped to improve their farms and their fortunes and enjoy the social standing that followed. Theirs were moral claims, yet still the claims of men who intended to keep their distance from poverty.

They had no intention of falling into the ranks of the landless poor; they feared being reduced to dependence on the labor market.

In this respect, "covetousness" was a precise accusation, for it condemned the proprietors not for ambition per se but for desiring that which allegedly already belonged to their neighbors. Even *Brief Vindication* did not denounce accumulation of every sort, in other words. Jenkins presumed that the ambitions of the yeomanry to maintain their holdings, to build improvements to pass on to their children—this qualified as materialism of another order.

That essential distinction, common to the arguments of many colonists, had some logical difficulties. Some of the tensions faced by American farmers were inherent in their goal of attaining a "decent competency." Daniel Vickers notes one key contradiction: farmers generally denied that seeking a competency in fact put them into competition with their neighbors and with other men in the colonies who held similar ambitions. They spoke as if there were sufficient land available for every like-minded rural household. In times of prosperity, moreover, farmers were susceptible to defining a sufficiency in expanding terms. And whatever the times, their methods of agriculture, large families, and systems of inheritance pressed many to search for additional resources and credit.[82] Even in economic depression, many middling households would feel such pressures, and then the presence of wealthy or grasping men made it particularly plausible to locate the threat to their interests in the excessive ambitions of others.

In Pennsylvania, as in many places, the threat to farmers' hold on their land—and the threat to small urban tradesmen's fortunes—took the form of debt. The Bible told men to lend to the needy, but the position of creditor and debtor each had moral hazards. Puritan divine Cotton Mather grappled with the dilemma. Men were tempted to delay or neglect repayment of loans (including stalling payment for work done by others in their employ). Creditors were tempted to demand excessive interest, Mather wrote, or perhaps to lend from malicious motivations, "to make others become their *Servants*, which you know, *Debtors* are." In effective terms, in other words, being in debt involved working on behalf of another person's gain.[83] It threatened the great good that so many households worked to attain: a status of controlling and benefiting from one's own work time and pace. Yet debt was endemic in this agrarian society. Debts within neighborhood networks might at times be settled in local institutions. More distant commercial exchanges commonly took men into courts of law. As commercial transactions multiplied in number, the courts in some colonies began to change in order to accommodate them. In Connecticut and

New York, at least, courts increasingly adjudicated claims between strangers rather than neighbors. Such matters were relatively formulaic: rather than sorting through the complex history of men's dealings they confined their deliberations to the validity of specific financial instruments such as promissory notes. Juries became less common elements of these proceedings, an admission that local knowledge was often inessential to finding justice between "man and man."[84]

Pennsylvanians in the 1720s grappled with the problems of debt in the midst of economic depression. Their disputes focused on elections for representatives to the legislature rather than on courts of law, but as in New Jersey's conflict, both sides in Pennsylvania also had recourse to the public press. As in Boston, moreover, men of some social distinction and political position took part on both sides of the issue. Yet again in both places the main elements of the two partisan groups divided along lines of social and economic standing. On the one hand were wealthier merchants; on the other an alliance of backcountry farmers and city artisans came together in support of policies that protected their interests. In this case, the latter group might be cast as the men with a project.

Like the other colonies, Pennsylvania suffered from shortages of coin, the drain of money to pay metropolitan dealers in Britain, and a shortage of a medium for trade. Various provinces tried to solve the liquidity problem by emitting paper bills, sometimes on the promise of future taxes (an expedient called "currency finance") and sometimes as mortgages on land. The lack of a medium inhibited trade at every level, so that most interests complained of the problem. Some merchants emitted bills of exchange of their own to facilitate their transactions; in addition, the shortage of cash put some of these men at an advantage. When most people needed cash, they had to procure it from well-placed "moneyed men," who might take advantage in such transactions of their effective monopoly.[85] A pamphlet writer named Francis Rawle decribed the inequity that resulted from a lack of paper bills and a shortage of specie: "The Farmer to pay a Debt was forc'd to sell twice as much as he needed to come at Silver, and take one part in such Goods as he did not want." Debtors found themselves pressed into exchanges that seemed unfair, and when even those did not suffice to pay debts, the result was "Law-Suits and barbarous Attachments [of men's property], the Bane of concord, Peace and civil society, and the Preludes of Poverty."[86]

Early in the 1720s, suffering from depressed trade, Philadelphia artisans met together at local taverns in a "Leather Apron Club," where they were joined by several political leaders who sympathized with their plight.

Even Governor Sir William Keith thought the government should act "to calm the Minds of the people." In 1723, a legislature chosen by the combined votes of backcountry farmers and urban mechanics emitted paper currency based on land. The rest of the decade saw pamphlet debates and political organizing over the prospect of extending the policy.[87]

Benjamin Franklin wrote in favor of further emissions, arguing that paper money supported the sort of society and the distribution of wealth that would benefit the majority. Franklin was an ambitious middling tradesman himself in 1729, a printer and writer with an ear for ordinary readers. In his view, new money would help clear away mortgage holders' claims to people's farms. It would benefit the many craftsmen who worked for merchants and were now forced to take payment in the form of imported goods rather than currency. Access to paper bills would help such men pay creditors of their own. City craftsmen and rural people could get it at reasonable rates, without going through middlemen who routinely overcharged.[88]

Who, then, could oppose paper money? Franklin listed four groups. First were "moneylenders," who could demand "exhorbitant Interest" when cash was scarce. Second were men amassing great holdings of land: "those who are Possessors of large Sums of Money, and are disposed to purchase Land, which is attended with a great and sure Advantage in a growing Country as this is; I say, the Interest of all such Men will encline them to oppose a large Addition to our Money." They would benefit from keeping the cost of land low and money high, so that "the Common People in general will be impoverished, and consequently obliged to sell More Land for less Money than they will do at present." Then there were lawyers, who would oppose "a plentiful Currency," for fear that ordinary people "will have less Occasion to run in Debt, and consequently less Occasion to go to Law and Sue one another for their Debts." Such men (and, finally, "their dependants") stood apart. As Franklin presented the case for paper money, the issue did not divide two sets of legitimate interests, but rather pitted the few against the many, the moneyed and ambitious against "the Common People in general."

By contrast, the interest of small farmers, craftsmen, and dealers could be taken to serve the good of the whole. What made sense of that view was the conviction that a society hospitable to the middle sort of people was to be desired. "Want of Money in a Country discourages Labouring and Handicrafts Men (which are the chief Strength and Support of a People) from coming to settle in it, and induces many that were settled to leave the Country, and seek Entertainment and Employment in other

Places, where they can be better paid."[89] After all, Pennsylvanians knew that free laboring and handicrafts men struggled in England and did not generally seek employment in the Chesapeake, where the institution of African and African American slavery closed opportunities and degraded labor. There was nothing necessarily lasting about the opportunities and the decent competencies such men had found in Penn's colony. Franklin's argument recognized the tendency of societies toward change, the tendency of property toward concentrated ownership, the tendency of men who enjoy advantage to oppress.

Franklin thus accused his opponents of holding a contrary social ideal. He wrote in the press in 1729:

> The whole Country is at this Instant filled with the greatest Heat and Animosity; and if there are yet among us any Opposers of a *Paper-Currency*, it is probably the Resentments of the People point at them; and tho' I must earnestly exhort my Countrymen to Peace and Quietness for that publick Disturbances are seldom known to be attended with any good Consequence; yet I cannot but think it would be highly prudent in those Gentlemen with all Expedition to publish such Vindications of themselves and their Actions, as will sufficiently clear them in the Eyes of all reasonable Men, from the Imputation of having a Design to engross the Property of the Country, and make themselves and their Posterity Lords, and the Bulk of the Inhabitants their Tenants and Vassals; which Design they are everywhere openly accused of.[90]

Franklin's view of the world was in some respects far different from the views of evangelicals such as Griffin Jenkins, but nonetheless he appealed to a similar social good: "If the People are once convinced there is no such Scheme on Foot," he wrote, "it may exceedingly tend to the Settlement of their Minds, the Abatement of their Heats, and the Establishment of Peace, Love, and Unity, and all the Social Virtues."[91] How could opponents of paper money oppose an outcome like that? Franklin may have accurately described a common perception that opponents of the paper money intended to amass lordships; alternatively, he may have been promoting that interpretation. Either way, opponents of paper money were vulnerable to the charge. It was an appeal to common knowledge of the English experience. Moreover, it was plausible even in Pennsylvania, "the best poor man's country," to imagine men with outsized ambitions might wish to reshape the society to their own interest. It was possible to mobilize many common men against them.

These, then, were arguments about society, claims about a community that was not part but "the whole," that would allow gain and self-seeking but retain moral limits. Some hedged the quest for material success with evangelical language, an insistence on neighborly duties, or an appeal to the allegedly shared good of all. In the decade following Boston's market riot, a young Samuel Adams saw the same social divisions underlying conflicts then unfolding in Boston and in society at large. In the pages of the newspaper the *Independent Advertiser*, Adams grappled with a palpable growth in social inequality. Although he came from a successful background and attended Harvard College, Adams allied himself with middling craftsmen, shopkeepers, and other ordinary men of Boston. He reprinted an essay by Cato that laid out the need for limits to men's ambitions. "I will readily own, that every Man has a Right and a Call to provide for himself, to attend upon his own Affairs, and to study his own Happiness. All that I contend for is, that this Duty of a Man to himself *he performs subsequently to the general Welfare, and consistent with it.* The Affairs of ALL should be minded preferably to the Affairs of One, as every Man is ready to own when his own Particular is embarked with the Whole, as indeed every Man's will prove to be sooner or later."[92] Still, the "sooner or later" made a great difference, and the distinction described the situation of the poor or middle sort, on the one hand, and the wealthy on the other. The bulk of the people had insufficient resources to cushion them from general economic difficulties; the fact that a general economic decline affected them in "Particular" was quickly apparent. Only a few men amassed fortunes on such a scale as to insulate them from the vagaries of the times; while the generality suffered, the few might profit, unmindful that their ultimate well-being was at one with the welfare of their neighbors. Adams encouraged the ordinary to remind them, as he himself was using the press to do. For the common inhabitants of a place could deploy their influence over public reputation. It was lucky that wealth was inadequate to happiness and that men also required "good repute" in their lives. Even the wealthy should pay heed to the opinion of their fellow townsmen, for men "insensible" to others' views put themselves "at Defiance of the community where they live," and thereby alerted community members "to be on their Guard against them." Such men earned the anathema of their neighbors. They "cut themselves off from society *and teach the People what to call them.*"

This was characteristic of Samuel Adams, the man: he encouraged the popular voice in the press, in town meeting, and in the streets of Boston. He urged ordinary men to speak up on behalf of what they saw as appropriate behaviors and even an appropriate distribution of wealth: "But some say, Is it a Crime to be rich? Yes certainly AT THE PUBLICK EXPENCE or to the Danger of the Publick." The king himself made a useful rhetorical factor in this line of argument. "A man may be too rich to be a Subject, even the Revenues of Kings may be too large." As everyone must agree with that, they could hardly defend unbridled ambition in lesser men such as themselves. Yet some individuals denied their fundamental commonality with their neighbors. Adams could have been thinking of the town's "projecting gentlemen" when he published Cato's view that the fundamental source of oppression lay in men's outsized goals: "Thus with great Men, it is Wealth and Empire; *to do what they list and to get what they can*; which is direct Faction, or promoting under the Colour of the Publick [good], those Views which are inconsistent with it. Thus with the Trader and Artificer, it is the encouraging only that Sort of Art or Ware in which he himself deals; and this is Monopoly and Engrossing, ever mischeivous to the Publick." Against these evils, Adams encouraged his readers to use the weapons of the weak: men were not in fact anonymous, much as transactions within the commercial marketplace might lead them to consider themselves as such. Adams reminded the wealthy: life was not a merely a market, and they were not in fact entirely insulated from the judgments of their neighbors. No one appreciated better than Samuel Adams: there was political power implicit in the standing of neighbors, and that power was needed when men tried "to put a whole Country in Two or Three people's Pockets."[93]

These disputes tell us a good deal about the commitments and resources of middling colonists in British North America. Colonists on all sides of these debates were promoting their own interests as they understood them. When they challenged the land claims of proprietors, promoted direct dealings between city and countrymen, or favored paper-money emissions, ordinary colonists were acting to protect their material well-being, social standing, and ability to help establish their children in similar lives. At the same time, they also expressed deeply held values in their actions and words. They testified about the sort of dealings they considered fair, the sort of economic and social policies they considered in the general interest, and the sort of society they considered good. Their views on these matters were in many respect English views, shaped by popular knowledge of English history and English law, as well as the evangelical Protestant fervor spreading on both sides of the Atlantic. At the same time, these were North American views, for they were grounded in a largely rural and middling society.

Most important, perhaps, many colonists expressed powerful ideals about the nature of their collective social life. They insisted that a good society was one with space for a good many of the middle sort—farmers, planters, tradesmen, and others like themselves. In part this was to emphasize an identity as industrious and productive members of the community. Thus Benjamin Franklin asserted that "Labouring and Handicrafts Men" constituted "the chief Strength and Support of a People." These producers improved the land and its products, raised foodstuffs and processed materials into manufactured goods, and transported provisions and goods to fill social needs. Similarly, Griffin Jenkins touted the property rights of farmers whose labor had made land in northern New Jersey productive, over and against the proprietors' merely paper titles. Sometimes implicitly, sometimes explicitly, these colonists distinguished themselves from those who idealized the life of the leisured gentry. Such a genteel social ideal undoubtedly held attraction for the middling as well as the wealthy. Countless commentators of the day noted the spread of fashion, the appeal of imported goods, a widespread enjoyment of the pleasures of consumption. As the eighteenth century progressed, the world of goods became more difficult to break down into neat categories of "necessaries" and "luxuries." Many middling households squared the pursuit of a competence with the purchase of "conveniences" and "comforts" of life.

Yet genteel consuming threatened to remove such households from a framework in which a man might rest secure with attaining a comfortable subsistence. That framework was under pressure in America and Britian alike, as some claimed social superiority by virtue of the wealth that provided them leisure, the learning and accomplishments that leisure allowed, and the social practices, consumer goods, and styles of life that learned, accomplished, polished men and women commanded. Confronting such claims, how difficult was it to hold faith in the possibility of lives neither measured solely by standards of gain nor characterized by constant competition? When challenged to articulate their ideas by the specter of "oppression," ordinary colonists and popular spokesmen often raised economic contribution rather than leisure as a virtue. By so doing they countered other men's exaltation of themselves as superior by virtue of their gentle status. They disputed the pretensions of many of their society's leading men.

Emphasizing an identity as producers was only one element of the popular arguments made in these disputes. For colonists might also resist the regime of work prescribed for them by men such as Rev. Benjamin Colman, who wished servants would keep busy and country farmers would aspire to greater profit. In response, some colonists defended lives not consumed by acquisition or measured in material terms. They insisted on the limits of their ambitions and, indeed, proposed that their embrace of such limits constituted a vital social virtue and palpable social contribution. They prided themselves on their commitment to mutuality and their identity as neighbors. Griffin Jenkins framed that identity in deeply Christian terms. He called on proprietors to love their neighbors, and he envisioned parties resolving their disputes without recourse to judges' ideas of law. Even Ben Franklin, distinctly more secular, more urban, and more conversant with commerce, wrote of economic life as an endeavor dedicated to mutual benefit rather than simply individual gain. The sort of exchange he pictured could be grasped by the ordinary reader: "As for Instance *A* may be skilful in the Art of making Cloth, and *B* understand the raising of Corn," he wrote. "*A* wants Corn and *B* Cloth, upon which they make an Exchange with each other for as much as each has Occasion, to the mutual Advantage and Satisfaction of both." Matters surely became more complicated, but neither the number of exchanges nor the introduction of money, a mere medium of exchange, should reasonably undermine the goal of achieving mutual satisfaction through commerce. Samuel Adams imagined a society with republican, "publick virtue," defined as "one Man's Care for Many, or the Concern of every Man for All."[94]

No doubt there would be differences of wealth and standing in the good society that ordinary colonists imagined when they engaged in these public disputes. Still, that society would limit private individuals who strove to become overmighty, and whose ambitions would not blink at expropriating their middling neighbors and reducing them to landlessness or reliance on a wage. It was not only that poor people should not suffer while the rich rioted in luxury; the middling should not be dispossessed merely to fulfill the undue ambitions of the few. Colonists invoked protection of the properties, legal rights, and social standing of the middling many. They argued on the grounds of their own legitimate (because measured) ambitions. Far from antimarket or anticommercial, this way of thinking merely but vitally sought to establish terms within which commercial exchange should take place.

At the same time, this way of thinking had profound political significance, implications for the fate of British liberty. Samuel Adams, like Cato, was forthright in hostility to great concentrations of wealth. He believed that government and society needed to restrain the acquisition of the few. Indeed, a variety of theorists in England suggested that societies might require an "Agrarian Law" that limited the amount of property one man might own, not only in defense of other men's well-being but on behalf of their very freedoms. "As Liberty can never subsist without Equality, nor Equality be long preserved without an Agrarian Law, or something like it, so when Men's Riches are become immeasurably and surprizingly great, a People who regard their own Security ought to make strict Enquiry, *how they came by them*, and oblige them to take down their own Size, for fear of TERRIFYING THE COMMUNITY, OR MASTERING IT." This was a matter of freedom as much as of equity, for there was a fundamental connection between the social order in which men lived and the freedoms they might enjoy therein. The link between distribution of property and political freedom was present in the property requirement that set voters and jurors apart from other adult men unqualified for a political voice in those institutions. Hard times in Boston or anywhere else in the colonies did in fact disenfranchise men, causing loss of freedoms in observable and obvious ways. Beyond that, the link between men's social standing and their portion of liberty was present in another way: freedom required a space from the compulsions of commercial society, a space that made dealings *within* the market more likely to be fair and consensual, less likely to be arbitrary.[95]

To promote their interests and ideas, men of the middle sort came together to vote in town meetings and other local gatherings, or in elections for their provincial houses of representatives. Beyond institutions of representation, they also assumed the right to a popular presence. They made use of their capacities to consent, both "before-hand" as voters and after the fact as executors of the law, to articulate such ideals. Well before the conflict with Britain, ordinary men (so often spoken of as not yet "politicized") sometimes practiced a popular politics. They commonly resorted to familiar political forms to make their notions of fairness felt in their societies.

Indeed, it is worth considering that colonists were accustomed to space for collective public consent not only in respect to issues that later generations would view as political matters but also in transactions that were by our standards economic in nature. Their capacity to consent to law extended where the law of their day extended, which is to say into decisions that a later age would insulate in a realm called "the economy." They expected a voice—as voters, jurors, and the people out of doors—in matters such as the supply and price of scarce goods, the limitation of monopoly, the institutions of town supply, the emission of paper money, and the workings of courts that adjudicated cases of debt. They considered popular ideas of fairness and right to be pertinent to the policies their society pursued on these matters. They assumed these matters were *their* business, not as individuals particularly learned or qualified to rule (for they were not) but as members of good standing on a particular social ground. When they celebrated British freedom, they meant this too, not just limits on monarchs but limits on would-be lords. In other words, when they thought of freedom, they thought of social relationships. For many colonists, this suggests, the other side of the coin of liberty was obligation.[96] Social connections provided them the capacity for covenants, associations, and relationships with one another by which they might know themselves (and be known as) "the people" of their society. When they drew on that capacity, they could make a revolution.

3

Declarations of Interdependence

Nearly every account of the Patriot movement of 1765 to 1776 includes ordinary colonists' capacity to frustrate official efforts to enforce the law. Patriots harried tax collectors, coerced officials into resigning, tarred and feathered informers and customs commissioners, rescued impounded vessels, threatened and demolished houses, and destroyed tea to prevent duties being paid on it. These demonstrations of popular power are familiar elements in the story of American resistance against Parliamentary rule. Yet we generally view these occasions when colonists assumed jurisdiction solely as necessary means to a substantially separate end. The *end* itself—a project of defending liberty and, eventually, seeking independence—seems defined by political elites somehow standing (and thinking) apart from their more mobbish, less distinguished neighbors.

So, although many historical accounts acknowledge popular political participation in the resistance years, most locate the *center* of the Patriot movement elsewhere: perhaps in official resolutions passed by provincial houses of assembly; in pamphlets and newspapers that promoted republican ideology or developed a vision of American empire. In this view, the people constituting themselves "out of doors" at mass public meetings and in crowd actions undoubtedly played a role. Ordinary participants in popular politics of the era surely counted as numbers. They filled the ranks. Yet it is still possible to imagine that they did not influence that movement in fundamental ways. Paradoxically, the broad public mobilization of the Revolutionary era may seem at the same time necessary for the Patriot movement's success and inessential to its meaning. By this logic, prominent, leading men actively defined the so-called "common cause" of America, while their lesser neighbors consequently and even subsequently joined.[1]

And what can be more obvious? Surely the leaders led, and the followers joined and followed.

Yet that may be a truth for ordinary times, and we are concerned with revolutionary ones.[2] This chapter tells a story in which the presence of the people out of doors vitally defined the colonies' resistance movement and shaped America's Revolution. It places the political forms that middling and lesser sorts brought to the movement at the heart of the matter. In critical ways, I argue, the Patriot movement of 1765–1776 was *about* the popular presence in execution of the law. Equally important, this account also places the social and cultural commitments of ordinary colonists at the center of the resistance. As it defended the popular presence, the Patriot movement also promoted the popular capacity to insist on prerogatives of ordinary knowledge and obligations of neighborhood. Indeed, it was the obligations of neighboring relationships that formed the truly *common* element in the "common cause," for Patriots created networks for dealing on neighborly terms and reinforcing neighborly oversight. To qualify as a Patriot in the resistance years, individuals had to recognize those terms and that oversight.

This chapter provides an account of Patriot networks, as they knit together colonists of different regions, beliefs, interests, and social ranks into a new and shared identity of "Patriot." Those networks surely reflected the thinking of members of the colonial elite, but they were remarkable for their embrace of middling participants and middling people's concerns. Elite purposes were neither sufficient to the Revolution nor neatly insulated from the purposes of others, in other words. Certainly many ideas and commitments circulated out (from cosmopolitan centers) and down (from the well read and elite to others less so). Yet the processes of "politicization" and "mobilization" also unfolded along another trajectory. Understandings of Patriotism also circulated up (representing the beliefs of an array of middling and lesser sorts) and in (from the parochial and the local into the official centers of political authority).

To look at the colonial resistance this way is not to discount or ignore the acts of the prominent Patriots celebrated by later generations. It is, however, to reinterpret those acts. It is to view them as acts *in relationship to* colonists of other social sorts. Throughout the resistance years, leading colonists were concerned not only with their relationship with Parliament, but with their relationship with fellow Americans. We mistake their achievement if we imagine them as creating a movement or developing a political ideology, then disseminating it to others. They did something more extraordinary than that. They joined in a commitment to neighboring and popular jurisdiction; they embraced an identity of "friends" to "their country"; they heeded vox populi. As a result, to a striking degree they accepted alterations in economic, social, and cultural relationships with their fellow free colonists. They acknowledged that their own economic ambitions, social aspirations, and cultural pretensions properly came under the jurisdiction of their neighbors.

Put differently, prominent Patriots generally remembered what some later Americans would (wish to?) forget: the powerful presence of their social inferiors. They acknowledged those inferiors' significance, their capacity to appear in numbers in public, to act collectively with discretion and agency as "the people." This interpretation thus turns the tables on many accounts of the Revolution. To a surprising degree, it suggests, elite Americans joined their lesser neighbors in this movement.[3]

Perhaps it was precisely that fact that made the Patriot moment revolutionary, a time when the world turned upside down.

Parliaments and Juries

The role of common men in execution of the law was a primary concern from the outset of the resistance movement.

The crisis began after the Seven Years' War, when British authorities faced a staggering war debt and assessed the resources that their colonists in North America might possibly provide to ease it. In 1764, Parliament passed the Sugar Act, which would skim some profit from the molasses and other sugars that colonial merchants routinely imported from foreign islands in the Caribbean. The new legislation actually lowered the duties levied on such sugars, but it established means to execute the law for the first time and announced a serious intention of doing so. The act promised a windfall to some British subjects, namely the owners of sugar plantations in the British West Indies. It was a blow to the interests of New England and Middle Colony merchants, who already bought up the sugar produced by British plantations but needed foreign sugars to fill their cargos and offset their balance of trade with England itself. With duties on foreign sugars, the price on British sugars would also undoubtedly rise.

Some North Americans accordingly objected. When Parliament regulated trade, they said, it was supposed to benefit the entire empire, rather than improving profits for one special interest. Still less should such regulations aim at lowering taxes on Parliament's constituents in Britain by taxing subjects in the colonies. To the extent that the Sugar Act explicitly sought to raise revenue, it constituted taxation of the colonists by a body of men they had never elected to represent them. In 1765, Parliament confirmed that raising revenue was its intention. It passed the Stamp Act, setting direct imposts on the sale of legal documents, newspapers, playing cards, and other items in the colonies. In response, many colonists quickly protested. They rallied around a fundamental principle of British rights: there should be "no taxation without representation."[4]

That principle has made sense to generations of Americans, in whose political world the institution of representation has played a central role. For eighteenth-century subjects of Britain, however, other concerns were equally vital. Colonists realized that Parliament's new policies would narrow the space for consenting to laws *after the fact*. Appointing its own officials and bypassing courts of common law, the ministry directly challenged the capacity of colonists out of doors to influence the law, whether in courtrooms or at sites of punishment. English authorities intended for justice to be determined by admiralty courts, where appointed judges paid by the Crown would preside unhampered by either local jurors or spectators. Parliamentary policy threatened *both* elements of British liberty so succinctly identified by Sir Henry Care—not only "1. Parliaments," but also "2. Juries." Many colonists defended the latter as fervently as the former.[5]

In published and private writings, countless colonists expressed concern for their familiar political institutions. As a student of English history, John Adams was not surprised that "the same restless Ambition, of aspiring Minds, which is endeavouring to lessen or destroy the Power of the People in Legislation, should attempt to lessen or destroy it, in the Execution of Lawes."[6] Would-be tyrants predictably targeted both arenas of popular consent. Other authors similarly objected that British authorities were overriding colonial rights to participate in execution of the law. They condemned the stamp distributors designated to enforce the new exactions and the admiralty judges designated to hear disputed cases. "How are our new laws to be adjudged and executed? Is not our property, after being seized by a numerous swarm of horse-leaches . . . to be thrown into a prerogative court? a court of admiralty? and there to be adjudged, forfeited, and condemned without a jury?"[7] Every provincial assembly on the continent objected to those provisions of the Sugar and Stamp acts that bypassed courts of common law. As Boston's voters explained, the addition of powers to admiralty courts "greatly weakens the best Security of our Lives, Liberties and Estates, which may hereafter be at the Disposal of Judges who may be Strangers to us, and perhaps malicious, mercenary, corrupt, and oppresive."[8] Far better to deal with judges known and rooted among them, in institutions through which colonists of different ranks were accustomed to negotiate with one another.

Writers and orators also maintained that both elements of Parliament's initiatives violated the British Constitution. Placing execution beyond the reach of common law courts was contrary to the rights of Britons: "Is not the distinguishing character of an Englishman, that he is free? Is he not born with an inherent right of assisting in the making of those laws by which he is to be taxed and governed, and of judging of them when they are made—Is not this the very spirit of the British constitution?"[9] Without a representative, how could the colonists assist in making laws? Without enforcement by familiar institutions of law, how could they judge the laws already made?

In arguing against these innovations, colonial writers insisted that local knowledge was essential to the law. The notion that members of Parliament, so distant, could tell what was best for the colonies was absurd: "Is it possible for any man in England to have such a knowledge of our internal circumstances, ever varying in an infant state, as to be capable of representing us?"[10] Representation, here, meant bringing local knowledge to the process of enacting laws and taxes. Nor should such knowledge be abstract, a matter of information alone: a representative should be inextricably bound up in the fate of his constituents, vulnerable as they were to all consequences, affected by the occurrences and policies that affected them. Wrote one observer: "The first birth-right of a Briton is, that he cannot be legally tried but by his Peers—One of the next is, that he cannot be taxed but by a parliament in which he is represented—or rather by gentlemen who pay a share of the tax they impose on him; for the law, not trusting too much to virtue, wisely proceeds on this supposition, that however inattentive a man may be to the concerns of others, he will probably pay some regard to his own interest; and it is in this view that the law requires a man to be possessed of a certain estate to entitle him to represent others."[11] Here was a widely held view of the essence of representation: it required sharing fundamental interests with one's constituents.

Similarly, local knowledge and accountability were essential to *execution* of the law. Carolinian Henry Gadsden evoked the ways in which law was necessarily located, when he named "our best inheritance" to be "trial by Jury and the Law *of the Land*."[12] In Virginia, leading planter Richard Henry Lee purposefully called the Sugar Act and Stamp Act merely "acts" of Parliament, "because laws I cannot call them." This was more than rhetoric; it was a careful choice of words from an experienced lawyer, legislator, and justice of the peace. Mere passage of a bill through the legislature was insufficient to the creation of binding authority. Lee helped establish a county organization that condemned Britain's efforts to lay and execute taxes in North America. Such measures violated colonists' rights, subverted their governments, and threatened their property. Some 115 signatories to the so-called Westmoreland County Association denounced and threatened supporters of the Stamp Act, agreed to gather "at the scene of the action" when they found someone trying to carry out the despised policy, and pledged to rescue one another from jail should the need arise. Such rescues and resistances were permissible and even proper, authorized as they were by the united voice of the vicinage. Making an "association," Westmoreland planters underscored their horizontal ties to one another and asserted the authority that inhered in those ties.[13]

In public demonstrations, colonists outside the ranks of the elite showed that Parliamentary policy was their concern, and they asserted their own competence to execute the law. Crowds made statements of political principle in many American towns. Some demonstrators dramatized their customary roles as jurors and punishers. Several crowds in Connecticut, for example, subjected effigies of the stamp masters not only to punishment but to "Tryal." In Lyme, men who called themselves "Proctors of Liberty" appointed from their own number an allegedly impartial judge and jury to try the stamp man in absentia. West Haven inhabitants encountered "a horrible Monster or Male Giant," twelve feet tall with a head "internally illuminated." "This Giant seemed to threaten Destruction to every Person and Thing around him," until captured by local men, who paraded him around the town accompanied by rough music, "the discordant Noise of Drums, Fiddles, and taunting Huzzas." The *Boston Evening Post* recounted the ensuing trial: "There the Giant was accused, fairly try'd and condemned by a special Jury and an impartial Judge, as an unjust Intruder, a Patron of Ignorance, a Foe to English Freedom, &c. and was sentenced to be burnt. The Sentence was accordingly executed, amidst the joyful and loyal Acclamations of near three Hundred Men, Women and Children."[14]

Portsmouth, New Hampshire, held "a special Court for the Trial of a Person in an unpopular Office," who appeared in effigy "at the Bar." The charge against the stamp master was this: "accepting a Promise of a Reward from his *Grandmother*, for using his Endeavour to impoverish and starve his *Mother* and her *Daughter*, of whom she had conceiv'd a *Jealousy* of her Growth and suppos'd Riches." Although he pled his innocence, and "put himself on his Country for Trial," the case was clear. "The evidence being so full, the Jury brought him in Guilty, without going off the Stand—The Judges then sentenced the Prisoner to be carried from hence to the place of Execution, and there to hang by the Neck till Dead; then his Ramains to be taken down and burnt to Ashes."[15]

Other localities dispensed with trials to proceed directly with punishment of effigies depicting stamp distributors or proponents of the act. The *North-Carolina Gazette* recounted events in Wilmington: on October 19, some five hundred people exhibited an effigy that represented "a certain Honourable Gentleman" who was known locally to favor the new tax. Having paraded the effigy, hanged it by the courthouse, and committed it to a bonfire, the crowd addressed itself to others: "After the Effigy was consumed, they went to every House in Town, and bro't all the Gentlemen to the Bonfire, and insisted upon their drinking, Liberty, Property, and no Stamp-Duty."[16]

Elizabeth-Town, New Jersey, also evoked the course of justice when its residents resolved that they would hang the first person to use stamps "without Judge or Jury."[17] Parliament might enact law without Elizabeth-Town; Elizabeth-Town threatened to execute justice without Parliament—or even, somewhat startlingly, without the participation of the proper colonial authorities. It must have been hyperbole (Jersey stamp master William Coxe did not put it to a test), but Elizabeth-Town certainly claimed jurisdiction over the Stamp Act.

Dramatic actions against effigies discouraged some appointed stamp masters from taking their posts. Other appointees resigned when crowds attacked their property. Marylanders pulled down the house of the stamp distributor there, and a Connecticut newspaper suggested that all the stamp distributors would be wise to insure their houses. In Boston, New York, Newport, and Charleston threatening crowds successfully forced appointed stamp men to resign. In Georgia, officials briefly managed to execute the Stamp Act but desisted when country people threatened to march on Savannah. Within a few months, the appointees had all pledged not to take up their posts, and no one dared to take their places.[18]

Using the forms of public trials and public punishments, Patriots reproduced occasions at which common men were accustomed to participate and spectators were invited to show detestation or approval. Those actions graphically claimed that rights of execution remained in the hands of colonial communities. Crowds denied the Stamp Act the status of law. Equally important, newspapers broadcast descriptions of these events, circulating the statements of "the people," or "the town" along with statements of houses of representatives and learned political essayists. The Patriot press extended the reach of local actions, as partisan newspapers presented their own pageant, depicting a broad, popular consensus to colonial and metropolitan readers alike.[19] Whether or not the colonists might be construed as having consented to these acts *before* they were passed by Parliament, public popular actions in the summer and fall of 1765 made it impossible to contend that "the people" were consenting to them *after* the fact.

Beneath this picture of unified opposition, however, there remained an unplumbed measure of dissent and discomfort. It was all very well for a gazette to report that "all the gentlemen" of a North Carolina town attended a Patriot bonfire. Admittedly, some attended only at the insistence of others. Probably, some attended only with mental reservations. Indeed, reports in Patriot newspapers provide imperfect indications of opinion on the ground, for these accounts were themselves part of the public proceedings. Patriot printers accepted or constructed partisan accounts of events, and they assumed the same rhetorical conventions as the demonstrations themselves; they omitted backstory and diverse commentary; and they represented a single, consensual position as that of "the people." They do not tell us, in other words, how or among whom that position was negotiated and maintained, or what dissenters might have thought, or when plans for demonstrations did not materialize. They recounted and extended a moment of vox populi.[20]

Across the colonies, moreover, many leading figures doubted that the right of the people to execute law extended to refusing the stamp duties. Prominent men as various as Benjamin Franklin, agent for the Pennsylvania assembly; Henry Laurens, merchant of South Carolina; and James Otis, Massachusetts pamphleteer, had to be convinced that colonists might forcibly oppose implementation of the Stamp Act. (Only Franklin's close friends among the Philadelphia shipwrights prevented a mob from convincing him.) Like Otis, other writers of pamphlets who found the act unconstitutional doubted that it might properly be resisted, only to find themselves pressed to support the middling and lesser people who *did* resist. They hastened to catch up with the thinking of their less prominent neighbors.[21]

And some, such as Thomas Hutchinson, chief justice of the Massachusetts Superior Court, did not respond to pressure from social inferiors. Hutchinson did not like the Stamp Act, but he intended to enforce it and refused even to answer when a group of townsmen asked whether he favored the law. Another group replied by demolishing his very fine house. The crowd's fury has not always made sense to historians. It made sense to workingmen of Boston, who were defending their capacity to execute or not execute law against a powerful authority who denied that capacity. They showed Hutchinson that he was, in the end, answerable to them. If he wished to rebuild in town, he would need to secure the services of those inferior city tradesmen and laborers whose questions about the Stamp Act he had spurned. Simply put, the crowd reminded Hutchinson of where he lived. Yet on this occasion, the crowd's destruction caused discomfort among Boston's "good People." Their disapproval reminded everyone that crowds had limits, and that the elite and respectable claimed significant say in defining what those limits were.[22]

For their part, not all "the people" supported their political elites or followed where elites tried to lead. We can see why colonial voters would generally endorse their representatives' authority; even men without the vote might reasonably prefer to be ruled by not-very-representative neighbors in Providence, Wilmington, or Annapolis rather than not-at-all-representative strangers in London. Yet not every popular action displayed proper deference toward the elected. One crowd of Connecticut "Sons of Liberty" besieged the stamp master in Wethersfield, when several elected assemblymen traveling through town to Hartford tried to intervene. Shouldn't the crowd wait for the sense of the government before forcing the stamp master's resignation? "Here is the sense of the government," replied one crowd member, referring to the crowd itself.[23] The assemblymen should proceed to Hartford, "where they might possibly be wanted." Later, having secured a sworn resignation, crowd members escorted the stamp master to Hartford as well, where they gathered around the statehouse and required him to resign again in the presence of assembled legislators.[24] These men seemed to think that their presence as "the people" trumped mere representation. They suggested they would not pay the stamp tax even *with* the consent of their elected legislature.[25] Popular disapproval reminded everyone that *governors* had limits, and that the commonalty claimed significant say in defining what those limits were.

Such events prevent us from assuming that even those colonists who opposed Parliament's new measures were in easy consensus. Agreement on principles did not make simple agreement on applications, and there were fault lines that could shatter the effort to present a united front. For although "the people" were surely a necessary conceptual presence in colonists' understanding of the British Constitution, at the same time, the people's physical presence in demonstrations and execution of the law had the potential to overwhelm and divide. By the same token, perhaps, elites also seemed necessary when lesser men thought of government; yet those elites' failure to consult or defer to demonstrations of popular sentiment could throw governing elites into disfavor. It was possible for a crowd to reject representation as insufficient and to replace it, for a critical political moment, with the popular presence.

Patriots who acted out of doors and Patriots accustomed to roles of leadership did not fully resolve these sources of tension over the following decade. They nonetheless managed an alliance with one another, a "coalition," in the words of one leading historian, or what many participants called "the common cause."[26] They did so by associating with one another in networks that regulated economic, social, and cultural life. Let us see how they mobilized and, for a critical and revolutionary period, managed to stand together.

The Common Cause

Patriots mobilized around pacts that they often called associations, establishing economic boycotts of British-made goods. These began as agreements to temporarily suspend British imports and their consumption, initiated by commercial interests in 1764. Although these pacts started small, they became increasingly inclusive and participatory over time. Parliament repealed the Stamp Act in 1766, but it laid new exactions and introduced new plans to execute its laws in the Townshend Acts of 1767, the Tea Act of 1773, and the Coercive Acts of 1774. Each new measure sparked new mobilizations. Growing numbers of colonists took part, and their associations regulated ever more aspects of life. Although they began as voluntary agreements, the pacts quickly became coercive, as participants cooperated to boycott and ostracize anyone who failed to join.[27]

Such agreements thus became the *common* element of the "common cause" of Patriotism: They were the arena where most ordinary men and women took part in the movement; equally important, they were where legislators, writers of pamphlets, qualified voters, and participants in street mobs all joined together, pledged to the same commitments and vulnerable to the same oversight. With these pacts, Patriots created networks for dealing on neighborly terms and reinforced neighborly jurisdiction over many transactions.

The pacts addressed the economic and social consequences that some colonists feared would result from Parliamentary rule. Even without the new taxes, we have seen, systemic shortages of specie and a circulating medium made it difficult for many households to avoid and discharge debt. A new drain of money would impoverish growing numbers of households. The Sugar Act "must break and subdue the hearts of traders here," wrote Boston merchant Oxenbridge Thacher, and storekeepers, tradesmen, laborers, and sailors all knew they would suffer along with the traders if he was right.[28] In all the colonies, paying for stamps on legal documents would load additional costs on debtors dragged into court or creditors pressed to sue by their own obligations. It promised disaster for poor "mortgagers, obligors, and defendants."[29] The new taxes would make themselves felt throughout colonial societies. "In arbitrary governments," worried one colonial writer, "tyranny generally descends, as it were, from rank to rank, through the people, til almost the whole weight of it, at last, falls upon the honest laborious farmer, mechanic, and day laborer. When this happens, it must make them poor, almost irremediably poor indeed!"[30] Political oppression would embitter social relations, as each rank defended its own interest at the expense of those beneath. Hardship would descend as it so often did: through the raising of rents, calling in of debts, legal actions followed by seizures and auctions of property, the loss of competences, the loss of livelihoods.[31]

At first, few worried that this was what Parliament intended. True, there were some in England who might not mind making the colonists "irremediably poor." The great absentee proprietors of sugar plantations in the British Caribbean, for example, lived the fashionable life in London, Bristol, or Bath. They showed little concern for the well-being of impoverished English inhabitants of the island colonies, let alone the countless enslaved Africans whose labor produced their fortunes. It would not bother such men if the mainland, too, were impoverished. They viewed the New World solely as a source of wealth for themselves.[32]

Yet Americans trusted that few Englishmen shared that view. Surely most Britons at home saw the free colonists of North America as their fellows and their equals. In adopting oppressive policies, the English were merely misinformed about the colonies' situation and the policy's likely effects. They would relent when duly informed. To enlighten the English, merchants in New York, Philadelphia, Boston, and other towns decided to suspend importations of British goods. Loss of business would influence British manufacturers and dealers who counted on American sales. It would remind English interests of the importance of colonial customers by giving them a foretaste of what would happen when the customers were reduced to penury. Those interests in turn could lobby Parliament for repeal of the offending taxes. Colonists appealed to Englishmen's self-interest, recalling them to the greater, shared interest that united every part of the empire. They also appealed to Englishmen's affection for the colonists as fellow Britons. "Are we not children of the same parent?" asked one anonymous writer in the press.[33] Most Americans believed that they were.

By the same logic, it became incumbent on elites *within* the colonies to establish that they also regarded their neighbors as fellow and equal subjects. To accomplish that end, the associations to limit imports and consumption called for conspicuous changes from political and social elites. Marylander Daniel Dulaney, for example, imagined a dramatic alteration should political leaders in that province appear clad in homespun rather than their usual imported finery: "The Sight of our Representatives, all adorned in compleat Dresses of their own Leather, and Flax, and Wool . . . would excite, not the Gaze of Admiration, the Flutter of an agitated Imagination, or the momentary Amusement of a transient Scene, but a calm, solid, heart-felt Delight."[34] Dulaney here described sensations induced by the sight of genteel dress, feelings of transience, agitation, and admiration introduced by the fashion system, a discomfiting lightness of being. Homespun, Dulaney believed, would transform the spectacle of genteel dress into one that evoked a sense of solidity and, indeed, solidarity. Like other accounts, this one imagined the colony's political elite as objects for the view of others. Changing their appearance, Maryland's representatives would present and experience themselves as something other—something more "solid"—than genteel consumers. The Assemblymen's New Clothes would reflect their fitness to rule, not through magnificence, but through their visible likeness and fidelity to constituents.

On more ordinary occasions, new clothes—not fashionable and costly but plain and domestic made—helped members of the privileged classes renounce their aspirations to wealth and superiority. At church, at the tavern, in the courtroom, in public streets, homespun garments testified to their wearer's commitments. A Virginian reported on the change to an English merchant:

When you traded here you well knew it to be the ambition of the people of this country to Endeavour who should be best dressed with the British Manufactures, but they are now quite on the contrary extreme, for their glory now is, to dress in their own manufacture . . . . Many people, who a few years ago, would not wear a shirt of less value than 2s6d or 3s sterling per yard, now put on a cotton shirt of their own manufacture.[35]

Students graduating from the College of New Jersey wore homespun when they received diplomas. Various traders pledged to do without all laces and ruffles in their clothing and to import only inexpensive cloths from Britain. Such choices demonstrated that plain and common could be good enough.[36]

The well-to-do also cut a less fashionable appearance at the funerals of their friends and family members. Beginning in 1764, Boston merchants announced they would stop importing the expensive gloves that mourners in prominent families customarily wore and gave to many in attendance at funeral ceremonies. In Elizabeth-Town, New Jersey, a group resolved to reduce costs by "dispensing with Scarfs, Gloves and Liquors," all of them imported items, on these occasions.[37] Residents of Philadelphia, Charleston, Annapolis, and other towns quickly followed suit. Changes in the observation of funerals remained popular throughout the resistance decade. Patriots publicly renounced a practice that marked some as prosperous; they adopted standards more comfortable for those with less to spend in honor of their loved ones.[38]

Patriots also abandoned other socially invidious practices. In the Middle and Southern colonies, they agreed not to patronize the theater, for it was a spectacle that attracted the fashionable wealthy and tempted tradesmen to squander their money. New Jersey Patriots discouraged horse races as well as stage plays in 1770–71, since at both venues, "vast Sums of Money are thrown away for no useful Purpose of Life."[39] In the South, Patriot gentry also decided to forego horse racing and cockfights, partly in deference to the sensibilities of a growing population of New Light Baptists in their midst. Everywhere, Patriot men and women alike gave up fancy entertainments, canceling their usual assemblies and balls. They dispensed with fashionable afternoon tea parties, held in the private parlors of the well-to-do.[40]

For members of the elite classes, these changes represented a retreat from the social ideal of gentility and an embrace of a social ideal of connection. The change is neatly captured by Patriot bans on tea and encouragement of rum. Tea was addictive, expensive, and exotic, hence easily deployed as a symbol of consumption of foreign imports in general. And though colonists of most ranks consumed it, only those with particular aspirations and leisurely afternoons consumed it in the genteel mode—in select groups of acquaintances gathered in private parlors. Tea parties were a source of fashionable information, a place for witty conversation, fine clothing and accoutrements. They were closed gatherings of men and women of similar social standing. Inclusive of both genders, they were nonetheless characterized by a certain conspicuous exclusion along lines of social rank and cultural style. Cultural historian Richard Bushman has located such genteel gatherings midway between the inclusive feasts of the late medieval village and the closed, familial gatherings of nineteenth-century homes. Eighteenth-century genteel occasions accommodated a middle group, a "select company" of near equals beyond family but exclusive of the ordinary folk. The tea table, in this view, stood between the boards of medieval feasts and the dining table of a nineteenth-century private family. Laden with queensware and silver, the tea table represented the rise of increasingly decorous, discriminate, and costly practices of consumption. For all these reasons, tea came under attack even before Parliament laid a tax on it, and it remained a powerful symbolic item in Patriot demonstrations and rhetoric through 1776.[41]

Rum, with its capacity for inspiring comradeship, its sealing of bargains, and its amenability to consumption by friendly passing of the bottle, quickly became the Patriotic drink. Sons of Liberty or local political leaders provided liquor to enhance the public celebrations of the Stamp Act repeal held in towns in Pennsylvania, New York, Georgia, and other provinces. Massachusetts Patriots celebrated the anniversary of the repeal with parades and gatherings. Rutland celebrated with skyrockets, bonfires, and the drinking of "Many Loyal Healths." In Dorcester, some 350 Sons of Liberty dined outside the Liberty Tree tavern in 1769 and drank forty-five toasts to express patriotic sentiments. Such celebrations, wrote John Adams, "render the People fond of their Leaders in the Cause"— that is, they helped render would-be leaders *leaders*. These events bridged gaps of social rank, cementing an alliance, establishing some men's bid for leadership, other men's recognition of commonality. They established shared commitments. Rum also played its role of promoting male solidarity at the growing number of militia musters that marked the early 1770s.[42]

By contrast, tea could hardly be more reviled. A few examples illustrate the great hostility against it. In January of 1775 Portsmouth, New Hampshire, reported these proceedings: "About 60 pounds of TEA was publicly burnt on the Parade in the Town at 8 o'clock in the Evening, last Wednesday, belonging to a person who bro't it from Salem, who was so far convicted of his own Error in attempting the Sale of that condemned Commodity, that he put it in the Fire himself in the presence of a large

Number of Spectators."[43] In Providence, Rhode Island, the town crier specifically described an upcoming tea burning as an occasion for demonstrating one's patriotism to the jury of one's peers: "All true friends of their Country, lovers of Freedom, and haters of shackles and hand-cuffs, are hereby invited to testify their good disposition, by bringing in and casting into the fire, a needless herb, which for a long time hath been highly detrimental to our liberty, interest, and health." It was important to Patriots to report that three hundred attended the bonfire in the marketplace, and that participants showed a laudable spirit. "There appeared great cheerfulness in committing to destruction so pernicious an article; many worthy women, from a conviction of the evil tendency of continuing the habit of Tea drinking, made free-will offerings of their respective stocks of the hurtful trash." As for those who did not volunteer: "Whilst the Tea was burning, a spirited Son of Liberty went along the street with his brush and lampblack, and obliterated or unpainted the word TEA on shop signs."[44]

Other Patriots also refused tea with public ceremony. Famously, forty-one women in Edenton, North Carolina, signed a pledge not to consume tea or wear expensive fabrics. In Wilmington, women conducted a public procession through the streets to announce their abandonment of tea. Individuals who persisted in the habit came under the discipline of Sons of Liberty. Faced with the threat of opprobrium, they apologized in public places and in the press. When rumors circulated suggesting that John Hancock was importing tea, he paid for printed handbills to deny the charge and circulated them in the streets and shops of Boston.[45]

The proliferation of such dramatic events and newspaper reports about them provides evidence that some consumer goods—and the social ideal of gentility with which they were associated—had created divisions in colonial societies. The Patriot movement coalesced by dispensing with such goods and by banning genteel social occasions. For it was only in mitigating invidious differences that political consensus was secured. Put slightly differently, we can measure the divisive effect of some forms of consumption and sociability on colonial societies by the strict suppression of those forms by Patriot agreements.

As with the disuse of other goods, the disuse of tea suggests that its consumption and expense could be the source of social tensions. Patriots' ban of tea parties suggests that those occasions aroused anxiety over new behaviors associated with the rise of commodity consumption. Becoming a consumer, the anthropologist Grant McCracken has pointed out, entailed new patterns in and meanings for one's daily routine. Well before factory work introduced new structures of time and work discipline, consumption reordered aspects of daily life. Eighteenth-century consumers spent more time in town, in shops, at teas and similar gatherings that provided fashion information.[46] For females in particular, this meant less time at the hearth and at productive labor at home. Patriots rejected this reordering; they identified time spent at consumption as wasted and indicted tea gatherings as conspicuous leisure. Trade boycotts and nonconsumption agreements thus moved women who had begun to enter the realm of consumption back into the realm of household production. Instead of drinking tea, Patriot women would manufacture cloth at home. "Bringing Women to the Wheel and the Loom is restoring them to their primitive and most ancient Dignity and Employment," noted an author in the *Newport Mercury*. He took special pains to reassure elite ladies that spinning was not an indignity to their class.[47]

These changes reveal the powerful meanings of cultural choices in eighteenth-century society. In pursuit of unity across lines of region, belief, social class, and occupation, the colonists who joined the Patriot movement found it useful, perhaps necessary, to suppress genteel occasions. They replaced them with spectacles of a different sort, public occasions that stressed solidarity and minimized social difference. The boycotts gave elite Americans the opportunity to establish that they cared about their neighbors' views. They could not only refrain from importing and consuming, they could publicly appear at new occasions—Patriot public meetings, tea burnings, and simple, unostentatious funerals—now transformed into occasions of conspicuous *non*-consumption. Much like government processions, court days, and public punishments, these new occasions presumed the critical presence of spectators.

How crucial this function was to well-to-do Patriots appears in the prominent coverage that "new-style" funerals received in the colonial press. The *South Carolina Gazette* reported one case: "Few had more friends than this amiable and excellent LADY, yet the latter clause of the eighth article of the Association was strictly adhered to at this funeral." Similarly, when a Philadelphia alderman died in early 1775, the *Pennsylvania Gazette* stressed both the virtue of the deceased, who had been known for "uprightness in his dealings," and the virtue of the mourners at the funeral, which was "conducted agreeable to the resolves of the Continental Congress."[48] The press also made a point of reporting when graduates from Harvard and the College of New Jersey had their degrees printed on locally manufactured paper and wore homespun suits at graduation ceremonies.[49] Publication in the press supplemented the dramatic occasions themselves, a new Patriot dramaturgy enacted on the streets, on town commons, and at public occasions ranging from graduations to tea burnings to funerals.

A dissenter from Patriot standards, William Wragg of South Carolina, offers a point of comparison. There was nothing wrong with the now-rejected funeral customs, Wragg argued in 1767. He would prefer to see "a decent external sorrow" in the garb of mourners. He would further prefer to find honest mechanics at home with their families rather than meeting in the streets. The Patriot regimen seemed to Wragg to invert the proper order: shouldn't there be sober workingmen, sipping tea, rather than boisterous gentry, swilling rum and sharing toasts with their inferiors? Schemes for nonconsumption would please Wragg if they reformed lower-class drinking habits instead of changing the behaviors of the respectable classes. "Instead of receiving offence, by passing the doors of numberless dram-shops, the bane of all order and sobriety, I shall with pleasure enter the decent habitations of honest mechanics."[50]

Wragg's rejection of Patriot views throws into relief the choices being made by other members of the colonial elite. Wragg wrote as observer and judge; he spoke of the way that social institutions—whether funerals or dram shops—appeared to *him*, and he comfortably passed judgment on his lesser neighbors' virtues and vices. By contrast, many of his contemporaries showed greater concern for the perceptions and opinions of the middling and poorer sort. It was elite behavior and appearance that came under closest scrutiny in these nonconsumption networks. Wragg's article reminds us that the normal state of affairs was for elites to preach austerity to others while living large themselves. In English historian E.P. Thompson's words, "Only a ruling class which feels itself to be threatened is afraid to flaunt a double standard."[51] Threatened by Parliament—and by the press of their neighbors' opinions—elite colonists who became Patriots renounced tokens of superiority. They reassured themselves and their neighbors: whatever differences and divisions existed within the free population of American societies, they were not differences and divisions of kind.[52]

Moreover, the transformations established by Patriot associations went beyond the symbolic to reshape colonial material and economic relationships. If in cultural terms Patriot pacts required elites to defer to middling values, in economic terms pacts required them to defer to the material interest of their lesser neighbors. Of course, middling colonists could also take part in nonconsumption. Most households of most incomes could save by resolving to consume less. Studies show that middling households were purchasing new items in the quarter century after 1740, not just necessities but conveniences and even luxuries, and in unprecedented numbers. Doing without such imports offered every family the opportunity to refine its virtue and cut back on expenses. The notion that all sorts were sinners was familiar in this society permeated by Protestant belief, and colonists accustomed to scouring their own hearts were likely to find a propensity for self-seeking and even opulent living there. More than a few male colonists said they found such propensity in their own household, among its female members. Many colonists had indulged at least a modest fondness for fashion in recent decades; now many colonists might change their ways.[53]

Yet middling and poorer Patriots took part in the pacts in a different role—as producer rather than nonconsumer. Here are the goods that towns in eastern Connecticut resolved to stop importing in 1768: "Carriages, Horse furniture, Hats, Ready Made Apparel, House furniture, shoes, laces, articles of jewelry, clocks, furs, broadcloth costing above 10s per yard, liquirs."[54] Although some banned items might qualify as potential purchases for middling households, many were luxury goods. Passing up this sort of consumption would hardly require a substantial change of buying habits among many Americans. Rather, these agreements promised custom for the producing classes. Cabinetmakers, spinners, weavers, hatters, tailors, dressmakers, shoemakers, tatters, goldsmiths, brewers of cider, and growers of apple trees all had a stake in Connecticut's program. Now their purchasing neighbor would patronize their shops, keep them and their journeymen employed, and help members of the trade cancel debts of their own.

So those who agreed not to buy imports also put money in the pockets of their producing neighbors. As merchants renounced imported gloves, for example, glove makers in New England boosted production of inexpensive plain gloves marked as manufactured in the region. Along with glovers, local tanners, butchers, and farmers would benefit. The Patriot shift in purchasing redistributed wealth within the empire. In one year's time, a contemporary estimated, Boston alone saved some £10,000 with its new-style funerals. The effect was also a modest redistribution of wealth within colonial societies. Some of the saved money remained with mourning families; some of it reached colonial artisans and their hires; and, if wealthy families followed the advice of Patriot writers, some lightened the burdens of the local poor.[55]

Moneyed and creditor households thus redirected their custom to help offset the debt of their producing neighbors. A gentleman who wore homespun did more than indicate his satisfaction with plain style, then. His clothing also represented specific local and regional acts of production and purchasing. True, in the South, cloth of the colonists' "own making" might be produced in fact by enslaved workers, with minimal impact on economic relations beyond the plantation. Yet in small planter households and in other regions, it was free women and children who spun thread, local weavers who made cloth, and local sewers who cut and stitched. Skilled men and women produced clothing in specialized trades as mantua-makers, tailors, tailoresses, seamstresses, and milliners.[56] Leather dressers and tanners processed the material for leather pants, aprons, and shirts. Patriots promoted production outside the household by setting up linen, wool, and tow cloth manufactories that employed poor women in Boston, Philadelphia, and New York. Homespun reflected employment and income for an array of colonial spinners, weavers, and tailors, along with farmers who raised flax and husbandmen who raised sheep. So programs *against* importation and consumption were also programs *for* domestic manufacture and for easing the plight of working households. By the close of 1765, New York and Newport had both instituted regular marketplaces to vend home manufactures. The patronage of well-to-do neighbors could help prevent colonial producers from descending to the "wretched state of Vassalage" that some English policy makers apparently intended.[57] By cooperating in these Patriot programs, Americans could fend off a state of subordination and impoverishment far beyond the narrowly political realm. These were boycotts of Britain; they were also positive movements to embrace "Oeconomy, Industry, and Manufactures" in British North America.[58] They were movements to secure the sort of society where ordinary men might reasonably maintain a middling competence.

Many colonists thus rethought the imperial relation by rethinking relationships closer to home. Nathaniel Ames's almanac for 1767, written not for the learned few but the many, depicted Patriot aims this way: to "prevent the execution of that detestable maxim of *European* policy amongst us, viz: that the common people, who are three-quarters of the world, must be kept in ignorance, that they may be slaves to the other quarter who live in magnificence." The way colonists mobilized over the following years testifies that many shared Ames's diagnosis of the threat. They shaped a movement in direct and purposeful opposition to the specter he evoked: they countered the magnificence of the few and the indebtedness, or "slavery," of the many. They worked against the ignorance of the common people by disseminating information about the crisis and the behavior of their fellows in that crisis.[59]

Indeed, Patriots committed themselves to a fundamental principle of public knowledge. Their pacts generated an extraordinary number of local meetings, official and unofficial, public gatherings in the streets, meetinghouses, and marketplaces of colonial towns. The sorts of crowds that had confronted stamp men now might confront suspected importers, retailers, or consumers of banned goods, or else celebrate at bonfires of the effigies of such men. On a less spectacular level, nearly every colonist was vulnerable to the surveillance of his or her neighbors. The pacts brought public attention to many arguably private choices. What one bought, what one sold, what one consumed, what one wore—all became subject to broad public knowledge. Violators of Patriot standards might find their names listed in the province newspaper or accounts of their transgressions posted in meetinghouses, taverns, mills, and other gathering places. Patriots agreed that individual informants should work with committees to discover violators of the pacts. A group of Connecticut towns explained the purpose of identifying everyone who would not join the movement: "that their names may be published, their conduct exposed, and their persons avoided."[60]

We see why these pacts became known as "associations."[61] Subscribers associated themselves with one another. They dissociated from anyone who refused to abide by their agreements. "We will not trade with anyone . . . ," "we will discountenance . . . ," and they would treat dissenters with "all the neglect they shall justly deserve."[62] Well-to-do Patriots promised to withdraw from the corrupt or avaricious to join themselves with the values and oversight of local publics. They dissociated themselves from Old World hierarchies and social divisions. Where they had sometimes set themselves apart and above, Patriots among the colonial elite now set themselves among their fellows. Their behaviors testified that they stood on a level—the level of local exchange, networks of mutuality, and the values and practices that inhered in those networks. The result was a series of Patriot circles within which participants would deal with one another in Patriot ways.

One leading historian has recently proposed that colonists founded their quest for liberty in these years on their identity as consumers in the Atlantic market. On the contrary, it seems to me, those who had begun to build identity on consumption of imports became Patriots precisely as they became *nonconsumers* in that market, as they returned to a more familiar role as patrons of their producing neighbors. For their part, countless mechanics, farmers, and laborers became Patriots primarily by embracing the role of *producer*. Members of all groups became Patriots by engaging with one another in economic, social, and political transactions. We miss the essence of the matter if we define Patriots solely by the way they recrafted relationships with tea or cloth or indeed with any goods. Of far greater significance, they recrafted their relationships *with one another*. If there was a single word that encompassed the Patriot identity established in the boycotts of trade, that word would be *"neighbor."*[63]

Women's participation in these networks supports this view of the Patriot movement as grounded in practices of neighboring. After all, colonial women as a group had been largely debarred from recognized political agency. That they so quickly found a role in the Patriot movement reflects the degree to which that movement defined all free neighbors as potential participants. Engaging free, white women as effective actors in public affairs was not the *last* resort of this society (which could not imagine engaging enslaved Africans), but it was certainly not the first. Despite all doubts about their political capacities, however, women quickly became active in Patriot networks. They banned tea from their tables; they adopted homespun; urban ladies took up spinning, and rural women devoted more hours to it. Those with money purchased domestic-made goods rather than imports; those without money found new employment and new markets for their products. Women took part in transactions, reported on them, gossiped, and excluded or ostracized. In some places, they signed their names to boycott agreements. Contemporary accounts report women's presence at public tea burnings, and surely they took part as well at other gatherings described only as consisting of "the people."[64]

Like other Patriots, women showed their political loyalties by rising above their desires for fashionable clothing and addictive tea. Three hundred Boston women, heads of families, signed an agreement not to drink tea until the Tea Act of 1770 was repealed.[65] And fifty-one ladies in Edenton, North Carolina, agreed likewise:

> As we cannot be indifferent on any occasion that appears to affect the peace and happiness of our country; and as it has been thought necessary for the publick good to enter into several particular Resolves . . . , it is a duty that we owe not only to our near and dear relations and connexions, but to ourselves, who are essentially interested in their welfare, to do every

thing as far as lies in our power to testify our sincere adherence to the same, and we do therefore accordingly subscribe this paper as a witness of our fixed intention and solemn determination to do so.[66]

The Edenton ladies here testified to their motives: they were not "indifferent" to the "happiness" of their country; they acted from "duty" to their "relations and connexions." Having long been charged with kinship obligations and the cultivation of neighborly feelings, women now acted on the strength of those feelings and to fulfill those obligations. Their acknowledged capacity in matters of household production, local exchange, and neighborhood relationship now made them political actors. The Patriot movement would shortly come to prize the sort of "manly virtue" displayed on militia fields, a virtue denied to women.[67] Yet insofar as Patriotism meant affection and connection, insofar as it required sacrifice and productive labor, it included space for female participants. Women could exhibit such virtues as well as any man.

At the same time, Patriots maintained a critique of femininity, for the feminine epitomized in many minds a certain natural dependence, a weakness of will in the face of tea or expensive laces, susceptibility to the sorts of social pretensions that brought households into excessive consumption and devastating debt. Fairly or unfairly, Patriot writers blamed wives and daughters for the hardships of many households. Patriot rhetoric found easy targets for disdain in women who flouted the new standards of association.[68]

As early as 1765, an author in the *Newport Mercury* expounded on what fashionable women should be *permitted* to wear: "While their Ornaments are the Work of their own Hands, let them wear and possess them as the honorable Rewards of their Labour and Toil; let the finest linen array them; may their Bosoms be covered with the most delicate Needle Work; and let us never profanely think of tearing the embroidered Tucker or Handkerchief from their lovely Necks or Breasts, if of their own handy Work."[69] This writer assumed his readers to be familiar with English history. In the late seventeenth and early eighteenth centuries, British weavers had blamed a rage for East India cottons for slack demand for woolens and their own unemployment. Crowds had indeed torn dresses off fashionable women in London streets, protesting their failure to buy British. Invoking those events, the *Mercury* raised the specter of mob action; it suggested that colonists inhabited a like situation, in which the well-being of some colonists was endangered by the fashionable tastes of others. He reminded colonists of an English tradition in which producing classes defended their interests against the allures of fashion and the weakness of females. He reminded women of their vulnerability to public insult should they fail to follow the popular maxim intended to guide the fairer sex, "Keep Within Compass."[70]

Ten years later, the *Pennsylvania Journal* showed that wayward women remained vulnerable to Patriotic insult. The paper published a satirical petition, ostensibly from "Diverse OLD WOMEN of the city," complaining about having to give up tea. "Your petitioners . . . fear it will be utterly impossible for them to exhibit so much patriotism as to totally disuse it." As a substitute, the petition alleged, chocolate was too heavy a drink for the ladies, and would "destroy that brilliancy of fancy, and fluency of expressions, usually found at tea tables, when they are handling the conduct or character of their absent acquaintances." The petition asked an indulgence, permission to continue drinking tea for "those spinsters, whom age and ugliness have rendered desperate in the expectations of husbands; those who are married, where infirmities and ill behavior have made their husbands long since tired of them, and those old women of the male gender who would be most naturally found in such company."[71] Here, clearly, was hostility toward men who drank tea with the women instead of rum with the men. Here was hostility toward gentility, including the "brilliancy" and "fluency" of conversation associated with it. And here, not subtly, was hostility toward the woman who did not dutifully join the Patriot program.

Contrast such expressions with published paeans to the spinning bees of "daughters of liberty." To cite one: in Providence, Rhode Island, eighteen "Daughters of Liberty" spun yarn at the house of Dr. Ephraim Brown from sunrise to sunset. The ladies consumed "a plain dinner that omitted TEA!" and resolved to oppose the Stamp Act, eschew British imports, and spurn all gentlemen who failed to do as much.[72]

Patriot rhetoric thus combined praise for liberty's "daughters" with condemnation for the "old," unmarried, or unproductive female. The *Pennsylvania Journal* article attacked women inadequate to the family circle, the unproductive and superfluous, women not integrated into the household economy. By contrast, the spinning party at Ephraim Brown's, attended by marriageable youth, approximated the ideal Patriot gathering. Its participants were young and productive. For women, these articles show, integration into domestic production was more than a desideratum; it was necessary to acceptable Patriot femininity. Put differently, Patriots were happiest with females when they were dutiful wives, mothers, and—commonly said—"daughters of liberty."

And what was true for female Patriots—that they avowed motives of affection; they were producers and not consumers; they influenced imperial affairs as they took part in neighborhood exchange; they faced powerful social pressure to take part only in prescribed ways—these things were also true for male Patriots. Men who joined the cause, after all, described themselves as dutiful "*sons* of liberty." *Every* Patriot had to stay within compass, for nowhere was Patriotism easily identified merely with pursuing self-interest or self-assertion, or maximizing liberal and individual rights. Men, too, in other words, mobilized as neighbors.

They said as much in public gatherings to secure Patriot associations and networks. Here was Thomas Barnard in Salem, Massachusetts: "A suspicion of being inimical to those with whom we are connected in society, and whom we esteem and love, cannot but give severe pain to a generous mind." And Enachy Bartlett, a merchant in Haverill: "My comfort in life does so much depend on the regard and good will of those among whom I live."[73] Comfort in life depended on one's fellows—their business at one's shop, their readiness to exchange labor and goods, their assistance in times of difficulty, their forbearance as creditors and good faith as debtors, their companionship at the tavern, their friendship and esteem. So men, too, acknowledged vulnerability to the oversight and judgment of others. Women's position of dependence was not utterly disqualifying in this movement, in other words, because the movement did not require distinctive individual independence even of its male participants. Instead, it required competence within local economies and neighborhood life.[74]

To view the Patriot movement as deeply shaped by neighborly ideals and practices is to propose a particular interpretation of the origins of the American Revolution. Many historians explore the ideas of leading Patriots, expressed in pamphlets, newspaper articles, private correspondence, and other literature. Whether influenced by a dissenting republican ideology, liberal political ideas drawn from thinkers such as John Locke, or Scottish commonsense philosophy, these leaders thought their way to revolution. The spread of their ideas to the rest of the population, so the argument goes, made the situation revolutionary. The sheer volume of publications that circulated in the resistance decade attests to that flow of ideas, from the relatively elite and educated to one another, as well as to the more middling and lesser sort of reader.[75] Yet such a view of the Revolution is incomplete. The pacts that most colonists joined allow us to see a strand of Patriotism that was created with and by the participation of ordinary colonists. The surviving records and publications of self-appointed or locally chosen committees provide a view of that Patriotism. The same partisan newspapers that carried political essays to common readers also recounted local gatherings that adopted associations and executed them. Patriot gazettes printed numerous individual apologies, promises to reform, protestations of innocence, and descriptions of crowd actions. Such publications spread information about the standards of Patriotism, negotiated in concrete cases within various communities, from one locality to another, to rural and metropolitan readers alike.[76] These concrete local events, and the oral and written accounts that circulated about them, were not the unadulterated voice of "the people"—any more than pronouncements of elite congresses or legislatures might be. Yet by viewing the way Patriotism unfolded on the ground, we detect some of the expectations and values that more ordinary colonists brought to the coalition with their superiors.[77] For if the middling people of British North America shaped the resistance movement, they did so most powerfully in these many specific actions. In the acts of adopting and enforcing associations, in other words, colonists *both* elite and ordinary thought their way to revolution. The networks they built expressed the *domestic* origins of American independence, using the term "domestic" in its double sense, to describe commitments that were to an appreciable extent "homegrown" within American societies, and to locate the grounds of such commitments in common practices of household production and neighborhood economy.

The language generated by Patriot pacts testifies to these commitments of many ordinary households. With the term "association," subscribers to Patriot agreements emphasized their social connections. Other phrases similarly suggested acts of affiliation. The phrase "solemn league and covenant"—adopted by New England town meetings for their pacts in 1774—echoed a seventeenth-century agreement that had brought Protestant Scots into alliance with Puritan English. Everywhere in the colonies, too, Patriot rituals showed the influence of ideals of Christian community. Such rituals drew on Protestant evangelical ideas that had been circulating through the continent for decades. Nonimportation and nonconsumption pacts embodied antimaterialist values familiar to the many colonists drawn to Baptist, Methodist, and other "New Light" preaching since the 1740s. An antiworldly impulse—to remove oneself from fashion, commercial debt, and corrupt entanglement in prideful consumption—appeared powerfully in Patriot pacts. And as some evangelical Christians of the era joined new communities of brethren, linked by mutual love, so Patriots joined new associations, linked by mutual commitment to one another's well-being. When they figured themselves as "sons" and "daughters" of liberty, Patriots forged a relationship with one another—not, perhaps, "brothers and sisters in Christ," but brothers and sisters nonetheless.[78]

Equally important, Patriots employed dramatic forms of renunciation that recalled some of the most expressive elements of evangelical awakenings. Tea burnings—often accompanied by the burning of offending laws or Tory publications—resembled the bonfire of books and finery inspired by New Light preacher James Davenport in New London in 1743. Patriot political orators sometimes drew from the rhetorical style of evangelical preachers who stirred listeners to new belief. Perhaps most striking, the public conversions that were central and defining events in evangelical awakenings found clear counterparts in the forms used by colonists who became Patriots in the 1760s and early 1770s, many of them standing before a gathered community.[79] Thus, in Cumberland County, Virginia, John Scruggs admitted to his county committee that "he had lately imprudently fallen into a Breach of the Continental Association, by Gaming." Scruggs appeared before assembled local Patriots, where he "made Concessions and exhibitted such Marks of true Penitence, that it is resolved that the said Scruggs be again considered as a worthy Member of this Community." The Reverend Asa Dunbar, of Weston and Sudbury, Massachusetts, publicly stated that he hoped to remain "in good fellowship with every friend to American liberty." In New York, Stephen Baxter admitted to blasphemy as well as Loyalist tendencies, for with "horrid cursing and profane swearing, I have opposed the . . . liberties of America." Baxter offered a public apology, "for all of which conduct of mine. I am sincerely sorry, [and] ask the forgiveness of all those I have abused personally, and also the friends of American liberty in general, to whom I desire my confession be made publick in one of the New-York papers."[80]

Such public acts of contrition, reform, or conformity were repeated countless times in countless localities. A New England committee made clear that its role was to secure and maintain good fellowship. "The great end of discipline," they wrote, was to "take away the sin and save the sinner."[81] Another showed its commitment to treating first-time violators as neighbors, to be recalled to harmony, rather than as criminals, to be exposed to public view. In Norfolk, Virginia, a committee acknowledged "the great caution with which public censure should be inflicted." The

Petersham, Massachusetts, town committee decided to publish the names of several opponents of the continent-wide association of 1774, but only after "all the friendly Expostulations and Intreaties which we have been able to make Use of" had failed to change their minds. These men were not just political dissidents, in this account, but members of a town or a fellowship who had strayed, appropriately treated with friendly address, but ultimately described, when unresponsive to their fellows, as betrayers and "parricides."[82] Patriot rituals of apology, reintegration, or exclusion resembled the discipline enacted within many Protestant churches. They made sense to a population accustomed to judging "true Penitence."

If some Patriot language was resonantly Protestant, other more secular expressions also emphasized the significance of fellow feeling within the movement. Time and again, Patriots described themselves as "friends" of their country. They called dissenters "unfriendly," "inimical," or "enemies" to the common cause. These terms explicitly figured Patriotism as a social relationship and a matter of affection. The word "country" when used in this phrase evoked a constituency or vicinage as much as nation or empire. It evoked networks of people as well as place. In Patriot discussions, "friends of their country" sometimes contrasted with "friends of the government." In speaking of their country, in other words, they were talking about their *society*.[83]

Many men's expressions of allegiance further emphasized that such motives as gratitude for established relationships and awareness of mutual dependence made them Patriots. John Armstrong of Isle of Wight, Virginia, described his reasons for joining the Patriot association there: "I should think myself guilty of the greatest ingratitude in acting against a Country, in which I have been treated with the greatest humanity and obtained a livelihood by the generosity of the inhabitants. I am sincerely sorry that I have forfeited the esteme of the good people of this Country and hope that my future behaviour will be such as to gain their good opinion."[84] When Philadelphia traders chided their counterparts in Newport for setting a different timetable for suspending trade, they condemned it as "ungenerous." The Newport merchants should change their agreement, "so as to be on a footing with your neighbours."[85] Similarly, New York merchants attested the importance of working to "harmonize with our brethren of Philadelphia" in their pacts.[86]

As defined by these pacts and associations, Patriotic virtue consisted precisely in marked willingness to conform to the opinions and standards of neighbors. Patriot politics thus relied on something rather different from the sorts of independence ascribed to virtuous republican individuals; it relied on the affection and connection of men and women bound to one another by social ties.[87]

The Patriot Economy

If reliance on social ties was the strength of the Patriot movement, that same reliance might also be said to be its weakness. Patriots created networks by drawing on people's capacities for cooperating, judging exchanges, tolerating negotiation, settling disputes, coming to a broad consensus about fairness, and coming to terms with one another. The movement relied on a popular ability to withdraw from the Atlantic market and engage on other, more neighborly terms. It drew on participants' experience of neighborhood transactions and on their commitment to the values and expectations that inhered in those transactions. As a result, the Patriot coalition incorporated and confronted the tensions of a society deeply influenced by the practices and values of the wider Atlantic market, a society in transition toward a market society.

All Patriots accepted some measure of public authority over a host of social and economic transactions. *Some measure*—but how much? How much say should the public have over the uses and value of people's property? And who was included in the term "public authority"? Whose judgment qualified? Who had jurisdiction?

Colonists intensely debated these questions when they debated Patriot networks and associations. In the past, merchants in various port cities had met to discuss and promote the interests of local trade. Thomas Hutchinson noted that those meetings included only merchants, and they did not create binding or mandatory agreements on anyone else. Soon after they first formed, the impetus for Patriot pacts shifted out of the hands of merchants. Many of the boycotts of 1767–70 originated not with traders but in mass gatherings and town meetings, where participants promised to boycott dealers until those dealers agreed to associate. In the plantation South, well-to-do planters powerfully shaped the movement, and in Northern seaports prosperous professional men spearheaded various Patriot programs. At the same time, tradesmen became increasingly active, and street crowds were vital to the enforcement of these pacts in many places. Tradesmen and other inhabitants increasingly took up the promotion of pacts. Merchants found themselves signing on under pressure and agreeing to suspensions of trade that were more sweeping, stringent, and ambitious than they would have preferred. Brunswick, New

Jersey, merchants denounced the disorders the pacts created as the "follies of less considerate men." By 1770, New York governor Cadwallader Colden reported, city merchants had had enough of such things as collective negotiation and public oversight of their business affairs. He predicted that they would avoid all associations in the future, since they were "so sensible of their danger, from Riots and tumults" that they would not "readily be induced to enter into combinations, which may promote disorder for the future, but will endeavour to promote due subordination to legal authority."[88] Colden may have been right, but New York merchants would not be in a strong enough position to avoid association when other inhabitants demanded they take part. On one occasion, storekeepers who did not join found that their "signs doors and windows were daub'd over in the Night time with every kind of Filth." In every colony, newspaper pieces, anonymous threats, personal admonitions and the occasional crowd action made clear that nonsubscribers' persons and property were under threat. Increasingly, too, the Sons of Liberty who inspected merchants' warehouses, stores, and account books to monitor compliance consisted of not only fellow traders but also petty dealers and tradesmen. From the outset, we have seen, some ordinary men had claimed that the constitutional crisis was their business and that defending American liberties and American societies was their project. As associations provided economic and social benefits for many tradesmen in particular, growing numbers of such men became active Patriots.[89]

In the face of these developments, even men who opposed Parliamentary policies sometimes reiterated the conservative principle that political competence was restricted to elite men. Over a five-month period in late 1769, a writer called "Free-man" contributed several essays to a debate over the nature of Patriot politics in the *South Carolina Gazette*. Free-man worried that the mechanics of Charleston had been far too prominent and powerful in forming the most recent town agreement. "When a man acts in his own sphere, he is useful in the community, but when he steps out of it, and sets up for a statesman! believe me, he is in a fair way to expose himself to ridicule." Surprisingly, some leading men deferred to tradesmen and acknowledged them as political partners. Why were some established political leaders taking part in a "harlequin medley committee," composed of equal numbers of merchants, planters, and mechanics? It was inappropriate to consult "with men who never were in a way to study, or to advise upon any points, but rules how to cut up a beast in the market to the best advantage, to cobble an old shoe in the neatest manner, or to build a necessary house. Nature never intended that such men should be profound politicians, or able statesmen." Free-man insisted on the gulf between statecraft, for which independent gentlemen were qualified, and daily affairs, at which tradesmen were competent.[90]

Moreover, the general committee of the town had presumed to enact and execute stringent standards incumbent on everyone. The whole process had slighted the assembly of the colony. "That body is, in effect, the legislative, whose rule and laws are put in execution and required to be obeyed." This Free-man had learned from John Locke. "When other laws are set up, and other rules pretended or enforced, than what the legislative, constituted by the society, have enacted, it is plain that the legislative is changed." When they met at Liberty Tree, the general committee usurped the powers of the colony's own representative and deliberative body. These were not, then, the objections of a man simply loyal to British authority. "Free-man" was William Henry Drayton, well-known lawyer and an elected member of his colony's house of representatives. He did not protest the Patriots' challenge to Parliament's prerogatives. He worried about the prerogatives of the Carolina political elite. "To stigmatise a man, even the meanest in a community, and brand him with the infamous name of *an enemy to his country*, can be *legally* done by no *authority* but by *that* of the *voice* of the *legislature*," he wrote. When "the people" acted as if they held authority, "the power of the general ass-bly is thereby disowned and overturned."[91]

Historian Robert Weir notes that Drayton recognized "the most fundamental fact" about the Patriot movement in these years: "that the main arena of politics was no longer the assembly."[92] Patriot politics increasingly took place in a space more inclusive and less bounded than assembly chambers. A New Yorker described himself as "a lover of Constitutional Liberty; but a sworn foe to Coblers and Taylors, so long as they take upon their everlasting and unmeasurable shoulders, the power of directing the loyal and sensible inhabitants."[93] Many others who hesitiated to endorse the movement cited these grounds: workingmen should stay in their place, and that place did not include shaping policy for the whole. These complaints reflect the extent to which the participation of men outside the ranks of the elite formed the common cause. Although men such as Drayton deplored it, Patriots among the province elite were joining their inferiors at Liberty Tree.

Some men justified their collaboration with cobblers on the basis of tradesmen's status as property holders, however small. Replying to Free-man, John MacKenzie asked, "Have not the mechanicks, whom you have treated so ungenerously, a right to be consulted, about their property, as well as you?"[94] In New York, "Brutus" went farther than that, ignoring property to invoke the social significance of tradesmen as a group. How could merchants decide by themselves? "What particular Class among us, has an exclusive Right to decide a Question of general Concern?" he asked.[95] In matters that affected the community, simple membership in the community might provide grounds for political agency. A self-described "Tradesman" spoke for his kind in the *Pennsylvania Chronicle* in 1770: "As we form a considerable, independent, and respectable Body of the People, we certainly have an equal Right to enter into Agreements and Resolutions *with others* for the public Good."[96] Colonists who claimed equal rights with Britons at home, and who insisted that American voices were essential to defining what was the "public Good" of the empire heard their own logic deployed to broaden participation in American political institutions. And in Charleston itself, tradesmen took to the press on their own behalf, to argue that men as lowly as they were in fact fitted for politics, on the grounds of that most basic qualification for social life: "common sense."[97] *Common* sense, here, was the possession of a certain social sort, the province of common men.

The shifting emphases of these pacts and their different impact on men of different occupations and interests help explain why historians have sometimes characterized the Patriot pacts as anticommercial, sometimes as procommercial. Patriot associations certainly recognized the significance and value of trade. When merchants first initiated nonimportation, they imagined it along these lines: a temporary respite from importing would allow them to secure their interests, to gather their resources and renegotiate terms so as to resume the trade on less disadvantageous grounds. They endorsed the power of commerce and the strength of their established trading relationships with English dealers and manufacturers. As the pacts became less amenable to mercantile interests, more influenced by planters and tradesmen, many merchants participated with less enthusiasm. Some considered the possibility of independence from England with an eye to the potential of trade and prosperity outside the British Empire. Some would embrace the opportunity to establish an American empire of trade. Others, such as many Philadelphia merchants, would become "reluctant revolutionaries," anxious about the extent of popular politics and the extent of popular claims to jurisdiction over economic life, aware that the middling men who were becoming influential did not entirely trust the world of commerce or respect its prerogatives.[98]

Indeed, some colonists who also promoted trade boycotts could be sweepingly critical of commerce as a way of life. Thomas Jefferson minced few words: "Merchants have no country," he said. (Hence, how could they be friends to it?) Yet planters who denounced Scots factors trading in the plantation colonies surely admitted the Patriotism of some native-born merchants in Philadelphia, Boston, or New York. Besides, like many other farmers, tobacco planters could hardly renounce the Atlantic trade on a lasting basis. George Washington noted that nonconsumption agreements served the interests of some of his class, who could reduce their debt without losing social face. Those planters' withdrawal from purchasing cannot be reduced to a simple opposition to commerce. And if many tradesmen preferred to stress domestic production over consumption of British goods, they were hardly hostile to exchange as a fundamental component of social life. Their economic and social security relied on it.[99]

Yet if the *fact* of commerce was not at stake—if everyone knew members of their society would continue to trade with one another and in the Atlantic market—nonetheless the *terms* of commerce were at issue. Patriots indicted Englishmen precisely for conducting trade based on motives that we might consider not only acceptable but normative: "with no other view than to enrich themselves."[100] Likewise, they renounced colonists who saw commerce as a competitive project guided solely by the desire for profit. A movement so suspicious of ambition, accumulation, profit seeking, and "magnificence" cannot simply be characterized as favoring "commerce," which after all relied on and normalized those qualities. Put differently, the Patriots did not promote trade *of just any sort*, and certainly not trade that was unregulated or unaccountable to social and political goals. They called for trade with England and trade among the several colonies that was constrained by mutual commitment to a larger, shared interest.

When they spoke of such an interest, uniting all Britons within the empire, Patriots made two rather different claims. One was empirical, the claim that the interests of different groups within the empire in fact depended on one another's well-being. Patriots pointed out, for example, that English manufacturers depended on the solvency of colonial customers. The second claim was a claim on Britons' allegiance, a claim on their loyalty, and a matter of choice. The empire depended on the commitment by various interests within it to subordinate narrow self-interest in order to construct a larger good. Such subordination was not required when Britons dealt with the Dutch, French, or Spanish; those exchanges might yield mutual benefits, but relationships between nations were avowedly competitive in ways that relationships within the empire were not. "Tradesman" discussed the proper nature of trade in the *Pennsylvania Chronicle* in 1770: "In the Race of Commerce, not only our own private Advantage, but also that of the Body of which we are Members, should be in View." Membership in the "Body," not individuality, was the salient guide to practices of exchange. In this framework, any political unit—the British Empire or an American one—appeared rather like a neighborhood writ large.[101]

Consistent with this view, Patriots' networks and associations created neighborly relations within their own bounds. They routinely overrode market forces when those forces undercut the colonists' social and political goals. To be Patriots in good standing, people had to renounce the unalloyed profit motive. What they preached to the English they would practice at home. So, for example, no one should take advantage of the difficulties of the times. Nonimportation could potentially generate windfall profits for those with scarce goods on hand. To prevent that, Patriot dealers and storekeepers promised, "to hold prices steady," to keep to "a reasonable price," and take only "a moderate profit." The Virginia Convention of 1774 decided that any merchant who took advantage of the predicted scarcity to raise his prices would be dubbed "an approver of American Grievances."[102] And the Continental Congress included similar provisions in the Association of 1774. Two key articles read: "Such as are venders of goods or merchandise will not take advantage of the scarcity of goods, that may be occasioned by this association, but will sell the same at the rates we have been respectively accustomed to do, for twelve months last past," and "That all manufactures of this country be sold at reasonable prices, so that no undue advantage be taken of a future scarcity of goods." The committee of Bucks County, Pennsylvania, put pressure on storekeepers to abide by price limits: "This Committee desires as much as possible to prevent every species of imposition and extortion which designing persons, prompted by a sordid attachment to private interests and present scarcity of sundry articles of merchandise, may be tempted to commit."[103]

Tradesmen and artisans, too, avowed limited ambitions. Leather dressers in Boston worried when a rumor impugned their patriotism, and they published a disclaimer in the *Gazette*: "To the Public: Wheras, it has been reported that the Leather-Dressers are endeavouring to increase their stocks of wool, and when they have got what will be taken off this season in their own hands, intend to raise the price. It is so far from the truth, that they are determined strictly to adhear to their former price." They urged town butchers to keep down the price they asked for skins, then

concluded: "Let the demand be ever so great, the leather dressers are determined not to raise the price."[104] These measures restricting prices reassured the public of all participants' good faith. They depended on and
reinforced the common idea that such a thing as "reasonable prices" existed and that people might expect (and sometimes demand) to pay them.

In other ways as well, Patriots directly disputed the authority of market
forces alone to determine value. Increasingly, writers in newspapers and
political pamphlets dismissed many British goods as mere "baubles," fashionable "fripperies," or "superfluities." These words could hardly please
importers, for they suggested a lasting and moralistic rejection of purchasing. Patriots clearly took one side in long-standing Anglo-American
debates about luxury. Moreover, distinguishing trifles from "necessaries,"
Patriot rhetoric explicitly rejected a conceptual development essential to
market societies, namely, the flattening of all desires into a single, undif-
ferentiated category of market "demand." Associators forcefully rein-
scribed the blurring line that distinguished luxuries from necessities. In
doing so, they refused the thought that the whims of the wealthy might
properly be cast in the same terms as poor people's hunger for bread.
They denied that market factors alone determined the meaning or value
of goods; instead, they placed commodities in the context of social need
and social impact. When New Jersey towns denounced the theater as
working "to no good purpose," or when newspaper writers dismissed
imports as "trifles," they replaced market standards with other standards
of worth. Patriots insisted on an expansive and consequential view of
countless acts that another era would consider merely and unremarkably
"economic." Patriot transactions regarded such factors as human need,
obligation, and social affection.[105]

This is to draw a line of connection between the crowds that regulated
nonimportation and nonconsumption pacts in America and the crowds
that regulated the price and supply of grain in eighteenth-century England.[106] True, the colonists' concern was not securing a sufficiency of
bread or any other necessity in these years (although, as the next chapter
recounts, crowd actions to claim and distribute scarce necessities would
soon become widespread). Destroying tea was not the same as distributing bread. Intimidating an importer into storing his goods under the control of Patriot committeemen was not the same as intimidating an exporter
into yielding up flour or grain to feed the local poor. Yet if Patriots did
not invoke the "moral economy of the eighteenth-century English
crowd," they certainly invoked what they considered moral dimensions
of individual economic transactions.[107] Prewar crowds, committees, and

local authorities who monitored imports, consumption, and prices formed what we might call a Patriot economy: conducting exchange within a network of Patriots who dealt solely with one another and solely according to Patriot terms. They drew on premises akin to the principles that informed the food riots so common across the Atlantic. They drew on the assumption that public authority—in the form of law or the people executing law—might properly regulate transactions. Whether governors with proclamations, magistrates with rulings, grand juries with indictments, petit juries with verdicts, town meetings with bylaws, or neighbors in association, the public might limit the coercions of individuals or the market. In times of crisis, dearth, or difficulty, when dealers engrossed, when oppressions threatened, ordinary people had resources on which to draw that allowed negotiation *with* the market. They had access to and confidence in notions of value authorized by local and common knowledge. They carried confidence in such knowledge into the common cause.

Sweeping claims that individuals' transactions lay within the purview of public rights as well as private ones made it difficult for some men of property to fully support the Patriot project. Many explained their antagonism by noting the pacts' assumption of jurisdiction over private property. Patriot merchant meetings and Sons of Liberty were "the greatest tyrants ever known, for they will suffer no man to use his property, but just in such a way as they approve of."[108] Individuals whose property was threatened by mobs wondered how a movement that cited an Englishman's sacred rights could sanction such treatment. Patriots laid extraordinary and arguably illegal restrictions on trade, they pointed out, as well as limits on the prices a property holder might ask for his or her goods, and limits on the prices a purchaser might pay. Given these realities, how could the Patriots "talk of Liberty, Property and Rights without a blush?"[109] Samuel Seabury, rector of St. Peter's Church in New Rochelle, New York, complained that, in enforcing nonimportation pacts, Patriots ignored property rights. "Individuals are deprived of their liberty; their property is invaded by violence." John Agnew, rector of a Virginia parish, criticized his local revolutionary committee: "The Committee of *Suffolk* has invaded private property; they have taken goods from a man of *Carolina* and sold them against his will."[110]

These critics—and there were many others—challenge Americans' view of the extent to which the eighteenth-century Revolutionaries defended rights of property. There is no doubt that Patriots explicitly championed property. In 1765 they had cried, "Liberty, Property, and no Stamp-Duty," and the term figured in countless toasts, documents, and orations.[111] At the same time, they ruled all sorts of transactions and goods in the realm of *public* affairs—even the realm of cobblers' affairs. They seized the tea or destroyed the carriages of individuals who stood against resistance measures. The same Patriot crowds and committees that insisted that British officials had no business seizing American property also insisted that neighbors might appropriately make regulations and sometimes seizures. Indeed, Patriots did not neatly equate property's immunity from official agents authorized by government with immunity from control of "the people." The way we have generally read their defense of property rights may suffer from this error, a blind spot created by later and more expansive conceptions of individual ownership not current among many Patriots.[112] So, when a colonial jury boldly returned a seized vessel to the smuggler who owned it, we see vindication of the rights of the vessel's owner. Colonists themselves may have also seen a vindication of *colonial* property—a reassertion that colonial juries in colonial courtrooms held jurisdiction over the ship in question. In such cases, it was not necessary to think of rights as *solely* pertaining to individuals. There were circumstances, after all, in which those same jurymen might approve popular seizure of a trader's cargo. As with commerce, so with property: Patriots defended it only as it was conceived within bounds. It was limited in its uses, because social and political in its consequences. However the meanings of property might later change, many Patriots of the resistance era insisted on the claims of neighbors and countrymen over and against claims of individualism and privacy. Patriots presumed that liberty and property entailed obligations.[113]

Such a conception of property as both individual and social had the potential to divide Patriots who emphasized one aspect from those who emphasized the other. Patriot committees and Patriot printers alike worked to minimize the ground for dispute. It is significant that, when Patriot newspapers reported tea burnings, they often emphasized the willing compliance of owners of the tea. The tea owners' "cheerful countenances," their decision to put their tea in the fire "themselves"—these elements of published accounts testify that consent from individual owners mattered. Patriots recognized that property was a sticking point to many men whose support they desired, a sore point to some who counted themselves as Patriots but hoped to moderate the movement's commitments. The local committee of Nansemond County showed their concern over offending the propertied in the pages of the *Virginia Gazette*. Committeemen had seized, advertised, and sold goods that John Thompson had imported, only to learn later that Thompson had properly observed Patriot guidelines after all. Thompson proved his Patriotism by announcing that he was happy with the committee's actions. The committee told readers that Thompson even invited them to the tavern and "insisted on our partaking of a cheerful bowl with him."[114] In this case, everyone could rest assured that individual consent and community authority had proved compatible. Thompson's behavior testifies to the distinctive values of this movement: he manifested his political identity not by standing out as an individual, sticking to his individual conscience, or defending his own due, but by generously conforming and giving way. All parties finessed the question of ultimate property *right*.

By contrast, it created a crisis in the movement when men did not finesse. In December 1773, in the course of enforcing a nonconsumption and nonimportation pact, Bostonians threw privately owned tea into the harbor. A Patriot newspaper in New York claimed that the event concluded "without the least Injury to private Property." Yet the dealers consigned to receive the tea could not be said by any stretch to have agreed to its seizure, and the event outraged many throughout the colonies.[115] In the aftermath, popular claims against property became even more notable in some areas. In Maryland, the surveyor of the customs William Eddis recounted negotiations that preceded burning of the ship *Peggy Stewart*. Eddis dismissed as "an absurdity" the Patriot claim that the owners had consented to the ship's destruction in "a voluntary election, unawed and unimitimidated by the multitude."[116] Surely threats from the common people gathered in Annapolis had forced destruction of the brig and its cargo of tea. Thus an observer in Bladensburg, Maryland, early in 1774: "The common sort seem to think they may now commit any outrage they please; some of them told the Merchants yesterday, that if they would not sell them Goods, they would soon find a way to help themselves." In other areas, committeemen rather than crowds acted on the values and expectations of the common sort. "A certain merchant at Georgetown, ten miles from this, imported from London, on his own account, a large cargo of Goods this Fall, and thought to sell them higher than common. We understand that on saturday a Committee is to examine them, and should they find the advance too much they say, he shall, and must sell them lower. What think you of this land of Liberty, when a man's property is at the mercy of any one that will lead the mob!"[117] The writer who posed this question clearly meant it rhetorically—a fact that, quite alone, marked him as unfriendly to the cause. Those who saw themselves as Patriots asked much the same question in true earnest. How far was property susceptible to public adjudication, and who composed the public that should adjudicate it? The coalition that united men and women of different regions, interests, and ranks seemed likely to founder on such questions in early 1774. Historians generally concur that only Britain's heavy-handed answer to the destruction of the tea—sending warships to close down the port of Boston—unified a movement that might otherwise have fallen into disarray.

To mediate the crisis, Patriots established a coordinating, central authority, a Continental Congress. Self-chosen groups of "Sons of Liberty," prominent from the time of the Stamp Act, gradually yielded to committees chosen by representative if often irregular local gatherings. Now Congress would assume the authority to promulgate a Continental Association. In September 1774, it called on every town or county to elect a committee of "inspection" or "observation." The result was mobilization on an unprecedented scale. Towns in the backcountry with few importers or merchants to oversee now elected committees for the first time. These committees, guided by the resolutions of the Continental Congress, would henceforth regulate the Patriot economy.

In the activities of these committees, we see again an ambiguity about precisely who joined whom in the common cause. Two forms of negotiation were crucial to the authoritative standing of committees. First, they united committee members of a variety of interests and social ranks. Many committees of 1774–76 resembled the "harlequin medley committee" of Charleston, incorporating lesser men and new leaders along with established elites, to ensure representation of significant interests within Patriot deliberations. Over time, a close study of Philadelphia's revolution finds, voters in that city selected committeemen with smaller property and less experience in provincial matters.[118] A Virginia Patriot noted that immense powers were "lodged with Men whom I should think must themselves be surprised at the great authority they have stepd into."[119] Decisions of committees would represent the combined voices of representatives of at least some of the different ranks within free colonial society.

Second, the system established negotiation between committee members and the population "out of doors"—in this case, outside *committee* doors. It built on colonists' familiarity with institutions for the execution of the law. Indeed, although committees took authority as elected "delegates" of the people, they most powerfully resembled courts of common law. They often met at county courthouses.[120] They summoned witnesses and suspects. They gathered information. They listened to testimony. They reached verdicts and pronounced sentences. They adjudicated disputes. A dissenter objected to the presumptions of New Haven's committee: "Our Committee of Inspection have proceeded to very unwarrantable lengths; they ordered summonses to be served on several persons who had not been altogether complaisant enough to the mandates of the Congress."[121] Some even issued warrants for the arrest of suspicious persons.[122] "Have we not . . . established courts of inquisitions in the colonies unparalleled in any age or nation?" asked "Martyr." "Where . . . was there ever an instance of men, free men, being summoned by illegal and mock authority to answer for acts and offenses, which are warranted by the laws of the land, the law of nations, and the law of God?"[123] As they modeled themselves on courts of law, Patriot committees invoked a common capacity to execute law.

The printer James Rivington, protected by occupying British forces in New York City in 1776, challenged the status of committees when he published this query about proceedings there: "Mr. Rivington: What is the Committee of Observation? By whom were they appointed? And what authority had they to order Capt Chambers or any body else, to attend them . . . ? Who says . . . that the sense of the city was asked, relatively, either to the sending away Capt. Lockyer, or the destruction of the tea aboard the [ship] *London*?" The writer charged that recent resolutions made by "the people" actually came from a gathering of fewer than one-twentieth of the population; and, although Patriot papers claimed that the city had celebrated by ringing *all* the bells of city churches, in truth only *some* of them had rung.[124] Here was a stickler for accuracy, indicting Patriots who constructed "the city" and "the people" out of a portion of the whole. And although this writer had his own ax to grind (denouncing the political activity of tradesmen), he accurately described the method of the Patriot press. Printers' acts of publication accepted the premises of vox populi, that there existed an authoritative and singular collective stand to be recognized as that of "the people."[125] In the period from 1774 to 1776, many Patriots agreed, that stand emerged from acts of popular committees.

Equally vital to committee authority, committees, like courts of law, accommodated spectators and relied on the possibility of popular action. Committee meetings were sometimes so heavily attended that it was difficult to tell just who had reached a decision there. For example, the committee of Charles County, Maryland, considered the case of John Baillie and Patrick Graham of Port Tobacco, accused of "infamous conduct" in importing dry goods and conducting surreptitious sales of same. "A very full and respectable number attended at the Court-house," and the gathering decided that the two men be "held up as foes to the Rights of *British Amer-*

ica," so that everyone would stop dealing with them.[126] Other accounts also leave uncertain where the jurisdiction of committeemen ended and that of the people began. When Jesse Dunbar of Halifax, Massachusetts, bought some fat cattle from an official of the Crown, the Plymouth committee took steps. "One of the Oxen being skinned and hung up" for sale in Plymouth, the committee put the ox in a cart, put Dunbar in its belly, and carted him four miles to Duxbury. The committee made Dunbar pay them one dollar, then delivered him to the "Kingston mob" and the "Duxbury mob," who pelted him with dirt and tripe "to the endangering his life." The crowd forced Dunbar to pay another sum of money, hung the offending beef in the road, and departed.[127]

Those who denied common sense and ordinary knowledge routinely interpreted such events as cases when leading men manipulated the mobility. A Loyalist who opposed the committees charged that one of them admitted it might deploy the mindless many. "What, do you drink Tea? Take care what you do, Mr. C., for you are to know the Committee command the mob, and can in an instant let them loose upon any man who opposes their decrees, and complete his destruction."[128] Yet while committees presumed the presence of the mob, the relationship between the two forms was not so simple. Take this transaction: William Aitchenson, a Virginia merchant who would not sign the Continental Association, described the method used to create compliance in Norfolk. The mob, he said, erected a pole near the capitol, where the committee met, and attached a bag of feathers to the top of the pole, and put a barrel of tar underneath. Individuals were forced to stand next to the pole in front of the committee and retract their opposition to associations and congresses. According to Aitchenson, two men who imported tea contrary to the Patriot agreement were almost tarred and feathered by the mob, and were saved only when a "gentleman" intervened on their behalf. In the end they had only to promise to deliver the tea to be burned.[129]

Other records, private and public, present a similar pattern of interplay between committees and crowds. In Norfolk, the gentlemen may well have preferred more lenient treatment than bystanders preferred, but these roles—punitive mob, lenient committee—seem to have been common enough to constitute a set piece. Hadn't these roles (or something like them) been learned and practiced at court days through the years? What was really happening in these cases is elusive to historians and may sometimes have been elusive at the time. How much was there cooperation between crowds and committees, how much negotiation, how much conflict and disagreement? Similar questions surround events that took place in Bridgetown, New Jersey. The Cumberland County committee found tea in a cellar in the market square and, not knowing if it had arrived before or after the deadline for ending importations, announced they would store it privately until they found out. When they gathered the following morning, they learned "to their surprise" that the tea had been destroyed "by persons unknown." The committee resolved their strong disapproval of the anonymous action. They would neither "conceal nor protect from justice any of the perpetrators of the above fact." Yet had the committee anticipated or even encouraged the persons unknown? Is it evidence of their complicity that they had conveniently announced to the public that they would start storing the tea at 10 A.M. the next day? Did their condemnations amount to the ritual that Thomas Hutchinson, watching the Boston town meeting, called "vot[ing] themselves innocent" in the wake of crowd actions? Or were they in this instance innocent and surprised indeed?[130]

Surviving committee records reveal some of the conflict and negotiation that took place between committees and "people." In Albany, New York, townspeople urged their committee to enforce the price limits set by the association. "We are in great measure imposed upon by the Merchants of the City contrary to the 9th and 13th Articles of the Continental Congress," they complained. Should the committee not reply within twenty-four hours, "we shall look upon it that you will not consider our oppression; and if we find that you will not Vindicate our doleful Circumstances, we will without doubt be obliged to remove these ruinous Circumstances ourselves." Albany Committee members defensively noted that petitioners had named no specific violators; they could only reassure the people that they would duly "hold up to the public everyone contravening" the agreement.[131]

And how are we to characterize what happened when some "constituents" attended a meeting of the committee of observation and inspection in Freehold, New Jersey, in 1775? The group presented committeemen with a Tory pamphlet and asked their opinion of it. The committee promptly declared the publication "a performance of the most pernicious and malignant tendency; replete with the most specious sophistry," and denounced its "detestable author" for his efforts "to damp that noble spirit of union . . . prevailing all over the Continent." Satisfied with the committee's support, "the people" took back the pamphlet, gave it "a suit of tar and turkey buzzard's feathers," then nailed it up "firmly to the pillory-post, there to remain as a monument of the indignation of a free and loyal people."[132] Like many other committee meetings, this one resembled a trial followed by punishment. It clearly drew on the popular capacity to "judge" and execute the law as jurors, punishers, and spectators of justice.[133] Who led whom on such an occasion—and who followed whose lead—was an ambiguous matter. People who brought with them to committee meetings a supply of tar and feathers were not without resources. Committeemen promptly did what was expected of them. Such interactions between men on committees and people outside committee doors were crucial, symbolic, and identifying events. In some respects, the question of who was authorizing whom is moot: "the people" and their leaders were authorizing each other.

These events offer new perspective on the choices made by the Patriot elite. It is easy to oversimplify the process by which leading men made up their minds. Few of them developed their political thinking in isolation, or only in secluded conversation with others. They did not create and then pass on a completed and coherent point of view to lesser colonists. On the contrary, the colonial elite, Patriot and Loyalist, were influenced at every step of their thinking by their own embeddedness in society— surely by their roles as representatives or magistrates or militia officers, but also by their position as neighbors, townsmen, and brethren. They felt at every turn the ideas and activity of more ordinary men, who influenced and sometimes pressed their superiors. We underestimate elite acts of leadership—by men in the Continental Congress, provincial congresses, and local institutions—if we think of them as merely creating, enacting, or disseminating a political program. In joining boycotts of trade, elite colonists took considerably greater risk than that: they joined their inferiors, endorsed the capacities of the local public, and admitted their own substantial vulnerability to that public's values and judgments. In the Revolutionary moment, elite Americans joined the people.

Declarations of Interdependence

Mass demonstrations, committee meetings, and crowd actions were more than central to the resistance movement. These experiences were also critical to Americans' capacity to imagine independence from Great Britain. We see this clearly in the text that many historians credit with placing independence in the forefront of American thinking: Thomas Paine's pamphlet, *Common Sense*.

In retrospect, the colonists may seem to have been slow to consider separation from the mother country. True, by the close of 1775, faith in

Britain was at low ebb. In April, British soldiers and colonial militiamen had clashed at Lexington and Concord. Men from throughout New England had gathered to contain the British troops in Boston. In June, both sides had suffered significant losses at the Battle of Bunker Hill. Over the summer, the Second Continental Congress found itself petitioning for peace but conducting a war. Congressmen quickly adopted New England's provisional forces into a Continental army and placed the Virginian, George Washington, in command. Through fall and early winter, Washington and his men held the hills around Boston harbor in a wary standoff with British forces occupying the city. Even still, many colonists treasured their ties to Britain. Then, in January 1776, Paine's pamphlet came off the press in Philadelphia. A second edition appeared in February, and printers in New York, Boston, Salem, Newport, Hartford, Lancaster, Norwich, Albany, and Providence all issued copies within a few months' time. With this publication, Paine helped shift colonial discussion from reconciliation with Britain toward independence.

One element of Paine's success was rhetorical: his work was brilliantly written and forcefully argued. Did some speak respectfully of the drama of the state? Paine wrote of government as a "puppet show," a genre known and understood by every apprentice who had wasted time in Philadelphia streets. Paine powerfully endorsed the capacities of ordinary Americans. Common men themselves might consider and decide matters of political right and political wrong, even to issues of empire, monarchy, and the very forms of government. Paine carried this conviction through four chapters, never explicitly confronting the conventional view of cobblers and farmers but rendering it moot. Rather than defend the commonalty, he wrote as if their competence were unquestioned.[134]

Yet Paine's success reflected as well an ability to fathom the extraordinary political process taking place around him and the unprecedented possibilities that it introduced. Over the resistance years, Americans witnessed, read about, and took part in repeated public negotiations that exercised and affirmed their capacities as neighbors and countrymen. In mass gatherings, local governments, and local committees, merely common men of merely common sense had become increasingly accustomed to exercising political discretion and wielding political power. New men had argued and acted along with more experienced local leaders in official and unofficial bodies. Common tradesmen and farmers had stood in judgment of men who were their social superiors, and they had grown accustomed to receiving deferential hearing from merchants, lawyers, and other educated members of the Patriot elite. When writers in the press scoffed at their abilities, ordinary men had found articulate replies and allies among their betters. For such men, *Common Sense* reverberated deeply. It assumed and extended the most liberating premise of Patriot practice: the sufficiency of ordinary men and ordinary knowledge.[135]

At the same time, *Common Sense* confirmed another belief central to the resistance: the power and virtue of affection, the security to be found in the social bonds that united disparate households into community and society. "Society in every state is a blessing, but government even in its best state is but a necessary evil." Later thinkers might employ Paine's phrase to argue for individual rights against the state or for policies of laissez-faire. Yet in 1776, Paine meant something rather different, and something rather more, for what mattered in that crucible year was the strength of colonial societies, understood primarily as arenas of obligation and mutual commitment rather than individuality.

For Paine, as for other Patriots, what was good about society was its web of commitments. Society "promotes our happiness positively by uniting our affections," he wrote. Unified affections were the very basis of any connection among people, the very ground of political identity. Paine accordingly argued that political allegiance depended on powerful social bonds that transcended mere interest to include sentiments of mutuality and sympathy. Paine offered reasons why the colonies should separate from England and reasons why their strength arose from union with one another. Did some colonists feel gratitude for occasions when Britain had protected the colonies? Their feelings were misplaced, for when Britain defended colonial borders and colonial shipping, "her motive was *interest*, not *attachment*."[136] In this logic, self-interest might bind individuals or groups into alliance, but true political unity depended on a deeper tie. Only attachment could join different neighborhoods, towns, counties, or provinces into a single people. "Present convenience" was not enough. Political unity derived from such "feelings and affections which nature justifies, and without which we should be incapable of discharging the social duties of life."[137] And though such feelings no longer subsisted between the colonies and Britain, colonists from different provinces, he maintained, did enjoy such confidence in and feeling for one another.[138]

Indeed, despite their manifest differences, had not many colonists of different regions, social classes, and religious beliefs forged a sense of sameness and commonality, precisely through their shared, public pursuit of the Patriot cause? There had been common resolutions of different provincial assemblies; committees chosen by hundreds of towns and counties in different parts of the continent; a gathering and acquiescence of different ranks in real and symbolic punishments, rituals that testified that every Son and Daughter of Liberty detested unconstitutional laws, overreaching officials, and invidious distinctions among neighbors and could be counted on to oppose them all. There had been renewed engagement with one another in commitment to fair and mutually beneficial exchange. In the pages of Patriot newspapers, colonists could read of one another's actions and resolutions; they could know themselves to be part of a larger movement, a community of the like-minded and the like-hearted. If Americans could dispense with loyalty to England, it was because they possessed an equally powerful allegiance that could take its place.[139]

Readers responded to *Common Sense* with a sense of recognition and liberation. And no wonder. Here is Paine's description of a hypothetical group of people (he called them "colonists") beginning in an original state of "natural liberty." Such people would quickly form a society, prompted by "a thousand motives" to "seek assistance and relief" from each other. Only when some individuals, weak in their "attachment" to their fellows, acted out of selfish motives would the colonists move toward the discipline of rudimentary government. Then, said Paine, "Some convenient tree will afford them a State-House, under the branches of which the whole colony may assemble to deliberate on public matters. It is more than probable that their first laws will have the title only of *Regulations*, and be enforced by no other penalty than public disesteem."[140] Could readers in British North America fail to recognize their own social and political movement in these lines? Here, surely, was the Patriot system of resistance, the meetings beneath Liberty Trees, assemblies of the many who regulated behavior with the threat of "public disesteem." What were Patriots doing, then, other than forming a new society, laying the ground for a new political union? Americans could imagine a future of unity, cooperation, mutual benefit, and widespread prosperity. Perhaps they might rest secure in their mutual social, economic, and political ties. Paine's pages made manifest this lesson of Patriot pacts, for all those who had been taking part in their towns, counties, and provinces. They stood at an extraordinary, pristine, and precious moment.

By spring of '76, Paine's words and the actions of George III worked together to convince many colonists of the need to separate from Britain.

From the first, colonists had sought to recall the British people to the special relationship that they had assumed bound them to one another. Surely, the colonists believed, when Englishmen realized that Parliament's policies would cause suffering among their brethren across the Atlantic, they would relent. But the intransigence of British policy makers prompted reconsideration. They came to realize, the Reverend Ezra Stiles said, that repeal of the Stamp Act had not come, after all, from "generous fraternal principles." With the Townshend Acts, wrote Benjamin Franklin from London, many colonists "reflected how lightly the interest of all America had been estimated here, when the interests of a few of the inhabitants of Great Britain happened to have the smallest competition with it."[141] The British set themselves apart by "their total unfeeling neglect of the most essential concerns of us Americans," wrote a South Carolinian. New Yorkers noted that the colonies had lost "confidence in the Tenderness of Great Britain."[142] Lingering hopes for reconciliation dwindled in the face of English policy. White southerners recoiled when they heard that the ministry was considering plans "for instigating the slaves to insurrection." And in the wake of bloody combat between regulars and civilians, there came the news that George III, "with the pretended title of Father of his People," was dispatching more troops against them.[143] From a Patriot perspective, the parent country was guilty of a fundamental failure of feeling. It was Britain that renounced the historic connection, through lack of affection, tenderness, and fraternity. Joined with that belief was another: the security that England failed to offer, the colonists might provide for one another. In June 1776, the Second Continental Congress delegated it to a Virginian, Thomas Jefferson, to find the precise words.

In this way the Declaration of Independence was made possible by countless prior declarations of neighborly *interdependence*, declarations made in local meetings, in committee chambers, beneath Liberty Tree, in the press, in the hearing of a broad public. These were declarations made when the well-to-do passed up fancy imported gloves for more common American-made; when colonial women held spinning bees, sacrificed imported tea, and spent their time processing flax instead of buying fine cloth from European merchants. They were declarations made by college students who gave up liquors and merchants and storekeepers who gave up profits when commodities were in short supply. Such acts testified to faith in an ultimately common interest, a common commitment to regard no private interest apart from the whole.

Let me be clear: Patriots surely *feared* dependency. Their worries about vassalage and slavery were real ones. They feared the seductions of addictive consumer goods. They worried about the dangers of femininity seen in some women's abandonment of household production and their entry into fashionable consumption. Dependence on the wealthy and powerful, indebtedness to strangers rather than neighbors—these would result in "the slavery and ignorance of the many." Yet Patriots developed in detail and in practice, and through coercion and publicity, a potent critique of the sort of *individual* independence that many Americans in the nineteenth century would celebrate. For though the ideal voter and the ideal representative were each independent—not servile, not beholden to great men—that idea did not imply boundless endorsement of private judgment, individual dissent, or private accumulation of property. On the contrary: as Patriots saw it, securing the independence of the many required limits on the independence of the few.

In this context, independence meant sufficient wherewithal to allow dissent from the mighty and powerful; it did not imply independence from the locality, from the opinions of one's neighbors, from a jury of one's peers, or "the Tribunal of the Publick."[144] Patriots thus endorsed independence from the powerful, the wealthy, the would-be oppressor, but they opposed—sometimes violently—the independence of individuals from the judgments, standards, and interests of their neighbors. The distinction was logical and necessary for anyone who understood freedom as a matter of social arrangements, a social distribution of property. "It will be highly politic, in every free state, to keep property as equally divided among the inhabitants as possible," said one Connecticut clergyman in 1773, "and not to suffer a few persons to amass all the riches and wealth of a country," for the wealthy would soon control everyone else.[145] Mutual dependence on neighbors represented the sole way for ordinary households to remain free of dependence on greater men. The alternative to "vassalage" and "lordships"—to the dependence of the lowly many on the exalted few—was the mutual dependence and association of the roughly equal. Within rough equality, there was room for rough inequality, so long as such inequality was countered by a shared status of inhabitant, subject, fellow, or neighbor, by constantly acknowledged and presumably continuing relationships with one another. So the tradesmen of New York might challenge the merchants: "Who is the Member of the Community that is absolutely independent of the rest?"[146] No one, was the answer, and it followed that no one group might pursue its way without reference to or consultation with the others. Patriots did not require social leveling; they did require arrangements and institutions that secured ongoing mutual commitment and accountability. The independent nation and the empire that many Americans imagined would look much like a neighborhood writ large. The liberty that they sought thus required more than the absence of parliamentary oppression; it required the presence and vitality of neighborly relationships in their own societies.

4

The Patriot Economy

We have reached the moment of declaring independence, the moment of revolution. It is tempting to leave matters there. The choice for independence was glorious. The military struggle that followed was glorious, too, but the truth of it includes campaigns that bogged down, economic turmoil, and sorry lack of support for the soldiery among many supposedly patriotic Americans. Perhaps it would be best to leave Patriots unified, poised for independence, bravely enlisting in the military ranks, envisioning their country's future greatness.

But there is still a great deal to explain. I have described a movement powerfully shaped by the views of ordinary men, infused with ideals of mutual dependence and neighborly relations. That movement both relied and insisted on the political powers of ordinary free colonists. It defended institutions of popular presence as strongly as it defended institutions of representation. How and when did that movement change? For if the Revolution began with those values and those political forms, surely it ended on different terms. Didn't America's Revolution pave the way for a regime of private property, individualism, unfettered free trade and free enterprise? In political terms, the Revolution certainly established governments based in representation, but what happened to the popular presence in executing the law? How are we to account for the commitments abandoned and goals redefined?

This chapter traces how the principles, ideas, and political forms of Patriotism fared from 1776 to 1780, during the high-water mark of what we might call the *first* Patriot coalition. As in the resistance decade, in the late 1770s men accustomed to roles of leadership and men accustomed to acting out of doors as voters and executors of the law managed a crucial alliance, relying on ideas and political networks developed before independence. The Continental Congress and Revolutionary state governments pursued policies aimed at maintaining the Patriot coalition and the Patriot economy. For their part, in many areas local governments and Revolutionary committees continued to exercise jurisdiction over economic and political transactions. Outside of official Patriot bodies, men and even women continued to mobilize in crowds to enforce popular understandings of fairness and Patriotism. With these acts they both supported their political leaders and pressed them to keep the Revolution true to popular ideals. To a striking degree, during these years Patriotism meant a primary commitment to social goals, opposition to substantial economic inequalities, and limits to the ambitions of property. At the heart of many Americans' Revolution there remained a social vision grounded in ideals of neighborhood, secured by the people's capacity to associate with one another.

Yet these years also saw growing rifts within Patriot ranks over that social vision and the extent of popular jurisdiction it authorized. Some leading men moderated their support for popular values and proposed alternative ways of understanding the continent's Revolutionary project. By 1780, Americans stood on the verge of change: the dissolution of the first Patriot coalition and its replacement by a second one—one that engaged substantially different interests and assumed substantially different terms.

Let's look at the fault lines along which Patriotism splintered.

.   .   .

We begin by charting an extraordinary degree of continuity, the persistence of prewar Patriot networks and commitments to Patriot social ideals.[1]

There were, of course, instabilities in the coalition that declared independence in July 1776. Patriots had established boundaries to their membership, limits to who, among all who lived in their society, might take a part. Most strikingly, few white colonists of any region or social rank understood themselves to be joining a coalition with African American slaves. Though they spoke of liberty and avowed a hatred of "slavery," white colonists blocked their ears to their own words; consciously and unconsciously, they worked to contain their ideas. Yet soon they would feel pressure against that containment, some of it stemming from British initiatives, some from Patriot insiders, and a good deal from enslaved African Americans themselves. As early as 1775, an inhabitant of Charleston, South Carolina, reported that slaves there "entertained ideas, that the present contest was for obliging us to give them their liberty." Many slaves would press their case for liberty during the Revolution. How far could a movement that united slavery and liberty manage to hold?[2]

Equally difficult, there were free white colonists who remained attached to Britain and many more who were simply *not* attached to the Patriot movement. Through the resistance years, it was perfectly possible to disapprove of Parliamentary policies yet also regret Patriot programs or distrust Patriot leaders. Well after July 5, there were skeptics, fence-sitters, and the determinedly uninvolved, people unprepared for whole-hearted commitment. Such people resisted the resistance movement, with its persistent pressure to resolve the world into two neat camps: "enemies" and "friends." Preferring the gray area in-between, these Americans would wait to see how events transpired. They placated Patriot committees with minimal cooperation and avoided their "liberty mad" countrymen. These colonists, too, had a stake in the future of their society and government. They too had ideas about liberty and justice, and in due course they would make their own commitments felt, some on the battlefield, many more on the home front. Through the war years and beyond, their presence, active or passive, provided a counterweight to the "presence of the people."[3]

Finally, even within Patriot ranks, there was critical ambiguity about the meaning of many of the commitments that everyone avowedly shared. Patriots might all embrace the practices and values of neighboring, but how far-reaching and lasting a commitment to those values did they imagine for their society? Patriots supported popular rights to representation in the creation of law and presence in its execution. But how responsive should new Patriot governments be to the desires, interests, and participation of the people? The coalition joined reluctant Patriots with fervent ones. It allied political, social, and economic elites with more ordinary farmers, tradesmen, small planters, and laborers. It included some established leaders who allied willingly with lesser men, others who regretted the mobilization of their inferiors and sought to minimize those inferiors' influence on public affairs.

Indeed, the commitments of many leading Patriots were in some respects ambiguous. When they spoke of the "common" man and the "sovereignty of the people," whom did they mean to designate, and how literally did they intend their rhetoric? How much did political insiders mean to authorize themselves, and how much did they mean to admit their lesser neighbors to agency? John Adams put the issue most succinctly: "It is certain, in theory, that the only moral foundation of government is, the consent of the people. But to what extent shall we carry this principle?"[4] And just whom did Adams mean to encompass in or exclude from that subject, "we"?

While political elites asked such questions of themselves, the middling and poorer ranks of Patriots faced complementary questions. Artisans, laborers, small farmers, and middling planters accepted that the rich and powerful could be Patriots. But suspicions remained. "Spartacus" wrote in the *New York Journal*: "There are always a number of men in every State who seek to rise above their fellow-creatures, and would be so much above them as to have them and their estates at their disposal, and use them as their footstools to mount to what height they please." Another writer was certain that some men in government espoused a similar principle, "that by keeping the Commonalty in a State of Poverty and Distress, they may have the greater Opportunity to gull Mankind."[5] It followed that all men who courted power were suspect. *Loyalist* writers repeatedly accused leading Patriots of acting out of personal ambition, in service of their own fortunes, besotted with their own rise to power. If the rank and file of Patriot Americans rejected those Loyalist characterizations of prominent Patriots, they still remained distinctly less than trusting of ambitious men. "There are many very noisy about liberty, but are aiming at nothing more than personal grandeur and power," according to one anonymous writer of 1776. "The people are now contending for freedom; and would to God they might not only obtain, but likewise keep it in their own hands."[6] The private soldiers of Pennsylvania spoke out in a broadside: "It is the happiness of America that there is no Rank above that of Freeman existing in it," they wrote, "and much of our future Welfare and Tranquility will depend on its remaining so forever, for this Reason, great and over-grown rich men will be improper to be trusted, they will be too apt to be framing Distinctions in Society, because they will reap the benefits of all such Distinctions."[7] Men who thought in such terms refused to leave direction of the Revolution to select groups of wealthy men or political insiders. They would keep a watchful eye on those who might seek to rule without due deference to the people out of doors. At times they would act forcefully to direct the movement as they saw fit.

In the face of these instabilities, Patriots adapted to the challenges of prosecuting a war and establishing governments in each of the new states. The outbreak of warfare affected Patriots' economic and social program even before the Declaration. The months following Lexington and Concord saw what one historian has called a "*rage militaire*," a bright and sweeping enthusiasm for martial service and martial glory. War had an immediate tendency to cast everything else in its shadow: whether or not one's neighbors drank tea understandably paled next to the issue of whether they rose in arms for the common defense. Wearing homespun became a less potent sign of Patriotism when other men began donning uniforms. In many areas, gatherings for militia exercise supplemented such Patriot public occasions as austere funerals, committee meetings, and tea burnings. The movement took on a more martial public face.[8]

Exigencies of war also undercut some tenets of the Association of 1774. In mid-July, 1775, Congress eased provisions of that pact to allow merchants to import war materiel and export goods to pay for it. In March 1776, Congress endorsed limited commercial activity by establishing regulations for privateering and, the next month, opened American ports to foreign trade. Connecticut delegate Oliver Wolcott told a correspondent that these changes would "do away imperceptibly the material parts of the Association, and the prudence of committees must necessarily lead them to observe the varying scene."[9]

Still, the key principles embodied in the Continental Association remained at the heart of the Patriot cause. Indeed, the war reinforced the idea that economic behaviors were a sure reflection of political allegiance. Some transactions were obviously patriotic, others not. In occupied Boston, people ostracized or mobbed dealers who supplied British troops and artisans who worked for them.[10] New Yorkers acted swiftly when they learned that ships in their harbor would sail north to supply the occupation. "There were two Sloops here loaded with Flour for the Soldiers at *Boston*, by Mr. *Watts*. The people went, <u>Sunday</u> as it was, and unloaded them in a hurry. . . . This was not done by the Magistrates, but by the people."[11] Throughout the war, there would be opportunities for profit by aiding the enemy and the challenge of suppressing such trade. In this context, every Patriot must have agreed that there existed a moral and Patriotic economy and—regrettably—an immoral and "Tory" one.[12]

Patriots in all the new states insisted on the spirit if not always the letter of prewar associations. The trade boycotts, disruptions of warfare, and Britain's naval blockade created shortages. As early as May of 1775, the General Committee for Charlestown, South Carolina, received a memorial from "the inhabitants of this Town," complaining of both "the dearness and the alarming scarcity of grain." The committee explored the problem and resolved to ban exports. "No *Indian* corn should be exported from this Province, except by persons who have plantations in *Georgia*, for their own immediate use upon such plantations; nor any rice, except to complete the lading of such vessels as had actually taken on board part of their intended cargoes of rice before the twenty-fourth instant."[13] Other committees or provincial authorities also reacted to "the changing scene" by imposing regulations. The Pennsylvania Committee of Safety supervised the salt supply; the New York Provincial Congress authorized committees to take custody of all tea held in greater than a five-pound quantity and to retail it in small amounts to the populace.[14] The Continental Congress carefully set the terms on which Bohea tea imported before the Association might be retailed.[15] Patriotism still established standards for retail, consumption, and pricing, subordinating individual opportunity for profit to the general well-being.

Moreover, Patriotism still involved the activities of crowds, which worked to offset shortages. In the course of 1776, there were "many riotous procedings" in New York City and disorders in the Hudson River towns of Fishkill and Kingston, where crowds—some spearheaded by women—seized and distributed recalcitrant retailers' stocks of tea. In New Jersey, crowds targeted dealers who withheld woolen cloths and other imports from the market. As winter approached, salt became vital for preserving butchered meats, and Virginia, Maryland, Massachusetts, and North Carolina all saw crowds act against hoarders of that necessity.[16]

In this context, crowds enforcing the claims of moral economy were consonant if not identical with the Patriot program. True, reports identified participants in one crowd in Maryland as "disaffected." (By contrast, another consisted of individuals "sincere in their Country's cause," who had "acted like men of Spirit and principle ever since these distressing times commenced.")[17] And at least one group of elite Patriots—the New Jersey Provincial Congress of 1775–76—disapproved of some crowds that seized goods. Mobs might "create divisions amongst us," they lamented, and appropriation of imports might deter merchants from undertaking the risk of trade to create even greater scarcities and suffering. Moreover, we cannot be sure how most crowd members in these cases thought of themselves. English people did not have to be in the middle of revolution to engage in food riots, we know, and these American crowds acted in the pattern of countless English crowds when they sometimes offered owners of goods payment according to what the commonalty considered fair. Yet since 1765, Patriots had championed familiar, customary English rights and liberties. They had endorsed common knowledge and common sense, and they had identified their cause with the renewal of neighborly obligations. By 1776 the distinction was not always very clear or even very important: whether as neighbors, Englishmen, or Patriots, people felt entitled to act against hoarders of goods. In narrow terms, such acts executed the price limits adopted by the Association of 1774, the requirement that "*no undue advantage be taken*" in event of scarcity. In broad terms, those acts expressed popular commitments of the Patriot movement by preventing individuals in positions of advantage from squeezing their neighbors and taking their property. Even those New Jersey leaders who discouraged crowds made appeals to neighborly sentiments and obligations: "This committee do at the same time request that all persons who may have any of those necessary articles to dispose of (and those who have large quantities are desired to do it,) will consider the poor people in this time of general calamity, and not exact extravagant prices, especially on such as have been procured at low rates, more particularly the article of Salt."[18] And New York Patriots made explicit the correspondence between Patriot principles and popular principles. The colonists' movement had always centered on opposition to coercive accumulation; monopolizers and hoarders were much the same as other would-be oppressors, ranging from Parliament to stamp masters to individuals who had refused to abide by prewar associations, for their aim was to "distress[] the people, [and] deprive them of their property."[19] When hoarders demanded unreasonable prices for necessities, they took people's property without their consent; accordingly, food riots against them reasonably appeared as acts and aspects of Patriotism.

More significant, while not every food rioter acted as a Patriot, every hoarder and monopolizer surely acted in ways that damaged the Patriot cause. The impact of withholding necessities in hopes of future profit was unmistakable. There was little dispute in 1776 over what Patriots should think about engrossers, monopolizers, and price gougers. A Maryland man named John Gibson put the matter most clearly when he denounced the gentlemen planters who stockpiled salt: "Was they real friends to their country as they stile themselves, would they ingross that necessary article salt, and keep it from the necessitous as they do in this county, which seems to be for no other purpose than to distress the needy (for what end?) to make the war in which we are engaged more irksome, occasion the people to mutineer and create divisions among them, these are the ends they answer."[20] There was something unarguable about that.

One final, critical factor fastened Patriots of all sorts to the principles of a Patriot economy. The continent needed to finance the war, and they had limited alternatives for doing that. They could try for loans from England's long-standing rivals, but France, Holland, and Spain were unlikely to risk much money until the upstart Americans had established plausible governments and mounted a military effort with some promise of success against British arms. Private American investors might also provide revenue, and Congress duly authorized the sale of interest-bearing bonds, called loan certificates, but those revenues, too, fell far short of what was needed. In the meantime, the army could appropriate goods as needed, in exchange for a certificate promising future payment. In times of emergency, farmers, artisans, and traders in the vicinity of battle could expect armies to seize foodstuffs, livestock, wagons, and other items. To control and facilitate the process, Congress authorized General Washington to impress teams of horses and other necessities on specific terms and observing careful procedures. Yet local crowds and committees acting with the common consent of the vicinage were one thing, armed forces indiscriminately impressing property were something else. Everyone considered impressment a distasteful and dangerous policy, an expedient "ever disagreeable to a free people . . . which nothing but necessity could authorize." To pay for the war, Patriot governments accordingly adopted the policy that had financed colonial military ventures: currency finance. At first, state authorities issued bills on their own authority, but Congress soon shouldered the bulk of the task. The continent emitted its first $2 million in paper money in June of 1775, added another million in July, then an additional $3 million by the end of the year.[21]

This policy of currency finance grew out of Americans' colonial experience, but it also reflected their revolutionary commitments. They mobilized their greatest asset: the networks that had formed to carry the Patriot cause and, since late 1774, to support Continental authority. In this context, the money acquired a particular meaning: the currency would circulate among a Patriot population already pledged to dealing with one another as neighbors and countrymen. That circulation would in effect map the contours of the Patriot coalition; it would rely on relationships and networks already established by a decade of Patriot trade agreements. Participants in those agreements had insisted on seeing acts of exchange as unavoidably social, political, and ethical acts. They had united in declaring interdependence. Now these same Americans would support the war by sustaining the value of the currency. With each transaction, people would reenact their commitment to independence and their trust in Revolutionary authorities. They could remind themselves that, in serving the common interest of all Americans, they best secured their own futures. Historian Richard Buel captures this ideal—a belief that transactions in wartime and in support of a revolutionary nation constituted a form of political participation. Buel calls the policy of currency finance a commitment to "consent in the marketplace." The phrase is apt on two counts: first, unlike military authorities who impressed goods, government agents armed with paper money would (so Patriots hoped) find willing sellers. Second, willing sellers would, with each transaction, declare their consent to Patriot governments and the capacity of those governments to confer value. They would support congressional authority. The policy of currency finance called on Americans to attest by their actions their willingness to share the risk of revolution. It presumed a virtuous, self-sacrificing, neighboring population. Patriots contrasted their own means of conducting the struggle with those used by an oppressive British government. The empire might wage war financed by taxes at home and fought by paid mercenaries; Patriots would fight through the willing participation of a united populace.[22]

Of course, such "consent in the marketplace" was a distinctly eighteenth-century type of consent, a collective consent that assumed and accommodated substantial community pressure on individuals. (Alternatively, we could say that the Patriots' policy assumed an eighteenth-century sort of marketplace, one that accommodated social and political goals and that comprehended its participants as a collective whole, rather than purely as individual and competitive parts.) From any perspective, the policy did not provide unlimited space for individual dissent or for expansive claims of private ownership. With little debate, Congress recommended that the new states enact legal tender laws to require creditors to receive the money in discharge of all private and public debts. These were the sorts of laws that Scottish philosopher Adam Smith would soon condemn as "tyrannical," yet throughout the states, provincial authorities waging war *against* tyranny duly enacted them. Paper bills "shall be received in all payments in this colony, and no discount or abatement shall be made thereon, in any payment, trade, or exchange whatever," resolved the Massachusetts Provincial Congress, and other provinces resolved the same. In many states, anyone who refused to take Patriot bills in payment of debt might have that debt legally extinguished. Patriots mobilized to support the buying power of the money.[23]

Indeed, currency finance brought "real friends of their country" face-to-face with their real enemies. As it provided Patriots a form of participation, the paper money also provided a weapon to the disaffected and the outright Loyalist. Tories would not willingly accept the money; some even counterfeited the bills in order to sap their value and hamper the Patriot war effort. Besides those who supported a British victory, other Americans had scruples against recognizing Revolutionary regimes. "We have great reason to think that the Quakers have determined to refuse our Continental Currency," wrote South Carolina delegate Edward Rutledge. "If they make a point of it, we must make a point of hanging them." To refuse Patriot paper, even from motivations of conscience rather than opposition, smacked of treason.[24]

Everywhere, refusal to accept the bills placed an individual outside the Patriot pale. In January 1776, the Continental Congress explicitly called on Patriots to boycott those who obstructed or discouraged the money's circulation. "If any person shall hereafter be so lost to all virtue and regard for this country as to refuse to receive the Bills of Credit emitted by the authority of Congress, or should obstruct or discourage the currency or circulation thereof, and be convicted by the Committee of the city, country, or district where he should reside; such person should be deemed, published, and treated as an enemy of his country, and be precluded from all trade or intercourse with the inhabitants of these Colonies." Newspapers circulated this and other similar congressional resolves, and state authorities echoed the judgment.[25] North Carolina's Council of Safety, for example, reported that persons "inimical to the liberties of *America*, have offered larger sums of the Bills of Credit emitted by the Congresses held at Hillsborough and Halifax, than at the rate of eight Shillings in exchange for *Spanish* milled Dollars"; and that others, "equally disaffected, have asked and demanded in payment for articles of merchandise, higher prices when to be paid in said Bills of Credit" than in specie or other bills. The council urged local committeemen to look carefully into what people owned and accumulated. In every town and county committees would visit every household, requiring of each "an inventory, on oath, of all and singular their Real and Personal Estate." Anyone who refused to give an account of his property should be apprehended and made to answer to the council itself.[26] Patriots in Carolina would keep close oversight over the accumulation of property.

Not every state went as far as North Carolina did in authorizing committees to inventory property. In every province, however, much as they had enforced the Association, local committees also enforced legal tender laws on behalf of Patriot money. Committeemen of Middletown, Connecticut, for example, published the names of John and Gersham Birdsey in the *Courant* for depreciating Continental bills. The newspaper also recorded an apology from Elijah Burr, who admitted selling Bohea tea for over three-quarters of a dollar per pound. "I am sorry for my offence, and will restore to all persons from whom I have taken more the overplus," Burr said. He promised to abide by all Patriot standards in future.[27] Baltimore County, Maryland, Patriots investigated complaints from three men alleging that James Clarke had refused to sell salt "at the price stipulated by this committee." Clarke explained that his salt was of high quality and noted that the buyer had agreed to the price. Might he now atone in some way? The chairman polled the committee, "whether any concession whatever from Mr. Clarke be accepted?" They voted eight to six against. The committee restated the familiar premise established in the resistance years: the consent of both buyer and seller was insufficient to a Patriotic transaction. In effect, committees assumed that they and their constituents, the people at large, were interested parties in exchanges.[28] John Cowgill, a Quaker farmer, offended his Delaware neighbors by refusing the congressional money "from conscience." The County Committees of Inspection and Observation urged Patriots gathered at the Liberty Pole to cut off contact with Cowgill. Reportedly, millers refused to grind his grain, teachers to instruct his children. Other friends to their country went further: they paraded Cowgill through the streets of Dover in a cart with a paper pinned to his back. It read, "On the circulation of the Continental Currency depends the fate of America."[29] That inescapable fact made every Patriot an interested party to countless transactions.

Despite the best efforts of committees and crowds, however, Continental and state bills suffered loss in value. Cuts in supply and redoubling of demand produced inflation, first in the price of imported goods, then—as farmers became soldiers—affecting farm produce as well. Britain's naval blockade so curtailed the supply of imports that farmers found less reason to produce for urban markets or military demand. Besides, warfare disrupted seasons of planting and harvest, and wherever they marched, British troops also took provisions from the fields and cattle from the pasture. Demand for labor and the products of many artisans soared. At the same time, the sheer quantity of bills in circulation caused them to depreciate. Circumstances precluded careful emissions or timely withdrawal of the money. Congress, which emitted most bills, could not tax, since its members were not directly elected by American voters. State governments, which had the theoretical authority to tax, either could not or did not. Equally devastating, the buying power of the money depended on faith in the success of American armies. For if Patriot governments were to crumble, then those left with paper bills on their hands would be the losers. You did not have to hope for British victory but merely doubt that Patriots would win to have reason to question the Patriot bills. With every American setback on the battlefield, the money declined in buying power. By the end of 1776, Congress had emitted a total of $25 million in paper, none of it called in by any of the states. Washington's army had retreated from Long Island and White Plains. There were few encouraging signs until the Continentals managed a victory at Trenton at Christmas.

By midsummer, some areas of the country were reporting a notable depreciation in the buying power of Patriot bills. Powerful agreement among Patriots was proving insufficient to supporting the currency; outside the coalition, too many Americans had the goods and the capital to compromise its value. Everywhere, there were some with the wherewithal and willingness to take advantage of the times. New Englanders in particular suffered acutely late in '76. Much of the early fighting centered in their region, and it had vitally disrupted both production and trade; moreover, Continental bills had flooded the area as authorities struggled to raise soldiers and pay for their supply. As a result, many markets began to experience disproportionate rises in prices.[30]

Over the summer and fall, crowds of farmers and tradesmen responded. In July 1776, a group sent a letter of warning to merchants in the area of Springfield, Massachusetts. Jonathan and Hezekiah Hale received the following message:

> Sirs: It is a matter of great grief that you should give us cause to call upon you in this uncommon way. Every man whose actions are unfriendly to the comon cause of our country ought to be convinced of his wrong behaviour and made to reform, or treated as an open enemy. We find you guilty of very wrong behaviour in selling at extravagant prices, particularly West Indian Goods. This conduct plainly tends to undervalue paper Currency which is very detrimental to the Liberties of America. We therefore as your offended brethren demand satisfaction of you the offender by a confession of your past conduct and a Thorough reformation for time to Come.

The Hales confessed, reformed, and accepted the prices that their neighbors suggested as "reasonable." A merchant in nearby Longmeadow, Samuel Colton, did not. A crowd of farmers and townsmen appropriated his supply of West Indies goods, entrusted them to the town clerk for retail sales, and later left the proceeds in Colton's house. They marked their act as part of the Patriot movement by wrapping themselves in blankets "like Indians," signaling their identity with a Boston crowd that had seized and destroyed tea in the harbor a few years earlier.[31]

There may have been other disturbances—there was surely the threat of them in the area. In August, thirty-two Middlesex towns sent delegates to a convention at Concord to confer about the crisis. "We hereby bear testimony against all mobs, riots, and disorderly proceedings," they declared. Yet inimical persons, the convention reported, conspired against American liberty by forging and altering bills or by discouraging others from accepting the money. Many had "used divers artifices and much low cunning, to depreciate the value of our paper currency, to the great damage of the good people of these States." The convention urged Patriots to confine enemies to their farms, disarm them, and make all efforts to enforce state laws that made paper money legal tender.[32]

Another convention of towns petitioned their provincial governments over similar problems. In November, committeemen from twenty-seven towns from along the New Hampshire–Massachusetts border gathered at Dracut to uphold the primary commitments of the Patriot movement. The body reminded state leaders and the public at large that the Association had specifically prohibited advancing prices since 1774, and that many other Congressional resolves indicated that Congress "intended that no unreasonable advantage should be taken" in economic dealings, but that "all should be sold upon reasonable terms." Now retailers in the area were raising prices, exacerbating tensions of social class by distressing mechanics, laborers, and soldiers. Without attention to these people's sense of equity, there might be disorder, or even "defection from the common cause of America."[33]

Military realities, meanwhile, made possibilities of "defection" even more threatening. By the close of 1776, Patriots everywhere were realizing that the British military would neither quickly lose nor quickly leave. Martial enthusiasm, so evident across the colonies in the early months of fighting, waned in the face of protracted war. Americans reluctantly concluded that military service would not prove a common ground of participation for all Patriots. Instead, the cause would rely chiefly on a continental army, its private members drawn from the ranks of the relatively poor and recompensed by a cash bounty at enlistment and the promise of a steady wage.[34] There were significant consequences to that fact. Thousands of private soldiers engaged in a waged relationship with continental authority. This was a striking change from employment in local economies where payment might often include produce or goods. With cash the medium of their payment, soldiers were suddenly and sweepingly vulnerable to predatory suppliers and to systemic decline in the value of Patriot bills. They would count on the value of Patriot money to purchase for themselves and their families. Depreciation of the bills put pressure on the continent to pay even higher rates to the soldiery. One regiment in Boston, for example, told Col. Thomas Crafts that it was difficult to march off to war leaving wives and children destitute of necessary goods due to sudden and rapid rises in prices. "Five Months ago Eight Dollars was better than Twelve now, by means of such abominable extortion, which if persisted in and our wages not rise in proportion to the prices of those things, we must purchase therewith, will inevitably serve to impoverish the soldiery (but not to enter on politicks) our daily experience proves the truth of it."[35] Under these circumstances, to fill the ranks, Patriot authorities needed to regard the poor man's sense of equity. And besides the pragmatic, there was the moral ground for concern: the soldiers' enlistment constituted a contract, and fairness surely required that their wages should retain the buying power they had commanded at time of enlistment.

Indeed, experience showed that the poor would fight, but they would not sign up without reasonable security, and they expected some sacrifice from their countrymen who avoided military service and tended to business at home. Both yeoman planters in Virginia and militiamen in Pennsylvania demanded that their well-to-do countrymen either enlist themselves or pay penalties to support their neighbors in arms.[36] In New England, recruiters had begun reporting sluggish enlistments over the course of the summer. In Boston, Thomas Cushing explained, "The price of Labour with us is very high and they can get better wages in the Field than in the Army."[37] As they relinquished the idea that all men would willingly serve as needed, Patriots found that their ideals of common participation depended on noncombatants' willingness to take part in some equivalent terms. In other words, with the waning of Patriots' *rage militaire*, noncombatants incurred a more significant economic obligation. Economic support for the cause would be the extent of some men's sacrifice, and for those men economic Patriotism became the sole mode of participation and measure of allegiance. Americans' capacity to maintain the value of the currency and their willingness to take part in exchange on terms that supported the war effort became all the more freighted. Military authorities called on civil authority and civilians to support the soldiery. "How cruel it is, that a few persons, at this time, should have the power to distress the farmer on the one hand, & the soldier on the other, & fatten on the spoils of both."[38]

While Massachusetts and New Hampshire considered Dracut's petitions, the Connecticut state government acted to redress similar grievances. Early in December, the state passed a law to fix maximum prices for wheat, rye, Indian corn, rum, sugar, pork, beef, cheese, and other items.[39] Henceforth it would be illegal to withhold these goods from sale, as well as to ask or to give prices beyond certain maximum levels established for each commodity in the act. Governor Jonathan Trumbull explained that the new law would answer several critical ends: "This is Done not only to Convince the Soldiers that while they are fighting for the Country they & their Families may not at the same time be Ruined by the Extravagant Demands of the People & further to check that Hated[?] Excess that seems to prevail among all Ranks in this Time of General Calamity and Distress & that overbearing Oppression so hateful to God Almighty as well as Ruinous and Destructive to all Civil Communities."[40] Patriots could hardly accept behaviors that were "hateful to God." If He was to decide the outcome of the war, as many believed, then the entirety of the cause might depend on Americans' broad, continued, and public opposition to oppression.

On Christmas Day, emissaries from Massachusetts, New Hampshire, Connecticut, and Rhode Island conferred in Providence. The immediate crisis was military: a British invasion of Rhode Island seemed imminent, and warfare in the middle states had cut off communication with Congress. Delegates at the interstate convention first disposed troops for Rhode Island's defense, then tackled the problem of Patriot money. States should halt emissions and tax to bring in Continental bills, they decided. While these remedies would help, the convention recommended that other state legislatures enact price ceiling laws similar to Connecticut's. Delegates suggested specific ceilings for sugar, molasses, and rum from the West Indies; wheat, rye, corn, cheese, butter, beef, and pork from New England farms; materials such as flannels and woolens; and products such as rawhides and shoes. The convention set a daily price for farm labor, on the basis of which the work of all tradesmen might be computed, "according to the wages & Customs, that have heretofore been adopted and practised in different Parts of the several States compared with Farming Labour." To alleviate distress of the "Poor Consumer," delegates suggested that goods costing £100 in Europe—now sold at 500 to 600 percent from prime cost—sell for a maximum of £250 wholesale, and that retailers—now marking up prices by 40 to 50 percent—be limited to 20 percent. That would "allow but a Reasonable Profit to the adventurers." Alongside price ceilings, the convention urged state authorities also to pass antiwithholding laws, requiring those who possessed supplies in any significant quantity to bring them to the open market. Such laws forbade monopoly and engrossing, particularly of the "necessaries" of life. They set conditions under which civil and military authorities might seize hoarded goods either to feed and clothe the troops or to alleviate distresses of the civilian poor. Finally, to prevent owners of goods from moving them to a more favorable market, the states should enact embargoes against exportation beyond state lines. Together, these measures aimed at making Americans accept paper money in all transactions, suppressing preference for specie, and damping speculation. These steps would combat the "unbounded Avarice" that threatened "Fatal and Pernicious Consequences" for the American cause. Within a few months, all four New England states passed laws—generally called "Regulating Acts"—incorporating these policies.[41]

The early months of 1777 thus saw renewed mobilization that engaged ordinary men in execution of the Patriot program. Lists of goods and services regulated by Patriots provide a sense of the ambition of the project. With the exception of military stores, New England capped the prices of almost all imported goods—cloths from woolens to osnaburgs, sugars and molasses, hardware and fancy goods—allowing for variation to account for costs of transport from eastern port cities to other parts of the region. New England states regulated wheat, rye, corn, beef, swine, salt pork, flax; farm produce such as cheese, butter, peas, beans and potatoes; products such as wood, hay, pine boards, plank joists, mutton, veal, and more. Rhode Island went beyond regulating daily farm labor, to specify maximum prices for the work of artisans connected with maritime trade—ships' ironworkers, ships' carpenters, and caulkers—as well as masons, tailors, barbers, and house carpenters.[42]

Massachusetts law empowered local officials to regulate goods and services not enumerated by law. Drawing on local knowledge, Worcester set prices proportional to those established for Boston and added other items to the list: apples, shoats, lodging, flip, leather breeches, hats, horseshoeing, scythes, pails, and more. Where they were uncertain about the proportional requirements and costs of various artisans, the selectmen and committeemen urged such prices "as are in a Just comon and usual proportion to the prices afixed to articles herein enumerated according to antient usage and custom." Other towns similarly relied on local knowledge of what would be fair. Newbury, Ipswich, and Salem all published detailed price ceilings in broadsides that circulated through the area. Leaders of Groton, Shirley, Townshend, Lunenburg, and Fitchburg met together in convention to set prices and wages for their towns. Committees of thirty-eight Connecticut Valley towns sent delegates to Northampton to establish uniform price ceilings for their area and devise ways to suppress inimicals who depreciated Patriot money. Eighteen Essex County towns sent committeemen to Ipswich, where they denounced "Selfish and mischievous men" who withheld goods from their neighbors, "in direct opposition to the calls of nature and their country."[43] Elsewhere town clerks wrote the prices recommended by selectmen and committeemen into the pages of town records, as regulations were adopted at town meetings. The regulating acts mobilized extensive activity on the local level.[44] Here was a Patriot economy indeed.

Once again, that economy generated and required extraordinary participation. Rhode Island Council President Stephen Hopkins observed: "The Equity and Necessity of the Measure are so obvious and striking that it meets with a most general Approbation."[45] Connecticut leader Elbridge Gerry also described a broad consensus: "The Execution of such Laws are undoubtedly difficult," he wrote, "but it being the Interest of such Multitudes to assist their operations, the Refractory will undoubtedly be diligently watched."[46] Gerry assumed the continued presence, necessity, and vitality of Patriot networks. Watchers and informants might prosecute violators of regulating laws in the courts of law. In many places, however, execution was entrusted to the sorts of committees that had overseen associations and boycotts. As in the prewar politics of resistance, committees might bypass the courts to publish the names of the recalcitrant, so that they became vulnerable to their neighbors' ostracism, persuasion, or even punishment. In many respects, in other words, New England in early 1777 presented a familiar picture of Patriot unity, organization, and ideological commitment. With these measures, New England governments put themselves behind policies that endorsed popular ideas of fairness, presumed continued popular engagement in enforcing those ideas, and honored the revolutionaries' contract with private soldiers and their families. Other states, experiencing different degrees of pressure on prices, nonetheless considered enacting similar measures in their own regions.[47]

As in the prewar era, Patriots mobilized in pulpit and press as well as on the ground. Soon writers in areas most suffering from monopoly, extortion, and currency depreciation were elaborating the rhetoric honed in the prewar years of resistance. They denounced those who would not participate in the Patriot economy in much the same terms as they had denounced those who would not participate in boycotts and associations. Men who sought a profit by weakening Patriot paper bills were guilty of the same greed and desire for power seen earlier in stamp men, officials, merchants, and others who would not abide by Patriot agreements in the decade of resistance. In newspapers, pamphlets, and other publications, writers embraced price ceilings and other regulations as essential to the common cause.

The common and obvious condemnation of price gougers was that they acted from avarice. Monopolists, engrossers, and discounters were "lost to all public virtue," motivated by "a sordid love of gain," the "Harpys of trade," and "greedy Muckworms crawling."[48] For many, these mercenary traits lay at the heart of the continent's economic and political ills. An anonymous contributor to the *Boston Gazette* explained: "Luxury engenders various wants: By these avarice is begot; and avarice to gratify her purpose, is obliged to league with Oppression."[49] Such explanations of price inflation did not mention factors of money supply but focused solely on the impact of selfish individuals within society. In the logic of those for whom relationships with neighbors stood foremost, what mattered were a man's motivations and character.

As we might expect, New England clergymen interpreted acts of hoarding and raising prices as age-old sins. "Extortion seems to be the progeny of an amazing avaricious lust after worldly gain," according to the Reverend Jonathan French.[50] Rev. Abraham Ketelas devoted thirty-eight pages, filled with biblical examples from the lives of the apostles, to showing his readers that "sordid avarice, that infamous love of money . . . is the root of all evil."[51] A third Massachusetts minister composed a satiric version of an extortioner's prayer: "May my merchandise still prosper, or my husbandry increase, but may scarcity and want still be the fate of my country, and more and more abound. May the time speedily come, when I shall be able to buy the poor for silver, and the needy for a pair of shoes. May all my countrymen be brought low and I be made Lord over them."[52] There was nothing subtle about that. Here was the ambition for lordship and the exploitation of neighbors that had prompted the resistance movement in the first place.

As Patriots saw it, the problem with avarice was that it was "boundless" or, more poetically, "as unbounded as the ocean." It threatened to swamp the society and the Patriot cause. Bounding it was the job of the Patriot governments and, in execution of Patriot policies, the job of Patriots everywhere. By contrast, when Boston's tanners petitioned for a higher legal price limit for their wares, they carefully denied that they acted from such motives. Other men's "unbounded avarice" was disrupting the war effort and the harmony of the interdependent Patriot society; the tanners wanted only "to obtain a reasonable and moderate Profit for the necessary support of themselves and Families"—or, just "a competent support."[53] Those sorts of ambitions were acceptable and even laudable. The danger, as everyone knew, came from men like the extortioner, who sought "lordship" over their countrymen. Americans who had opposed men of such ambition since the time of the Stamp Act should hardly stop opposing them now.

Other writers also invoked the need to oppose men's ambition for lordships. They recognized not just age-old sins but Toryism, which is to say, precisely the tendency to squeeze property from other Americans that Patriots had organized against since the time of the Stamp Act. "This is the same oppression we complain of Great Britain," wrote "A Farmer." Hoarders and monopolists closed the space in which their neighbors were accustomed to consent, so that prices represented some men's coercive power rather than all men's collective and negotiated sense of value. Wasn't the war precisely opposed to the taking of men's property without their consent? Minister Jonathan French made the point that oppression and extortion were fundamentally the same. People tended to speak of oppression as something done by governments, as when they taxed unfairly, stripped inhabitants of the fruits of their labors, and caused them suffering. Extortion, by contrast, usually suggested similar acts by individuals against their neighbors. The distinction was minor at best.[54] Timothy Stone argued the same point in a sermon on selfishness: "We may see states which have grown up to a great height of power, influence, and authority; who have by various means, heaped up to themselves great wealth, vainly puffed up with a fond conceit of their own power and importance." Such nations were likely to grasp at empire, to view themselves the rightful rulers of other peoples, and to end up at war. Readers would surely recognize Great Britain in this. Yet when Americans withheld from the market, engrossed goods, or bled their poor neighbors, were they not much like those selfish Britons? "In short, we are practicing the same things in kind upon one another every day."[55]

In another sermon, Nathaniel Whitaker fiercely denounced those who followed self-interest, even if they supported the cause when it suited them. Some Americans, he wrote, "wish well to the public cause," but placed its success second to their own interest. "They are high sons of liberty, till her cause crosses their private views, and even then they may boast in her name, while like George III, they stab her to the heart, by refusing submission to those regulations which are essential to her preservation."[56] By this logic, avarice might compromise the would-be Patriot. Indeed, Toryism and avarice, self-seeking, or ambition were so linked in Patriots' thinking that writers only sometimes felt compelled to spell out the argument that discounting the money, withholding goods from market, or overcharging were clear signs of Tory sympathies. There were echoes throughout these writings of John Gibson's view of salt hoarders: "Was they real friends to their country, as they stile themselves," surely they would act differently toward their neighbors and accept and support Patriot bills.

A second genre of writings also framed the problem of money and prices in deeply social terms. These were dialogues, short dramas that ranged from a few lines published in a newspaper or broadside to pamphlets of greater length. They presented conversations among familiar types—"A Countryman and a Soldier," or "a *poor* Widow and an *honest* Farmer."[57] These publications assumed a shared social framework: they presented characters who lived with one another in society and were carrying out a revolution together. The genre itself made the case that prices existed as a relationship among those characters. The dialogue contained the matter of prices by situating the topic in purely social terms. As such, it reassured all readers of their own capacity to adjudicate recognizable social disputes. It argued for common sense.

One remarkable pamphlet, *The downfall of justice; and the farmer just return'd from meeting on Thanksgiving Day*, went so far as to give the voice of common reason to "Jack," an African American slave who spoke in heavy dialect. The setting was a simple one: a wealthy farmer, his barns filled with corn, his cellars with cider, sat down to dine with his family. He had been offered $5 for cider, he told his household at a sumptuous dinner, but of course he had refused to sell; the price, he predicted, would soar to $15 by spring. After all, "the times are now in our hands, and if we don't improve this opportunity I don't see which way in the world we could ever answer to ourselves with good conscience." That said, the farmer offered grace, expressing pity for "the poor and needy throughout the world." In the course of the feast, the farmer's children discussed the morning's sermon. What had it meant, they wondered? "He that withholdeth corn, the people shall curse him," had been the text. Might it have some application? Ah, explained the farmer, the meaning was largely "spiritual"; in pragmatic terms, it meant that men such as he should sell corn when offered hard cash. Only "Jack," an African American slave, saw through the family's flat-footed hypocrisy:

> Well, Masser, I don't tink 'tis fair ting when poor fok he canno get no noting in he belly; Masser every ting. I do no no what Masser mean; he pray, he pray, he tells Lord he pity poor ebery where; he no give; he no sell; what he du? Masser got rye enuf, wheat enuf, cyder enuf, ebery ting enuf; Jack he trash, he trash, dis bin full, dat bin full, ebery bin full, poor fok he no lette have, what he du, what poor fok du; ah Masser! Jack pitty poor fok.[58]

Modern readers may squirm at the dialect and wonder at some eighteenth-century meanings ("Jack he trash, he trash").[59] Still, it is clear that the author of "The Farmer Returning" expected readers to recognize Jack's perspective as the plain and common sense of the matter. Jack posed common knowledge of fairness over and against the learned logic of the farmer and his family. The author of the drama assumed that it would not overstretch readers to allow an untutored, enslaved black man speak their part. Jack, unqualified for even the status of one of the "three disinterested men" called in to arbitrate disputes within a community, nonetheless could grasp the obvious: he could recognize avarice when he saw it. The character of Jack was accorded a capacity to pronounce on his master, the farmer who was "Lord over" Jack, as he might wish to be lord over his neighbors. Of all the figures who appear in "The Farmer Returning," Jack came closest to qualifying as neighbor or Patriot. Here, in a New England publication, was a muted critique of slaveholding and a loud critique of the miserly well-to-do. Here was the specter of the magnificence of the farmer and the slavery of the many.

Nothing made the case that justice was recognizable to the most ordinary of men more strongly than the character of Jack. Yet in this literature of patriotism and prices, Jack was only one of a number of characters representing the relatively humble view of life and revolution. To read these pamphlets, newspaper pieces, and paragraphs in almanacs is to encounter soldiers, widows, hardworking tradesmen, and laborers, all of them with claims of justice to make. In some articles those claims were addressed to merchants, in others to farmers, as various authors variously identified the source of the problem; yet authors agreed on the core of the matter. Indeed, they could hardly think of it in other terms: the problem was social, a question of the relationships among social beings, all of them located, recognizable, identified as particular members within a larger whole.

   With that way of casting the problem came obvious solutions that in-volved the participation of the many to set social relationships right. "The Farmer Returning" noted the crowds that sought popular justice against the miserly. One of the farmer's sons looked over their bounteous store of provisions and noted that "town folks" might "rise and take this away." Such crowds were unlikely to face punishment or even disapproval from leading men. "I doubt but the authority would justify them in it," the son mused, a remark that could surely have been taken by some readers as provocation. In "The Farmer Returning," an enslaved African American, food rioters, and the authorities of the state appeared in agreement and potentially allied. The author invoked a coalition that allied Patriot au-thorities with the people "out of doors," acting in a mob and in agreement with the lowest class in the province. He described the first Patriot coali-tion at its broadest.

.   .   .

An alternative way of thinking about money appeared when Congress discussed New Englanders' Patriot economy early in 1777. Only a mi-nority questioned the emerging policy of regulation, but their questions presaged a gulf of outlook and understanding that would later become significant. The differences explored between Patriot leaders in early 1777 would make themselves felt more powerfully within a few years. Their debates suggested alternative ways of thinking about not only money and prices but also economic exchange, Patriotism, and popular initiative in the Revolution. Implicitly, at least, a few congressmen raised the possibil-ity that the activity of committees and crowds, and the common commit-ment to overseeing economic transactions among Patriots, might not remain essential to the commitments of the continent. As we shall see, these debates prefigured more divisive and more public disputes that would sorely test the Patriots' original coalition of 1774. They show us the ex-tent to which even undoubted Patriots might come to disagree over what being a Patriot required.
   The Continental Congress declared its fundamental agreement with the New Englanders' Providence convention in February of 1777. "Cer-tain persons, devoid of, and in repugnance to every principle of public virtue and humanity, instigated by the lust of avarice, are, in each State, assiduously endeavouring by every means of oppression, sharping, and extortion, to accumulate enormous gain to themselves."[60] Given that real-ity, state actions to prevent such oppression were surely Patriotic. When congressmen decided not to vote "approbation" of the Providence pro-

ceedings, it was not lack of confidence in regulating laws but rather dif-
fidence toward state governments, who might object if Congress presumed
the right *either* to approve or disapprove state acts. As for the substance of
the regulations proposed, Massachusetts delegate Samuel Adams wrote
home to report that Continental leaders thought the proposals "wise and
salutary." John Adams, who disagreed with the recommendations for regulating laws, admitted that they were nonetheless "extremely popular in
Congress."[61]

A handful of delegates dissented from the general approval. The partial accounts that remain of congressional debates suggest that three or
four men at least viewed such measures as unlikely to help. Laws were not
sufficient to control prices, as John Adams saw it: even the absolute government of France had failed in that project. Accordingly, he expressed
doubt about "the justice, policy, and necessity" of regulatory laws. He
noted that high prices resulted from a scarcity of goods and that setting
ceilings for prices was most likely to make matters worse by discouraging
production and importation.[62] James Witherspoon of New Jersey had
worries that were less philosophical, more circumstantial. In 1776, the
price of imports had skyrocketed, while the price of farm produce had
risen less dramatically. If laws forbade all further increases, they would
freeze the current relationship of domestic and imported goods and disadvantage the many farmers who formed the bulk of his constituency.
Witherspoon did not object to regulations per se, but he objected to what
he saw as disproportion in price ceilings.

Pennsylvania delegate Benjamin Rush went further, questioning the
most basic premises of regulations. He proposed a variety of ways to
conceptualize the colonies' situation. Prices, Rush said, acted much like
buoyant objects floating in a basin of water. How could a person make
those objects go lower? Certainly it was possible to push the objects to
the bottom of the basin and hold them there, but the simpler and surer
expedient would be to drain the water out of the basin itself. If Revolutionary governments would likewise drain bills from the economy through
taxes, the argument ran, prices of goods would naturally fall. We can easily follow Rush's logic, but we should pay particular attention to his metaphor. Without mentioning the persuasive or coercive powers of common
opinion, and without questioning popular committees and crowds, Rush
nonetheless drew attention to the unwieldiness of the visible hand of
popular activity that worked to lower prices. Rush framed the problem so
that it might be solved by policy makers in legislatures, not by committees and crowds. His approach implicitly undercut ordinary Patriots'

claims to jurisdiction over prices and supply. In the same debate, Rush used a medical metaphor that worked in much the same way. Price inflation and currency depreciation were symptoms of a disease that afflicted American societies. In the midst of a "universal disorder," he continued, regulations of marketing and prices would only be "an opiate." Instead, Patriot authorities should apply "a radical cure" by taxing the excess paper out of circulation. There was a logic drawn from contemporary medical practice in this prescription: like the body physical, at times the body social needed to be bled.

Casting depreciation and inflation as diseases proved to be one of the most compelling and widely used tropes in the continent's debate about prices. This way of figuring the problem of prices neatly transformed Rush, a medical doctor, into an expert on fiscal policy. Equally important, it framed depreciation and price inflation as disorders rather than evils, amenable to systemic rather than local treatment. Other members of Congress spoke of high prices as an indication of a decline in Patriotic fervor and public virtue. By contrast, Rush explicitly denied that prices for goods or labor had much to do with such matters as patriotism, affection, or virtue. Rush urged his fellows to discount the public clamors lamenting "rapacity and extortion" in dealings between men. "This has led some people to decry the public Virtue of this country. True Sir there is not so much of it as we could wish, but there is much more than is sometimes allowed on this floor. We estimate our Virtue by a false barometer when we measure it by the price of goods."[63] A "false barometer"—in other words, there was a false linkage between virtue and money. In a movement committed to a Patriot economy, it was a tricky argument: Rush did not explicitly deny that those who raised prices were often Loyalists or else men who worshipped their own self-interest, hence without virtue. Rather, he suggested that it was not only possible but desirable to consider prices as something other than the product of political allegiance, personal motives, or social relationships. Rush urged his fellow Congress members to dissociate virtue and Patriotism from the prices demanded in the marketplace. To accept that proposal would be to narrow the meaning of Patriotism.

In light of later developments, we should note that neither Adams, Rush, or Witherspoon clearly proposed that price controls infringed on individual rights, or that the purpose of the Revolution was individual economic freedom.[64] Adams seems to have raised the matter of equity: as Rush's diary recounted it, Adams questioned the "justice" of the measures recommended by the Providence convention. Still, it isn't clear what Adams meant by that, and the bulk of his argument apparently stressed that regulations were impractical. For his part, although Rush thought the visible hand of price control laws was inefficient, he did not argue that it was unjust. This was not itself opposition to crowds and committees. It was not yet—or not entirely—an alternative view of liberty or the purpose of the Revolution. Moreover, these Patriots knew and deplored the fact that Tories devalued the money out of animus to the cause. Nonetheless, Rush's way of formulating the problem effectively relieved individuals from the imputation of avarice. It suggested no failure of Patriotism just because they refused to take the money at face value. Indeed, individual actors hardly appeared in Rush's view of the matter at all. The closest that Rush came to blaming individuals for the money's loss of value was when he offered an example to illustrate why controls would not work. In Philadelphia, he recounted, merchants had evaded price limits established by the Association by a stratagem, technically selling their goods as required, but charging large fees for the barrels in which the goods were delivered. Staying within the letter of the regulation, they had violated its spirit. If others denounced the merchants as venal or unpatriotic, Rush did not: for him the virtue of the individual merchants did not arise. It was not salient to view them as either friendly or unfriendly to the cause; it was not significant—to forging financial policy at least—to calibrate their relationship to their neighbors.

Historians have generally shared Rush's reasoning. This is the way prices behave, we believe, within given market structures and conditions. Adam Smith's brilliant work, *The Wealth of Nations*, was just appearing in Dublin and London, and if no one in Philadelphia had a chance to read the book as yet, men such as Benjamin Rush were thinking in Smithian ways. Still, if the vast majority of congressmen and leaders in many states approved legislated price limits and related legislation, their position did not reflect simple innocence of the market. Few were as well-read as Adams and Rush, but most surely knew that the supply of money and its purchasing power were related.[65] Richard Henry Lee of Virginia, for example, agreed that Patriot governments should draw down the volume of paper money when possible. Yet he defended regulatory legislation: even the best physicians treat the symptoms of disease with a "palliative," he said, thus gaining space for improvement in a patient's condition while waiting for a more fundamental cure to take hold. And John Adams's older cousin Samuel focused on ways to rein in monopolizers and hoarders: "If the popular Indignation can once be raisd to a suitable Pitch as I think it can it will become dangerous for them to withhold their Goods or demand an exorbitant Price for them and the Evil will be cured. I think every Step should be taken for the Downfall of such Wretches, and shall be ready to jyn in any Measure within Doors or without which shall be well adapted to this Effect."[66] These men's disagreement with the critics of regulation did not stem from naïveté about supply and demand so much as from concern about hearts and minds. It wasn't (as some historians have implied) that they could not grasp the market; it was that they preferred to keep hold of something else. Opponents of market controls discussed the behavior of *money*; Samuel Adams and Richard Henry Lee were concerned about the behavior of *people*.[67]

That fundamental difference carried starkly contradictory implications for the sorts of political actors who might claim jurisdiction over economic life and the sorts of political actions that they might use to do so. After all, what *was* a price—a relationship between supply and demand, or a relationship between neighbors and countrymen? One's answer to that question bespoke a fundamental philosophical choice. There was no adjudicating such a difference; one view was not right and the other wrong, to be proven as such by "the market" or the course of events.[68] In 1777, however, one was the consensual Patriot view, the other was not. Although Adams and Rush urged their fellows to reconsider the issue, they acknowledged that theirs was very much a minority opinion. Neither member took his dissent from the floor of Congress to the public press. If they were correct in thinking that legislative price controls would not answer, after all, they might wait for time to prove their point. Nor was it politic or Patriotic for them to broadcast their views while Congress sought to rally strong popular support for its measures and its money. Whatever their doubts, these leaders surely hoped that New England's economic regulations would have positive effects. Dissent from price controls would surface in the Patriot press only after some months in which Patriots pursued regulatory policies with limited success.

Outside the halls of Congress, there was a second source of change in Patriot thinking. Some reconsidered the role of the Revolutionary committees that executed the Patriot economy. From one perspective, it was reasonable to imagine that, just as such bodies had been crucial to the adoption of independence, so they would be to its achievement. The Continental Congress and Revolutionary state authorities continued to rely on committees and the participation they mobilized through 1776 and beyond. Such committees acted as administrative arms of those authorities in many areas; they publicized government resolves, coordinated initiatives, oversaw enlistments, took charge of estates abandoned by Tories, and policed both disaffected Americans and British prisoners of war housed in the area.[69]

Yet committees could challenge as well as support authorities above them. We've seen that some prewar committees provided a vehicle for the growing political consciousness and mobilization of artisans, petty shopkeepers, and others among the middling sort of men. In various provinces, committees continued to play that role. True, throughout the new states, there was a fundamental shift in the nature of governments. No longer appointed in any part by a monarch or proprietor, provincial governments now had all their branches depend directly or indirectly on the consent of the people. However, new governments varied widely in the degree to which they actually reflected popular desires. Different provinces broadened the suffrage, shifted greater power to the lower house of assembly, reproportioned their legislatures so as represent back-country districts more fully, curtailed the powers of governors, and made other alterations to make government more closely reflect the popular will. In most places, nonetheless, conservative interests managed to hold off popular claims for greater change, so that many freemen still found their voices excluded from provincial institutions. (In Virginia, said Thomas Jefferson in 1776, the new government maintained suffrage restrictions so high that most men "who pay [taxes] and fight" would still be debarred from the vote.) Some states—New York, Massachusetts—were unable to settle on new governments before the end of the decade. Everywhere, some Americans considered their governments to be unfinished and hoped to secure further change.[70]

In this context, popular committees served to promote interests and ideas not fully represented in government. In Pennsylvania, Philadelphia militiamen and private soldiers in the various counties formed their own "Committees of Privates" to voice the concerns of the soldiery and the common man. In Maryland, too, Committees of Privates formed to press for a broader suffrage in the new state. In Annapolis and in Boston as well, self-appointed groups organized to take action against Tories and extortioners.[71] In Baltimore, a self-selected "Whig Club" took on "not only Legislative but even Executive powers," when they sent papers threatening supposed Tories. (They signed the papers "Legion.")[72] Other towns and counties continued to elect bodies to pursue the war, and Patriots in New York established a series of Committees for Detecting Conspiracies to deal with the many Loyalists in their state. Public meetings appointed ad hoc committees for various ends. Committees could fill a gap in political institutions by organizing and promoting the interests and views of Americans who believed themselves insufficiently represented without them.[73]

At times, then, Patriots predictably clashed with one another over the role of committees. In Massachusetts, for example, conservative commercial interests remained influential in the General Court, but they did not enjoy the confidence of many Patriot towns in the western counties. Through the late 1770s, westerners refused to recognize the court's judicial appointments or allow county courts of common pleas to sit. A supporter of state government in Berkshire County complained, "Enthusiastick People . . . (having got themselves into the office of Committees of Correspondence and Inspection) inculcate into the minds of their Votaries Both by their Examples and Doctrines that they ought to pay no more obedience to the Acts and Doings of the General Court than they themselves think proper."[74] Such enthusiasts were admittedly firm supporters of the common cause, however, and they had "got themselves" onto committees by being elected in their towns. By the logic of the Patriot movement, weren't these committees (and not the General Court) the speakers of vox populi? Until the state established a new government on terms acceptable to farmers in Berkshire and other counties, towns and their committees would assume that mantle. They would rule on local disputes and execute—or not execute—both provincial and Continental resolutions. The Court's appointed justices would find no jurymen in the western counties willing to recognize the appointees' commissions and so convene a court of law. Even in the east, where law courts slowly reopened, the state government could not assume simple agreement and cooperation from towns and committees that voters established.[75]

Problems became evident when the Court tried to bring order to the situation. First, the court resolved, towns should consolidate responsibility for all provincial matters in the hands of a single committee, so that most officials could confine their attention to merely local concerns. Many towns accordingly chose a single joint committee of correspondence, safety, and inspection. Second, localities should choose proper men to their committees. Some state leaders fumed that popular prejudice against holding more than one office prevented them from sitting on local bodies as well as in the government. It was important, they resolved, that "the most discrete, prudent, firm persons" (men at least *like* themselves) should serve on committees that ruled over the liberties, property, and possibly even the lives of individuals. Fewer committees and better men on them— together, these two measures might reestablish a line that had been blurred between those qualified to fill provincial elective office and those whose place was in local offices or merely out of doors. They might end the proliferation of revolutionary forms.

It was more difficult for the General Assembly to establish or explain its superiority to those political forms. The House described the history of local committees in a way calculated to contain their continued Revolutionary potential. In the past, the House wrote, "these Committees, existing originally by Sufference, acted discretionally, until the Resolves of Congress dictated to them, & many times according to their discretion only, where the Committees could not procure the Resolves, & in Cases not referred to by any Resolves."[76] That committees often acted discretionally was unarguable; but what did it mean to say they originally existed "by Sufference"? The phrase sidestepped a critical question: by whose "sufference" had committees taken shape? Who had allowed them their powers? There was surely a sense in which the Continental Congress had authorized local committees when it issued the Association of 1774, even if some local committees in the province existed before Congress had first met. There was also the historical fact: committees arose from the *suffrage* of town voters and, often, other inhabitants as well. But men trying to establish government on the state level could not afford to emphasize the representative character of committees. On the contrary, they needed to avoid comparison between such committees' status and their own. After all, how might a House of Representatives, itself now fully dependent for its authority on the local constituencies, claim logical priority or jurisdiction over committees if committees were also and equally—or even *more*—representative of the local ground? To finesse the question, the Massachusetts House obscured voters in their towns; suffrage became "sufference." In this way the notion that committees existed "originally by Sufference" evoked continuity where there had in fact been rupture, as if the General Court itself—although out of session at the time and based in a rejected royal charter of government anyway—had somehow permitted committees to form. The court invented continuity in provincial institutions where there had been interruption, a fiction that suggested provincial authority's ongoing, necessary existence and priority.[77]

One writer in the public press developed these arguments when he observed committees gathering to support the power of Patriot bills. "Speculator" doubted that local committees had the right to send their own delegates to countywide conventions to consult and make policy, such as the ones that resolved against enemies or in favor of economic regulations. Much like William Henry Drayton, who, as "A Free-man," had criticized the Charles Town committee in 1767, Speculator believed that committees usurped legislative prerogatives. Speculator characterized committeemen as officers of the law, much like "constables," whose business consisted of "inspecting the political behavior of inhabitants" of their towns. They should not "assemble in a body like a court or congress, . . . making resolutions beyond their sphere."[78] Such institutions outside the state government might generate ideas, pressures, and dissent. They might become an alternative locus of popular loyalty. The threat was real enough: everyone knew that, in 1775, an elected convention had effectively supplanted the conservative assembly in the loyalties of the Pennsylvanian people. In Massachusetts, county conventions had organized popular refusal to recognize the new officials appointed by Parliament in 1774.[79] Similarly, Patriots all knew that mobilization of committees and conventions since 1774 had given voice to unsettling popular ideas about equality and claims on property. Given that experience, assemblies had reason for vigilance toward any other representative body that might gather. At the time that Speculator wrote, other thinkers were proposing shifts of power away from the provincial government, through such institutions as elected county assemblies, which might lay taxes and assume other duties, thereby keeping power close to the voting and executing public. It was possible to imagine that local committees would feel beholden to conventions rather than the General Court if ever the two authorities promoted divergent policies. Speculator concluded: "I hope and trust as the General Court are the <u>creators</u> of committees, that they will define their power, and limit their jurisdiction." Yet were committees truly creatures of the House, or were they (like the General Court itself) creatures of the people?[80]

These questions arose in a series of conflicts that broke out as Boston dealt with shortages, monopolists, and regulations in 1777. The city faced difficulties of scarcity and rising prices from early in the year.[81] According to the town meeting, many problems could be blamed on the extortionate demands of suppliers from the country, as well as others "whose Principles are known to be *unfriendly* to our present Contest with Britons," and others still willing to sacrifice the cause to gratify their own "Lust & Appetites." The town labeled those who depreciated Patriot bills as "Public Enemies," and voters called on the Committee of Correspondence, Safety, and Inspection to find their names and "represent them in the Public News Papers, as dangerous Enemies to the United States of America, by endeavouring not only to lessen but destroy the Medium of Trade."[82] Yet there is evidence that the committee, composed primarily

of merchants, retailers, and other men of substance, was not able or willing to execute the law with sufficient rigor to bring prices down.[83] Presumably it was doubts about the existing committee's commitment that
led voters to add thirty-six men "not in Trade" to the committee, specifically to oversee transactions in the town's twelve precincts.[84] Voters explicitly sent the new committeemen to confront merchants and "require of
them a direct Answer to the following Question—Will you take the Price
set by this State?" Merchants' replies would be published.[85] The February meeting totally bypassed the committee to manage a shortage of
flour. The meeting summoned local flour dealers to report the extent of
their holdings in the face of their assembled townsmen. (Various dealers
discovered they had rather more on hand than first they had thought.)
Despite these measures, difficulties of harvest, transport, and trade continued to plague the city. In March, bakers began rationing bread, one
loaf per household. The prices of other goods moved even higher, as the
merchants and retailers who normally sold West Indies imports to country
suppliers either lacked those items or stored them and withheld.[86]

In April, a crowd bypassed both committee and town meeting. Abigail
Adams described what happened to five men who had engrossed goods,
then refused paper money or taken it at a discount:

> About 11 o'clock yesterday William Jackson, Dick Green, y Harry Per-
> kins, and Sergent of Cape Ann, a Carry of Charlestown were carted out of
> Boston under the direction of Joice junr, who was mounted on Horseback
> with a Red coat, a white Wig and a drawn Sword, with Drum and fife fol-
> lowing; a Concourse of people to the amount of 500 followed. They pro-
> ceeded as far as Roxbury where he ordered the cart to be timped up, then
> told them if they were ever catched in Town again it should be at the ex-
> pense of their lives. He then ordered his gang to return which they did
> immediately without any disturbance.

Had Thomas Hutchinson been in Boston that day (rather than safe in
London), he easily would have recognized the scene. "Joice Junior" had
appeared in prewar Popes Day celebrations and in crowds that intimidated the tea consignees in 1773. Joice evoked by his name and costume
the historic figure of English tailor George Joyce, a member of Cromwell's army and—so it was believed—the man who captured and beheaded
King Charles I. His appearance in support of the Regulating Acts and
town supply in 1777 dramatically represented the popular understanding
of the continuing resistance movement. Joice's presence produced a nar-

rative that linked the overthrow of an oppressive king to the foiling of a popish plot against Parliament, the discipline of tea importers and, now, the banishment of price-gouging engrossers. The crowd acted on the popular right to participate on the common ground. By carting the men and tipping the cart, Bostonians enacted the forms by which condemned criminals were customarily hanged on Boston Neck.[87]

Some evidence suggests that, beneath the costume, "Joice jun" might have been John Winthrop, merchant and member of the dilatory town committee.[88] If so, his presence in Boston streets might have signaled division within the Patriot committee itself (Winthrop for action against engrossers, others not). Alternatively, it might have signaled committee efforts to channel popular bitterness and intimidate uncooperative dealers at the same time. In either case, the action created controversy. A fair number of Bostonians apparently disapproved of the mob of April 16. The merchant Isaac Smith lamented the fate of its victims in private correspondence: "To be seized when seting down to breakfast and ludgd. into a Cart with his wife and children hanging round him, not knowing but he was a going to the Gallows, must be shocking to any one that has the sparks of humanity in them." The proceedings had been highly irregular, as the crowd banished the five men "without even the shadow of an Accusation."[89] There were similar remarks in taverns and parlors around town. Joice and other writers answered the criticism in published notices. Some replies were caustic: "Well Mr. Joyce, jun. what have you been doing? How could you find it in your Heart to frighten 2 or 3 poor Women and Cart so cruelly five lunatick Tories, only because they are enemies to their Country?"[90] For his part, "Joice" insisted that crowds were necessary because Patriot authorities were inactive. Price control violators had "their Cause supported by Persons of a certain Class, called Moderate Men alias Hypocrites," and those were "Persons who I know never were blest with the best Characters in political Matters." In the April 23 *Gazette*, Joice issued warnings to hoarders, naming some names and referring to others in general terms. He asked citizens to keep him informed of those who withheld from the market by dropping a note at the offices of the *Gazette*. To all appearances, Joice and the people out of doors stood ready to replace the inactive Committee of Correspondence, Safety, and Inspection. When men who saw themselves as leaders of the Revolution did not act, other men and even women could assume the common ground.

Yet despite his bravado, Joice did not appear at the head of a Boston crowd again. Opposition from others of the town's merchants and traders may have been too strong. In May, commercial interests carried the town meeting to call for repeal of the Regulating Acts. In instructions to the town representatives, the meeting introduced a new way of looking at the relationship between committees, crowds, and liberty. Their argument against the laws emphasized several points. It was proving too difficult to enforce regulations. "However well designed," such a policy was "a growing source of Animosity and ill will" between city and countryside, each of which blamed the other for high prices. If only the public would distinguish between honest, upstanding merchants, and the "mushroom traders," new to the business, who appeared overnight to take advantage of economic turmoil. Gentlemen merchants bred to the trade upheld its proper conduct and supplied their customers as best they were able. By contrast, newcomers to commerce stooped to deceitful practice, so that government should focus specifically on controlling them. With fraud prevented, trade might be left free of all restrictions, and free trade would soon bring plentiful supply to the state. Regulating laws encouraged withholding and so created scarcity, which caused higher prices. Trade should be "freed from the cruel Shackles, with which it has lately been injudiciously bound." "For it has been a known and acknowledged Truth, by all Nations, which were *wise enough to encourage Commerce*, that Trade must regulate itself [and] can never be clogged but to its ruin." Beyond the practical, moreover, there was principle at stake: the law ran "directly opposite to the idea of Liberty."[91] Within a few weeks, the town of Providence, Rhode Island, echoed Boston's new position. Regulating laws were unwieldy, inequitable, and counterproductive, they stated. The policy caused scarcities and sparked animosity between country and town, buyers and sellers. Providence blamed the law itself for the appearance of "sharpers and mushroom pedlars," opportunistic dealers prone to "Evasions Quibles and Lies." Equally damning, the laws were proving nearly impossible to execute, save by "a degree of rigour and severity heretofore unknown in these Free states." Like Boston, Providence proposed a notion of liberty that would hold no space for such coercions. Enforcing the law would "render a Man's House and Store liable to be opened and searched in a Manner most ignominious and unworthy of a Freeman."[92] Some execution of some laws, however popular with "the people," nonetheless constituted unacceptable infringement on men's individual liberty.

Other towns disputed that view. A few weeks later in May, towns in Plymouth County gathered in convention to resolve on the Patriot crisis. Avarice and extortion were the causes of the region's shockingly high prices, the convention decided. Price inflation constituted "a triple headed mischief, as it tends to weaken the springs of government, to ruin the currency & to discourage the soldiery." To counteract monetary decline, the convention arrived at two clear resolutions: "Resolve: That an equitable exchange of the fruits of the earth, or a commutation on one man's labour, in due proportion to that of another, is the basis on which the felicity, freedom, and happiness of a community greatly depend." And, to counter directly the mercantile position that execution of the law infringed on the liberties of propertied men, they adopted a second point: "That the highest degree of political and civil liberty consists in the living under the protection of an equal government, or the administration of laws framed by the people themselves (who are to be governed by them) or their representatives." Men could not ask to be free of all coercions or rid of all committeemen who might open and search their house and store.[93]

Indeed, Boston itself could not establish a consensual position in this dispute about regulation, committees, and liberty. In September, commercial interests finally secured repeal of the Regulating Acts by the General Court. Yet despite their reservations, conservatives in Boston accepted town and committee regulation on a substantial scale over the months that followed. Sugar merchants were withholding from the market, so that farmers were not bringing in food and provisions. A crowd of nine hundred from the North End of town marched on the warehouse of sugar dealer Jonathan Amory. Mr. Amory, a participant later wrote, "to prevent his property being taken from him without pay," agreed to entrust his sugars to a committee, which would oversee its retail in small quantities to countrypeople who brought in supplies for the city. More crowds and the threat of them led other dealers to add their stores of molasses and sugar to the public holding. With regulating laws off the books, then, mobs successfully forced private dealers to cede their store of sugars to public control. Local leaders, whatever their preferences for continued regulation by law, accepted continued regulation by the people out of doors and the town meeting. Those who might, in the best or calmest times, object to committees searching men's stores and warehouses now accepted committee jurisdiction. Committee control had proved necessary in order to avoid direct seizures and uncompromising implementation of popular claims by Bostonians outside committee doors. In other words, committee control was made necessary by crowds.[94]

As one participant recalled, the measures taken during the sugar shortage "kept down the price of flour and wood for about a year." Despite that success, it had to be admitted that Patriots were at loggerheads. Were their crises in provision and inflation to be explained by lax execution of the monopoly and price ceiling laws, or—as many traders in town had concluded—by execution that was overly stringent? No one questioned that the city suffered from spiraling costs and inadequate supply, but different Patriots drew different lessons from the experience. As Boston headed into new difficulties in 1778, the town meeting once again called for uncompromising legislation against hoarders and monopolizers.

These divisions of thinking in the late 1770s raised fundamental questions about the nature of Patriotism. Joice junior had called his victims "Tory villains." Abigail Adams dissented only slightly from that analysis: "If tis not Toryism, tis a Spirit of Avarice, a Contempt of Authority, an inordinate Love of Gain, that prevails not only in Town, but every where I look or hear from."[95] Toryism or avarice—Adams seemed to suggest that there was little to distinguish the two and little to choose between them. Yet in one respect the distinction was potentially vast: avaricious men committed crimes for which they paid fines or suffered other punishment; Tories committed treason, and they might plausibly be excluded from Patriot society altogether. Massachusetts and the other states were already debating: what were the wages of being a Tory? And what were the crimes that surely identified a man as being one? Put differently, what were the requirements of Patriotism?

Of course, Patriots were those willing to fight for the cause, and others who would support the military, sacrifice self-interest, sell goods and labor fairly, bearing in mind the needs of the poor. Moderate men promoted the possibility of abandoning that measure of Patriotism as it came to seem onerous, divisive, and unrealistic. The Massachusetts General Court explained its desire to broaden the Patriot movement in late 1777: "The taking the money of particular persons in our funds," it said, would "engage the abilities of such persons to the American interest."[96] Put differently, people who lent money to Patriot governments would then have a powerful stake in the stability and success of those governments, and in the states' capacity to pay interest on their loans. To gain such allies, the General Court was willing to redefine Patriotism as something compatible with the pursuit of interest. For many who owned property, surely, it was tempting to broaden the movement so as to conciliate those of their fellows who still held aloof from Patriot efforts. A new policy would woo the moneyed even if recently disaffected. Men who had not supported the Association and men who had not supported declaring independence might now join in supporting Revolutionary state governments and the

Continental effort against British troops. And maybe the moneyed would be willing to enter a coalition with the more conservative of Patriots. Even Tories who had removed from Boston to Halifax began considering a return, once they realized that British forces would not quickly subdue the rebellion and that repossessing their abandoned estates would require coming to terms with the new authorities. Once the French became America's ally in 1778, moreover, the idea grew more plausible that the fledgling states would win their independence. In that case, money loaned to those governments at interest might prove a good investment. Here were grounds for a new coalition.[97]

Even the Patriot press began to explore those grounds, as opponents of regulations developed arguments against Patriot economy and against popular jurisdiction. Dialogues and dramas that situated readers among familiar social actors did not appeal to these writers. These authors bypassed the common reader to address and construct a more learned readership in substantial, reasoned essays in newspapers. They employed little Revolutionary rhetoric, spoke little about Toryism, and focused on money rather than sin. Their arguments required discarding a social framework in order to develop a different way of thinking.

"A Countryman," a prolific spokesman for redefining Patriotism, wrote articles in the New England papers starting in June 1777. "Countryman" noted that the price-regulating projects were very popular, but he thought they worked against the value of the money. The value of Continental money, he explained, depended solely on the relationship between demand for bills and the quantity in circulation. "The abundance of bills we have now makes them cheap." So the legislature should lay taxes to bring paper in. This was by no means a defense of private accumulation: "Publick poverty, and private opulence," he wrote, "is the fatal disease which has put a period to the greatest empires of the world." It was regrettable that wealthy men were hoarding their wealth, when it should be available to the critical needs of the government. There was familiar Patriotism in this concept, then, yet Countryman radically refigured the place of self-interest in both polity and society. Good policies, he thought, would align the self-interest of individuals with the public interest, rather than require men to sacrifice. He recommended bringing the wealthy to support government not (or not only) as an obligation, but as a good investment.

Along with opinions about prices and financial policy, Countryman presented opinions about popular mobilization and the liberties of the people. He raised the question of which members of society ought to establish economic policies in the new governments. He began with a right on which all Patriots relied. The right of revolution, he wrote, arose at that moment when government struck at the foundation of the people's rights and liberties. "This maxim fully shows," he deduced, "that there is one common line between the governing and governed, which is dangerous for either to pass." Everyone agreed that government ought not to trespass on the liberties of the people; fewer followed Countryman in declaring that, by the same token, the people ought not to trespass on the prerogatives of government. Like Speculator, Countryman disapproved of committees, conventions, and crowds. *Laws* were institutions appropriate to and reserved for governments, he wrote—implying, not to localities, or committees, or county conventions with their voluntary pacts and resolutions. For while the people might also act to change the behavior of their neighbors, their proper realm was "*custom*" rather than law. The great difference between legal and customary power related to individual dissent and individual choice. Possessing jurisdiction only over the realm of custom, the people might voluntarily set good examples for their fellows, but they should not presume to coerce.[98] The case for limiting the people and the case for freeing self-interest were logically separable but historically coincident in this moment. Countryman wrote at a time when, by general understanding, a well-positioned, advantaged minority stood to gain from trade that was freed of obligations and social meaning, so that many of "the people" of Revolutionary America would oppose such a policy. The author accordingly cast an argument for the elite to overrule policies that had the powerful and sometimes overwhelming support of the majority of free male colonists.

Other denunciations of popular politics also appeared. One article that ran in newspapers in both New England and the Middle states specifically re-created the gray area between extremes of black and white. An anonymous author renounced the long-standing conviction that the population comprised two groups, either "friends" or "enemies" to the common cause. Instead, the author divided Americans into five categories. Some were "Rank Tories," who actively worked to depreciate the currency in order to cripple the war effort. "Moderate Men" were those whose connections with royal government or the Church of England led them to hope for a return to the status of the colonies in 1763, at which their own positions and privileges would presumably be restored. While "love of slavery" motivated Rank Tories, most Moderate Men acted out of excessive fondness for the finer things of life—"the fish, . . . the cu-

cumbers, and the melons, and the leeks"—available to those who were well situated within the hierarchy of empire. "Timid Whigs" composed a third category of American, those who trembled at every feint of the British Army while wringing their hands at the shocking expense of the war. Behind such timidity was surely avarice. With the final two categories the author spoke pointedly to the current scene: "Staunch Whigs" hated the British and loved liberty, good government, and order. These were the best leaders for the community, for they were "both just and merciful in the exercise of power." Such judicious leadership marked them apart from the final category, called "Furious Whigs." Their fervor carried them to absurd and dangerous policies that threatened to injure the cause of the continent as greatly as the fears of Timid Whigs might do. The Furious sort of Whigs had faulty perspective: they considered "the destruction of Howe's army of less consequence than the detection of the most insignificant Tory." They lost sight of the larger struggle for independence, caught up in the narrow concerns and petty squabbles of their own locality. Perhaps most dangerous, they were willing to suspend even "the common forms of justice" against those they considered enemies. By doing so, they damaged the American cause.[99]

Unsurprisingly, Staunch Whigs were the heroes of this piece, but it must be noted that Timid Whigs, though beset by avarice, counted as Patriots nonetheless. (Even Moderate Men, who did not "wish well to independence," did not do too badly in this article, compared to Joice Jun.'s depiction of them: "Moderate Men, alias Hypocrites.") Here was an analysis for those who saw the many shades of gray, an argument for a resorting of the population, allowing for new coalition. Perhaps monopoly and extortion were not Toryism, but only avarice. Staunch Patriots would not act out of avarice, and they would surely condemn it in others; nonetheless, they might come to accept it (and those avaricious others) as part of America. Here was a discounting of the dangers of self-seeking, hence a refiguring of "the American cause" that might broaden its membership and also narrow its ambitions. Patriots needed to win the war and establish their independence. In this version of the common cause, weeding out Tories (or some of them) was now inessential, a revision that effectively dismissed many of the social goals so popular with middling and poorer Patriots. Was there not a view of Patriotism that could accommodate wealthy, ambitious, and moneyed interests?

Finally, later in the year, one writer elaborated the case that, far from promoting American liberty, regulating acts and the acts of the people in their execution were violations of that liberty. "Tertius Cato" advocated a scientific approach to money matters. Citing Isaac Newton, he explained that money was merely a measure of the value of goods and that the measure might easily vary. When prices changed, in other words, it represented no necessary injustice. By this logic, there existed no such thing as "true value" for goods and services. In a given community, people's estimation of the value of many goods might tend to coincide, but it was also perfectly possible for evaluations to differ. "Value" was extrinsic to goods and labor, and there could be no expectation of consensus as to what constituted "reasonable" prices or profits. This view not only explained but also depoliticized the conflicts between such interests as merchants and consumers, who merely valued things differently. Tertius Cato undercut supporters of popular action and regulation of exchange by refusing to privilege vox populi. Correspondingly, what appeared to others as collective rights seemed to Tertius Cato to belong to individuals: "Men, by nature, have a right to property, and what they justly acquire, they have a natural right to value and esteem as they please; none but themselves can estimate the labor and toil in procuring it; this is the very essence of our natural disposing right." Only the person who produced or procured an item could put a price to it.[100]

Compare Tertius Cato to the committeemen assembled at Plymouth to institute a program of price ceilings for their towns. The convention declared it the "duty" of all who had necessaries "to supply such as are destitute at the stated prices, with so much of them as they may not reasonable want for their own consumption." The destitute did not figure in Tertius Cato's world: "Men have also a natural right, either to dispose of their property or not." That natural right existed somehow prior to relationships and their obligations, and without reference to social need.

Indeed, the "men" imagined by Tertius Cato were distinctly isolated from society. The labor that such a man performed in producing or procuring was private, invisible to his neighbors and inestimable by them. He was not a member of the familiar community evoked and assumed by price control advocates. Readers could assume that Tertius Cato was speaking of a merchant, since he listed his hypothetical individual as owning hypothetical rum or molasses, items not grown in the country or produced in urban workshops. Yet Tertius Cato wrote as if all economic actors were the same; there was no need to specify whether a man were trader, tradesman, or farmer. The "individual" he depicted lacked social identity, or, more precisely, that individual's membership in the larger social whole was inessential. He did not stand in relation to others unless and until he voluntarily entered into exchange by offering goods for sale. Such isolation dramatically distinguished the man pictured by Tertius Cato from the peddlers, merchants, widows, soldiers, farmers, and tradesmen pictured by other writers. "Wherein consists the nature of my offence, o[r] what is the degree of it, when I estimate the value of my own property, I am at a loss to conceive." That loss was the product of abstraction, the result of removing acts of estimation and valuing from their social and political milieu. This was thinking possible and appropriate to a man for whom markets were not *marketplaces*, which is to say, not physical locations filled by neighboring or nearby buyers and sellers with visible characteristics, needs, and capacities. Equally, it was thinking that did not include such actual figures as army suppliers, who represented the taxpayers, the soldiery, and a common cause.

Tellingly, where most defenders of commerce urged the public to distinguish the established and upstanding merchant from the transient "mushroom pedlar," Tertius Cato did not. He defended the transient man, the man without connections. Like "A Countryman," Tertius Cato provided new arguments about the law in order to create a space for individuals to evaluate and sell their goods free from the demands of popular consent. He went beyond Countryman in one critical respect: he denied the power of the people's consent as it was expressed not merely in crowds but even in legislatures. Tertius Cato noted a familiar maxim that limited British and now American governments: "New laws make no new crimes, but only ascertain the nature and degree of them, and threaten punishment." He insisted that the people's representatives should not recast acts accepted as private and legitimate into public crime or treason. He omitted that monopoly and oppression were in no respect "new crimes." He provided for a second objection by excepting soldiers from the free market. Their depreciating wage admittedly remained a public concern; the states might establish storehouses, collect necessary supplies, and then retail them to soldiers and their families at a set price. Other transactions were properly left to themselves.[101]

Some Patriots made fun of these arguments: "I would ask you in a free and independent State, whether every Person has not a Right to do everyThing in his Power to Ruin the Country with Impunity, and distress every Department by Monopolizing? You cannot deny but that they can, and have a Right to do it, and it is our Part to yield to them and suffer the Minor to swallow the Major."[102] In other words, what about when the supposed rights of the minority truly damaged the cause of the majority? Other writers, such as "On Liberty with Respect to Trade," constructed careful rebuttals. "Men have no more right, under pretense of using their liberty, to be fraudulent, unjust, injurious and oppressive in trade, than they have to 'steal freely,' or to commit 'robbery' on the high way." Trade would no more regulate itself than burglary would. The author of "On Liberty" rejected the effort to refocus discussion onto the behavior of goods and returned to the actions and motivations of people. People, he assumed, were situated in social relationship: at stake was not an individual deciding the value of things he owned, but the fundamental nature of the interchange that took place "between man and man." In the context of society thus imagined, liberty referred to something other than individual freedom to indulge one's "will and pleasure," to "take a boundless latitude in getting gain." Instead, liberty had valence for individuals and their community alike. Men acted freely only when they acted under their moral and intellectual capacities, free not from their neighbors' oversight but from self-will and avarice. Using his reason, a man would realize that he and his countrymen shared a common interest. Here was the leap of faith that had been basic to Patriot resistance and necessary to Patriot revolution, an identification of self not with personal or particular interest but with a whole, even an empire, knit together by just such leaps by a virtuous people. "On Liberty" declared interdependence once again.

The ideas introduced by Tertius Cato did not displace more familiar denuciations of avarice and calls for Patriotism in the press. Many contributors to publications proceeded without reference to his claims about liberty, and few of the like-minded immediately supported his views. We must remember that the contents of the press reflected thinking in other public arenas (and in private correspondence) only in part. Even Patriot authorities who now opposed or despaired of regulatory policies could not welcome dissemination of the idea that legislators, as much as street crowds, lacked jurisdiction over economic exchange. In 1778 and 1779, those leading the war effort had every reason to continue to view production, marketing, and pricing as measures of Patriotism. In repeated calls for enlistment in the army and for military supply, the Continental Congress, state governments, and military authorities all continued to speak of "reasonable" prices and transactions. States from New England through Maryland limited prices. Independence could not be secured if Americans all saw themselves as isolated individuals, free of social obligation. In these respects, Tertius Cato's conception of liberty did not yet fit the Patriot movement or the Patriot press. It was not possible to detach the "common" from the "cause" quite yet.

Nathaniel Low's almanac for 1778 reiterated a key reason why: Low described a war that was increasingly fought by a single class of men, and he identified the class divisions that were undermining the common cause:

> It is the rich that are principally affected by this dispute. The poor have little to loose [sic]; but you depend on these to to defend your country and fight your battles. They have ventur'd their lives and shed their dearest blood for you. And yet it is the poor chiefly that feel the calamitous effects of monopoly and extortion; tho' it is evident these men were never more necessary than now, never more useful, and their services were never yet of greater importance.[103]

What would happen should so many Americans continue to pursue their own gain by withholding the necessaries of life merely for private profit? Low did not describe the potential disaster for the cause, and it would not have been politic to depict it too graphically in print. The poor were necessary and useful, their services of importance. What if their services did not continue? In 1778, a soldier detailed the logic that might plausibly guide the military men at Valley Forge: "The Gentleman of the Army who cannot purchase from his Country, what he wants, at Prices as reasonable as the Wages he has consented to receive, for his Services in the Army, will reasonably suppose his Obligations to his Country, in that Way, are at an End."[104]

What Low described, what others deplored, and what Tertius Cato came close to defending was a reality that Patriots were loathe to admit— that there were limits to the interdependence many Americans would embrace, and that, for some, the neighborly society imagined in 1776 was receding from view. I spoke at the beginning of this chapter of the depth of popular suspicions of wealthy and ambitious men. There were unquestionably those among the wealthy and those among the political elite who remained firm Patriots by any measure, sacrificing self-interest and personal ambition on behalf of the greater cause. Even many who thought specific regulation policies unwise or inequitable still condemned avaricious Tories and monopolists, supported the efforts of regulating committees, and sympathized with the acts of many crowds. And they keenly felt an obligation to the soldiery. It was possible to think vox populi mistaken about this or that regulation and yet genuinely honor "the people."

Despite that, the coalition forged in the resistance years and embodied in the Association of 1774 was weakening. It was not only that the poor were doing the fighting; too few other Americans were sacrificing in kind. Could men making vast profits claim to be conducting the war at home? Could "timid Whigs" be described as firmly resisting the ignorance of the many and the magnificence of the few? Could enough Americans qualify as Patriots by the standards of the original coalition? No answer was obvious, but the issue would be joined at the very center of the movement, in Philadelphia, in summer and fall of 1779. Committed popular forces—militiamen and committeemen—faced conservative men in the state and in the Continental Congress. Patriot policy toward finance, prices, and monopoly had presumed a virtuous, self-sacrificing, neighboring population. Could Patriots still hold themselves and others to those ideals?

.   .   .

Pennsylvania's Patriots had been divided since the adoption of a state constitution in 1776.[105] Commercial and propertied interests hoped to replace the constitution with a more conservative frame of government. There were other divisions as well. The Quaker population of eastern Pennsylvania had worried Patriots since the beginning of the conflict. In 1777, the capital city had been occupied by British forces. Congress itself had decamped, and some Pennsylvanians who remained in the city had shown themselves willing to fraternize, trade, and profit with the occupying forces. After the British left, Patriots who retook the city confronted those not fully loyal to the Patriot cause. The very man in charge of liberated Philadelphia in 1778, General Benedict Arnold, offended many with his lavish style of life, his preference for socializing with wealthy collaborators and Loyalists, and—as they discovered—his use of public office for private profit by dealing in British goods. Arnold was rebuked by Pennsylvania state authorities for the last of these, disliked and distrusted by countless ordinary inhabitants for the rest. (Arnold's treachery of 1780 shocked but did not surprise Philadelphians, who had seen him put self above *patria* in 1778.)[106]

Like Arnold, other well-positioned men seemed taken with the many possibilities for profit. They were willing to limit the voice and the jurisdiction of their ordinary countrymen. Bitterness against such trimmers rose in early 1779, as an extraordinary rise in prices in the city forced the issue. Once again Patriots mobilized to combat withholding, shortages, and acts of price gouging. In January the state's Executive Council urged officials to search out and prosecute monopolists as "most heinously criminal." In April the General Assembly again outlawed forestalling and regrating of provisions by statute. When, on April 20, the ship *Victorious* arrived in port, Philadelphians welcomed the prospect of sales of dry goods from its hold. As townspeople waited, however, the *Victorious* stood laden at anchor. Its cargo had been entrusted to merchant and conservative congressman Robert Morris. Rumor circulated that Morris was holding sales until the Continental money depreciated further and he could charge even higher prices.[107]

Early in May, the First Company of the Philadelphia Militia Artillery addressed a memorial to the Supreme Executive Council. They were deeply aggrieved, they wrote, for while they were serving their country, others were getting rich, depreciating the money, preying off the soldiers' families. When the soldiers returned from service they found themselves ruined. Equally unfair, the assembly had set fines for anyone delinquent from military service, but a monopolizer—so the militiamen claimed— could make enough to pay his annual fines in a single day of immoral trading. The militia memorial suggested two possible solutions: delinquents needed to be fined in proportion to their estates, or else the government might leave fines aside and let the militia itself find means to make the able-bodied do their military duty. Coming from men who held arms and could use them, it was effective lobbying. Christopher Marshall, a leading constitutionalist, agreed to join the militia's cause: he called a mass meeting on May 24 in the city to consider the town's dire situation. On the day before the meeting, persons unknown posted flyers that threatened monopolizers and other Tories. When some people tore the flyers down, a crowd of militiamen escorted them to jail. The next morning, men carrying clubs visited merchants at their houses and stores demanding that they lower prices. In the afternoon, Philadelphians gathered in mass meeting and elected Daniel Roberdeau, brigadier general of the militia and staunch constitutionalist, to preside.

Roberdeau insisted on the fundamental need for popular consent in the marketplace: high prices on necessary commodities constituted a "tax," laid on the people by engrossers and speculators. Here, surely, was a central premise of the American resistance since 1765: such taxes required the consent of the people or their representatives. The meeting thus established the "common consent of the community" to price regulations. The problem was clear: clandestine groups that plotted to engross and overcharge were evading public oversight. The meeting resolved: "That the public have a right to enquire into the causes of such extraordinary abuses, and prevent them." The gathering promptly established two committees: one would investigate Robert Morris for withholding cargo from the *Victorious* from the city market. A second or "general" committee would determine price ceilings in equitable proportions, then work to lower them, month by month. It was also to press Congress to discipline any of its officials that might have abused the public trust. Finally, the meeting resolved that no Tories be allowed to reside in the city. The militia as a whole promised to assist in enforcement of all resolutions. Some reports suggest they continued their own arrests and jailings after the meeting adjourned.[108]

In response to these events, state authorities carefully negotiated their relationship with the militia and with the city's mass meetings. The Supreme Executive Council denounced forestallers as "abettors of the tyranny of Great Britain," but at the same time announced that city magistrates should review all arrests that had taken place outside "the ordinary course of justice." On June 1, the general committee published its intention to meet publicly on Sundays to hear reports of violations of its resolves, then investigate and announce its findings. Within the month, a grand jury had spoken out against the policy of allowing wives of British sympathizers to stay in town, on the grounds that such women spread divisive rumors and worked to undermine Patriot money. At this moment, many aspects of the law were in the hands of the people. An approving article in the *Boston Gazette* characterized Philadelphians as running a "Coran Popula," an "athenian court" that found every defendant guilty and sentenced all to jail. Philadelphia's radical Patriots allegedly planned to gather "the whole herd" of extortioners together, then send them over to the enemy's lines. On June 28, the militia published its own statement in support of committee actions. They were willing to rise to arms, they said, to enforce committee resolves and regulations. And they made an unmistakable claim for partnership in directing the Revolution: "We wish not to have the preeminence; but we will no longer be trampled upon."[109]

Over spring and summer, the crisis mobilized local committees and sparked new efforts at price regulation through much of the North. In Massachusetts, towns elected committees, petitioned for new legislation, and sent delegates to intertown conventions that adopted voluntary price ceilings much as they had adopted the Association a half decade earlier. New Hampshire and Connecticut towns also moved against forestallers, monopolizers and discounters. New Hampshire held a convention in

Concord to adopt regulations. In New York the mobilization began in urban centers such as Albany and Fishkill, then spread through their surrounding counties as well as to some towns in Orange and Ulster. These towns established new committees or reinvigorated the old; they set prices for goods, took charge of distributing scarce produce, and blocked export of necessities to unregulated neighboring states. The movement now particularly defended the needs of urban consumers. Its breadth and ambition were impressive.[110]

Back in Philadelphia, Robert Morris duly presented his case in person and in writing to representatives of the mass meeting. The investigating committee blamed one of Morris's associates—a Baltimore merchant—for forestalling the cargo of the *Victorious*, as he "set the terms" of the deal with Morris. Yet some of the committee felt the congressman was too involved in the matter to be fully innocent. "However unwilling Mr. Morris may be to acknowledge the term engrossing, or monopolizing, yet, as he did not import the cargo and did, in partnership with Mr. Solliekoffe, get the whole into his possession, we are at a loss to find any other name." Still, Morris's rapid sale of the flour "abates the rigorous sense generally applied to those words."[111]

The general committee announced a second mass meeting for late July, when those present would choose a committee of 120 to pursue those who monopolized or overcharged. In the days prior to the meeting, conservatives and radicals in Philadelphia mobilized. Each group printed up a ticket naming a slate of candidates for the committee election, one slate in favor of price regulation and ridding the city of its enemies, the other opposed. The slate that favored regulations swept the poll—2,115 to 281. For all that, opposition to the committee was growing, not only among merchants and conservative men, but among some tradesmen and others as well.

Matters came to a crisis late in September. Militiamen voted to send away the wives of inimicals and asked constitutionalist leader Charles Willson Peale to lead them in the task. After Peale declined, handbills circulated on city streets. On October 4, they called for militia meetings to act against enemies. Although Peale and other radical leaders discouraged action, the militia seized four opponents of price controls and marched them through the town. What else they intended would never be clear. Historians know that they marched with arms by the house of James Wilson, a lawyer who defended Tories, and that Wilson, Robert Morris, and some twenty to forty other gentlemen had gathered inside the house. As the militia passed, firing between house and street somehow began. A total of six or seven men received fatal wounds. Dozens more were less seriously wounded. The melee ended only when the elite City Troop of Cavalry and some Continental cavalrymen arrived on horseback and rode into the crowd.[112]

In the aftermath of what became known as the "Fort Wilson" affair, Patriot authorities hastened to defuse tensions. Militiamen mustered to rescue their fellows who had been jailed. Pennsylvania officials freed the prisoners on bail and took steps to distribute flour to the poor, especially to the families of militia members. In addition, the state swiftly enacted laws to remove some popular grievances. They made fines on military delinquents proportionate to their wealth; they charged officials to act vigorously against the "inimicals" in the city.

Reports of events in Philadelphia shook Patriots in New England and the South. The violence both reflected and hastened the waning of elite Patriots' support for the original coalition, their commitment to popular institutions, the crowds, committees, and assemblies "out of doors" that assumed jurisdiction over law and its execution.

In September, Continental leaders decided to put an end to paper emissions and rely on taxes and loans for the revenue needed to continue the war. There were countless reasons to do so. Congress had poured money into the war effort: as much as $160,000,000 by the beginning of September, when delegates decided to cap emissions at $200,000,000. Price inflation, currency depreciation, and countless disrupting factors of wartime had brought expenses to an extraordinary pitch, and Congress realized they would reach their spending cap by the end of the month.[113] The bills fell so greatly in value that some imagined they would soon become worthless. Congress felt their authority in the matter at an end. Henceforth, the war effort would rely on expenditures from the various states and from immediate impressment by the army and its agents in exchange for certificates from the Continental loan office. Over the summer, Congress had seen mounting turmoil on the streets outside their own dwellings and meeting place. They had seen one of their own members accused of putting profit before Patriotism, forced to answer a radical committee and publish an explanation in the public press. Such experience surely affected their willingness to adopt a radical change in policy.

Whatever the causes, we can turn to Thomas Paine for an astute account of the consequences for the Patriot movement. In mid-1780, he wrote: "While the war was carried on by emissions at the pleasure of Congress, any body of men might conduct public business, and the poor were of equal use in government with the rich. But when the means must be drawn from the country the case becomes altered, and unless the wealthier part throw in their aid, public measures must go heavily on."[114] Here was a startling and precise description of the passing of a Revolutionary moment, and it is right that we pause and consider it. While Congress financed the war with paper money, said Paine, two conditions prevailed. First, "any body of men might conduct public business"—any body, not only provincial or continental bodies of representatives, men claiming the stature of rulers, men winnowed through the process of elections and selected to be wisest among their fellows. Instead, says Paine, even ordinary men, endowed only with local and common knowledge, might form themselves into a public "body" and make their concerns and resolutions felt. They might gather, speak, and act to public effect, in public time.

And this capacity of ordinary men was part and parcel of a second condition that Paine identified with the years when currency finance was the policy of Congress. The second condition was this: "The poor were of equal use in government with the rich." Paine's phrase bears repeating, for surely few of us today can remember a time that even approximated such a state of affairs, and it takes an effort to imagine it. If he exaggerated for rhetorical effect, it was not by too much. Since 1765, members of the poor and middling ranks had made themselves felt in the Patriot movement. Since 1775, the willingness of the poor to enlist in the Patriot cause and to serve on the battlefield had been critical to the colonies' bid for independence. Patriot authorities asked that soldiers accept paper money and that civilians of all social ranks, in turn, give it currency and recognize its value. Such recognition required a leap of faith—faith in the power and determination of Patriot authorities to give the money value, faith in the virtue of one's fellows and brethren in the common cause.

Perhaps, in the longer run, that faith was proved misplaced. In any event, many Americans would lose or abandon such faith in the face of the experiences of 1776–80.[115] Yet even as they abandoned specific price ceilings, marketing laws, and other regulations, some Patriots retained their desire for greater fairness and a sense of obligation to the poor. Many surely retained the deeply rooted belief that monopolizing, hoarding, and speculating were sinful, unpatriotic, and unneighborly. The common understanding persisted: "Was they real friends of their country, as they stile themselves," men would not do these things. Were they real friends, they would show greater regard for public good than for private interest. From 1775 to 1779, Patriots' understanding of their movement had shifted in important ways but also held true. They knew that Patriots were those willing to fight for the cause, and others who would support the military, sacrifice self-interest, sell goods and labor fairly, and bear in mind the needs of the poor. But men who were not real friends were plentiful, and they had a role to play in the new societies and governments emerging from revolution.

5

The Freedoms They Lost

At last we are ready to see how political liberties that had been essential to British subjects became dispensable—even impermissible—to citizens of the new American states. How did popular practices of participation in execution of the law disappear? Equally important, how did the collective capacity to influence the terms of exchange and the meaning of property diminish? What happened to the power of "common consent"? To answer those questions, we look at the way that commitments to neighboring and accountability, so vital to the Patriot movement of 1774–80, became unnecessary to the identity of many Patriotic Americans of the 1780s and beyond.

We closed the last chapter with Thomas Paine's insight: the continent's policy of issuing paper money had presumed and maintained the coalition that joined common farmers, artisans, and free laborers ("the poor") with Patriot leaders in the Congress and in state governments. Forged in the years of resistance, that coalition had depended on the rights of ordinary freemen to participate on the common ground. It had required such men to act with vigilance in committees and crowds in order to support the buying power of Patriot paper. Accordingly, it had expressed the commitments of those men, their common view of fairness, insistence on shared burdens, concern for poor soldiers and their families, and deep suspicion of undue individual ambition for profit. Like the prewar boycotts and the Association of 1774, policies of currency finance had located countless economic transactions under a public jurisdiction.

By backing their bills with tender laws and other regulatory measures, Patriot governments put their authority behind such principles. During the years 1775–80, currency finance had assumed consensual participation by large numbers of Americans in a coordinated, regulated Patriot economy.

The 1780s saw a profound change in the Patriot movement. As Paine had predicted, new financial policies signaled new priorities among many leaders. Men who had joined their social inferiors in associations during the early war years increasingly became disenchanted with that connection. Other leading men, less enamored of popular politics from the outset, came to the fore in the Continental Congress. With that changing of the guard came a shift in the definition of Patriotism, as new leaders tried to mute the popular voice and secure an alliance with more moderate Americans. Henceforth the ideas and commitments of small farmers, planters, tradesmen, and others would have less influence within Patriot circles of policy making. In the 1770s, the central experience of many Americans had been one of *association*. The 1780s, by contrast, was an era of *dissociation*, when some who had joined with their middling neighbors now withdrew from that commitment.[1]

This brief concluding chapter recounts that dissociation and the extraordinary turmoil that it engendered. Patriots who had once united for independence now measured their differences. The liberty of Englishmen, as Henry Care had phrased it, depended on "1. Parliaments 2. Juries." Patriots had agreed in 1776: liberty required representation of the people in the body that framed the law as well as the presence of the people in the institutions that executed it. In the 1780s, Americans bitterly contested the extent and limits of representation, the extent and limits of the popular presence. They discovered within Patriot ranks gulfs of understanding and interest that were increasingly unbridgeable.

Two related issues—the return of Tories to American societies and adoption of financial policies to retire the Revolutionary debt—became the focus of conflict.

Congress appointed Robert Morris "financier" of the Revolution and delegated sweeping powers to him to reorganize Continental finances. Morris hoped to use those powers to create a new alliance. He described his project in private correspondence in 1781: he wanted to "unite the several States more closely together in one general money connexion," he wrote. A money connection would dramatically depart from the ideals of 1776, when Patriots envisioned mutual affection and shared sacrifice as the grounds for their union. Morris saw the need to engage the many Americans inadequately motivated by affection and uninspired by the call to sacrifice. He understood the motivations of such Americans, men less fearful than some other Patriots of social and economic inequality, less dedicated to the vision of a middling society and the interests of that middling many. Morris pursued the support of the group that Thomas Paine had called "the wealthier part." He would craft policies designed "indissolubly to attach many powerful individuals to the cause of our country by the strong principle of self-love and the immediate sense of private interest." These powerful individuals would support state and central governments because it was worth their while. Morris hoped that this second Patriot coalition would give new energy to the war effort and to nation building. It would strengthen the authority of government and adopt policies to promote commerce. Such policies would recognize those "principles of liberty" that assured each man of "the free disposal of his property on such terms as he may think fit." Visions of a powerful commercial empire would re-place the vision of a Patriot economy.[2]

The financier began by reassuring the wealthier part that they would not be required to join their social inferiors. He reined in the activities of Revolutionary committees. In 1780, Morris urged the states to repeal all antimonopoly laws that forced marketing or disallowed withholding goods from the war effort or the poor, set ceilings to prices, or made the money legal tender. "I wish and pray that the whole detestable tribe of restrictions may be done away," he wrote.[3] "The whole detestable tribe"—the phrase explicitly referred to economic regulations, but Morris was clearly thinking of the committees that enforced those regulations when he summoned the image of overly consensual and troublesome Native American polities. As the states complied with the new financial program, local committees that had administered regulations did not all disappear; yet those that remained would henceforth act without the congressional imprimatur they had enjoyed since 1774. By removing government back-ing from paper money, Congress had effectively ended the Association that had served as linchpin between popular participation, on the one hand, and the central Patriot authority, on the other.

Indeed, in the new decade Congress would depend not on committees so much as on the states. First, Congress relied on the states to supply the army, calling on each provincial government to provide supplies accumu-lated by any means they chose. States could accept taxes in the form of produce and goods, so that money, having become nearly worthless, need not play a role in military supply. Second, Congress called on the states to enact and execute a new financial policy. For a time the states sought to maintain the circulation of paper bills, but by spring of 1781 the currency had lost all value and only rarely came into use in trade. To replace the bills, the new coalition would require a new form of money that would work in new ways.[4]

As we have seen, the paper money issued by Patriot governments had spread the burden of Patriots' struggle in symbolic and psychological ways as well as material ones. For individual Americans, to take the money was to acknowledge the authority of "the public" and its Revolutionary bodies, ranging from Congress at the center to new state governments to countless committees and crowds at the local level. To accept it in payment of a debt was to experience oneself as part of a Patriot community, accommodating one's neighbor who was tendering paper bills and supporting the soldiery as well. In countless interactions, many who did not fight in the militia or army could still know themselves to be Patriots.

In material ways, the paper money had been an effective means of spreading the burden of Revolutionary struggle throughout the population. No Patriot had intended the paper to depreciate, of course, but in retrospect some reflected that the depreciation had acted as a tax on the countless individual transactions in which paper was offered and accepted; it was a tax through which most of the struggle for independence had been successfully financed. Benjamin Franklin, for example, wrote affectionately about the paper money whose value had dwindled away to nearly nothing, for in that dwindling he saw a necessary tax that had paid for the war in its most difficult years. "This Currency, as we manage it, is a wonderful Machine. It performs its Office when we issue it; it pays and clothes troops, and provides Victuals and Ammunition; and when we are obliged to issue a Quantity excessive, it pays itself off by Depreciation," he wrote in 1779.[5] Depreciation took its toll on all those who accepted the money and then spent it again at a lesser rate. Just how equitably this mechanism had spread the cost of the war might surely be debated, but currency finance had carried the Revolution through long and difficult years. In 1781, Thomas Paine reflected that, once the money had passed out of circulation, many still thought of it as having accomplished a vital part. "Common consent has consigned it to rest with that kind of regard, which the long service of inanimate things insensibly obtains from mankind." The meaning of the money, as its value, thus rested on the highest Patriot authority, "common consent."[6]

By contrast, the new dispensation relied on the consent of the few and uncommon. Morris and his allies set about creating a money that would secure the confidence of those interests. One plan was to replace Continental bills with currency from the Bank of North America, a private body incorporated by Congress in 1781. The bank would hold government funds, borrow capital from men throughout the nation, and emit bills that would become—so Morris hoped—the national currency. Unlike the paper money of the currency-finance years, the bank's notes would depend on an inner coterie of bank directors. (The bank president was Morris's longtime business partner, Thomas Willing.) The bank would lend its money to those men who "could render it most productive." It thus espoused a clear social aim: it would not primarily aid the many small farmers trying to establish their children in a competence as popular land banks had done, but serve those enterprising men— especially merchants—who used capital to accumulate capital. The bank also served Morris's political vision: henceforth money would be private rather than public. The Bank of North America could ignore popular political pressures that sometimes convinced legislatures to issue paper bills and make them legal tender in payment of debts. Insulated from popular politics, it would pursue sound policies unaccountable to the majority. Its ties would be with a different class of men, and it would promote policies that the enlightened and informed minority saw as best for the national interest. No more would bills be tied to political allegiance: accepting or refusing them was purely a matter of business rather than a result and a sign of affiliation.[7] In a sense, the bank removed money from the Revolution and removed Revolutionary implications from money in turn.

As it happened, too few of the wealthy decided to entrust their funds to Morris's bank. There was another alternative, however, and it became more attractive as the war wound down. The victory at Yorktown in 1781 eased Congress's need for immediate revenues from the wealthy, but it undercut Morris's hopes for building up the power of Congress. Without pressing military danger, the states were unlikely to yield greater authority to the central government. Morris decided to bolster congressional authority by taking responsibility for remaining debt from the war. For if Congress could be made responsible for discharging the debt, it could lay claim to the authority and the power to accomplish that end.

Briefly put, by the early 1780s, much of the "debt" consisted of loan office certificates, the interest-bearing notes issued originally as investment securities, rather than to fill needs for a circulating currency. Congress had never realized enough revenue from them, even after raising the interest rate from 4 to 6 percent. In practice, many loan certificates had been issued not to lenders of capital but to suppliers, farmers, and others whose goods were impressed by the army. Government agents had given out loan office certificates in order to convince dealers to part with necessary goods; as a result, there were far more certificates in circulation than capital available to the government that issued them. Moreover, where state and Continental bills had reached the small farmer who produced only a modest amount for the market, the loan office certificates, issued only in large denominations, generally went to large suppliers. When Morris took the helm of financial planning, the majority of certificates were concentrated in the hands of a limited number of commercial men in the states north of Maryland.[8]

For advocates of a stronger central government, the situation offered an opportunity: by giving the certificates value, Congress could gain the support of these men. As the need for revenue waned, Morris and his allies set out to forge a new alliance with the moneyed by declaring the government in debt to them. The "grand money connection" would be in this respect fictive: even where the moneyed had been unwilling to lend, they could still be won over by a government that recognized an obligation to them. What mattered was not whether they had ever provided a service to the Congress or the common cause that deserved recompense at the face value of the certificate, but whether a debt to them could be constructed. As the British national debt had bolstered that empire's growth and power, so an American debt might bolster America's central government. The strategy recognized the truth of Cotton Mather's warning to the people of Massachusetts many years before: debt made a man a servant to his creditor. By this logic, the Congress would become servant to the holders of the debt.[9] That was precisely why many Americans objected to the policy; yet Morris and many others noted that a Congress that served the moneyed classes might thereby prove itself invaluable, necessary, and worthy of support. Holders of certificates would perforce promote initiatives to increase Congress's powers. The policy of amassing and redeeming the debt would create a powerful interest group out of government creditors. It would serve their interest to press for a competent and authoritative central government.

Indeed, government creditors formed a "numerous, meritorious and oppressed body of men," according to Morris. He urged them to mobilize as a vocal interest group.[10] Merchants and their allies should organize, form associations, and lobby both the Congress and state legislatures to provide Continental authorities with the power to pay interest on the debt. Such payments would require that Congress control "regular and certain" revenues, and such regularity and certainty required the power to tax. At the same time, certificates not yet concentrated in the hands of commercial interests could be gathered there. Morris and his associates shared the information that Congress was likely to honor these certificates at full face value, so investors quickly bought them up at their depreciated rate. What remained was to establish surely the certificates' status as debt. Morris wanted the government to pay both interest and principal, all calculated on the face value of certificates often bought for a mere fraction of that amount. Only such an action would establish the public credit, he argued—meaning the capacity of the Congress to borrow from the wealthy classes. Morris's colleague, Benjamin Rush, urged fellow congressmen to convince the wealthy that Congress had turned over a new leaf: "Let the Congress only make it the interest of individuals to trust them, by providing funds for redemption of the principle and the payment of the interest of their debts, and they will immediately forget all their broken promises. It will be to their interest to trust them, and interest governs the world." Rehabilitatation of self-interest was a necessary step toward establishing government authority and social stability. "I do not speak of interest here as a sordid passion. Interest, rightly understood, is duty; duty, when practised, is virtue; and virtue is happiness."[11] Yet this was a different virtue than that imagined by the republican political theorists so influential in the years of resistance, and it implied substantially different notions of liberty and obligation. It meant the end of the Patriot economy.

It was evident to the men who proposed these changes that their programs were not going to be popular and would not look to most Americans like Patriotism. They turned to the public press to plead the legitimacy of their views and combat received ideas. Rush, writing as "Leonidas" in the *Pennsylvania Gazette* in 1782, sought to revise common perceptions of recent history. Many Americans believed that the years 1776 and 1777 had marked the high point of Patriotic virtue, he admitted, and that the spirit of self-sacrifice and mutual affection had steadily declined through the trials of the war years. Yet if there had been "more of passion in our patriotism" in '76, Leonidas contended, "there is more of principle in it now." Early Patriots had fallen by the wayside, he charged: "Who led many of us to the places for drilling?—and who were the foremost in tarring and feathering a tory, or burning a king's tender?—who talked loudest at town meetings?" Rush claimed that many such men were now taking refuge with the enemy in New York or Halifax, or even fighting in Loyalist regiments. It was an extreme and even absurd argument; presumably some early Patriots had shifted sides, but it was hardly true that "all" such men now stood "among the most bitter enemies of the United

States." More plausibly, Rush argued that times had changed and that early Patriot leaders had failed in some respects. The first and second Continental Congresses "knew nothing of the arts that were necessary to preserve liberty alive amidst the anxiety and tumults of a most difficult and complicated war." Their paper money policies had proved untenable over the longer run and, according to Rush, had actually harmed the nation. "I believe most of the evils in government, with which we are now contending, have been bequeathed to us by the disaffection of some of them, by the timidity of others, and by the ignorance of them all."[12]

Rush may have convinced some readers, but his article spoke to a broad popular sense that congressmen of the early '80s were not the equals of earlier leaders, and that the new appeals to self-interest did not amount to earlier forms of Patriotism. That some were openly revising earlier ideals became glaringly apparent when they supported the return of undeniable Tories to American societies. The prospect of Tory return dramatically divided Patriots with different visions of the social, economic, and political relations they hoped to establish through their Revolution.

Disputes had appeared as early as 1778 in parts of New England. As the front of warfare shifted south in 1780, most Northern states faced would-be returnees. With the victory at Yorktown in 1781, controversy raged everywhere over the ultimate disposition of abandoned estates and confiscated property and the status of men who had been disaffected from the Patriot side. Even the Treaty of Paris, securing the peace in 1783, did not settle the matter. The treaty assured creditors in England and America against any "lawful impediment" to recovering their prewar debts at "the full value in sterling money." It called on Congress to "earnestly recommend" to state legislatures that they "provide for the restitution of all estates, rights, and properties which have been confiscated belonging to real British subjects," and to repeal confiscation laws adopted during the war. Although it said nothing specifically about rights of inhabitancy, it provided for Loyalists who had fled America to return for up to a year's time, during which they would be "unmolested in their endeavors to obtain the restitution of such of their estates, rights, and properties as may have been confiscated."[13] When Congress ratified the treaty in January 1784, it committed itself to those obligations.

Yet there remained questions of jurisdiction. Congress could recommend to the states; the states could pass laws accordingly, and some of them did. But could the states execute these laws permitting Tory return if the voice of the people opposed them? The issue was unavoidably local in its impact and its resolution. Revolutionary crowds and committees had assumed the premise that ordinary men in the localities of the continent had a voice in adjudicating the terms of neighborhood life and policing its boundaries. Having defended that premise over and against the English Parliament and colonial authorities, Americans were unlikely to abandon it now.[14]

Tory return also violated some Patriots' standards of economic fairness. The restoration of confiscated property, apparently equitable to the commissioners in Paris, looked rather different when viewed from the closer perspective of many localities. To begin with, many Tories had abandoned their estates, refusing to fight to defend their property alongside their Patriot neighbors. Those neighbors had shed their blood and won the war. Should Tories now merely resume ownership? Besides, Patriots had supplied the army, accepted depreciating paper bills, and sacrificed portions of their own property in order to support the war effort. In that context, confiscation of Loyalist property had seemed only fair. The army might impress *Patriot* property, after all. Should Patriots who watched their own property taken have carefully preserved the acres, livestock, and stores of men who promoted a British victory? Use and sales of Tory estates had provided the states with a means of supporting the war. Were Tories now to enjoy their prewar holdings intact, even at the cost of Patriot taxpayers?

Finally, political power as well as economic principle was at stake. Many Tories who recovered their property and resettled in their old localities would presumably qualify to vote. Few doubted that they would throw their numbers and their influence behind the conservative forces seeking to moderate state governments, strengthen the central government, and limit popular control. Progress toward a broader suffrage since 1776 now might be offset—or even undone—by including returnees into the voting population. Conservative Patriots who would welcome returning Tories as members of a new alliance found it easy to counsel their countrymen to Christian charity. By contrast, popular forces who might forgive the Tories' transgressions still refused to forget what Patriotism had originally meant to them.[15] Admitting Tories into the community would undermine the social visions embodied in the resistance since the 1760s.

That fact was particularly poignant in Pennsylvania, where popular antipathy to great concentrations of wealth had led some Patriots to promote an "agrarian" provision to the Constitution of 1776, limiting the amount of land a single owner might accumulate. Now Pennsylvanians faced the possible return of their largest landlord, the colonial proprietor.

In 1779, Pennsylvania's state legislature had divested the Penn family of their unsettled landholdings—roughly 24 million acres—and abolished collection of quitrents on settled lands. The peace settlement provided that the family keep their substantial personal estates and granted a modest payment of £130,000 sterling as compensation for their other losses. Yet there was no guarantee that this was to be the final settlement, that quitrents would not be restored, or that households that acquired some of the public lands could rest secure in their possession.[16] In the early 1780s, rumors circulated that the proprietor might negotiate a return to the province. The Penn family actively sought greater compensation, and organized opponents of the popular state constitution of 1776 hoped to welcome numerous other returnees as reinforcements to their project of revising the frame of government.

To combat that prospect, Pennsylvanians mobilized the popular presence. Philadelphians gathered in mass meeting at the statehouse again in 1783, resolving to prevent Tories from returning and to confront town residents who harbored "despised traitors." The meeting appointed a committee to convene hearings and order the inimical to leave the city. Countryside towns in Bucks and Philadelphia counties sent representatives to their own conventions and echoed Philadelphia's resolution against all exile Tory return. Militia battalions in three other counties met, renewed their commitment to one another, and agreed that the gains of the Revolution were by no means secure. As Bucks County saw it, they still faced "a powerful, unbroke political combination" that opposed popular power. Men who had tried to prevent independence to begin with might now return to roll back changes that had made the state government responsive to majority views. Having lost the war, the Tories might yet win the peace. That possibility mobilized widespread debate and broad participation in state elections in 1783. Pennsylvania voters rallied to choose representatives pledged to oppose Tory return.[17]

Elsewhere, too, Americans worried that peace might bring a flood of returning exiles, each to take up property, sue for debts, and reclaim positions of political influence. People accordingly mobilized to block Tory return, acting through their representatives or, when unsuccessful, through the popular presence. Connecticut's legislature encountered widespread local refusal to execute its policies on the subject. Leaving in place confiscation laws, the government repealed statutes that had outlawed infiltration of the population by Tories in the late 1770s. The town of Stratford worried that "whole shoals" of Tories who had spent the war in occupied

New York might now flock to Connecticut. Other towns—Fairfield, Middletown, Norwich, and Stamford among them—elected new committees of inspection to prevent the return of "that class of gentry." Richard Smith, a merchant barred from returning to his home province of Massachusetts, secured permission from the Connecticut legislature to settle in New London. Patriotic citizens mustered to prevent Smith from bringing his stores of goods into Connecticut; besides being objectionable in himself, Smith would profit from sales while Patriot merchants, who had waited for peace to send orders to Britain, stood idle. In nearby Chester, Connecticut, inhabitants voted that they would treat Smith as an enemy and patronize only Patriot retailers. People revived the political forms that had secured Patriot networks since the outset of resistance. Danbury, for example, rode one Tory out on a rail. Nor did it deter popular action when Congress ratified the Treaty of Paris in January 1784. Windham appointed a committee of inspection to root out Tories as late as 1785.[18]

Massachusetts society also divided over the prospect of Tory return. In 1783, the General Court responded to popular sentiment by passing "an Act to prevent the return to this state of certain persons therein named." Among others, it banished nearly three-quarters of the mercantile community of prewar Boston. In the commercial east, some mercantile interests hoped returnees might bolster their influence in local and provincial affairs. Yet artisans supported exclusion, and sentiment against Tories was strong in other parts of the state. Many towns instructed against allowing returns or restitution of confiscated property through the mid-1780s, and newspaper articles opposing Tory return outnumbered publications espousing the other side.[19] South Carolina saw extensive popular mobilization as well. Once peace arrived, British merchants who had sat out the war in Charleston as neutrals now hoped to resume trade. They received some support from planters looking for agents to market their crop. Yet mechanics protested that these supposedly "neutral" dealers had depreciated the Patriot currency and refused to sell their wares for the produce that poor country people brought to exchange. A general meeting in 1783 asked the governor to investigate enemies remaining in the state, while crowds forced the notorious out of town and paraded effigies of returning Tories. The next year, a group of mechanics and merchants in the city created the Marine Anti-Britannic Society to coordinate the movement. One anonymous group posted thirteen names in public places and demanded that the named Tories leave the state within ten days' time. This, despite the fact that twelve on the list had been "lately restored by their country to their property, and rights of their citizenship," while the remaining individual was a British subject, "received here for the 12 months to settle his affairs, as per treaty." Governor Benjamin Guerard accused the anonymous opposition of "annihilating and usurping the legislative, executive and judicial powers" of the state by publishing "a most scandalous, imperious, tyrannical, seditious and treasonable notification and mandate." As in other states, crowds and committees were pitted in immediate opposition to policies established by the people's representatives in state government.[20]

Occupied until the very end of the war, New York experienced acute conflict. The state had banished nearly sixty Tories in 1779, allowing for confiscation of their estates. Many others remained in possession of their properties behind British lines. Should these Loyalists now vote in elections, while many of their less well-to-do Patriot neighbors could not? A 1784 law provided that inspectors of elections should allow the vote of a man who had cooperated with the enemy only if he had acted from "fear or compulsions" rather than advocacy of the British cause, but that was not always an easy or popular judgment. Many writers in New York painted a picture of renewed mobilization and bitter conflict between Patriot governments and Patriot committees in the counties and towns. In Dutchess County, said one observer, "the Country in general is under the Domination of Committees, and there can be no Confidence even in the new created Government, which the Committees despise." Even the governor of the state could not assure returnees of their rights. "Mr. Clinton indeed talks favorably to those who are oppressed and against the usurped Power of Committeemen, but they find no Relief."[21] After all, the people could withhold consent to policies even after state authorities had adopted them. As had happened in the years of resistance, then, conflict appeared between representatives elected by the people and the people themselves in crowds and committees. Some people apparently even spoke of local committees as the true representatives of the people. "The Language of the Committees is that none shall rule but the Majority of the People, and that the committees represent the Majority; that the Acts and Agreements of the Congress, the Legislatures, Governors and Rulers are all to be subject to the will of the People expressed by the Committees, as the Representatives of the Majority of the People." Such logic threatened the rule of the states and the authority of Congress. "The Congress and Assemblies look on tamely and want either the Will or the Power to check these Proceedings. In short, the Mob now reigns as fully and uncontrolled as in the Beginning of our Troubles and America is as hostile to great Britain at this Hour as she was at any Period during the War."[22]

Here were two opposing views: on the one hand, why shouldn't public policy be determined closer to the ground and by the public "out of doors"? Crowds, popular meetings, instructions to representatives, petitions and resolutions—all had been part of a familiar political system in the colonial era. Those accustomed to being "the people" and "the town" saw no reason to doubt their capacity to act in such terms now. In "things of their knowledge," the people's voice was "as the voice of God." The inhabitants of a given county, town, or neighborhood might surely claim knowledge of the recent history and fair outcome of local relationships and transactions. Yet such a situation did not much approximate the institution known as government. Without government, "the greatest blessing of mankind," what power could protect the people in their liberties and their property? Advocates of government power hoped to mediate the popular voice, ensuring a measure of consent to the people but containing their capacity to challenge and change the law by resort to crowds, committees, and conventions.

Local and particular settlements, not all of them equitable, not all of them uniform, resolved many disputes over Tory return by the later 1780s. People integrated into their old communities or abandoned the attempt, recovered some portion of their property or petitioned the Crown for recompense instead. Tory conflict made clear how intractable the differences dividing Americans were. Bitter divisions continued as the issues of taxes, debt payment, and hard money policy moved to center stage. Conflicts over these issues might plausibly ease when times were less difficult, trade less depressed, prices for farm goods more robust; yet unlike Tory return, economic policy would surely be a recurrent bone of contention.

There was sharp conflict over the role of common knowledge in the laws that settled claims of debt. Petitioning their legislature for an emission of paper money in 1786, Albemarle, Virginia, planters insisted on the authority of common memory regarding the terms of debts in the past. They began by endorsing creditors' claims. "We Consider it just and right, that old british debts should be paid that was contracted before the War." Yet they insisted on making repayment at something approximating the *value* those obligations had represented when incurred. "We remember that when those debts was contracted, that there was a paper Currency among us that they [i.e., creditors] generally was willing to recover, therefore we wish to pay them off in paper money, and then they will be willing to allow us a reasonable price for our Tobacco Etc."[23] In this logic, debt was not a number printed on the face of a bill, but a real, historically knowable transaction. Planters did not want to discharge debts incurred in one monetary regime in a very different one; under changed circumstances, a debt's nominal value did not fairly reflect past transactions. So, they reasoned, a man who borrowed cash to purchase fifty acres of land should not owe two hundred acres' worth to the lender a few years later, simply by virtue of changes in money. Albemarle planters stubbornly refused to remove economic value from the context of its actual, known history, presuming instead that such history provided a guide to men's original understandings and that such understandings were constitutive of value. Whether considering Tory return or the substance of a debt, they insisted that a specific, commonly known past was pertinent to determining justice.[24]

Many people throughout the states insisted that ordinary men's collective and common sense produced the standards of worth that should prevail in their society. A popular sense of fairness—not the mere market—had jurisdiction over value. Listen to the logic of the writer of "On Public Faith," in 1787: any creditor who had sold his public notes below face value had transferred to the buyer only a portion of the value of the note. He effectively remitted to the government "such a part of his original right" as exceeded the price he received for it now. The buyer, paying the agreed-upon price, thereby accepted that the note held precisely that value. For the buyer now to ask that government regard the face value of the bill was "cruelly injurious." In fact, "the purchaser is to be considered an extortioner, as much as a man who takes advantage of his neighbour's necessity, to exact excessive usury for the loan of money." Such purchasers should certainly not combine together with other holders of certificates to secure congressional intervention. It was the judgment of the public that gave public securities value; when securities "generally pass, among the citizens of a commonwealth, under par, their sense is declared, and their consent given in the plainest manner, for the redemption at the same rate." The people having spoken by general agreement as to price, governments "have not even a <u>right</u>"—let alone an obligation—to redeem them at "the original value." Such an act by government would "contradict this sense of the people and the principles of justice." From this view, to pay off loan office certificates at face value was to violate common consent.[25]

Beyond that, of course, paying the debt would take revenues, and revenues would doubtless come from taxes on the small and middling people.

Critics of the policy of paying interest and principal of the debt at face value pointed out that many holders of the certificates had acquired them at a steep discount from the original holders, who had indeed performed a service to the union. There was "no reason why the yeomanry, who are the life of the country, because they have not leisure or ability to speculate in funds, should be taxed to the last shilling, only to increase the already superior fortunes of a few in the trading towns; no reason why the poor soldier, whom necessity has constrained to sell a whole year's public service for twelve dollars, should be taxed to make that sum rise to eighty dollars in the hands of the purchaser."[26]

To commercial men, that sort of thinking indicated that too many of their countrymen had no "just sense of the sacredness of public Credit." Public credit required securing for recent bond purchasers precisely the returns for which they had not paid. By contrast, it seemed more reasonable to the bulk of the people to connect payment to some palpable social and economic contribution. At the end of the 1780s, conservatives lamented that they could not dislodge that way of thinking. "We have still an Idea meeting us in Conversation and publication that a Discrimination must be made between original Creditors and speculators as they call them."[27] It was the popular insistence on making distinctions that frustrated many conservatives. People stubbornly held to their experience: just as some men had been Loyalists, some men had merely purchased government debt on speculative grounds. A discrimination must be made. Nothing so powerfully blocked efforts of nationalist leaders to create public credit, ally with moneyed men, and strengthen the hands of government as this popular insistence on the actual, known history of transactions, contributions, and relationships. That insistence expressed a deeply grounded conviction that "the people" of a vicinage might claim ultimate jurisdiction over disputes regarding debt. It expressed the fundamental commitment of many ordinary Patriots to the principles of the Revolution: there must remain a space for the people as a collectivity to consent to taxation and to the operations of the law. Moreover, when Albemarle planters petitioned for paper money, they reiterated the social ideal that they thought should guide state government policies. With new paper emissions some depreciation would occur, the planters admitted, and that would be to the detriment of large creditors. Yet, "it is better for a few to suffer little than a majority of the State to become Servants to the rest, and [as?] it appears to your petitioners likely to be the case."[28]

Together with Tory returns, the efforts of leading men to enact hard money policies convinced many that the Revolution they had begun years earlier was not yet won. Conservative policies reinforced their conviction that the vigilance and participation of ordinary men, acting as "the people," were necessary if America was to defend its rights and liberties.[29] It made little difference that the oppressor was not now Parliament or George III, but the "internal" enemies or returning Tories who had supported English authority and opposed independence. Joined with the moneyed, the aristocratic, and the timid Whigs, the Tories formed "a powerful unbroke combination." These interests were still intent on muting the popular voice. The oppression that loomed in the 1780s was thus, as oppression had always been, an economic, social, and political specter. A minister in New Hampshire pointed to the connection that every freeman of modest means knew full well: "When persons are so poor as to become dependent, their freedom of voting at elections is gone."[30] Policies that impoverished the middling sort removed their claims of consenting to government "before-hand." Men who promoted restoring "the Public Faith" by laying extraordinary, hard money taxes on small farmers, planters, and artisans were willing, perhaps even happy, to reduce many taxpayers to political ciphers. One Massachusetts town worried that the property requirements for voting in the state constitution of 1780 laid the groundwork for future tyranny. Every adult man should vote, thought Dorchester's town meeting, for the number who did not possess a £3 freehold or a £60 estate was "daily increasing." Soon the number "possibly may increase in such proportion, that one half the People of this Commonwealth will have no Choice in any Branch of the General Court."[31] As economic depression and tight money worsened, men watched their neighbors lose their land and their political status as voters. In the desperate straits of 1785–86, a New Jersey writer expressed the common fear: "We may awake in fetters, more grievous, than the yoke we have shaken off."[32]

Everywhere, in fact, the press of new taxes laid to pay principal on the debt caused distress. In petitions, instructions, and publications, farm communities objected.

The common response was to call for new paper money emissions that would, as they had in the past, allow debtors to pay at a rate they could tolerate, without losing so much of their productive resources, land, tools, or livestock as to reduce them to the status of laborers for others. Voters petitioned their governments, asking that they be permitted to pay taxes in commodities rather than specie. Where agrarian interests were numerous and strong enough, they secured relief through their representative governments. Voters won paper emissions and tender laws in New Jersey, for example. Agrarian interests also organized in Rhode Island, where they pressed to lower the property requirement for voting, reapportion taxes, and moderate hard money policies. When unable to influence the passage of laws, people took charge of their execution. Men rescued cattle taken for nonpayment of taxes; farmers refused to bid on their neighbors' seized property. Voters in Washington County sent delegates to a convention to oppose hard money taxes in 1784. Promptly on winning the legislature, agrarian interests adopted paper money again. Debtors would pay taxes with the currency, and the state, in turn, would use the bills to satisfy the principal and interest on its wartime debt. This issue animated campaigns for state office; spring elections in 1786 swept agrarian interests into power in Rhode Island.[33] In other states as well, massive taxes laid to pay public creditors fastened voters' attention on legislative choices. They made clear that representation in the legislature mattered, that the right to vote was consequential. Where legislatures did not ease the situation of the rural poor, the late 1780s saw spreading disturbances. A South Carolina judge told a grand jury that it was necessary to execute the law. "No society ever long endured the miseries of anarchy, disorder, and licentiousness," he said. "The period is not far distant, when the laws of the state must be voluntarily obeyed, or executed by force."[34]

Conflict in Massachusetts dramatized in the most graphic terms the decline of the coalition that had once joined together to pursue independence. The state struggled to reconcile the outlook and interests of a powerful, eastern mercantile group with the views and interests of small and middling farmers in western counties. Many of those farmers only grudgingly recognized the authoritative claims of the General Court through the late 1770s. They had insisted on a statewide convention to formulate a proper frame of government, and they remained skeptical about the constitution supposedly ratified by the voters in 1780. Eastern and commercial interests dominated the court, and their policies fed farmers' skepticism in the 1780s. Western towns used elections, petitions, conventions, and court closings to voice their grievances with the hard money policies those interests adopted.[35] "The Scarcity of Money is beyond your Conception," wrote one observer who described the severity of depression in the west. "Trade is stagnated, Lands will not sell. . . . Bankruptcies, and unexpected ones too, are Common. No Man can pay his Debts, and if the Moderation or good Policy of the Creditors does not prevent, Anarchy may be the Consequence."[36] Yet the state government resisted all pressure to allow tax payment in kind or to emit paper money and make it legal tender. Mobs arose against collectors and the sheriffs who distrained property for tax payments.[37] Early in 1786, the General Court laid a high direct tax, payable only in hard money, on the commonwealth.[38] Farmers in Berkshire and Hampshire counties responded by closing the courts of common pleas, where both debts existing and debts sure to follow from the new tax would be prosecuted. Conflict escalated as some took up arms. In January, a group of men sought to seize the federal armory in the town of Springfield. Historians debate many aspects of the conflict; they do not resolve—any more than contemporaries could do—the opposition between two incompatible views of money, government, and revolution.[39]

In response to the crisis, Boston men raised funds to finance the mustering of eastern militia. Major General William Shepard led the march westward to subdue the farmers, and, in Shepard's words, "to rivet in their minds a compleat conviction of the force of government and the necessity of an entire submission to the laws."[40] *An entire submission to the laws?* It was not a phrase that a good Patriot would have used twenty years earlier. It tells us that we have reached a critical moment, when gradual and cumulative changes in the Revolution suddenly became a transformation.

To grasp that transformation, we look to the reaction of one Masschusetts man, Samuel Adams.[41] His views powerfully illuminate for us the changes overtaking the Revolution. No one had been more closely tied to popular politics among Patriot leaders in the years before independence. Adams had championed the people's right to gather in the streets, inquire into the doings of their governors, and assume discretion and agency in the execution of the law. He had encouraged colonists to establish committees and gather in conventions to consult on public affairs. He promoted the right of the public to see and oversee the policies enacted by their representatives in the legislature. Unlike some other Patriots, Adams had fervently embraced a vision of a virtuous and interdependent society. In 1778, he was shocked that the Massachusetts House even considered allowing Tory return. "Shall these Traitors who first conspired the Ruin of our Liberties; Those who basely forsook their country in her Distress and sought Protection from the Enemy when they thought them in the Plentitude of Power . . . Shall these Wretches have their Estates reservd for them at the conclusion of this glorious struggle in which some of the richest Blood of America has been spilled?"[42] There was nothing lukewarm about *that* Patriotic feeling. Not surprisingly, Adams had limited sympathy for the policies of Robert Morris. He withheld his ballot when the rest of the Continental Congress voted to make Morris financier in 1781.[43]

Despite all that, however, in 1787 Adams powerfully denounced the actions of Massachusetts farmers in the western counties. He called what they did "treason," and expressed the hope that the governor would press for courts of law to punish leaders of the rebellion in no uncertain terms.[44]

We may attribute his views in part to parochialism: Adams was a man of the commercial east, hence with a limited idea of the sufferings of western farm communities. Yet there was more to it than that. Well before the "insurrection" of 1787, Adams had criticized the western counties for organizing in opposition to taxes and other policies. In 1784 he wrote:

> County Conventions and popular committees served an excellent purpose when they were first in practice. No one therefore needs to regret the share he may then have had in them. But . . . that as we now have constitutional and regular governments and all our men in authority depend upon the annual, free elections of the people, we are safe without them. To say the least, they are become useless.[45]

There were two key ideas here that shaped a new way of looking at the participation of the people. First, since 1780, Massachusetts boasted a "constitutional and regular" government. The frame of government had not descended from a distant past but emerged from a popular convention that embodied, so Adams believed, the will of the people. In ratifying that constitution, Massachusetts inhabitants had accepted constraints. This constitutionalism placed elements of consent in the past; in 1780, the logic went, the people had consented to consent in certain ways, most especially through the vote. They had created and accepted an altered situation.[46]

Through this process, moreover, conventions of the people had evolved into a form recognized as more basic than the existing government. People had gathered in conventions not merely to organize, petition, or protest; they had met in conventions to create, alter, and overrule the government itself. Conventions had rapidly evolved from lesser, local, and partial gatherings to meetings located "above the whole legislature." Given that very recent history, a resort to conventions now raised constitutional issues.[47] Groups that convened to petition, remonstrate, or otherwise address their governors might appear as a constitutional challenge to the very legitimacy of the state. Such a view left unanswered a good many questions about the nature and legitimacy of political assembly or popular organization. In the nineteenth century, Americans would feel less threatened when people or their delegates might "assemble in a body like a court or congress,"[48] as such assemblies came to seem simple gatherings of individuals rather than acts of a collective "people." Yet in the crisis of the 1780s, in the immediate wake of the Revolution, conventions seemed to some a dangerous step outside the bounds of normal and acceptable politics.[49]

Samuel Adams's second point put the focus on voting as the primary form of participation: "All our men in authority depend upon the annual, free elections of the people," he had said. *All* our men in authority—not just members of the House, but governors and lieutenant governors, senators, and those whom they appointed. Adams thus heralded and described a significantly new situation. No branch of the state government was now grounded in claims of monarchy or hereditary aristocracy. The executive as well as legislative took its authority from the people and its office from the electorate. For Adams, this new basis for government provided significantly different parameters for popular action. In toppling the monarchy, in other words, Americans had set a new logic in motion. To a substantial degree, they had traded in the popular presence and chosen unprecedented, more thoroughgoing representation.

Indeed, from the moment of declaring independence, Americans had realized that elections had taken on new importance. A New Jersey man wrote in 1776: "Elections are now of greater Importance, if possible, than heretofore," since "the Source of all Government originates with the People at large."[50] Indeed, Adams suggested, representative governments effectively made elections the central public moment.

> If the public affairs are illy conducted, if dishonest or incapable men have crept unawares into government, it is happy for us, that under our American constitutions the remedy is at hand, and in the power of the great body of the people. Due circumspection and wisdom at the next elections will set all right, without the need of any self-created conventions or societies of men whatever.[51]

Political action might wait until election day. Others proposed similar views: the people were sovereign; they set up constitutions; now they should follow the law. They should participate, we might say, as citizens rather than subjects. Their primary role became more distinctly episodic.

One writer explained it: no doubt it was true that "the sovereignty and all other power . . . is derived *from* the people." But no one should mistake that for the idea that the people might continue to wield power. "They possess it only on the days of their elections. After this, it is the property of their rulers, nor can they exercise or resume it, unless it is abused."[52] What was new in this formulation was not the idea that ordinary men should act as voters, but rather that that identity should encompass the bulk if not the whole of their political identity. Voting appeared here as the sole moment of popular power. Here is Adams in the mid-1790s, responding to Pennsylvania farmers' measures to block the whiskey excise: "What excuse can there be for forcible opposition to the laws," when "if any law shall prove oppressive in its operation, the future deliberations of a freely elected representation will afford a constitutional remedy?"[53] In this new system, constitutional government required that people speak via elections. The vote was sufficient to the freedom of the people.[54]

As Samuel Adams saw it, the Revolution had been a world-changing event. American states were not the colonies sans the king; rather, they were something entirely new. With no king, and with a different sort of government, there must be a different sort of "people." That people must give its consent primarily through the vote. This was reminiscent of the Reverend George Micklejohn, denouncing a different set of regulators in North Carolina some twenty years before, enjoining obedience to the acts of the legislature: "We not only yield our consent before-hand to whatever laws they may judge it expedient to enact, but may justly be said to have had a principle share in enacting them ourselves, inasmuch as they are framed by their wisdom, and established by their authority, whom we have appointed for that very purpose."[55] However arguable this view may have been in 1768, by the 1780s the very basis of American governments had altered. Now this logic extended even to the executive part of the constitution, hence even to execution of the law.

From this view, the regulators in western Massachusetts had mistaken their situation. When they marched on courts of law, they thought they were negotiating with a government still imagined as instituted somehow apart from themselves. By contrast, authorities in Boston saw them as rebelling against the popular will. When "all authority is from the people," then resisting authority was resisting the people themselves.[56]

It is important to emphasize that Samuel Adams did not intend to dismiss the whole of the popular presence. He denounced conventions, not crowds and juries.[57] He continued to prize those latter forms and no doubt expected them to endure. Neither he nor his contemporaries fully followed out the premises of representative government: if the people now fully consented "before-hand," on what grounds could the people act to judge the laws after they were made? That question would take many decades to answer. Well into the nineteenth century, Americans would sometimes use legal and social institutions in terms familiar to their colonial forebears. Yet sweeping changes would follow from the fact that, after the Revolution, governments now acted as "the people." In broad strokes, the changes included:

The Public Punishment of Criminals

As early as 1787, Dr. Benjamin Rush, who had questioned the intervention of popular bodies in regulating prices or disciplining Tories, now raised the question of whether the presence of the people at the punishment of criminals was a good thing.[58] For in such proceedings, a criminal might evoke the "contempt or indignation" of the assembled spectators, or else his "distress" might produce "sympathy, and a disposition to relieve it" among them. Either way, Rush argued, the transaction that took place between these participants did not serve the ends of government. It did not serve the ends of the state, whose laws "cannnot be resisted," for such occasions to engage the moral judgments of the community at all. Indeed, in some respects, Rush believed, it was better for crimes and punishments to remain unknown to the body of the people. The public would be left out of this element in the transaction of justice, and what had been acts of the society might now seem to be acts of the state alone. As such, they might best be moved out of public view. It would take some decades to accomplish Rush's enlightened and humanitarian reforms in punishment. Gradually, "the gallows, the pillory, the stocks, the whipping-post, and the wheel-barrow" would be replaced with the substantially less visible regime of incarceration. This regime would be less accountable but still sufficient to accomplish the purpose of punishment: in Rush's words, to create "terror among the people."

Crowds

Americans continued to gather in crowds and to act forcefully for many decades after the Revolution. Yet scholars who have looked most closely at crowds report a significant change in their nature. Crowds of the "classical" sort became markedly fewer. Such crowds had had a broadly accepted public role. They typically reached their ends while deploying limited violence against persons and even limited damage to property. They had taken place in dialogue and negotiation with elites, who accepted the legitimacy of such practices. In the aftermath of the Revolution, the popular presence seemed more dangerous and anomalous. Social changes would also have a profound impact. Irish and German immigrants swelled the population of American cities, and it became more difficult for popular gatherings to formulate themselves as "the people out of doors." Crowds came to express particular ethnic or class grievances, rather than plausibly speak as "vox populi." Elites became less willing to negotiate with crowds, less likely to recognize them as "the people."[59]

Courtrooms

In courtrooms, jurors no longer unquestionably represented the voice of the people, for now *prosecutors* of criminals spoke in the courtroom, not on behalf of *rex* or *regina*, but on behalf of "the people" of the state or nation.[60] As the prosecution now represented the people, juries must surely play a lesser role. The decades after the Revoluton saw a more rapid "transformation" of American law, replacement of common law with statute, and decline in the discretion by which jurors came to verdicts. Jurors would no longer decide law as well as fact, as judges became the repository of legal authority. We see the impetus mounting toward this transformation even in debates over the U.S. Constitution, when some doubted that the federal system should guarantee jury trials in cases of debt. Practices that had been key to British liberty—for the jury to serve as the voice of the people, and for juries to decide the law as well as fact—no longer seemed entirely necessary.

The status and behavior of jurors changed slowly and unevenly.[61] In the 1830s, the French observer Alexis de Tocqueville described the American jury as an institution of political participation for many citizens. The jury, he said, "preserves its republican character, in that it places the real direction of society in the hands of the governed, or of a portion of the governed, and not in that of the government."[62] Yet others noted that juries that decided law created "mischievous uncertainty" about what the law in various parts of the nation actually *was*. "In all instances where trial by jury has been practiced, and a separation of the law from the fact has taken place, there have been expedition, certainty, system and their consequences, general approbation," according to a Massachusetts lawyer. "Where this has not been the case, neither expedition, certainty, nor system have prevailed."[63] There was a form of freedom that resulted from certainty and system. Over time, growth of that sort of freedom under-mined the role of courtrooms as arenas of collective participation.[64]

Policing

Finally, the people would find more representatives to act for them in the law. In England and America alike, reformers increasingly imagined new, more regular, and more consistent forms by which governments might maintain the peace and regulate the moral order. Just as punishment became removed from the ordinary citizen, so policing would become less a matter of collective vigilance and participation. Urban municipalities in particular gradually came to rely on hired and professional forces of the police. A citi-zenry composed of free individuals would no longer have an obligation to aid constables and sheriffs. Responsibility and authority that had been dif-fused among the king's subjects as a collective whole would now fall to des-ignated public agents instead. With discretion removed from execution of the law, the project became one of mere enforcement, requiring set skills perhaps, but not the common judgment of the people or the town.[65]

Taken together, these changes begin to portray the very different world of nineteenth-century American freedom. The institutions by which a colo-nial people had taken part in execution of the law changed. Precisely how these institutions would evolve was not obvious in the 1780s. The basis of change, however, lay in a realization of that decade: a people that had treasured the capacity to be present in execution of the law might no longer assume that same liberty. When *government* originated in the peo-ple and fully assumed that mantle, there was less space for *people* to act as "the people." Representation became the heart of political life and the focus of political contest.[66] The people would be present less often, rep-resented far more. Their ideals and their views would be filtered and mediated. Vox populi would be replaced by *public opinion*, formulated at the polls and in the press.[67] Whether they liked it or not, whether they had intended it or not, Americans were differently free.

What are we to make of such change?

From one perspective, there is evidence that Samuel Adams had been right in 1787. The vote *could be* sufficient to farmers in western Massas-chusetts. They could elect a legislature and an executive that supported their views. They proved it in the state elections of 1787, when the harsh response by authorities to the Regulation met with strong rebuke from the voters. The electorate turned out Governor James Bowdoin and Lt. Governor Adams, and the new General Court quickly enacted laws to ease the grievances of farmers. Not every state had annual elections or equitable apportionment of representatives, and not every farmer or trades-man qualified for the vote, but where elections were frequent and where representation was proportional, voting for one's governors could indeed make ordinary men's ideas of fairness felt in the making of laws. Why should they think of themselves as subjects, who were ruled, when they were citizens, who chose their rulers?[68]

From a second perspective, however, Adams was wrong. That same year delegates from twelve states gathered in Philadelphia to form a new federal constitution. The new frame of government would be representa-tive, with a lower house elected by voters qualified in each of the states; yet it would not be so representative as to easily accommodate or reflect ordinary men's interests and ideals. One of its framers, James Madison, assured readers of the *Federalist* that the large districts established for the new federal government would prevent all but the wealthy and well-known from gaining election. "When we call on thirty or forty thousand inhabitants to unite in giving their votes for one man, it will be uniformly impracticable for them to unite in any men, except those who have be-came [sic] eminent for their civil or military rank, or their popular legal abilities." As a result, there would not be many middling men even in the lower house of the federal legislature.[69] Equally important, the Constitu-tion moved various decision-making powers from the states. It reserved the authority to emit money and establish legal tender laws to the federal government. In these and other respects, the Constitution limited the effects of the democratic and participatory politics that had emerged through the course of Revolution. Once the Constitution was ratified, the desires of popular majorities would not easily determine government policy. (We might say that Massachusetts farmers' capacity to vote was "enough" in 1787, but perhaps it was not by 1789.)[70]

The new guard of leaders in Congress and many states would seek to revise the meaning of Patriotism. As a crucial part of the change, they set about making economic life less vulnerable to vox populi. They depoliti-cized money. The new regime would insulate "the economy," constructed by law and policy, from popular ideas of what was good and fair. That project required narrowing what had been conceived as political and so-cial policies to a policy that was merely economic, meant to produce sol-vency or maybe prosperity, but not to provide an eighteenth-century ideal of liberty or embody the popular will. One view of the U.S. Constitution would place it at the outset of a long narrative in political struggle, between movements to expand the suffrage and make voting consequential, on the one hand, efforts to limit participation and make the vote empty, on the other.[71]

Yet it is not my purpose to replace a Revolutionary narrative of unalloyed gain with a narrative of unalloyed loss. I have no wish to argue with the many historians who have charted significant gains in freedom—expansion of the vote, a burst of antislavery thought and activity, new republican ideas that shaped families and society as well as political institutions, new spheres for public debate, and a turn toward individual rights—in the age of the American Revolution. Such gains were profound. When I speak about freedoms lost in the Revolutionary era, I mean specific forms of participation, collective social arrangements, and cultural expectations that many Americans valued and even mobilized around in order to defend. In the simplest sense, there had been space in British North America for consent *after the fact*, collective discretion in the execution of the law. In the aftermath of the Revolution, that space would dramatically contract. I want to stand by the title of this book: whatever else may have happened, whatever else was surely gained, significant forms of freedom were lost.

That said, some modification is in order. For it was not, strictly speaking, *we* who lost those freedoms. Many generations and many changes have come between the Revolutionaries of the late eighteenth century and the readers of this twenty-first-century book. It is critical to emphasize as much, because even today some Americans hark back to Revolutionary committees of safety or inspection, to colonial militias and Sons of Liberty, and to local common law juries that used local knowledge to determine law as well as fact. Some argue that Americans ought to reclaim such eighteenth-century forms today. Perhaps so. Yet I have been at some pains to recover the extraordinarily different social, economic, and cultural framework that gave meaning to those forms. They were not the sort of liberal, individual *rights* to which later Americans would grow accustomed. Americans who executed the law in the Revolutionary era did not act as individuals in mere pursuit of self-interest, assertion of minority rights, or individual freedom from regulation. On the contrary, what made sense of the popular discretion was the capacity of individuals to shed their individual identity and merge into a unified and consensual "body of the people." A gulf separates us from these Americans, whose ties with their king, neighbors, and countrymen sometimes allowed association and interdependence. We presume forms of individuality, dedication to rights, and principles associated with rule of law—all of them the product of the centuries and generations that have intervened.[72] Even were it possible, few Americans today would choose to dispense with much of that heritage. We operate on a different common ground.

Under these circumstances, if we merely reclaim the Patriots' political *forms*, we may still be lacking the *substance* of their liberties. Indeed, in some respects the U.S. Constitution embodied the legacy of 1776 with fidelity. What had been extraordinary in the Revolutionary moment had been twofold: Patriots had declared *independence*, in order to secure governments more representative of and responsive to the needs of the people in their North American societies. They had also declared *interdependence*, both as neighbors and as countrymen. They acknowledged themselves to be connected with one another beyond the boundaries of town, county, neighborhood, province, or even region. Many of them did so in order to defend what space they retained within social and economic transactions for collective consent, assuming an established authority of the public to set terms for individual accumulation and the use of property. Given that, it seems to me mistaken for twenty-first-century Americans to conclude that the Revolutionary heritage amounts to protecting individual freedoms in neighborhoods writ small.

Indeed, it is worth noting that Americans with other political views have also cited the example of the eighteenth-century "people." They also claim the mantle of early America who look to public power to restrain the depredations of the ambitious few, who insist that government might work *for* the people and express the majority's sense of right and wrong. They argue that such government is needed (as the king once was) to restrain those who would oppress the many, to use public institutions, in the eighteenth-century phrase, to *regulate*. In this perspective, what many twenty-first-century Americans have lost is an awareness of the breadth of the Revolutionaries' eighteenth-century project, which asserted public power to counteract the coercions of the market. We have lost the memory of the Patriot economy, with its unsettling implication that some Americans located freedom precisely in a popular capacity to determine the use and value of property within a framework of social purpose and human need.

Whether or not Americans should reclaim the precise forms that made an eighteenth-century Revolution, surely they should care about the substantial liberty that Patriots sought—and that the settlement of the Revolution, in the U.S. Constitutional order, promised to embody and secure. The question of whether the vote is a sufficient form of participation for securing liberty remains a vital one. The answer will depend on the degree to which voting in fact empowers a truly representative government of, by, and for those people. However much twenty-first-century Americans can celebrate the expansion of suffrage, more proportional representation, and other, similar gains, they still face constraints of continued disenfranchisement, suppression, inequality, and the influence of money. Surely these questions will matter as long as there are rulers tempted to disregard the well-being of the people for their own emolument; they will matter as long as men aspire to lordships, those private concentrations of economic power that, in Cato's words, threaten to terrify or master the community.

Notes

Preface

1. On freedom as the exception among immigrants to colonial America, see Aaron S. Fogleman, "From Slaves, Convicts, and Servants to Free Passengers: The Transformation of Immigration in the Era of the American Revolution," *Journal of American History* 85 (1998): 43–76.

2. *Boston Evening Post*, August 6, 1739. The quotation is from "Cato," or Trenchard and Gordon, the English writers. See also Pauline Maier, *From Resistance to Revolution: Colonial Radicals and the Development of Opposition to Britain, 1765–1776* (New York: Random House, 1974), chap. 2. On Cato, see Caroline Robbins, *The Eighteenth-Century Commonwealthman: Studies in the Transmission, Development, and Circumstances of English Liberal Thought from the Restoration of Charles II Until the War with the Thirteen Colonies* (Cambridge, MA: Harvard University Press, 1959). J.A.W. Gunn notes that Trenchard and Gordon expressed more confidence in the people's ability to see through government corruption and deception than many other writers who also worried about these ills. Gunn, *Beyond Liberty and Property: The Process of Self-Recognition in Eighteenth-Century Political Thought* (Kingston and Montreal: McGill-Queen's University Press, 1983), 19.

3. Bartlett Jere Whiting, *Early American Proverbs and Proverbial Phrases* (Cambridge, MA: Harvard University Press, 1977), 78. The quoted form is from the *Pennsylvania Chronicle*, 1768. Whiting notes slight variations in the adage, ranging from Samuel Ward's use of it, in 1647, to General John Sullivan's, in 1775, and beyond. The humble cobbler or shoemaker served as a familiar type in French as well as English commentary about the state. See, for example, Suzanne Rodin Pucci, "The Spectator Surfaces: Tableau and Tabloid in Marivaux's Spectateur Français," *Yale French Studies* 92 (1997): 159.

4. William Moraley, *The Infortunate: The Voyage and Adventures of William Moraley, an Indentured Servant*, ed. Susan E. Klepp and Billy G. Smith (1743; repr., Uni-

versity Park: Pennsylvania State University Press, 1992), 51–52. Moraley specified that he meant the charity with which "hospitable Inhabitants" favored "the Poor and Needy" who were "subjects of *Great Britain*," as well as the presence of good wages for journeymen in many trades. A Virginian applied the phrase "best poor man's country" to his colony as well. Lyon G. Tyler, "Virginian Voting in the Colonial Period," *William and Mary Quarterly* 6 (1897): 8, note 2. Those who used the phrase described the prospects of poor Englishmen, not poor African ones; obviously, its accuracy in describing the situation of poor European immigrants was also open to argument.

1. The Common Ground of Colonial Politics

1. Rev. George Micklejohn, "A Sermon to Governor Tryon and His Troops" (1768), in *Some Eighteenth-Century Tracts Concerning North Carolina*, ed. William K. Boyd (Raleigh, NC: Edwards & Broughton, 1927), 408.

2. On Bostonians' sympathy with North Carolina regulators, see Novanglus, Response to Massachusettensis, *Boston Gazette*, February 20, 1775.

3. Suzanne Rodin Pucci, "The Spectator Surfaces: Tableau and Tabloid in Marivaux's Spectateur Français, *Yale French Studies* 92 (1997): 149–70. Pucci notes an earlier meaning of "public" as an assembly to see or hear a performance, an audience (154).

4. Pemberton quoted in David W. Conroy, *In Public Houses: Drink and the Revolution of Authority in Colonial Massachusetts* (Chapel Hill: University of North Carolina Press, 1995), 65–66.

5. Benjamin Whitaker, "The Chief Justice's Charge to the Grand Jury for the Body of This Province," Records of the Court of Chancery of South Carolina, at a Court of the General Sessions, Charleston, October 1, 1741, 10. Strictly speaking, these were the sentiments of St. Paul's Epistle to the Romans (Rom. 13: 1–2). It is hard to imagine that every colonist outside the ranks of rulers did not get tired of hearing these verses.

6. Edmund S. Morgan, *Inventing the People: The Rise of Popular Sovereignty in England and America* (New York: W.W. Norton, 1988), chap. 1.

7. On Elizabeth, see Grant McCracken, "The Pre-Coronation Passage of Elizabeth I: Political Theatre or the Rehearsal of Politics?" *Canadian Review of Sociology and Anthropology* 21 (1984): 47–61; McCracken, "Politics and Ritual Soto Voce: The Use of Demeanor as an Instrument of Politics in Elizabethan England," *Canadian Journal of Anthropology* 3 (Fall 1982): 85–100; Clifford Geertz, "Centers, Kings, and Charisma: Reflections on the Symbolics of Power," in *Local Knowledge: Further Essays in Interpretive Anthropology* (New York: Basic Books, 1983), 125–29; Roy Strong, *Splendor at Court: Renaissance and the Theatre of Power* (London: Weidenfeld & Nicolson, 1971); Strong, *The Cult of Elizabeth: Elizabethan Portraiture and Pageantry* (London: Thames & Hudson, 1977); David Bergeron, *English Civic Pageantry, 1558–1642* (London: Edward Arnold, 1971); Peter Borsay, "'All the Town's a Stage': Urban Ritual and Ceremony, 1660–1800," in *The Transformation of English Provincial Towns, 1600–1800*, ed. Peter Clark, 228–58 (London: Hutchinson, 1984); David Bergeron, ed., *Pageantry in the Shakespearean Theatre* (Athens: University of Georgia Press, 1985). On spectacle and politics, see also Jean-Christophe Agnew, *Worlds Apart: The Market and the Theatre in Anglo-American Thought, 1550–1750* (New York: Cambridge

University Press, 1986); R.O. Bucholz, "'Nothing but Ceremony': Queen Anne and the Limitations of Royal Ritual," *Journal of British Studies* 30 (1991): 288–323.

8. Bernard Capp, "Popular Literature," in *Popular Culture in Seventeenth-Century England*, ed. Barry Reay (London: Croom Helm, 1985), 227.

9. William A. Whitehead et al., eds., *Documents Relating to the Colonial, Revolutionary, and Post-Revolutionary History of the State of New Jersey*, 42 vols. (Trenton and Newark, NJ: MacCrellish & Quigby, 1880–1949), 20:236–40 (also titled *Archives of New Jersey*). On events at Perth Amboy, Burlington, and Elizabeth, see 226–27, 235, 225–26, 230; *Pennsylvania Journal*, March 3, 1763.

10. Thomas Hutchinson, *The History of the Colony and Province of Massachusetts-Bay*, ed. Lawrence Shaw Mayo, 3 vols. (Cambridge, MA: Harvard University Press, 1936), 3:60. On "pomp and circumstance" and processions to welcome governors, see Leonard Woods Labaree, *Royal Government in America: A Study of the British Colonial System Before 1763* (New Haven, CT: Yale University Press, 1930), 85–91; Richard Bushman, *King and People in Provincial Massachusetts* (Chapel Hill: University of North Carolina Press, 1985), chap 1. Boston celebrated the king's birthday and the anniversary of his coronation every year (to 1773). Bushman notes that in the aftermath of the Knowles riots, "the governor was conducted to his house with as great parade as when he first assumed the government" (45). See also the account of the militia and popular greeting of Governor William Shirley in the *Independent Advertiser*, January 4, 1748; John G. Palfrey, *History of New England to the Revolutionary War*, 5 vols. (Boston: Little, Brown, 1859–1890), 3: 589–90, describes Boston's celebration of William and Mary. The prominence of militias in welcoming governors to South Carolina is recorded in the *South Carolina Gazette*, March 24, 1759, and December 26, 1761.

11. Winthrop quoted in Timothy Breen, *The Character of the Good Ruler: Puritan Political Ideas in New England, 1630–1730* (New Haven, CT: Yale University Press, 1971), 67; Anne Rowe Cunningham, ed., *Letters and Diary of John Rowe, Boston Merchant 1759–1762, 1764–1779* (Boston: W.B. Clarke, 1903), 225, entry for February 19, 1772; Saltonstall quoted in James M. Poteet, "Unrest in the 'Land of Steady Habits': The Hartford Riot of 1722," *Proceedings of the American Philosophical Society* 119 (1975): 227.

12. "Extracts from the Records of York County," *William and Mary Quarterly* 25 (1917): 30.

13. "Kingship organizes everything around a high centre. Its legitimacy derives from divinity, not populations who are, after all, subjects, not citizens." Benedict Anderson, *Imagined Communities: Reflections on the Origin and Spread of Nationalism*, rev. ed. (New York: Verso, 1991), 19.

14. David S. Lovejoy, "Equality and Empire: The New York Charter of Libertyes, 1683," *William and Mary Quarterly*, 3rd ser., 21 (1964): 494–515. Quotation is on p. 496.

15. "The Fundamental Constitutions of Pennsylvania," in *William Penn and the Founding of Pennsylvania, 1680–1684: A Documentary History*, ed. Jean R. Soderlund (Philadelphia: University of Pennsylvania Press, 1983), 99.

16. Soderlund, *William Penn and the Founding of Pennsylvania*, 268–69. Cf. "The First Frame of Government," ibid., 124–26. On William Penn's complicated and changing ideas about representation and popular participation in government, see J.R. Pole, *Political Representation in England and the Origins of the American Revolution*

(New York: St. Martin's Press, 1966), 76–93; Gary B. Nash, "The Framing of the Government in Pennsylvania: Ideas in Conflict with Reality," *William and Mary Quarterly*, 3rd ser., 23 (1966): 183–209; Richard R. Beeman, "Deference, Republicanism, and the Emergence of Popular Politics in Eighteenth-Century America," *William and Mary Quarterly*, 3rd ser., 49 (1992): 401–30.

17. Edward McGrady, *The History of South Carolina under Proprietary Government, 1670–1719* (New York: Macmillan, 1901), 102; John E. Pomfret, *Colonial New Jersey: A History* (New York: Charles Scribner's Sons, 1973), 30–31; Labaree, *Royal Government in America*, 220–22.

18. William Penn to Jasper Blatt, February 5, 1683, quoted in Soderlund, *William Penn and the Founding of Pennsylvania*, 199. See also Nash, "Framing of the Government."

19. Pole, *Political Representation in England*, 86–87. See also Nash, "Framing of the Government," 199. On the expectation of monarchs and proprietors that governors, along with their councils, would be the center of political rule in the colonies, see Jack P. Greene, "The Role of the Lower Houses," in *Negotiated Authorities: Essays in Colonial Political and Constitutional History* (Charlottesville: University Press of Virginia, 1994), 163.

20. J.H. Hexter, "Power Struggle, Parliament, and Liberty in Early Stuart England," *Journal of Modern History* 50 (1978): 1–50. The quotation is on pp. 33–34.

21. John Guillim, *A Display of Heraldry, to Which Is Added, a Treatise of Honour Military and Civil . . . by Capt. John Logan* (London: Printed by T.W., 1724), 266.

22. Norman H. Dawes, "Titles as Symbols of Prestige in Seventeenth-Century New England," *William and Mary Quarterly*, 3rd ser., 6 (1949): 69–83; Arthur M. Schlesinger, "The Aristocrats," in *The Birth of the Nation: A Portrait of the American People on the Eve of Independence* (Boston: Houghton Mifflin, 1968), 128–47; Richard Bushman, "American High-Style and Vernacular Cultures," in *Colonial British North America: Essays in the New History of the Early Modern Era*, ed. Jack P. Greene and J.R. Pole, 345–84 (Baltimore: Johns Hopkins University Press, 1984).

23. Mary Patterson Clarke, *Parliamentary Privilege in the American Colonies* (New Haven, CT: Yale University Press, 1943), 93–97; Jack P. Greene, *The Quest for Power: The Lower Houses of Assembly in the Southern Royal Colonies* (Chapel Hill: University of North Carolina Press, 1963), treats the rise of the assembly. In South Carolina, the right of the appointed upper house, or Council, to introduce and influence money bills remained in sharp dispute through the 1740s and 1750s. M. Eugene Sirmans, *Colonial South Carolina: A Political History, 1663–1763* (Chapel Hill: University of North Carolina Press, 1966), 257–58, 279–80, 303–5, and passim.

24. Pole, *Political Representation in England*, 415.

25. W. Roy Smith, *South Carolina as a Royal Province, 1719–1776* (New York: Macmillan, 1903), 90.

26. Ned C. Landsman, "'Of the Grand Assembly or Parliament': Thomas Rudyard's Critique of an Early Draft of the Frame of Government of Pennsylvania," *Pennsylvania Magazine of History and Biography* 105 (1981): 480. See also "Letter of Thomas Rudyard," in Soderlund, *William Penn and the Founding of Pennsylvania*, 114–16. On Rudyard, see Nash, "Framing of the Government," 195–97.

27. Massachusetts governor Shute, in 1720, is quoted in Breen, *Character of the Good Ruler*, 223; Governor Horatio Sharpe to Lord Baltimore, June 6, 1754, in *Archives of Maryland*, ed. William Hand Browne et al. (Baltimore: Maryland Historical Society), 6:68 (hereafter *Maryland Archives*).

28. Pole, *Political Representation in England*, 33–178; Robert Zemsky, *Merchants, Farmers, and River Gods: An Essay on Eighteenth-Century American Politics* (Boston: Gambit, 1971), 28–38; Jackson Turner Main, *The Social Structure of Revolutionary America* (Princeton, NJ: Princeton University Press, 1965); Main, "Government by the People: The American Revolution and the Democratization of the Legislatures," *William and Mary Quarterly*, 3rd ser., 23 (1966): 391–97.

29. Landsman, "Grand Assembly or Parliament," 479–80. See also Soderlund, *William Penn and the Founding of Pennsylvania*, 115–16.

30. Connecticut minister Joseph Moss, in Breen, *Character of a Good Ruler*, 219.

31. William Douglass, *A Summary, Historical and Political, of . . . the British Settlement in North America* (Boston, 1749), 507.

32. Richard D. Brown, *Knowledge Is Power: The Diffusion of Information in Early America, 1700–1865* (New York: Oxford University Press, 1989), 16–41; Alan Tully, *Forming American Politics: Ideals, Interests, and Institutions in Colonial New York and Pennsylvania* (Baltimore: Johns Hopkins University Press, 1994); J.A.W. Gunn, *Beyond Liberty and Property: The Process of Self-Recognition in Eighteenth-Century Political Thought* (Kingston and Montreal: McGill-Queen's University Press, 1983), 104–5.

33. After 1688, Parliament was in this same position of being "not only a watchdog of government but part of the government itself." John Brewer, *The Sinews of Power: War, Money, and the English State, 1688–1783* (London: Unwin Hyman, 1989), 159.

34. On the Massachusetts excise tax, see Zemsky, *Merchants, Farmers, and River Gods*, 150–51, 277–81. Daniel Fowle's offense was the pamphlet *Monster of Monsters* (Boston, 1754), and he gives an account of his imprisonment in *A Total Eclipse of Liberty* (Boston, 1754). Massachusetts Assembly actions (and the denunciation of Fowle's work as a "false, scandalous Libel") are in *Journals of the House of Representatives of Massachusetts* (Boston: Massachusetts Historical Society, 1919–1990), 40:63–64. New York prosecutions against printer Hugh Gaine, in 1753, and author James Parker, in 1756, are in Leonard W. Levy, "Did the Zenger Case Really Matter?" *William and Mary Quarterly*, 3rd ser., 17 (1960): 40–41. Levy notes that, vis-à-vis the press, assemblies were "most suppressive by far" (39).

35. Peter C. Hoffer, "Law and Liberty: In the Matter of Provost William Smith of Philadelphia, 1758," *William and Mary Quarterly*, 3rd ser., 38 (1981): 681–701. The Pennsylvania Assembly went so far as to order the sheriff to resist the writ of habeas corpus to keep Smith in jail for the duration of the legislative session.

36. They acted, for example, like the Council of Pennsylvania when it called the publisher Andrew Bradford before it in 1722 to tell him not to publish pamphlets "relating to or concerning" government affairs "without the permission of the Governour or secretary of this province." Richard A. Lester, "Currency Issues to Overcome Depressions in Pennsylvania, 1723 and 1729," *Journal of Political Economy* 46 (1938): 332. Even constituents who wrote petitions could be charged with "breach of privilege" by the House should their language offend. Clarke, *Parliamentary Privilege in the American Colonies*, 128–31.

37. James Wilson, *Considerations on the Nature and the Extent of the Legislative Authority of the British Parliament* (Philadelphia, 1774), 5–6.

38. On gentlemen identifying themselves in terms of their access to knowledge beyond the local, see Brown, *Knowledge Is Power*, chap. 1–4.

39. Josiah Quincy Jr., *Reports of Cases Argued and Adjudged in the Superior Court of Judicature of the Province of Massachusetts Bay, between 1761 and 1772*, ed. Samuel M. Quincy (Boston: Little, Brown, 1865), 38–39.

40. Christine Daniels, "'Liberty to Complain': Servant Petitions in Maryland, 1652–1797," in *Many Legalities of Early America*, ed. Christopher L. Tomlins and Bruce H. Mann (Chapel Hill: University of North Carolina Press, 2001), 230. This was so widely known that, reportedly, "the People Crieth Shame thereat."

41. Charles Hemstreet, *Nooks and Corners of Old New York* (New York: Charles Scribner's Sons, 1899), 34.

42. Joseph P. Reidy, "Negro Election Day and Black Community Life in New England, 1750–1860," *Marxist Perspectives* 1 (1978): 102–17.

43. Quoted in Pauline Maier, "Boston and New York in the Eighteenth Century," *American Antiquarian Society Proceedings* 91 (1982): 182.

44. "A Merchant," *Connecticut Courant*, October 14, 1765.

45. On "skill" in a trade understood primarily as social relationships, or a sort of property in "public membership," see Margaret R. Somers, "The 'Misteries' of Property: Relationality, Rural-Industrialization, and Community in Chartist Narratives of Political Rights," in *Early Modern Conceptions of Property*, ed. John Brewer and Susan Staves, 62–94 (New York: Routledge, 1996).

46. *Connecticut Courant*, July 22, 1765; Brown, *Knowledge Is Power*, chap. 6.

47. Laurel Thatcher Ulrich, *A Midwife's Tale: The Life of Martha Ballard Based on Her Diary, 1785–1812* (New York: Knopf, 1990), 12.

48. Timothy H. Breen, *Tobacco Culture: The Mentality of the Great Tidewater Planters on the Eve of Revolution* (Princeton, NJ: Princeton University Press, 1985).

49. Marcus Rediker, *Between the Devil and the Deep Blue Sea: Merchant Seamen, Pirates and the Anglo-American Maritime World, 1700–1750* (Cambridge: Cambridge University Press, 1987); Brown, *Knowledge Is Power*, 3–4, 132–59.

50. Of course, a fair amount of elite and informed opinion may also have been inaccurate. On one aspect of popular knowledge, see Alfred F. Young, "English Plebeian Culture and Eighteenth-Century American Radicalism," in *The Origins of American Radicalism*, ed. Margaret Jacob and James Jacob, 185–212 (London: George Allen and Unwin, 1984).

51. J.H. Hexter, "Power Struggle, Parliament, and Liberty in Early Stuart England," *Journal of Modern History* 50 (1978): 1–50. The quotation is on pp. 33–34.

52. In this they were both like and unlike the English of their day. The colonial situation may have made it easier for ordinary free men to believe that they retained a space to consent to the law. Colonial laws were subject to review by the Board of Trade and the Privy Council, whether to "confirm" or "disallow" the acts of provincial governments. Such review took place in the name of the king, who thus maintained a right to veto colonial legislation even after it had been accepted by a governor the king himself had appointed. For if the governor represented the king, he *only* represented him; a governor did not remove the king from the picture. Might not the same be said of those elected as delegates to provincial assemblies? If they represented their constituents, they *only* represented them. In such circumstances, it may well have seemed logical for "the people" to expect to have a say after their representatives had spoken—a chance to overrule their representatives as well. We may speculate, then, that these elements specific to the colonists' situation might have made "after-the-fact" powers of the people to review the law seem more logical than at home. (Labaree, *Royal Government*, 223–24, 254–55; Joseph Henry Smith, *Appeals to the Privy Council from the American Plantations* [New York: Columbia University Press, 1950]. Smith discusses also the appellate claims and practices by which the king-in-council might nullify colonial legislation.) On processes of law as forms of participa-

tion, see Cynthia B. Herrup, *The Common Peace: Participation in the Criminal Law in Seventeenth-Century England* (Cambridge: Cambridge University Press, 1987).

53. Sir John Somers, *The Security of English-Men's Lives, or, The Trust, Power, and Duty of the Grand Juries of England* (London, 1681), 4.

54. James Logan, *The Charge Delivered from the Bench . . .* , April 13, 1736 (Philadelphia, 1736), 18–19.

55. Anonymous, *The Nature and Importance of Oaths and Juries* (New York, 1747), 18.

56. Thomas Hutchinson, "Charge to the Grand Jury," 1765, in Quincy, *Reports of Cases Argued*, 110.

57. Robert Breck, *The Only Method to Promote the Happiness of a People and Their Posterity* (Boston 1728), 41, cited in Conroy, *Public Houses*, 79–80.

58. Whitaker, "Chief Justice's Charge to the Grand Jury," 15.

59. On resistance to the Tobacco Inspection Act of 1730, see David Alan Williams, "Political Alignments in Colonial Virginia Politics, 1698–1750" (PhD diss., Northwestern University, 1959).

60. In North Carolina the sheriff was routinely opposed in execution of his duty. Julian P. Boyd, "The Sheriff in Colonial North Carolina," *North Carolina Historical Review* 5 (1928): 151–80; Donna J. Spindel, "The Administration of Criminal Justice in North Carolina, 1720–1740," *American Journal of Legal History* 25 (1981), esp. 147–52.

61. Alison G. Olson, "Colonial Legislatures and Their Constituents," *Journal of American History* 79 (1992): 550.

62. Cases of "refusal to assist a constable," "contempt Cast upon authority by opprobrious speeches," forcibly "Takeing away a beast Destrained," "Abuseing Striking & Evily Intreating the sd Constable," and similar failures to cooperate can be seen, for example, in the *Province and Court Records of Maine* (Portland: Maine Historical Society, 1928–1975), 1:284, 6:17–18, 140, and 140n43.

63. Kenneth Scott, *Counterfeiting in Colonial America* (New York: Oxford University Press, 1957), 4, 223–24.

64. The seventeenth-century English village constable similarly relied on the consent of the people in executing law. Joan Kent, *The English Village Constable, 1580–1642: A Social and Administrative Study* (New York: Oxford University Press, 1986).

65. Richard Gaskins, "Changes in the Criminal Law in Eighteenth-Century Connecticut," *American Journal of Legal History* 25 (1981): 328.

66. Frank Wesley Craven, "An Introduction to the History of Bermuda: VI, The Revised Plan of Settlement," *William and Mary Quarterly*, 2nd ser., 18 (1938): 32.

67. Selden Daskin Bacon, "The Early Development of American Municipal Police: A Study of the Evolution of Formal Controls in a Changing Society" (PhD diss., Yale University, 1938), 335.

68. Henry Care, *English Liberties, or the Free-Born Subject's Inheritance* (London, 1682), 4.

69. Sir John Hawles, *The English-Man's Right: A Dialogue Between a Barrister-at-Law and a Jury-Man* (London, 1680), 6–7.

70. Jonathan Sewall considered and rejected indicting John Hancock by information in 1768. His reasoning is at Oliver M. Dickerson, "Opinion of Attorney General Jonathan Sewall of Massachusetts in the Case of the *Lydia*," *William and Mary Quarterly*, 3rd ser., 5 (1947): 499–504; Carol Berkin, *Jonathan Sewall: Odyssey of an American Loyalist* (New York: Columbia University Press), 51.

71. Hutchinson, "Charge to the Grand Jury," 177–78. Grand jury actions relat-

ing to problems of poverty in Gary B. Nash, "Poverty and Poor Relief in Pre-Revolutionary Philadelphia," *William and Mary Quarterly*, 3rd ser., 33 (1976): 17, 21.

72. Hutchinson, "Charge to the Grand Jury," 110.

73. Middlesex Grand Jury, in Quincy, *Reports of Cases Argued*, 110–11; South Carolina Grand Jury, *South Carolina Gazette*, February 7, 1771.

74. The Duke of York to Governor Andros, January 28, 1676, quoted in Henry B. Dawson, *The Sons of Liberty in New York* (New York: Arno Press and the New York Times, 1969), 17–18; Lovejoy, "Equality and Empire," 498–500.

75. Lois Green Carr, "The Foundations of Social Order: Local Government in Colonial Maryland," in *Town and County: Essays on the Structure of Local Government in the American Colonies*, ed. Bruce C. Daniels (Middletown, CT: Wesleyan University Press, 1978), 95. An example of grievances from a grand jury to the council in 1757 is at *Maryland Archives*, 6:555.

76. On grand juries as "representative," see J.R. Pole, "Reflections on American Law and the American Revolution," *William and Mary Quarterly*, 3rd ser., 50 (1993): 123–59, and the following responses.

77. Richard D. Younger, *The People's Panel: The Grand Jury in the United States, 1634–1941* (Providence, RI: Brown University Press, 1963), chap. 2. In Virginia, small and middling planters sometimes served on grand juries, according to Gwenda Morgan, *The Hegemony of the Law: Richmond County, Virginia, 1692–1776* (New York: Garland, 1989). See also Gwenda Morgan, "Law and Social Change in Colonial Virginia: The Role of the Grand Jury in Richmond, County, 1692–1776," *Virginia Magazine of History and Biography* 95 (1987): 453–78.

78. Livingston quoted in Bernard Friedman, "The Shaping of the Radical Consciousness in Provincial New York," *Journal of American History* 56 (1970): 786.

79. Whitaker, "Chief Justice's Charge to the Grand Jury," 28.

80. Thomas Hutchinson, "Charge to the Grand Jury, 1768," in Quincy, *Reports of Cases Argued*, 313–14.

81. Bruce C. Daniels, "The Political Structure of Local Government in Colonial Connecticut," in Daniels, *Town and County*, 66–68. In Connecticut, "grand jurors" elected from the towns assisted the justices in such matters as nominating worthy men and women for tavern keepers, licensing tanners, and levying taxes. John T. Farrell suggests that county courts functioned as a sort of subordinate General Assembly, with justices taking the place of an upper house, grand jurors playing the role of a lower, representative house. Farrell, ed., *The Superior Court Diary of William Samuel Johnson, 1772–1773, with Appropriate Records and File Papers of the Superior Court of the Colony of Connecticut for the Terms, December 1772, through March 1773* (Washington, DC: American Historical Association, 1942), xv.

82. Whitaker, "Chief Justice's Charge to the Grand Jury," 11–12.

83. *New York Weekly Journal*, no. 23, April 8, 1734, cited in Stanley Nider Katz, ed., *A Brief Narrative of the Case and Trial of John Peter Zenger, Printer of the New York Weekly Journal by James Alexander* (Cambridge, MA: Harvard University Press, 1963), 137. Historian J. R. Pole's contention that colonial grand juries might carry a representative function (especially in conflicts with the Crown) met with mixed responses from other scholars. See Pole, "Reflections on American Law," esp. 127–37; and responses by Peter Charles Hoffer, Bruce H. Mann, and James Henretta and James D. Rice, *William and Mary Quarterly*, 3rd ser., 50 (1993): 160–80. Henretta and Rice in particular deny that juries, "chose by the Sheriff" and consisting of only a subset of the pool of qualified voters, were representative of the people in any

meaningful sense. See pp. 176–79. Yet if colonial juries would fail to satisfy later ideas of what constitutes an adequately representative institution, there was nonetheless a distinctly eighteenth-century sense in which they often were described as representative.

84. Somers, *Security of English-Men's Lives*, 11.

85. Logan, "Charge Delivered from the Bench," 19.

86. Morgan, *Hegemony of the Law*.

87. Logan, "Charge Delivered from the Bench," 19.

88. Rhys Isaac, *The Transformation of Virginia, 1740–1790* (Chapel Hill: University of North Carolina Press, 1982), 30, 88–94; Jackson Turner Main, *Society and Economy in Colonial Connecticut* (Princeton, NJ: Princeton University Press, 1985), 323, 329–31, 348; Douglas Greenberg, *Crime and Law Enforcement in the Colony of New York, 1691–1776* (Ithaca, NY: Cornell University Press, 1974), 174–77.

89. James DeLancey Esq., *The Charge of the Honourable James DeLancey Esq . . . to the Gentlemen of the Grand-Jury for the City and County of New-York, January 15, 1733* (New York, 1733), 4.

90. James Parker, *Conductor Generalis; or, The Office, Duty and Authority of Justices of the Peace* (Philadelphia, 1722), 520.

91. Brendon McConville, *These Daring Disturbers of the Public Peace: The Struggle for Property and Power in Early New Jersey* (Ithaca, NY: Cornell University Press, 1999), 25.

92. A.G. Roeber, *Faithful Magistrates and Republican Lawyers: Creators of Virginia Legal Culture, 1680–1810* (Chapel Hill: University of North Carolina Press, 1981), 79.

93. Quoted in Roeber, *Faithful Magistrates*, 31.

94. Ibid., 75

95. *Maryland Archives*, 75:680.

96. Somers, *Security of English-Men's Lives*, 11.

97. Parker, *Conductor Generalis*, 519. A defendant might also benefit from "his good Reputation" when tried by a jury of the vicinity, according to the town meeting of Charlestown, Massachusetts, in *Boston Evening Post*, January 4, 1773. William Keith emphasized the protection that juries provided the individual accused in *A Letter to His Majesty's Justices of the Peace for the County of Chester . . . April 15, 1718* (Philadelphia, 1718).

98. Parker, *Conductor Generalis*, 297, 519, 522–23. Because jurors were expected to bring local knowledge to the courtroom, rules of evidence did not exclude either hearsay or information about prior convictions from court. John H. Langbein, "The Criminal Trial Before the Lawyers," *University of Chicago Law Review* 45 (1978): 298–99.

99. Also making point that the "country" was the jury was Hawles, *English-Man's Right*, 8.

100. Bruce H. Mann says it is "artificial and impossible to maintain in practice." Mann, "The Evolutionary Revolution in American Law: A Comment on J.R. Pole's 'Reflections,'" *William and Mary Quarterly*, 3rd ser., 50 (1993): 170n4.

101. Parker, *Conductor Generalis*, 521–25; William E. Nelson, *Americanization of the Common Law: The Impact of Legal Change on Massachusetts Society, 1760–1830* (Cambridge, MA: Harvard University Press, 1975). In New York, Governor Cadwallader Colden encountered opposition from lawyers and the broader public when he tried to expand the grounds for appeals from jury verdicts. Milton H. Klein, "Pre-

lude to Revolution in New York: Jury Trials and Judicial Tenure," *William and Mary Quarterly*, 3rd ser., 17 (1960): 453–60.

102. Parker, *Conductor Generalis*, 523.

103. John Prentice, *King Jehoshaphat's Charge* (Boston, 1731), 7–8.

104. Quincy, *Reports of Cases Argued*, 84, 564–65.

105. Care, *English Liberties*, 205.

106. [Jonathan Blenman] *Remarks on Zenger's Tryal* (Philadelphia, 1737), 9.

107. "A Narrative of a New and Unusual American Imprisonment of Two Presbyterian Ministers" (1707), in *American Archives: Fourth Series, Containing a Documentary History of the English Colonies in North America, from the King's Message to the Parliament, of March 7, 1774, to the Declaration of Independence of the United States*, ed. Peter Force (Washington, DC: M. St. Clair Clarke and Peter Force, 1837–39), 4:23. A grand jury made up of "opulent and substantial" New York gentlemen was allegedly "hand picked" to secure an indictment of Alexander McDougal for libel against the assembly. Levy, "Did Zenger Matter?" 47–49.

108. Allan Kulikoff, *Tobacco and Slaves: The Development of Southern Cultures in the Chesapeake, 1680–1800* (Chapel Hill: University of North Carolina Press, 1986), 281–82.

109. Tully, *Forming American Politics*, 102.

110. Parker, *Conductor Generalis*, 519. On the "project . . . of clothing judges and lawyers in robes" in Massachusetts, see Quincy, *Reports of Cases Argued*, 35.

111. Quoted in Quincy, *Reports of Cases Argued*, 307.

112. McConville, *Daring Disturbers of the Peace*, 116.

113. "Narrative of a New and Unusual American Imprisonment," 44.

114. *Maryland Archives*, 53:xxii.

115. John Adams quoted in Nelson, *Americanization of the Common Law*, 20–21. Julius Goebel Jr., "Law Enforcement in Colonial New York: An Introduction," in *Essays in the History of Early American Law*, ed. David H. Flaherty (Chapel Hill: University of North Carolina Press, 1969), 379, notes attendance at court as part of a freeman's duty.

116. Joel Bernard, "The Transit of 'Small, Merry' Anglo-American Culture: Sir John Barley-Corne and Sir Richard Rum (and Captain Whiskey)," *American Antiquarian Society Proceedings* 100 (1990): 81–136. Accounts of trials were widely familiar to ordinary readers in Anglo-America. On chapbooks published in London that recounted sensational (but actual) trials for the lay reader during the Tudor-Stuart years, see John H. Langbein, "The Origins of Public Prosecution at Common Law," *American Journal of Legal History* 17 (1973): 326–34.

117. Anonymous, *The Indictment and Tryal of Sir Richard Rum* (Philadelphia, 1724). "Sir Richard Rum" expected that readers would know the courtroom as a site of negotiation, a site where the people of a given locality might have a voice and even—in the form of the jury—have the final say.

118. Clifford Geertz, "Local Knowledge: Fact and Law in Comparative Perspective," in *Local Knowledge*, 173.

119. David Liberman, "Blackstone's Science of Legislation," *Journal of British Studies* 27 (1988): 117–49. Jury trials historically have kept "in the hands of the people that share which they ought to have in the administration of public justice" (135).

120. *Pennsylvania Gazette*, February 7, 1738.

121. "Criminal trials, in the common law world, were essentially local affairs regardless of the problem of prejudice," says Thomas D. Morris, *Southern Slavery and*

the Law, 1619–1860 (Chapel Hill: University of North Carolina Press, 1996), 221. See also J.H. Baker, "Criminal Courts and Procedure at Common Law 1550–1800," in *Crime in England, 1550–1800*, ed. J.S. Cockburn, 15–48 (Princeton, NJ: Princeton University Press, 1977).

122. Parker, *Conductor Generalis*, 523.

123. *The Nature and Importance of Oaths and Juries* (New York, 1747), 18.

124. "Narrative of a New and Unusual American Imprisonment," 43–44.

125. One English jurist who urged limits to the discretionary powers of grand juries in the late seventeenth century nonetheless argued his case from both "law and reason." Zachary Babington, "Advice to grand jurors in cases of blood . . ." (London, 1680), title page.

126. Parker, *Conductor Generalis*, 520–23. Josiah Quincy observed in Pennsylvania "a certain Quaker interest which operates much against the proprietor in land causes, in the courts of law, where the jury frequently give verdicts against the opinion of the judges." Josiah Quincy, *Memoir of the Life of Josiah Quincy* (ca. 1825; repr., New York: Da Capo Press, 1971), 135–36.

127. John M. Murrin, "The Legal Transformation: The Bench and Bar of Eighteenth-Century Massachusetts," in *Colonial America: Essays in Politics and Social Development*, ed. Stanley N. Katz and John M. Murrin), 540–72 (New York: Knopf, 1983).

128. "Petition of Reuben Searcy," 1763, in Boyd, *Some Eighteenth-Century Tracts*, 181.

129. Hawles, *English-Man's Right*, 9.

130. Roeber, *Faithful Magistrates*, 118–20.

131. On the English case, see J.M. Beattie, "Scales of Justice: Defense Counsel and the English Criminal Trial in the Eighteenth and Nineteenth Centuries," *Law and History Review* 9 (1991): 221–67.

132. Ray W. Pettengill, trans., *Letters from America, 1776–1779; Being Letters of Brunswick, Hessian, and Waldeck Officers with the British Armies During the Revolution* (1924; repr., Port Washington, NY, 1964), 37.

133. Isaac, *Transformation of Virginia*, 92.

134. Bruce H. Mann, *Neighbors and Strangers: Law and Community in Early Connecticut* (Chapel Hill: University of North Carolina Press, 1987), 8; Gail S. Marcus, "'Due Execution of the General Rules of Righteousnesse': Criminal Procedure in New Haven Town Colony, 1638–1658," in *Saints and Revolutionaries*, ed. David D. Hall et al., 99–137 (New York: W.W. Norton, 1984). On spectators in courts, see E. Merton Coulter, ed., *The Journal of Peter Gordon, 1732–1735* (Athens: University of Georgia Press, 1963), 14; Isaac, *Transformation of Virginia*, 88–94.

135. Judges' black silk gowns or, in capital cases, scarlet robes, were intended to create a "dignified appearance" and leave an "impression of reverence for authority of the law." "Memoir of Governor Increase Sumner," *New England Historical and Genealogical Register* 8 (1854): 116; Roeber, *Faithful Magistrates*, 75–79, 118; Carl Lounsbury, "The Structure of Justice: The Courthouse of Colonial Virginia," *Perspectives in Vernacular Architecture, III*, ed. Thomas Carter and Bernard L. Herman, 214–26 (Columbia: University of Missouri Press, 1989); Martha J. McNamara, *From Tavern to Courthouse: Architecture and Ritual in American Law, 1658–1860* (Baltimore: Johns Hopkins University Press, 2004); Cornelia Hughes Dayton, *Women Before the Bar: Gender, Law, and Society in Connecticut, 1639–1789* (Chapel Hill: University of North Carolina Press, 1995).

136. New York Governor Cadwallader Colden stressed the need to insulate judges from popular opinion in these terms, quoted in Greenberg, *Crime and Law Enforcement*, 176; Pettengill, *Letters from America*, 137. John Adams noted when spectators smiled and whispered at court. L.H. Butterfield, ed., *Diary and Autobiography of John Adams* (Cambridge, MA: Harvard University Press, 1961), 1:69; Lounsbury, "Structure of Justice."

137. Peter George Buckley, "To the Opera House: Culture and Society in New York City, 1820–1860" (PhD diss., SUNY Stony Brook, 1984), esp. 119–24.

138. Quoted in Scott, *Counterfeiting in Colonial America*, pp. 223–24.

139. Prentice, *King Jehoshaphat's Charge*, 23, 21.

140. William Lincoln, *History of Worcester, Mass. from its Earliest Settlement to September, 1836* (Worcester: Charles Hersey, 1862), 58, on public attendance at sessions of court and punishments.

141. In Philadelphia whipping post and pillory display generally took place on a market day, and the price of eggs rose when a criminal was particularly unpopular. John F. Watson, *Annals of Philadelphia and Pennsylvania, in the Olden Times*, 3 vols. (Philadelphia: Edwin S. Stuart, 1884), 1:103.

142. *Pennsylvania Gazette*, January 18, 1733.

143. "Narrative of a New and Unusual American Imprisonment," 8. On the purpose of shaming in punishment, see John Wright, *The Speech of John Wright, Esq; One of the Magistrates of Lancaster County, to the Court and Grand-Jury* (Philadelphia, 1741), 3.

144. James Boswell, *The Life of Samuel Johnson, LL.D.*, 4 vols. (London: T. Cadell and W. Davies, 1807), 4:202.

145. Negley K. Teeters, "Public Executions in Pennsylvania, 1682 to 1834," *Journal of the Lancaster County Historical Society* 64 (1960): 97.

146. Daniel A. Cohen, "In Defense of the Gallows: Justifications of Capital Punishment in New England Execution Sermons, 1674–1825," *American Quarterly* 40 (1988): 147–64; Ronald A. Bosco, "Lectures at the Pillory: The Early American Execution Sermon," *American Quarterly* 30 (1978): 156–76; Lincoln B. Faller, *Turned to Account: The Forms and Functions of Criminal Biography in Late Seventeenth- and Early Eighteenth-Century England* (New York: Cambridge University Press, 1987), xi, notes that popular literature of crime "re-used" criminal executions.

147. Proceedings of the Maryland Assembly, *Maryland Archives*, 2:425–26.

148. *Pennsylvania Gazette*, January 20, 1730.

149. Craven, "History of Bermuda," 35.

150. Joseph H. Smith, ed., *Colonial Justice in Western Massachusetts (1639–1702): The Pynchon Court Record* (Cambridge, MA: Harvard University Press, 1961), 110, 284–86.

151. Greenberg, *Crime and Law Enforcement*, 180–81, 167.

152. Young, "English Plebeian Culture," 190.

153. Cunningham, *Letters and Diary of John Rowe*, 213. John Murrin, "Anglicizing an American Colony: The Transformation of Provincial Massachusetts" (PhD diss., Yale University, 1966), 128, mentions the case of a soldier dismissed for "Pulling up the wiping post and Carrying it o[ff]."

154. Gaskins, "Changes in the Criminal Law," 322n56.

155. Pauline Maier, *Resistance to Revolution*, chap. 1; Edward Countryman, "Out of the Bounds of the Law: Northern Land Rioters in the Eighteenth Century," in *The American Revolution: Explorations in the History of American Radicalism*, ed. Alfred F.

Young (De Kalb, IL: Northern Illinois University Press, 1976), 37–70. The impressment riot is in *Pennsylvania Gazette*, June 27, 1765. Douglas Hay explores occurrences of ridicule or riot at executions in England in "Property, Authority, and the Criminal Law," in *Albion's Fatal Tree: Crime and Society in Eighteenth-Century England*, ed. Douglas Hay et al., 50–55 (London: Allen Lane, 1975).

156. Popular sympathies might stimulate well-timed announcements of mercy from a governor: "The urgent solicitations of the public at the place of execution" spared a soldier from hanging for burglary in May 1655 in New Amsterdam. Occasions when a hangman was not available or when threats of rescue occurred are in Philip English Mackey, *Hanging in the Balance: The Anti-Capital Punishment Movement in New York State, 1776–1861* (New York: Garland Publishing, 1982), 7, 7–8, 17–18, 24–25. Julius Goebe Jr. and T. Raymond Naughton, *Law Enforcement in Colonial New York* (New York: Commonwealth Fund, 1944), 8, 754–59. Juries also found their own valuation of stolen goods, which affected whether the crime amounted to a felony or a misdemeanor, a distinction that could save a criminal from hanging. An expected rescue, popular feeling against the convicted, and subsequent execution appear in *The New-York Gazette or The Weekly Post-Boy*, January 8, 1767.

157. Parker, *Conductor Generalis*, 196–97. Such a rescue constituted a felony in cases where the prisoner rescued "hath committed Felony, and was arrested for it"; preventing the apprehension of a man not yet arrested might constitute only a misdemeanor. This left a critical opening, for if the prisoner proved to be innocent of the crime for which he was being arrested, it is at least implied that it was not a crime, where prisoner not "attainted" (i.e., convicted and sentenced).

158. This interpretation relies on important work by English scholars who have recast our understanding of eighteenth-century English law by recovering its eighteenth-century purposes and parameters. Thus, if historians can now abandon the term "extra-legal" in talking about popular participation in execution of the law, it is partly thanks to scholars who have shown us more about what the term "legal" meant. See John M. Beattie, *Crime and the Courts in England, 1660–1800* (Princeton, NJ: Princeton University Press, 1986) and *Policing and Punishment in London, 1660–1750* (Oxford: Oxford University Press, 2001); Norma Landau, *Law, Crime, and English Society, 1660–1830* (Cambridge: Cambridge University Press, 2002) and *The Justices of the Peace, 1679–1790* (Berkeley: University of California Press, 1984). Also critical, of course, is earlier work by E.P. Thompson, Douglas Hay, and Peter Linebaugh.

159. One case when the law found a mob to have been illegal is that of Joseph Wanton, a royal customs officer in Rhode Island. In August 1742 a mob assailed him after he seized goods from a ship for nonpayment of duties. He successfully prosecuted six of them for assault. Jarvis M. Morse, "The Wanton Family and Rhode Island Loyalism," *Rhode Island Historical Society Collections* 31 (1938): 33–44.

160. Those actions were not "extra-institutional," but rather institutions themselves; they were not a substitute for political action, but rather politics itself; they were not indications of the *absence* of a professional police, but rather the *presence* of a space for collective and popular consent. Cf. Kimberly K. Smith, *The Dominion of Voice: Riot, Reason, and Romance in Antebellum Politics* (Lawrence: University Press of Kansas, 1999), esp. 11–12, 20–21.

161. This is akin to the two notions of the law that John Phillip Reid depicts as present or perhaps emerging in eighteenth-century colonies: on the one hand, "Tory law," which saw law as what was established by Parliament and hence saw resistance

to acts of Parliament as simply illegal; on the other hand, "Whig law," which saw law as needing to be received, in an active sense, by the people. Over and against those who speak of popular actions as "extra-legal," Reid emphasizes that Whig leaders in the colonies did not justify crowds by reference to supposedly overriding social, moral, or even political ideals, but on legal grounds. However, Reid is generally concerned with the thinking of leading legal theorists and practitioners; his "Whigs" were leading men. I am writing here of the ideas or agency of more ordinary men, relatively unlearned and unsophisticated in their understanding of the law. What interests me are ways that common men acted on their own behalf, out of their own understandings of the law, which might or might not tally with leading Whig thinkers. Reid, "'In Accordance with Usage': The Authority of Custom, the Stamp Act Debates, and the Coming of the American Revolution," *Fordham Law Review* 45 (1976–77): 335–68. On attributing mobs to the "absence" of a police, see Pauline Maier, "Popular Uprisings and Civil Authority in Eighteenth-Century America," *William and Mary Quarterly*, 3rd ser., 27 (1970): 19, 29–30; Gordon S. Wood, "A Note on Mobs in the American Revolution," *William and Mary Quarterly*, 3rd ser., 23 (1966): 639.

162. This is also to quibble with historians who understand the people out of doors as sometimes "taking the law into their own hands," for that phrase, appropriate to a later era, suggests that law normally received execution without their engagement. William Pencak, Matthew Dennis, and Simon P. Newman, eds., *Riot and Revelry in Early America* (University Park: Pennsylvania State University Press, 2002), 5.

163. Greenberg, *Crime and Law Enforcement*, 160.

164. "Extract of a Letter from Lower Smithfield, to a Gentleman in the Jerseys, Dated January 2, 1756," *New-York Mercury*, February 2, 1756.

165. On "public time," see J.G.A. Pocock, "Modes of Political and Historical Time in Early Eighteenth-Century England," in *Virtue, Commerce, and History* (New York: Cambridge University Press, 1985), 91.

166. Still, one newspaper writer ambiguously denounced the "Rabble, the very dregs of the People, black and white," *Boston Evening Post*, November 11, 1745. A few occasions of women's activity prior to the Revolution stand out; see Alfred F. Young, "The Women of Boston: 'Persons of Consequence' in the Making of the American Revolution, 1765–76," in *Women and Politics in the Age of the Democratic Revolution*, ed. Harriet B. Applewhite and Darline G. Levy (Ann Arbor: University of Michigan Press, 1990), 192–93. Henry Bamford Parkes, "Morals and Law Enforcement in Colonial New England," *New England Quarterly* 5 (1932): 431–52, suggests women's activity in rural crowds.

167. Nelson, *Americanization*, 13.

168. Murrin, "Legal Transformation."

169. On discretion in the criminal law in England, see Peter P. King, "Decision-Makers and Decision-Making in the English Criminal Law, 1750–1800," *Historical Journal* 27 (1984): 25–58.

170. Arlette Farge, *Subversive Words: Public Opinion in Eighteenth-Century France*, trans. Rosemary Morris (Cambridge: Polity Press, 1994), 35.

171. Ibid.; McCracken, "Pre-Coronation Passage of Elizabeth I," 52.

172. Young, "Women of Boston," 194–95, suggests spectatorship as a form of power. Robert B. Shoemaker, "'The London Mob' in the Early 18th Century," *Journal of British Studies* 26 (1987): 273–309, notes the fine line between spectators and participants in many mobs.

173. Bucholz, "Nothing But Ceremony," 295; Elizabeth Janeway, *The Powers of the Weak* (New York: Knopf, 1980).

2. The Commitments They Brought

1. This was James, Duke of Monmouth, reworded somewhat and reprinted by Samuel Adams in Boston's *Independent Advertiser*, January 11, 1748.

2. On government's obligation to protect the people, see John Walter, "Public Transcripts, Popular Agency, and the Politics of Subsistence in Early Modern England," in *Negotiating Power in Early Modern Society: Order, Hierarchy and Subordination in Britain and Ireland*, ed. Michael J. Braddick and John Walter (Cambridge: Cambridge University Press, 2001), 124–28.

3. Paul Seaver, "Symposium: Controlling (Mis)Behavior; Introduction," *Journal of British Studies* 37 (1998): 234; Allan Kulikoff, *From British Peasants to Colonial American Farmers* (Chapel Hill: University of North Carolina Press, 2000). Steve Hindle, "A Sense of Place? Becoming and Belonging in the Rural Parish, 1550–1650," in *Communities in Early Modern England: Networks, Place, Rhetoric*, ed. Alexandra Shepard and Phil Withington, 96–114 (Manchester and New York: Manchester University Press, 2000), illuminates community as process and ideal. Hindle writes that an earlier ideal of neighborliness became "fragmented and marginalized" in this era (108–9).

4. Whig writers of the early eighteenth century agreed that France was "the region of slavery," in the phrase of Joseph Addison and Richard Steele in the *Tatler* in 1710, cited in Lawrence E. Klein, "The Figure of France: The Politics of Sociability in England, 1660–1715," *Yale French Studies* 92 (1997): 31–32. David Underdown, *A Freeborn People: Politics and the Nation in Seventeenth-Century England* (Oxford: Clarendon Press, 1996), explores the broad popular conviction of inherited understandings between kings and other superiors and the ordinary "people" of the seventeenth century.

5. Marjorie K. McIntosh, *Controlling Misbehavior in England, 1370–1600* (Cambridge: Cambridge University Press, 1998), challenges the view that there was a clear break between a stable "medieval" England and "early modern" experiences of social disorder. For a useful symposium on McIntosh's book, see *Journal of British Studies* 37 (1998): 231–305.

6. Robert Brenner, "The Agrarian Roots of European Capitalism," *Past and Present* 97 (1982): 16–113; Brenner, "Agricultural Class Structure and Economic Development in Pre-Industrial Europe," *Past and Present* 70 (1976): 30–75; William George Hoskins, *The Making of the English Landscape* (London: Hodder and Stoughton, 1977); J.M. Neeson, *Commoners: Common Right, Enclosure, and Social Change in England, 1700–1820* (Cambridge: Cambridge University Press, 1993). Kulikoff, *British Peasants*, emphasizes the impact of the European experience on emigrants to the New World of being displaced from the land in the old.

7. W.E. Tate, "Parliamentary Counter-Petitions during the Enclosures of the Eighteenth and Nineteenth Centuries," *English Historical Review* 59 (1944): 392–403.

8. On the development of capitalist rationality, see Brenner, "Agrarian Roots"; Brenner, "Agricultural Class Structure." Cf. T.H. Aston and C.H.E. Philpin, eds., *The Brenner Debate: Agrarian Class Structure and Economic Development in Pre-Industrial Europe* (Cambridge: Cambridge University Press, 1985).

9. Keith Wrightson, *English Society, 1580–1680* (London: Hutchinson, 1982); Wrightson, "The Social Order of Early Modern England: Three Approaches," in

The World We Have Gained: Histories of Population and Social Structure, ed. L. Bonfield, R.M. Smith, and K. Wrightson, 279–91 (Oxford: Oxford University Press, 1986); H.R. French, "The Search for the 'Middle Sort of People' in England, 1600–1800," *Historical Journal* 43, no. 1 (2000): 277–93; French, "Social Status, Localism, and the 'Middle Sort of People' in England," *Past and Present* 166 (February 2000): 66–99.

10. Robert W. Gordon, "Paradoxical Property," in *Early Modern Conceptions of Property*, ed. John Brewer and Susan Staves, 95–110 (New York: Routledge, 1996); M.M. Goldsmith, "Mandeville and the Spirit of Capitalism," *Journal of British Studies* 17 (1977): 63–81.

11. C.E. Searle, "Custom, Class Conflict and Agrarian Capitalism: The Cumbrian Customary Economy in the Eighteenth Century," *Past and Present*, no. 110 (February 1986): 106–33.

12. In the eighteenth century, when enclosures often proceeded by legislative act, opponents composed petitions to counter proposals for change. Tate, "Parliamentary Counter-Petitions." But see also J.M. Neeson, "The Opponents of Enclosure in Eighteenth-Century Northamptonshire," *Past and Present* 105 (November 1984): 114–39.

13. Steve Hindle, "Exhortation and Entitlement: Negotiating Inequality in Rural Communities, 1550–1650," in Braddick and Walter, *Negotiating Power*, 117; Wrightson, *English Society*, 266–67; Roger B. Manning, *Village Revolts: Social Protest and Popular Disturbances in England, 1509–1640* (Oxford: Clarendon Press, 1988); W.E. Tate, "Opposition to Parliamentary Enclosure in Eighteenth-Century England," *Agricultural History Review* 19 (1945): 137–42; Tate, "Parliamentary Counter-Petitions," 392–403. On hedgebreaking, see Neeson, "Opponents of Enclosure," 129–32, 138. Neeson observes that opposition in the eighteenth century was often local and prolonged, with the result of delaying or modifying terms of enclosure in Northamptonshire. Searle, "Custom, Class Conflict, and Capitalism," 125.

14. On ideas about wages, see A.W. Coats, "Changing Attitudes Toward Labour in the Mid-Eighteenth Century," *Economic History Review*, 2nd ser., 11 (1958–59): 35–51. Joyce Appleby, *Economic Thought and Ideology in Seventeeth-Century England* (Princeton, NJ: Princeton University Press, 1978); Appleby, "Ideology and Theory: The Tension between Political and Economic Liberalism in Seventeenth-Century England," *American Historical Review* 81 (1976): 499–515; Goldsmith, "Mandeville and the Spirit of Capitalism."

15. Paul Slack, *Poverty and Policy in Tudor and Stuart England* (London: Longman, 1988); Wrightson, *English Society*, 271; Ellen Meiksins Wood, "From Opportunity to Imperative: The History of the Market," *Monthly Review* 46 (1984): 14–40.

16. Robert W. Malcolmson, "Workers' Combination in 18th-Century England," in *The Origins of Anglo-American Radicalism*, ed. Margaret C. Jacob and James R. Jacob, 149–61 (London: George Allen and Unwin, 1984). Quotation is from pp. 152–53.

17. E.P. Thompson, "The Moral Economy of the English Crowd in the Eighteenth Century," *Past and Present* 50 (1971): 76–136, repr. in Thompson, *Customs in Common: Studies in Traditional Popular Culture* (New York: The New Press, 1991), 185–258; Thompson, "The Moral Economy Reviewed," in *Customs in Common*, 259–351; Andrew Charlesworth, ed., *An Atlas of Rural Protest in Britain, 1548–1900* (London: Croom Helm, 1983). Robert W. Malcolmson, *Life and Labour in England, 1700–1780* (New York: St Martin's Press, 1981), reviews the moral economy literature as well. Underdown, *Freeborn People*, 9, 47–48.

18. On the claims of the poor on the law, see Peter King, "Gleaners, Farmers and the Failure of Legal Sanctions in England, 1750–1850," *Past and Present* 125 (1989): 116–50; Andy Wood, "The Place of Custom in Plebeian Political Culture: England, 1550–1800," *Social History* 22, no. 1 (January 1997): 46–60; Douglas Hay, "Moral Economy, Political Economy, and Law," in *Moral Economy and Popular Protest: Crowds, Conflict and Authority*, ed. Adrian Randall and Andrew Charlesworth, 93–122 (New York: St. Martin's, 2000); Susan E. Brown, "'A Just and Profitable Commerce': Moral Economy and the Middle Classes in Eighteenth-Century London," *Journal of British Studies* 32 (1993): 305–32; R.H. Britnell, "Forstall, Forestalling, and the Statute of Forestallers," *English Historical Review* 102 (1987): 89–102; John Brewer and John Styles, eds., *An Ungovernable People: The English and Their Law in the Seventeenth and Eighteenth Centuries* (New Brunswick, NJ: Rutgers University Press, 1980). On the fourteenth century, see Malcolmson, *Life and Labour in England*.

19. Richard Ashcraft, "Lockean Ideas, Poverty, and the Development of Liberal Political Theory," in Brewer and Staves, *Early Modern Conceptions of Property*, 43–61; Jacqueline Stevens, "The Reasonableness of Locke's Majority: Property Rights, Consent, and Resistance in the Second Treatise," *Political Theory* 24 (1996): 423–63. William James Booth, *Households: On the Moral Architecture of the Economy* (Ithaca, NY: Cornell University Press, 1993), 127–38, explores Locke's assumptions about the commons. See also Richard Ashcraft, "The Politics of Locke's *Two Treatises of Government*," in *John Locke's Two Treatises of Government*, ed. Edward H. Harpham (Lawrence: University Press of Kansas, 1992), 14–19.

20. Hay, "Moral Economy, Political Economy, and Law," 93–122.

21. Michael Ignatieff and Istvan Hont, "Needs and Justice in the *Wealth of Nations*: An Introductory Essay," in *Wealth and Virtue: The Shaping of Political Economy in the Scottish Enlightenment*, ed. Ignatieff and Hont (Cambridge: Cambridge University Press, 1983), 13–18; Christopher L. Tomlins, *Law, Labor and Ideology in the Early American Republic* (Cambridge: Cambridge University Press, 1993), 35–47.

22. Randall Nielson, "Storage and English Government Intervention in Early Modern Grain Markets," *Journal of Economic History* 57 (1997): 1–33, quotations on pp. 2, 3. See also Robert W. Gordon, "Paradoxical Property," in Brewer and Staves, *Early Modern Conceptions of Property*, 95–110.

23. "From the Public Ledger, March 14," reprinted in *Boston Post Boy*, May 18, 1767.

24. Even the poor in their riots did not oppose the market per se, for how else, after all, would they eat? "Moral economic" ideas were attuned to a world of commerce. Thompson, "Moral Economy Reviewed," 272.

25. Brown, "Just and Profitable Commerce," 305–32.

26. Emphasizing the desire for land is Kulikoff, *British Peasants*, 3, 71, 74, 139–40, and passim. For the complex nature of colonists' identity, see Michael Zuckerman, "The Fabrication of Identity in America," *William and Mary Quarterly*, 3rd ser., 34 (1977): 183–214. A view of related issues of identity in England is Craig Muldrew, "From a 'Light Cloak' to an 'Iron Cage': Historical Changes in the Relationship Between Community and Individualism," in Shepard and Withington, *Communities in Early Modern England*, 156–72.

27. Ilana Krausman Ben-Amos, "Gifts and Favors: Informal Support in Early Modern England," *Journal of Modern History* 72 (2000): 309.

28. James Horn, *Adapting to a New World: English Society in the Seventeenth-Century Chesapeake* (Chapel Hill: University of North Carolina Press, 1994); James R.

Perry, *Formation of a Society On Virginia's Eastern Shore, 1615–1655* (Chapel Hill: University of North Carolina Press, 1990). "Neer-neighbouring" was the phrase of Rev. John Wise of Ipswich, Massachusetts. Wise, "Instructions for Emigrants from Essex County, Massachusetts, to South Carolina, 1697," *New England Historical and Genealogical Register* 30 (1876): 64–67.

29. Virginia DeJohn Anderson, *New England's Generation: The Great Migration and the Formation of Society and Culture in the Seventeenth Century* (New York: Cambridge University Press, 1991); Ida Altman and James Horn, *"To Make America": European Immigration in the Early Modern Period* (Berkeley: University of California Press, 1991); Patricia J. Tracy, "Re-Considering Migration Within Colonial New England," *Journal of Social History* 23 (1989): 93–114, stresses migration by kin groups rather than individuals. David Cressy, *Coming Over: Migration and Communication Between England and New England in the Seventeenth Century* (New York: Cambridge University Press, 1987); David Grayson Allen, *In English Ways: The Movement of Societies and the Transfer of English Local Law and Custom to Massachusetts Bay in the Seventeenth Century* (Chapel Hill: University of North Carolina Press, 1981); Marianne S. Wokeck, *Trade in Strangers: The Beginnings of Mass Migration to North America* (University Park: Pennsylvania State University Press, 1999); Ned C. Landsman, *Scotland and Its First American Colony, 1683–1765* (Princeton, NJ: Princeton University Press, 1985).

30. Virginia adopted the shire in 1634, Massachusetts in 1692, North Carolina only in 1739. Myron C. Noonkester, "The Third British Empire: Transplanting the English Shire to Wales, Scotland, Ireland, and America," *Journal of British Studies* 36 (1997): 251–84, quotation on p. 259. The shire "provided a unifying procedurial element amid diversity" (265). Julian P. Boyd, "The Sheriff in Colonial North Carolina," *North Carolina Historical Review* 5 (1928): 151–80; quotation on p. 153.

31. Peter King, "Decision-Makers and Decision-Making in the English Criminal Law, 1750–1800," *Historical Journal* 27 (1984): 25–58, notes that law was susceptible to modification by a wide variety of groups in England.

32. Edmund S. Morgan, *American Slavery, American Freedom: The Ordeal of Colonial Virginia* (New York: W.W. Norton, 1975).

33. Richard B. Morris, *Government and Labor in Early America* (New York: Columbia University Press, 1946), chaps. 1, 2. Morris emphasizes the decline of "general" programs to fix wages and prices and the continuation of piecemeal regulations in the eighteenth century (77–91). See also Jon C. Teaford, *The Municipal Revolution in America: Origins of Modern Urban Government, 1650–1825* (Chicago: University of Chicago Press, 1975). Debate over the abandonment or continuation of economic regulations has generally focused on the sporadic nature of "enforcement" in the colonies, a point that a new understanding of "execution" of the law puts in new perspective. As with most other aspects of English life, the colonists both abandoned some and continued other regulations; their ability to disuse some forms (such as trade guilds) makes their retention of other forms (such as the assize on bread) *more* significant as a measure of intention.

34. Cathy Matson, "'Damned Scoundrels' and 'Libertisme of Trade': Freedom and Regulation in Colonial New York's Fur and Grain Trades," *William and Mary Quarterly*, 3rd ser., 51 (1994): 401; *Archives of Maryland*, ed. William Hand Browne et al. (Baltimore: Maryland Historical Society, 1883–), 25:491–92, 28:127 (hereafter *Maryland Archives*).

35. There was irony here, and a good deal more. There were people being pressed from the land in North America, people who could plausibly claim to have lived from and with that land since time immemorial. In some parts of the New World, such as much of New Spain, European settlers became Creole elites, living off the labor of local indigenous peoples; they maintained a sense of identity in relation to the metropolitan culture and the subordinate local population. By contrast, the scholar Michael Warner notes, many European immigrants in British North America came to think of *themselves* as the locals, rooted in the land. Michael Warner, "What's Colonial About Colonial America?" in *Possible Pasts: Becoming Colonial in Early America*, ed. Robert Blair St. George, 49–72 (Ithaca, NY: Cornell University Press, 2000).

36. Crimes of forestalling, ingrossing, and regrating were described in authoritative publications in North America, such as James Parker, *Conductor Generalis; or, The Office, Duty and Authority of Justices of the Peace* (Philadelphia, 1722), 192–94. "Any endeavours whatsoever to enhance the common price of any merchandize, and all kind of practices which have an apparent tendency thereto . . . are highly criminal, and punishable by fine and imprisonment."

37. Matson, "'Damned Scoundrels' and 'Libertisme of Trade,'" 389–418; Daniel Vickers, "Competency and Competition: Economic Culture in Early America," *William and Mary Quarterly*, 3rd ser., 47 (1990): 3–29. "Competency and Competition" suggests that the idea of "moral economy" had little valence in the lives of farm households in northern British America. Only Native American societies, Vickers argues, truly questioned political economy. Their defense of their lands "was the only pure expression of moral economy in American history" (19). Such a view is useful for underscoring the gulf between indigenous peoples' and European newcomers' ways of seeing, but it has the disadvantage of changing the meaning of "moral economy" so that it would no longer describe the beliefs of the English poor whose actions in food riots led E.P. Thompson to coin the phrase in the first place. As Thompson himself framed it, "moral economic" ideas made sense *within* the framework of markets in grain and other goods. Ruth Bogin, "Petitioning and the New Moral Economy of Post-Revolutionary America," *William and Mary Quarterly*, 3rd ser., 45 (1988): 392–425, suggests that Americans' ideas encompassed the bread nexus so central in England, even as bread was less central an issue (424).

38. Vickers, "Competency and Competition," 3–29. See also Kulikoff, *British Peasants*, 3 and passim.

39. Ronald Schultz, "The Small-Producer Tradition and the Moral Origins of Artisan Radicalism in Philadelphia, 1720–1810," *Past and Present* 127 (May 1990): 84–116.

40. This widely accepted view of neighborhood exchange grew out of a substantial debate among historians. Allan Kulikoff, "The Transition to Capitalism in Rural America," *William and Mary Quarterly*, 3rd ser., 46 (1989): 120–44, offers a summary of the literature. Important works include Michael Merrill, "Cash Is Good to Eat: Self-Sufficiency and Exchange in the Rural Economy of the United States," *Radical History Review* 3 (1977): 42–71; James A. Henretta, "Families and Farms: *Mentalite* in Pre-Industrial America," *William and Mary Quarterly*, 3rd ser., 55 (1978): 3–32. See also Christopher Clark et al., "The Transition to Capitalism in America: A Panel Discussion," *History Teacher* 27 (1994): 264–88; Richard Lyman Bushman, "Markets and Composite Farms in Early America," *William and Mary Quarterly*, 3rd ser., 55

(1998): 351–74. James A. Henretta, "The War for Independence and American Economic Development," in *The Economy of Early America: The Revolutionary Period, 1763–1790*, ed. Ronald Hoffman, John J. McCusker, Russell R. Menard, and Peter Albert (Charlottesville: University Press of Virginia, 1988), 52–58, notes the significance of manufactures as part of the rural household's practices of exchange. On dispute resolution, see William E. Nelson, *Dispute and Conflict Resolution in Plymouth County, Massachusetts, 1725–1825* (Chapel Hill: University of North Carolina Press, 1981); Grant Evans, "From Moral Economy to Remembered Village: The Sociology of James C. Scott" (working paper 40, Centre of Southeast Asian Studies, Monash University, Australia, 1986).

41. The market was an ever greater presence in most areas. Ellen Meiksins Wood helps cut through historiographic debates over whether European settlers in British North America were pro- or antimarket by observing that "the market" offered *both* opportunities and coercions. People generally preferred one to the other. Wood, "From Opportunity to Imperative." Emphasizing farm households as consumers of imported manufactures is Thomas M. Doerflinger, "Farmers and Dry Goods in the Philadelphia Market Area," in Hoffman et al., *Economy of Early America*, 166–95. On rural merchants, see Gregory Nobles, "The Rise of Merchants in Rural Market Towns: A Case Study of Northampton, Massachusetts," *Journal of Social History* 24 (1990): 5–12.

42. As I have suggested elsewhere, the uncertainty of dealings in the wider market might make practices of local exchange more meaningful, rather than less so, even as farmers and tradesmen became increasingly engaged in market exchange. Smith, "Food Rioters and the American Revolution," *William and Mary Quarterly*, 3rd ser., 51 (1994): 3–38. See also Mary McKinney Schweitzer, "Contracts and Custom: Economic Policy in Colonial Pennsylvania," *Journal of Economic History* 45 (1985): 463–65; James F. Shepherd, "British America and the Atlantic Economy," in Hoffman et al., *Economy of Early America*, 4–19; Doerflinger, "Farmers and Dry Goods," 166–95; Henretta, "War for Independence," 45–87.

43. Wise, "Instructions for Emigrants," 66.

44. On neighborliness as an ideal of social relations between "effective equals" in England, see Wrightson, *English Society*, 51; William H. Seiler, "Land Processioning in Colonial Virginia," *William and Mary Quarterly*, 3rd ser., 6 (1949): 416–36. Court records depict the value of neighbors as witnesses of character, witnesses to exchanges, and "evidences" of land boundaries. Sandra Sherman, "Promises, Promises: Credit as Contested Metaphor in Early Capitalist Discourse," *Modern Philology* 94 (1997): 327–49, explores a relationship between growing reliance on credit and the closing down of conceptual space for "moral agency" (335).

45. Timothy Breen, "An Empire of Goods: The Anglicization of Colonial America, 1690–1776," *Journal of British Studies* 25 (1986): 467–99.

46. John M. Murrin, "The Legal Transformation: The Bench and Bar of Eighteenth-Century Massachusetts," in *Colonial America: Essays in Politics and Social Development*, ed. Stanley N. Katz and John M. Murrin, 540–72 (New York: Knopf, 1983); Cornelia Hughes Dayton, *Women Before the Bar: Gender, Law, and Society in Connecticut, 1639–1789* (Chapel Hill: University of North Carolina Press, 1995).

47. "A Dialogue Between a Boston Man and a Country Man," appearing in 1714, reprinted in *Publications of the Colonial Society of Massachusetts* 10 (1907): 345–46.

48. Gary B. Nash, *The Urban Crucible: Social Change, Political Consciousness, and the Origins of the American Revolution* (Cambridge, MA: Harvard University Press, 1979), 129–38.

49. Justin Winsor, *The Memorial History of Boston*, 4 vols. (Boston: James R. Osgood & Company, 1882–83), 2:462.

50. Karen Friedman, "Victualling Colonial Boston," *Agricultural History* 47 (1973): 189–205. I explored the Boston market controversy in "Markets, Streets, and Stores," *Autre temps, autre espace: Etudes sur l'Amérique pré-industrielle*, ed. Elise Marienstras and Barbara Karsky, 172–97 (Nancy: Presses Universitaires de Nancy, 1986).

51. "At a meeting of the Freeholders . . . for setting up and regulating a Public market, April 24, 1734" (Boston, 1734).

52. The issue was revived briefly in 1740, when Peter Faneuil left money in his will for a market. Boston town meeting agreed to accept the gift only with the understanding that no dealers would be forced off the street; even then, there was close voting in town meeting.

53. Nash, *Urban Crucible*, 129–38, puts the market issue properly in context not only of proposed town meeting reforms but of conflicts over paper money. Smith, "Markets, Streets and Stores"; G.B. Warden, *Boston, 1689–1776* (Boston: Little, Brown, 1970), 115–24. Teaford, *Municipal Revolution in America*, chap. 3, offers a different perspective.

54. Albert O. Matthews, "Attempts to Incorporate Boston," *Publications of the Colonial Society of Massachusetts* 10 (1907): 352–56; "Dialogue Between a Boston Man and a Country Man," 346.

55. "Dialogue Between a Boston Man and a Country Man," 347, 348.

56. "My Son, Fear Thou the Lord, and the King: and Meddle not with Them that are Given to Change," Boston, 1714/15, reprinted in *Publications of the Colonial Society of Massachusetts* 10 (1907): 345–52, quotation on p. 351.

57. Ibid., 352.

58. On not identifying regulated marketplaces with moral economy, see Thompson, "Moral Economy Reviewed," 288.

59. Benjamin Colman, *Some Reasons and Arguments Offered to the Good People of Boston and Adjacent Places for the Setting Up Markets in Boston* (Boston, 1719), 7.

60. Ibid., 8.

61. Ibid., 6.

62. Ibid., 5.

63. Ibid., 7, 8.

64. "Dialogue Between a Boston Man and a Country Man," 348. Portsmouth, New Hampshire, inhabitants protested when shopkeepers engrossed produce coming into town in 1765, according to Bogin, "Petitioning and the New Moral Economy," 398–99.

65. There is some evidence that market opponents *from outside the town* may have done something close to that. The country people who brought victuals to town clearly opposed the new restrictions. Surely, wrote Colman, "it can scarce be supposed that any will think this comely and useful Order can be a breach upon their natural rights and liberties" (8). Surely, since Colman felt compelled to write about it, some thought precisely that. Suppliers now traveled freely to different neighborhoods and would feel constrained by the markets. They were wary about the expensive licenses and fees that might follow. Yet what ultimately deterred country suppliers was not that they were too attached to liberties in trade but (as Colman acknowledged) too *unattached* to producing and selling for maximal profit.

66. "Dialogue Between a Boston Man and a Country Man," 346.

67. Colman, "Some Reasons," 11.

68. "Dialogue Between a Boston Man and a Country Man," 348.

69. Colman, "Some Reasons," 9.

70. This according to Governor Jonathan Belcher, in a proclamation printed in the *Boston Newsletter*, April 14–21, 1737.

71. Nash, *Urban Crucible*, 134.

72. Colman, "Some Reasons," 2.

73. Rowland Berthoff and John M. Murrin, "Feudalism, Communalism, and the Yeoman Freeholder: The American Revolution Considered as a Social Accident," in *Essays on the American Revolution*, ed. Stephen G. Kurtz and James H. Hutson, 256–88 (Chapel Hill: University of North Carolina Press, 1973). We find Marylanders in 1739 complaining of new fines imposed by the proprietor's "rent receiver" in much the same terms as those used in England: the receiver had "Extorted from many his Majestys liege People" so-called "Alienation Fines on all Lands Decised." "Such Fines was a thing unheard of since the Settlement of this province by British subjects till within three years past." It was "Against Law, Custom, Reason, and the express Tenor of the Grants, made by his Lordship and his Ancestors to the good people this province and their predecessors," an act that was not only "an Innovation, but an Invasion of the rights of the People, and a great Aggrievance and oppression." *Maryland Archives*, 40:361.

74. James M. Poteet, "Unrest in the 'Land of Steady Habits': The Hartford Riot of 1722," *Proceedings of the American Philosophical Society* 119 (1975): 223–32.

75. On growing tenantry, see Gregory A. Stiverson, *Poverty in a Land of Plenty: Tenancy in Eighteenth-Century Maryland* (Baltimore: Johns Hopkins University Press, 1977); Sung Bok Kim, *Landlord and Tenant in Colonial New York: Manorial Society 1664–1775* (Chapel Hill: University of North Carolina Press, 1978); Bruce C. Daniels, *The Connecticut Town: Growth and Development, 1635–1790* (Middletown, CT: Wesleyan University Press, 1979).

76. This account of New Jersey's disputes relies heavily on Brendan McConville, *These Daring Disturbers of the Public Peace: The Struggle for Prosperity and Power in Early New Jersey* (Ithaca, NY: Cornell University Press, 1999). Most important, perhaps, McConville demonstrates that New Jersey yeoman farmers had long-standing and sophisticated ideas about their property and their liberties well before political disputes with Britain began. They would bring their ideas with them into the Revolution. Edward Countryman, "Out of the Bounds of the Law: Northern Land Rioters in the Eighteenth Century," in *The American Revolution: Explorations in the History of American Radicalism*, ed. Alfred F. Young, 37–69 (DeKalb, IL: Northern Illinois University Press, 1976).

77. McConville, *Daring Disturbers of the Peace*, 40; [Griffin Jenkins], *Brief Vindication of the Purchassors Against the Proprtors, in a Christian Manner* (New York: P. Zenger Jr., 1746).

78. McConville, *Daring Disturbers of the Peace*, 132.

79. Ibid., 155; Thomas L. Purvis, "Origins and Patterns of Agrarian Unrest in New Jersey, 1735–1754," *William and Mary Quarterly*, 3rd ser., 39 (1982): 600–627.

80. [Jenkins] *Brief Vindication*, vii–xii, 3, 4, 5, 16, 17.

81. Ibid., 17; McConville, *Daring Disturbers of the Peace*, 133.

82. Vickers, "Competency and Competition," 28–29. We see here the seeds of the ideologies that supported expansion across the continent in the nineteenth century. A second critical tension in the ideal of a competency lay in the degree of control of labor that was needed as farms became prosperous.

83. Cotton Mather, *Fair Dealing Between Debtor and Creditor* (Boston, 1716), 27. See also Mather, *Concio ad Populum: A Distressed People Entertained by Proposals for the Relief of Their Distresses* (Boston, 1719). Craig Muldrew, "The Culture of Reconciliation: Community and the Settlement of Economic Disputes in Early Modern England," *Historical Journal* 39 (1996): 915–42, notes stress on reconciliation in early seventeenth-century England. On the subject of informal settlements and litigation, Muldrew, *The Economy of Obligation: The Culture of Credit and Social Relations in Early Modern England* (New York: St. Martin's, 1998), 152–56, 173, 182–85, and passim, explores credit as a form of knowledge in this era.

84. Bruce Mann, *Neighbors and Strangers: Law and Community in Early Connecticut* (Chapel Hill: University of North Carolina Press, 1987); Sherman, "Promises, Promises," 327–49.

85. Roger W. Weiss, "The Issue of Paper Money in the American Colonies, 1720–1774," *Journal of Economic History* 30 (1970): 770–84; Theodore Thayer, "The Land-Bank System in the American Colonies," *Journal of Economic History* 13 (1953): 145–59. Paper money allowed farmers and artisans easier access to a means of paying taxes and debts. Without paper currencies, these groups could generally obtain specie only on disadvantaged terms. Richard A. Lester, "Currency Issues to Overcome Depressions in Pennsylvania, 1723 and 1729," *Journal of Political Economy* 46 (1938): 324–75; Lester, "Currency Issues to Overcome Depressions in Delaware, New Jersey, New York, and Maryland, 1715–1737," *Journal of Political Economy* 47 (1939): 182–217.

86. Francis Rawle, *Ways and Means for the Inhabitants of Delaware to Become Rich* (Philadelphia, 1725), quoted in Lester, "Currency Issues in Delaware," 183, 184.

87. Schultz, "Small-Producer Tradition," 96. On Governor Keith's support for paper money and his indictment of "the Lawyers and a few Rich Usurors" who opposed it, see Lester, "Currency Issues in Pennsylvania," 335–36. See also Gary B. Nash, "Social Change and the Growth of Prerevolutionary Urban Radicalism," in Young, *American Revolution*, 12–13.

88. Benjamin Franklin, *A Modest Enquiry into the Nature and Necessity of a Paper-Currency* (Philadelphia, 1729). Tradesmen in other towns also complained of receiving pay in the form of goods or "Notes on Shops for Money and Goods." In Boston, town caulkers decided to accept only "good lawful publick Bills of Credit, Manufactory Bills, Merchants Notes, Corn, Wheat or other Grain Pork Beef or other Provisions, Rum, Sugar, Molasses, or other West-Indies Goods, at the Price current, or market price." Robert Francis Seybolt, ed., "Trade Agreements in Colonial Boston," *New England Quarterly* 2 (1929): 307–9. This fact cautions historians not to draw *direct* conclusions about tradesmen's and small farmers' desires for imported consumer goods from the mere presence of such goods in their inventories. It complicates the easy equation of consumption and "choice."

89. Reprinted in Andrew McFarland Davis, *Colonial Currency Reprints*, 2: 336–57.

90. Benjamin Franklin, *American Weekly Mercury*, March 27, 1729, in *The Writings of Benjamin Franklin*, vol. 2 (Philadelphia, 1726–1757), http://www.historycarper.com/resources/twobf2/paper1.htm (accessed November 17, 2009).

91. Ibid.

92. "On Publick Spirit," *Independent Advertiser*, January 25, 1748.

93. Ibid.

94. Franklin, *American Weekly Mercury*; "On Public Spirit."

95. Ibid. See also *Independent Advertiser*, March 14, 1748.

96. Nancy J. Hirschmann, "Freedom, Recognition, and Obligation: A Feminist Approach to Political Theory," *American Political Science Review* 83, no. 4 (December 1989): 1227–44, notes that a fully voluntarist understanding of obligation assumes people to be inherently separate and fragmented.

3. Declarations of Interdependence

1. One symptom of this thinking appears in Gordon S. Wood's leading synthesis of the era, which recounts the coming of the Revolution without mentioning the presence of ordinary and middling sorts of Patriots prior to 1776. Readers are likely to conclude that such people mobilized (or mobilized effectively) only *after* the colonies had otherwise stumbled into war or reached a decision for independence. Wood, *The Radicalism of the American Revolution* (New York: Knopf, 1992).

2. If it is a truth at all. On power as a relationship, see Elizabeth Janeway, *Powers of the Weak* (New York: Knopf, 1980). Also: "Tolstoy was right. . . . A crowd may move a mountain; a single man cannot. If therefore, we say of a man that he has moved a mountain it is because he has been credited with (or has appropriated) the work of the crowd, that he claimed to command, but that he also followed." Bruno Latour, *The Pasteurization of France*, trans. Alan Sheridan and John Law (Cambridge, MA: Harvard University Press, 1988), 22–23.

3. Accustomed to seeing execution of the law as *mere enforcement*, we can dismiss the frustration of Parliamentary policies from the Stamp Act to the Tea Act as *mere nonenforcement*, as if struggles over execution were subordinate or incidental to arguments about the nature and necessity of representation. The historian whose interpretation I am contesting most centrally here is Pauline Maier, *From Resistance to Revolution: Colonial Radicals and the Development of Opposition to Britain, 1765–1776* (New York: Random House, 1974). Historians who have led the way in viewing popular participation from the perspective of the agency of ordinary participants appear in the notes below. In regard to early America, they particularly include John K. Alexander, Edward Countryman, Dirk Hoerder, James H. Hutson, Jesse Lemisch, Gary B. Nash, Steven Rosswurm, Richard Alan Ryerson, and Alfred F. Young.

4. Edmund S. Morgan and Helen M. Morgan, *The Stamp Act Crisis: Prologue to Revolution*, rev. ed. (London: Collier MacMillan, 1963), 36–58, 105–12, 117, 123–24, 137–38, and passim. John Dickinson emphasized that Parliamentary regulation of trade properly worked for "a mutually beneficial intercourse between the several constituent parts of the empire," in *Letters from a Farmer in Pennsylvania: To the Inhabitants of the British Colonies* (Philadelphia, 1767), letter 2.

5. Morgan and Morgan, *Stamp Act Crisis*, 40, 55–56, 153; L. Kinvin Wroth, "The Massachusetts Vice-Admiralty Court," in *Law and Authority in Colonial America*, ed. George Athan Billias, 32–73 (Barre, MA: Barre Publishers, 1965); Carl Ubbelohde, *The Vice-Admiralty Courts and the American Revolution* (Chapel Hill: University of North Carolina Press, 1960).

6. John Adams, *The Legal Papers*, 229, quoted in John Philip Reid, "Civil Law as a Criminal Sanction," in *Studies of Comparative Criminal Law*, ed. Edward M. Wise and Gerhard O.W. Mueller (Springfield, IL: Charles C. Thomas, 1975), 228n.

7. "To the Printer," *Boston Gazette*, July 15, 1765.

8. "Instructions to the Representatives from Boston," *Pennsylvania Gazette*, October 3, 1765.

9. "To the Printer."

10. Ibid.

11. Will. Alfred, "From a Late London Paper," *Boston Gazette*, January 27, 1766.

12. Gadsden quoted in Keith Krawczynski, *William Henry Drayton: South Carolina Revolutionary Patriot* (Baton Rouge: Louisiana State University Press, 2001), 42.

13. The Westmoreland Association appears in Robert L. Scribner, ed., William J. Van Schreeven, comp., *Revolutionary Virginia: The Road to Independence*, vol. 1, *Forming Thunderclouds and the First Convention, 1763–1774* (Charlottesville: University Press of Virginia, 1973), 22–26.

14. Lawrence Henry Gipson, *Jared Ingersoll: A Study of American Loyalism in Relation to British Colonial Government* (New Haven, CT: Yale University Press, 1920), 170–71 on events in Lyme, and 172–73 on New Haven and West Haven. The latter account is by "Antonius," New-Haven, *Boston Evening Post*, September 23, 1765.

15. Events in Portsmouth, New Hampshire, are in the *Boston Post-Boy*, September 16, 1765. A pageant depicting Prime Minister George Grenville in chains is recounted in the *New-Hampshire Gazette and Historical Chronicle*, January 10, 1766.

16. The account is from the *North-Carolina Gazette*, November 20, 1765, which is reproduced in Donna J. Spindel, "Law and Disorder: The North Carolina Stamp Act Crisis," *North Carolina Historical Review* 57 (1980): 9.

17. Maier, *From Resistance to Revolution*, 73.

18. Morgan and Morgan, *Stamp Act Crisis*, 162–65, 179–81, 187–204; Richard Walsh, *Charleston's Sons of Liberty: A Study of the Artisans, 1763–1789* (Columbia: University of South Carolina Press, 1959); Henry Dawson, *New York City During the American Revolution* (New York: Mercantile Library Association, 1861). *Connecticut Courant*, January 6, 1766, recounts events in New Bern, North Carolina, Providence, Rhode Island, and Taunton, Massachusetts.

19. It is not so important that newspaper accounts were partisan (they were), or that they may have been inaccurate (they may), as that they must be read as part of the political action itself. The same may be said of the Loyalist press, which made different claims about and on "the public." David Waldstreicher, "Rites of Rebellion, Rites of Assent: Celebrations, Print Culture, and the Origins of American Nationalism," *Journal of American History* 82 (1995): 49, suggests we view newspaper accounts of Patriot celebrations "less as objective reportage than as pieces of rhetoric, a genre designed to define what it ostensibly describes."

20. Waldstreicher, "Rites of Rebellion," 51–61, notes that newspaper accounts of actions by "the people" worked to deny the presence of divisions and dissent and to create unity.

21. On Otis's opinion that "we must obey" the acts of Parliament, see Edmund S. Morgan, "Thomas Hutchinson and the Stamp Act," *New England Quarterly* 21 (1948): 464; Ellen Elizabeth Brennan, "James Otis: Recreant and Patriot," *New England Quarterly* 12 (1939): 691–725. On Franklin, James H. Hutson, "An Investigation of the Inarticulate: Philadelphia's White Oaks," *William and Mary Quarterly*, 3rd ser., 28 (1971): 4–25; Verner Crane, "Benjamin Franklin and the Stamp Act," *Publications of the Colonial Society of Massachusetts* 32 (1933–37): 56–77. Benjamin L. Carp notes the role of Philadelphia's voluntary fire societies in preventing destruction of Franklin's house in Carp, "Fire of Liberty: Firefighters, Urban Voluntary Culture, and the Revolutionary Movement," *William and Mary Quarterly*, 3rd ser., 58 (2001): 781–818. Gary Kornblith and John Murrin suggest that most of the political elite who wrote

pamphlets agreed that the Stamp Act was unconstitutional but thought the colonies had to obey it. The middling sort (e.g., the Loyal Nine) and lower sort (such as Ebenezer McIntosh) disagreed. Kornblith and Murrin, "The Dilemmas of Ruling Elites in Revolutionary America," in *Ruling America: A History of Wealth and Power in a Democracy*, ed. Steve Fraser and Gary Gerstle (Cambridge, MA: Harvard University Press, 2005), 34–35. The *Newport Mercury*, May 18, 1767, published an article from the *London Gazetteer* that satirized colonial opposition to admiralty courts.

22. Bernard Bailyn, *The Ordeal of Thomas Hutchinson* (Cambridge, MA: Harvard University Press, 1974), 35–39, 65–69; Morgan, "Thomas Hutchinson and the Stamp Act," 461–92 (reference to Boston's "good People" is on p. 471); Bernard Bailyn, ed., "Thomas Hutchinson's 'Dialogue Between an American and a European Englishman,' 1768," *Perspectives in American History* 9 (1975): 390–94; Dirk Hoerder, *Crowd Action in Revolutionary Massachusetts, 1765–1780* (New York: Academic Press, 1977).

23. Or perhaps referring to the cudgels they carried?

24. Gipson, *Jared Ingersoll*, 177–90. Quotations from pp. 182, 183.

25. On "resistance to representation" in the French Revolution, see Susan Maslan, "Resisting Representation: Theater and Democracy in Revolutionary France," *Representations* 52 (Fall 1995): 27–51.

26. Edward Countryman has profoundly shaped our understanding of the Revolution as the product of changing political and social coalitions, especially in *A People in Revolution: The American Revolution and Political Society in New York, 1760–1790* (Baltimore: Johns Hopkins University Press, 1981). See also Countryman, *The American Revolution*, rev. ed. (New York: Hill and Wang, 2003).

27. I have dealt with one of these associations, the Continental Association of 1774, in an earlier article, some of whose examples and conclusions appear in the following pages. Barbara Clark Smith, "Social Visions of the American Resistance Movement," in *The Transforming Hand of Revolution: Reconsidering the American Revolution as a Social Movement*, ed. Ronald Hoffman and Peter J. Albert, 27–57 (Charlottesville: University Press of Virginia, 1996). T.H. Breen, *The Marketplace of Revolution: How Consumer Politics Shaped American Independence* (New York: Oxford University Press, 2004) provides a different view. See also David Ammerman, *In The Common Cause: The American Responses to the Coercive Acts of 1774* (Charlottesville: University Press of Virginia, 1974); Arthur M. Schlesinger, *The Colonial Merchants and the American Revolution, 1763–1776* (1918; repr., New York: Atheneum, 1968).

28. Boston's prediction of dire economic decline as an outcome of the Sugar Act also appeared in the town meeting's instructions to representatives, petitions to Parliament, and pamphlets. John W. Tyler, *Smugglers and Patriots: Boston Merchants and the Advent of the American Revolution* (Boston: Northeastern University Press, 1986), 83–88. Thacher quote on p. 89.

29. Quoted in Schlesinger, *Colonial Merchants*, 69. Charles M. Andrews, "The Boston Merchants and the NonImportation Movement," *Publications of the Colonial Society of Massachusetts* 19 (1918): 204–6. The Virginia stamp distributor, George Mercer, testified before Parliament that "most persons" in the colony thought the Stamp Act "would fall chiefly upon poor people . . . principally upon debtors and creditors," partly because there was not enough specie to pay it. Fletcher Norton, attorney general under Grenville, urged use of force against "resistance made to the execution" of the Stamp Act in America, citing prosecutions in England when "the clamour of the people" had prevented execution of a militia law there. Lawrence Henry Gipson, "The Great Debate in the Committee of the Whole House of Com-

mons on the Stamp Act, 1766, as Reported by Nathaniel Ryder," *Pennsylvania Magazine of History and Biography* 86 (1962): 33, 27–28.

30. Walsh, *Charleston's Sons of Liberty*, 54.

31. In West Florida, authorities reported, settlers were "hardly able to pay the common fees of office on taking up land, much less any additional charge on it." Since they were "deprived of the necessary currency for circulating," the colonies' "lower class of inhabitants" felt the distress. "Their murmurs were extreme." Wilfred B. Keen, "The Stamp Act in the Floridas, 1765–1766," *Mississippi Valley Historical Review* 21 (1935): 463–70.

32. On West Indies planters and lobbyists in England, see Andrew Jackson O'Shaughnessy, *An Empire Divided: The American Revolution and the British Caribbean* (Philadelphia: University of Pennsylvania Press, 2000), chap. 1. Boston merchants suggested that undue influence of West Indies interests inspired the Sugar Act in their "State of Trade," 1763, quoted in Tyler, *Smugglers and Patriots*, 71.

33. Quoted in Krawczynski, *William Henry Drayton*, 98.

34. Morgan and Morgan, *Stamp Act Crisis*, 118.

35. Margaret W. Willard, ed., *Letters on the American Revolution, 1774–1776* (Boston: Houghton Mifflin, 1925), 157–58.

36. Schlesinger, *Colonial Merchants*, 63–64 on Boston. On the College of New Jersey, see Larry R. Gerlach, *Prologue to Independence: New Jersey in the Coming of the American Revolution* (New Brunswick, NJ: Rutgers University Press, 1976), 117.

37. *Archives of the State of New Jersey*, 1st ser., vol. 24, *Extracts from American Newspapers, Relating to New Jersey*, vol. 5, 1762–1765 (Paterson, NJ: Press Printing and Publishing, 1902), x.

38. Schlesinger, *Colonial Merchants*, 63–64, 77, 86; Anne Fairfax Withington, *Toward a More Perfect Union: Virtue and the Formation of American Republics* (New York: Oxford University Press, 1991), 94–143; Breen, *Marketplace of Revolution*, 213–17.

39. *Archives of the State of New Jersey*, 1st ser., vol. 27, *Extracts from American Newspapers, Relating to New Jersey*, vol. 3, 1770–1771 (Paterson, NJ: Press Printing and Publishing, 1905), vii.

40. On the conflict between gentry and New Light ideals in Virginia, see Rhys Isaac, *The Transformation of Virginia, 1740–1790* (Chapel Hill: University of North Carolina Press, 1982), esp. 264–69. A different interpretation of the suppression of theater in 1774 appears in Withington, *More Perfect Union*, chap. 2.

41. Richard Bushman, "American High-Style and Vernacular Cultures," in *Colonial British North America: Essays in the New History of the Early Modern Era*, ed. Jack P. Greene and J.R. Pole (Baltimore: Johns Hopkins University Press, 1984), 352. See also Bushman, *The Refinement of America: Persons, Houses, Cities* (New York: Knopf, 1992), 3–180.

42. Richard J. Hooker, "The American Revolution Seen Through a Wineglass," *William and Mary Quarterly*, 3rd ser., 11 (1954): 52–77 (Adams quote is on p. 54); Peter Thompson, *Rum Punch and Revolution: Taverngoing and Public Life in Eighteenth-Century Philadelphia* (Philadelphia: University of Pennsylvania Press, 1999); David W. Conroy, *In Public Houses: Drink and the Revolution of Authority in Colonial Massachusetts* (Chapel Hill: University of North Carolina Press, 1995). For events in Rutland, see Lee Nathaniel Newcomer, *The Embattled Farmers: A Massachusetts Countryside in the American Revolution* (New York: Columbia University Press, 1953), 22. Toasts were important expressions of allegiance to Loyalists as well. See, for example, *Rivington's Gazette*, July 6, 1775, in Frank Moore, *Diary of the American Revolution, from Newspapers*

and Original Documents, 2 vols. (New York: Charles Scribner, 1860; repr., New York: Arno Press, 1969), 1:107–8.

43. *Boston Gazette*, January 1775.

44. Providence, Rhode Island, March 4, 1775, in *American Archives: Fourth Series, Containing a Documentary History of the English Colonies in North America, from the King's Message to the Parliament, of March 7, 1774, to the Declaration of Independence of the United States*, ed. Peter Force (Washington, DC: M. St. Clair Clarke and Peter Force, 1837–1846), 2:15. For New Jersey tea burnings, see Gerlach, *Prologue to Independence*, 197–200.

45. "Edenton Ladies Association, October 25, 1774," in Force, *American Archives: Fourth Series*, 1:891–92; Schlesinger, *Colonial Merchants*, 168–69.

46. Grant McCracken, *Culture and Consumption: New Approaches to the Symbolic Character of Consumer Goods and Activities* (Bloomington: Indiana University Press, 1988), 20–21.

47. *Newport Mercury*, July 29, 1765; Marla Miller, *The Needle's Eye: Women and Work in the Age of Revolution* (Amherst: University of Massachusetts Press, 2006).

48. *South Carolina Gazette* quoted in Ammerman, *Common Cause*, 117; *Gaine's Mercury*, January 30, 1775, reprinted in Moore, *Diary of the American Revolution*, 1: 16–17.

49. Schlesinger, *Colonial Merchants*, 110; Gerlach, *Prologue to Independence*, 117.

50. William Wragg, September 21, 1769, in *The Letters of Freeman, Etc.: Essays on the Nonimportation Movement in South Carolina, Collected by William Henry Drayton*, ed. Robert M. Weir (Columbia: University of South Carolina Press, 1977), 28, 29.

51. E.P. Thompson, *Customs in Common: Studies in Traditional Popular Culture* (New York: The New Press, 1991), 55.

52. See Woody Holton, *Forced Founders: Indians, Debtors, Slaves and the Making of the American Revolution in Virginia* (Chapel Hill: University of North Carolina Press, 1999), for an interpretation that sees Virginia's elite as pressed into Revolution both from below and from outside their society. I am arguing something slightly different: not only did middling Patriots generally lead the way in some aspects of the resistance (for example, blocking execution of the Stamp Act and not just denouncing it), but elites who became Patriots acquired that identity by taking as their own the values (at times, the appearance) of their more middling neighbors. In this movement, there was often necessary ambiguity about who was joining whom.

53. On the amount of consumption among middling colonists, see Breen, *Marketplace of Revolution*; Breen, "An Empire of Goods: The Anglicization of Colonial America, 1690–1776," *Journal of British Studies* 25 (1986): 467–99. Cf. James A. Henretta, review of Breen, *Marketplace of Revolution*, in *William and Mary Quarterly*, 3rd ser., 61 (2004): 765–69.

54. Gipson, *Jared Ingersoll*, pp. 268–69.

55. Withington, *More Perfect Union*, 97, 106–7, and on costs, 115–24.

56. Miller, *Needle's Eye*; Marla Miller, "The Last Mantuamaker: Craft Tradition and Commercial Exchange in Boston, 1760–1849," *Early American Studies* 4 (2006): 375; James A. Henretta, "The War for Independence and American Economic Development," in *The Economy of Early America: The Revolutionary Period, 1763–1790*, ed. Ronald Hoffman, John J. McCusker, Russell R. Menard, and Peter Albert (Charlottesville: University Press of Virginia, 1988), esp. 58–68.

57. On the manufactories, Richard B. Morris, *Government and Labor in Early*

America (New York: Columbia University Press, 1946), 13–14n61; Schlesinger, *Colonial Merchants*. The *Pennsylvania Journal* reported an appeal posted in Philadelphia in August 1775, soliciting spinners from city, suburbs, and country to work for the American Manufactory on Market Street, both for the income for their households and "the public good." Moore, *Diary of the American Revolution*, 1:123–24. *Newport Mercury*, November 18 and December 23, 1765, reported the markets. The quotation is from the *Connecticut Gazette*, March 29, 1766, cited in Gipson, *Jared Ingersoll*, 164.

58. Using the phrase of the Carolinians, in Krawczynski, *William Henry Drayton*, 41. Others in Schlesinger, *Colonial Merchants*.

59. Ames is quoted in Morris, *Government and Labor*, 53. See also James L. Huston, "The American Revolutionaries, the Political Economy of Aristocracy, and the American Concept of the Distribution of Wealth, 1765–1900," *American Historical Review* 98 (1993): 1079–105.

60. Connecticut towns also promised "Neglect, Disesteem and Contempt" for non-associators; David H. Villars, "Loyalism in Connecticut, 1774–1783," in *Loyalists and Community in North America*, ed. Robert M. Calhoon, Timothy M. Barnes, and George A. Rawlyk (Westport, CT: Greenwood Press, 1994), 18.

61. On associations as morally binding agreements that allowed an independent space for "the public" to appear in English politics, see Eugene Charlton Black, *The Association: British Extraparliamentary Political Organization, 1769–1793* (Cambridge, MA: Harvard University Press, 1963).

62. Josiah Gilbert Holland, *History of Western Massachusetts* (Springfield, MA: Samuel Bowles, 1855), 208.

63. I am dissenting here from Timothy Breen, *Marketplace of Revolution*, who suggests that colonists' "shared experience as consumers provided them with the cultural resources needed to develop a bold new form of political protest" (xv–xvi). It seems to me that it was not consuming that formed the common experience but rather practices that asserted local and common jurisdiction, including jurisdiction over exchange. Similarly, I want to stress that the sources of Patriot thought were not consumer goods themselves, as Breen argues in "Baubles of Britain: The American and Consumer Revolutions of the Eighteenth Century," *Past and Present* 119 (May 1988): 73–104, but rather cultural traditions apart from the goods. See also Jean-Christophe Agnew, "Coming Up for Air: Consumer Culture in Historical Perspective," in *Consumption and the World of Goods*, ed. John Brewer and Roy Porter, 19–39 (New York: Routledge, 1993).

64. Women's participation reveals some of the boundaries of the movement, to the extent that they "have been traditionally the creatures furthest removed from the ability to act effectively in the external world." Janeway, *Powers of the Weak*, 117. Historians who have recovered the participation of women in the resistance movement include Mary Beth Norton, *Liberty's Daughters: The Revolutionary Experience of American Women, 1750–1800* (Boston: Little, Brown, 1980), esp. 156–70 on trade boycotts; Linda K. Kerber, *Women of the Republic: Intellect and Ideology in Revolutionary America* (Chapel Hill: University of North Carolina Press, 1980), 36–42; Alfred F. Young, "The Women of Boston: 'Persons of Consequence' in the Making of the American Revolution," in *Women and Politics in the Age of the Democratic Revolution*, ed. Harriet B. Applewhite and Darline G. Levy (Ann Arbor: University of Michigan Press, 1993), 181–224; Smith, "Social Visions of the Resistance," 52–55.

65. Francis S. Drake, *Tea Leaves: Being a Collection of Letters and Documents Relating to the Shipment of Tea to the American Colonies in the Year 1773 by the East India Tea Company* (Boston: A.O. Crane, 1884), ix.

66. "Edenton Ladies Association."

67. Ruth H. Bloch, "The Gendered Meanings of Virtue in Revolutionary America," *Signs* 13 (1987): 37–58.

68. Norton, *Liberty's Daughters*, 156–70; Breen, *Marketplace of Revolution*, 172–82.

69. *Massachusetts Gazette*, September 20, 1764.

70. Joyce Appleby, "Ideology and Theory, the Tension Between Political and Economic Liberalism in Seventeenth-Century England," *American History Review* 81 (1976): 499–515. On a London calico riot of 1720, see Robert B. Shoemaker, "The London 'Mob' in the Early Eighteenth Century," *Journal of British Studies* 26 (1987): 289.

71. "Communicated by E.B.," *Pennsylvania Journal*, March 1, 1775, in Moore, *Diary of the American Revolution*, 1:30–31.

72. *Connecticut Courant*, April 7, 1766.

73. Rev. Thomas Barnard to the Committee of Safety for Salem, May 25, 1775, in Force, *American Archives: Fourth Series*, 2:710; Enachy Bartlett, September 9, 1774, *Miscellaneous Bound Collection*, Massachusetts Historical Society, Boston, MA.

74. Joan R. Gundersen, "Independence, Citizenship, and the American Revolution," *Signs* 13 (1987): 59–77, makes the critical point that dependence was not powerlessness in the colonial period.

75. Michael Zuckerman, "A Different Thermidor: The Revolution Beyond the American Revolution," in *The Transformation of Early American History: Society, Authority, and Ideology*, ed. James A. Henretta, Michael Kammen, and Stanley N. Katz (New York: Knopf, 1991), 173, suggests it was the "diffusion" of republican ideas from leaders to other Americans that "turned resistance into revolution." Bernard Bailyn, *The Ideological Origins of the American Revolution* (Cambridge, MA: Harvard University Press, 1967), drew on the outpouring of pamphlet publications to argue for the centrality of elite ideas. Robert E. Shalhope, "Toward a Republican Synthesis: The Emergence of an Understanding of Republicanism in American Historiography" *William and Mary Quarterly*, 3rd ser., 29 (1972): 49–80, reviews this interpretation.

76. Cf. Richard D. Brown, *Knowledge Is Power: The Diffusion of Information in Early America, 1700–1865* (New York: Oxford University Press, 1991), which describes information as largely flowing in one direction. Thomas C. Leonard, "News for Revolution: The Exposé in America, 1768–1773," *Journal of American History* 67 (1980): 26–40, notes that the early stages of resistance organizing pushed local news into the newspapers of all the colonies to a much greater extent than previously (27).

77. It seems to me useful if we think of Patriot newspapers as a meeting ground where two different sources of public authority sometimes came together (not necessarily in equal measure). Besides presenting authoritative writings of elites, marked by Latin epigrams and references to famous British political thinkers, the newspapers carried the authoritative pronouncements of communities and self-created groups. Some elite men no doubt had a hand at least in many of those pronouncements; but these pronouncements were adopted in public meetings where there was, to varying degrees, space for popular participation, dissent, or mere nonattendance. David Waldstreicher, "Rites of Rebellion, Rites of Assent," *Journal of American History* 82 (1995): 37–61. See

also Michael Warner, *The Letters of the Republic: Publication and the Public Sphere in Eighteenth-Century America* (Cambridge, MA: Harvard University Press, 1990).

78. Edmund S Morgan, "The Puritan Ethic and the American Revolution," in *The Challenge of the American Revolution* (New York: W.W. Norton, 1976), 88–138.

79. Harry S. Stout and Peter Onuf, "James Davenport and the Great Awakening in New London," *Journal of American History* 70 (1983): 556–78; Isaac, *Transformation of Virginia*, 266–69; Marilyn Westerkamp, *Triumph of the Laity: Scots-Irish Piety and the Great Awakening, 1625–1760* (New York: Oxford University Press, 1988), stresses the public nature of conversion in the awakening in the Middle Colonies.

80. H.R. McIlwaine, ed., *Proceedings of the Committees of Safety of Cumberland and Isle of Wight Counties, 1775–1776* (Richmond: Virginia State Library, 1919), 12. See also Robert L. Scribner, ed., William J. Van Schreeven and Robert L. Scribner, comps., *Revolutionary Virginia: The Road to Independence*, vol. 2, *The Committees and the Second Convention, 1773–75: A Documentary Record* (Charlottesville: University Press of Virginia, 1975), 302; *Boston Gazette*, December 18, 1775.

81. Rehoboth Committee, *Boston Gazette*, September 11, 1775.

82. Withington, *More Perfect Union*, 223–24; Petersham Committee, *Boston Gazette*, January 16, 1775.

83. On shifting meanings of the word "country," see Clive Holmes, "The County Community in Stuart Historiography," *Journal of British Studies* 19, no. 2 (Spring 1980): 70–71.

84. McIlwaine, *Proceedings of the Committees of Safety*, 49.

85. Merchants of Philadelphia to Merchants of Newport, November 17, 1769, Brown Papers, P-P6, Rhode Island Politics, John Carter Brown Library, Providence, RI.

86. "From the Merchants Committee of New-York," July 10, 1770, *Pennsylvania Magazine of History and Biography* 6 (1882): 118.

87. Alternatively, perhaps we should give more weight to the degree of *dependence* on neighbors and even social inferiors assumed by eighteenth-century writers who wrote of *independence* as an ideal for republican leaders.

88. Schlesinger, *Colonial Merchants*, 92n2. Cadwallader Colden to Earl of Hillsborough, July 7, 1770, quoted in Milton M. Klein, "New York Lawyers and the Coming of the American Revolution," *New York History* 60 (October 1974): 383–408, 395.

89. Pressures on merchants to join appear in Francis Bernard to Lord Hillsborough, May 8, 1769; George Mason to John Harrison, October 20, 1769; extract letter of Nath. Rogers, October 25, 1769, in *Sparks Manuscripts*, ms. 10, vol. 3, Houghton Library, Harvard University, Cambridge, MA, 24, 40, 44. The quotation is on p. 40. On the increasingly prominent role of tradesmen in the movement, see Charles S. Olton, *Artisans for Independence: Philadelphia Mechanics and the American Revolution* (Syracuse, NY: Syracuse University Press, 1975), 41–47, 54–63; Maier, *From Resistance to Revolution*, 87–89, 116–118.

90. Weir, *Letters of Freeman*, ix–xxxvi; William Henry Drayton, "To *Libertas et Natali Solum*," October 12, 1769, and Drayton, September 21, 1769, both in Weir, *Letters of Freeman*, 49, 30, 31.

91. William Henry Drayton, August 3, 1769, and Drayton, "A Letter to the People," October 26, 1769," both in Weir, *Letters of Freeman*, 7, 55. Drayton also warned: "Remember! that the same authority which obliged many members of this community, to surrender their native liberty, can also lay a tax of 20s for each negro

that you own, and the same sum, for every hundred acres of land which you possess, and resolve, that those, who refuse to pay it on such a day, shall be deemed enemies to their country" (ibid., 57).

92. Weir, *Letters of Freeman*, xxviii–xxix.

93. William Nelson, ed., *Documents Related to the Colonial History of the State of New Jersey, Extracts from American Newspapers, Relating to New Jersey*, vol. 3, 1770–1771 (Paterson, NJ: Press Printing and Publishing, 1905), 29, 371–72 (hereafter *New Jersey Archives*).

94. Christopher Gadsden, November 30, 1769, in Weir, *Letters of Freeman*, 40.

95. Cited in T.H. Breen, "Narrative of Commercial Life: Consumption, Ideology, and Community on the Eve of the American Revolution," *William and Mary Quarterly*, 3rd ser., 50 (1993): 492.

96. Ibid., 488.

97. Krawczynski, *William Henry Drayton*, 51–52; "The Mechanics of the General Committee to Drayton," in Weir, *Letters of Freeman*, 111–14. The reference to "common sense" is on p. 112.

98. Morgan, "Puritan Ethic," 90–108, suggests the movement was anticommercial; cf. Timothy Breen, *Marketplace of Revolution*; Thomas M. Doerflinger, *A Vigorous Spirit of Enterprise: Merchants and Economic Development in Revolutionary Philadelphia* (Chapel Hill: Univeristy of North Carolina Press, 1986), 189–96 and chap. 4.

99. Jefferson quoted in Morgan, "Puritan Ethic," 98. Washington quoted in Maier, *From Resistance to Revolution*, 119. See also Emory G. Evans, "Planter Indebtedness and the Coming of the Revolution in Virginia," *William and Mary Quarterly*, 3rd ser., 19 (1962): 511–19. Bruce A. Ragsdale, *A Planter's Republic: The Search for Economic Independence in Revolutionary Virginia* (Madison, WI: Madison House, 1996), interprets nonimportation and nonconsumption pacts as aiming at economic change in Virginia, in addition to their political purpose. Holton, *Forced Founders*, chaps. 3, 4.

100. Boston merchants "State of Trade," Tyler, *Smugglers and Patriots*, 71.

101. *Pennsylvania Chronicle*, May 16, 1770. This understanding of the colonies as a potential empire or country that was imagined as a neighborhood "writ large" is not to be confused with mere localism, or the habit of mind that focused primarily on the well-being of one's own neighborhood rather than to the larger objects of country or province or empire. That element of thought doubtless existed in the colonies, perhaps particularly in the backcountry. Nonetheless, what I am describing here is a willingness to imagine a larger, more all-embracing political identity, yet casting that identity as an extension of neighboring relationships. Cf. Albert H. Tillson Jr., *Gentry and Common Folk: Political Culture on a Virginia Frontier, 1740–1789* (Lexington: University Press of Kentucky, 1991).

102. Virginia Convention, in Force, *American Archives: Fourth Series*, 1:688.

103. "Minutes of the Committee of Safety of Bucks County, Pennsylvania, 1774–1776," *Pennsylvania Magazine of History and Biography* 15 (1891): 270.

104. *Boston Gazette*, January 16, 1775.

105. On the denunciation of luxuries, see J.E. Crowley, *This Sheba, Self: The Conceptualization of Economic Life in Eighteenth-Century America* (Baltimore: Johns Hopkins University Press, 1974); Morgan, "Puritan Ethic," 90–108. "Those who have not Virtue enough to deny themselves superfluities which are ruinous to their country, are unworthy to live in a land of Freedom," *Edes and Gill Almanac*, Boston, 1769, cited in N.W. Lovely, "Notes on New England Almanacs," *New England Quarterly* 8 (1935): 276.

106. Bostonians could read an account of English riots over marketing corn and cheese in "Extract of a Letter from Gloucester," in *Boston Post Boy*, February 23, 1767; an account of legal consequences in "London, December 5," *Boston Post Boy*, March 2, 1767; an analysis in "From the Public Ledger, March 14," *Boston Post Boy*, May 18, 1767.

107. Withington, *More Perfect Union*, 11–12, views the Association of 1774 as "an intercolonial agreement to regulate moral behavior," although she associates that morality not with popular ideas of exchange but with Scottish moral philosophy as read by leading members of the Continental Congress and with a colonial heritage of seventeenth-century Puritan moralism.

108. Quoted in James K. Hosmer, *The Life of Thomas Hutchinson* (1896; repr., Boston and New York: Houghton, Mifflin, 1972), 166.

109. Schlesinger, *Colonial Merchants*, 170.

110. Thomas Gustafson, *Representative Words: Politics, Literature, and the American Language, 1776–1865* (Cambridge: Cambridge University Press, 1992), 219–20; "Nansemond County (Virginia) Committee, March 24, 1775," in Force, *American Archives: Fourth Series*, 2:227.

111. *North-Carolina Gazette*, November 20, 1765, in Spindel, "North Carolina Stamp Act Crisis," 9.

112. Jacqueline Stevens, "The Reasonableness of John Locke's Majority: Property Rights, Consent, and Resistance in the Second Treatise," *Political Theory* 24 (1996): 423–63. E.P. Thompson, *Customs in Common*, 138, notes the problem of the "anachronistic imposition of subsequent property categories."

113. That meaning so distressed some Americans in the early nineteenth century that they omitted all reference to such events as the destruction of tea from their accounts of the Revolution. Alfred F. Young, *The Shoemaker and the Tea Party: Memory and the American Revolution* (Boston: Beacon Press, 1999), 88–89, 108–20.

114. Nansemond County (Virginia) Committee, March 24, 1775, in Force, *American Archives: Fourth Series*, 2:227.

115. "Tuesday Night Express News," broadside, New York, December 23, 1773, New-York Historical Society. According to an "Impartial Observer," the tea party was remarkable because "such attention to private property had been observed." Larry D. Kramer, "Foreword: We the Court," *Harvard Law Review* 115, no. 1 (November 2001): 28–29.

116. William Eddis, *Letters from America, historical and descriptive . . . 1769 to 1777* (London, 1792), 182–84.

117. "Extract of a Letter from a Gentleman at Bladensburg Md., November 1, 1774," in Force, *American Archives: Fourth Series*, 1:953; David Curtis Skaggs, "Maryland's Impulse Toward Social Revolution: 1750–1776," *Journal of American History* 54 (1968): 771–86. Cf. Eddis, *Letters from America*, 169, 215–16.

118. Richard A. Ryerson, "Political Mobilization and the American Revolution: The Resistance Movement in Philadelphia, 1765 to 1776," *William and Mary Quarterly*, 3rd ser., 21 (1974): 565–88; Pauline Maier, "The Charleston Mob and the Evolution of Popular Politics in Revolutionary South Carolina, 1765–1784," *Perspectives in American History* 4 (1970): 173–98; Edward Countryman, "Consolidating Power in Revolutionary America: The Case of New York, 1775–1783," *Journal of Interdisciplinary History* 6, no. 4 (1976): 645–77, 674.

119. Ammerman, *Common Cause*, 121.

120. Ryerson, "Political Mobilization"; Charles S. Olton, *Artisans for Indepen-*

dence: *Philadelphia Mechanics and the American Revolution* (Syracuse, NY: Syracuse University Press, 1975).

121. "Extract of Letter from New-Haven to Mr. Rivington, New-York, Dated April 1, 1775," in Force, *American Archives: Fourth Series*, 2:252–53.

122. Drake, *Tea Leaves*, xx, iv.

123. "Martyr," quoted in Schlesinger, *Colonial Merchants*, 170–71.

124. *New Jersey Archives*, 29:371–72.

125. This was not "public opinion" as in our day, for that is quantitative, a tabulation of individual responses: 65 percent approve, 30 percent disapprove, 5 percent don't know. Vox populi would not be expressed in such terms. It could accommodate some dissenters, individuals who might be dismissed if they could not be convinced. Yet it claimed to be more than the sum of individual parts. When they published Patriot events, Patriot printers accepted and endorsed the terms of those events.

126. "Charles County (Maryland) Committee, May 29, 1775," in Force, *American Archives: Fourth Series*, 2:727.

127. Dunbar recounted in "To the Provincial Congress of Massachusetts, Boston, February 23, 1775," in Force, *American Archives: Fourth Series*, 1:1266. See also Moore, *Diary of the American Revolution*, 1:41.

128. "Extract of Letter from New-Haven to Mr. Rivington."

129. Morgan and Morgan, *Stamp Act Crisis*, esp. 250–51, notes that public gaze on actions of moderates had its effect on their actions from 1765. Woodbridge, New Jersey, for example, kept a supply of tar and feathers for importers, stored openly in the center of town near "Execution Dock" and "Liberty Oak." *New Jersey Archives*, vi, 280.

130. Papers on the "New Jersey Tea Party" of 1773–74, in the *David Rankin Barbee Papers*, Georgetown University Library, Washington, DC, box 9, file 496. Hutchinson quotation from "Extract letter gentleman in New England to Jos. Harrison, Esq., November 18, 1769," *Sparks Manuscripts*, ms. 10, vol. 3, 57. Hutchinson himself had participated in a town meeting that voted Bostonians innocent in the aftermath of anti-impressment riots in the late 1740s. The town meeting "unanimously pass'd such a Vote as Vindicated the Town from the Charges made against them," according to the *Independent Advertiser*, January 4, 1748.

131. James Sullivan and Alexander C. Flick, eds., *Minutes of the Albany Committee of Correspondence, 1775–1778*, 2 vols. (Albany: University of the State of New York, 1923–25), 1:282–83. (Volume 2 comprises *Minutes of the Schenectady Committee, 1775–1779*.)

132. "Freehold (Monmouth County, New-Jersey) Committee, March 6, 1775," in Force, *American Archives*, 4th ser., 2:35–36. The pamphlet was James Rivington's "Free Thoughts on the Resolves of the Congress by A.W. Farmer."

133. Other actions against Rivington's pamphlet took place. Force, *American Archives*, 4th ser., 1:1013 and 2:15. "Orange County Committee," in Van Schreeven and Scribner, *Revolutionary Virginia*, 386.

134. Regarding the number of pages in *Common Sense*: the first edition, dated January 10, 1776, ran roughly two-thirds the length of the second edition, which appeared about a month later with additional arguments. Isaac Kramnick, "A Note on the Text," in Thomas Paine, *Common Sense* (New York: Penguin Books, 1986), 59.

135. Eric Foner, *Tom Paine and Revolutionary America* (New York: Oxford University Press, 1976); Edward Larkin, *Thomas Paine and the Literature of Revolution* (New

York: Cambridge University Press, 2005), 5–6, 22–48; Olivia Smith, *The Politics of Language, 1791–1819* (Oxford: Clarendon Press, 1984).

136. Paine, *Common Sense*, 84. Emphasis in original.

137. Ibid., 89.

138. Ibid., 84, 89.

139. On the emergence of American nationalism through the interplay of local celebrations and accounts about them in newspapers, see Waldstreicher, "Rites of Rebellion," 37–47.

140. Paine, *Common Sense*, 66–67.

141. Ezra Stiles quoted in Hooker, "Revolution Seen Through a Wineglass," 59n27. Benjamin Franklin, "Causes of the American Discontent Before 1768," in Guy Stevens Callender, *Selections from the Economic History of the United States, 1765–1860* (New York: Ginn, 1909), 140–41.

142. Christopher Gadsden, October 26 and November 9, 1769, in Weir, *Letters of Freeman*, 61; William Smith Jr., New York Assembly address to House of Lords, 1770, quoted in Milton M. Klein, "New York Lawyers and the Coming of the American Revolution," *New York History* 60 (October 1974): 383–408, 400–402.

143. John Drayton, *Memoirs of the American Revolution*, 2 vols. (Charleston: A.E. Miller, 1821), 1:231; Paine, *Common Sense*, 92.

144. "The Tribunal of the Publick" is the phrase of Lieutenant Governor William Bull, quoted in Weir, *Letters of Freeman*, xxxv.

145. Alice Mary Baldwin, *The Clergy of Connecticut in Revolutionary Days*, Tercentenary Commission of the State of Connecticut, Committee on Historical Publications, Publication No. 56 (New Haven, CT: Yale University Press, 1936), 13–14. James L. Huston views the ideal of a roughly equal distribution of wealth as an aspect of the republican ideology of Revolutionary elites in "The American Revolutionaries, the Political Economy of Aristocracy, and the American Concept of the Distribution of Wealth," *American Historical Review* 98 (1993): 1079–94.

146. Breen, "Commercial Narrative," 492.

4. The Patriot Economy

1. Historians have often written as if committees, crowds, and the Association stopped in July, 1776, since—from a later perspective—they had served their purpose of carrying Americans to the Declaration. Yet independence was not in any sense the *end* of popular activity in committees and crowds, but rather a means to achieving social and political ideals that remained in play throughout the war and after.

2. The quotation is from John Drayton, *Memoirs of the American Revolution*, 2 vols. (Charleston, SC: A.E. Miller, 1821), 1:231. See also *South Carolina Gazette*, November 7, 1775; Peter H. Wood, "The Dream Deferred: Black Freedom Struggles on the Eve of White Independence," in *In Resistance: Studies in African, Caribbean, and African-American History*, ed. Gary Okihiro (Amherst: University of Massachusetts Press, 1986), 161–87; Sylvia Frey, *Water from the Rock: Black Resistance in a Revolutionary Age* (Princeton, NJ: Princeton University Press, 1991); Cassandra Pybus, *Epic Journeys of Freedom: Runaway Slaves of the American Revolution and Their Global Quest for Liberty* (Boston: Beacon Press, 2006); Woody Holton, *Forced Founders: Indians, Debtors, Slaves, and the Making of the American Revolution in Virginia* (Chapel Hill: University of North Carolina Press, 1999), chap. 5; Ira Berlin and Ronald Hoffman, eds.,

Slavery and Freedom in the Age of the American Revolution (Charlottesville: University Press of Virginia, 1983). Ronald Hoffman, *A Spirit of Dissension: Economics, Politics, and the Revolution in Maryland* (Baltimore, MD: Johns Hopkins University Press, 1973), 147–48, 152–54, 156–57, 188, treats alliances between whites and blacks in that state. See also Arthur Zilversmit, *The First Emancipation: The Abolition of Slavery in the North* (Chicago: University of Chicago Press, 1967).

3. The phrase "liberty mad" was used by merchant Samuel Colton in the year 1781, describing his neighbors in a crowd action of 1776. Colton, "Reply to the General Court, c. February 1, 1781," in *Massachusetts Archives*, Massachusetts State House, Boston, 231:143. My account of the Colton crowd appears in Barbara Clark Smith, *After the Revolution: The Smithsonian History of Everyday Life in the Eighteenth Century* (New York: Pantheon Books, 1985), 3–42.

4. John Adams quoted in Willi Paul Adams, *The First American Constitutions: Republican Ideology and the Making of the State Constitutions in the Revolutionary Era* (Chapel Hill: University of North Carolina Press, 1980), 119.

5. "The Interest of America—Letter III," signed Spartacus, *New-York Journal*, June 20, 1776, quoted in Adams, *First American Revolutions*, 148. William Bordon, "An Address to the Inhabitants of North-Carolina, &c." (Williamsburg, VA, 1746), describing some members of the provincial legislature, in *Some Eighteenth-Century Tracts Concerning North Carolina*, ed. William K. Boyd (Raleigh, NC: Edwards & Broughton, 1927), 71.

6. Anonymous, *The People the Best Gove[r]nors; or, A Plan of Government Founded on the Just Principles of Natural Freedom* (n.p., 1776); Henry Alonzo Cushing, "The People the Best Governors," *American Historical Review* 1 (1896): 284–87.

7. Eric Foner, *Tom Paine and Revolutionary America* (New York: Oxford University Press, 1976), 129–31.

8. Charles Royster, *A Revolutionary People at War: The Continental Army and American Character, 1775–1783* (Chapel Hill: University of North Carolina Press, 1979), chap. 1.

9. Oliver Wolcott to Samual Lyman, April 17, 1776, in Edmund C. Burnett, ed., *Letters of Members of the Continental Congress*, 8 vols. (Washington, DC: Carnegie Institute of Washington, 1936), 1:425.

10. See, for example, actions against the ironmonger, Joseph Scott, reported in the *Boston Gazette*, October 3, 1774.

11. "Letter from New-York to a Gentleman in Philadelphia, Dated April 24, 1775," in *American Archives: Fourth Series, Containing a Documentary History of the English Colonies in North America, from the King's Message to the Parliament, of March 7, 1774, to the Declaration of Independence of the United States*, ed. Peter Force (Washington, DC: M. St. Clair Clarke and Peter Force, 1837–46), 2:364. A similar action on behalf of the colonists was undertaken at Halifax, where people destroyed a quantity of hay purchased and ready to be shipped to dragoons in Boston, in *Holt's Journal*, May 18, in Frank Moore, *Diary of the American Revolution, from Newspapers and Original Documents*, 2 vols. (New York: Charles Scribner, 1860; repr., New York: Arno Press, 1969), 1:80–81. Patriots arrested a Connecticut man for sending provisions to the royal troops. *Constitutional Gazette*, May 8, 1776, in Moore, *Diary of the American Revolution*, 1:239–40.

12. Not quite every Patriot merchant thought trading with the enemy was wrong. Robert A. East, *Business Enterprise in the American Revolutionary Era* (New York: AMS Press, 1969).

13. Committee for Charleston, May 26, 1775, in Force, *American Archives: Fourth Series*, 2:710.

14. Pennsylvania Committee of Safety, Force, *American Archives: Fourth Series*, 5:74; Provincial Congress of New York, *American Archives: Fourth Series*, 1:682; Richard B. Morris, *Government and Labor in Early America* (New York: Columbia University Press, 1946), 92–93.

15. *Boston Gazette*, April 29, 1776.

16. Barbara Clark Smith, "Food Rioters and the American Revolution," *William and Mary Quarterly*, 3rd ser., 51 (1994): 3–38; Larry G. Bowman, "The Scarcity of Salt in Virginia During the American Revolution," *Virginia Magazine of History and Biography* 77 (October 1969): 464–72; Hoffman, *Spirit of Dissension*, on Maryland. William L. Saunders, ed., *The Colonial Records of North Carolina*, vol. 10 (1775–76) (Raleigh, NC: Josephus Daniels, 1890), 670–71, 685, 701, 703.

17. Journals of the Council of Safety of Maryland, January 1–March 20, 1777, *Archives of Maryland*, ed. William Hand Browne et al. (Baltimore: Maryland Historical Society, 1883–), 11:449–51, 552–53; 16:4–5; 12:371–77 (hereafter *Maryland Archives*).

18. "New Jersey Provincial Council of Safety, May 1776," in Force, *American Archives: Fourth Series*, 6:467–68.

19. Provincial Congress of New York, in *American Archives: Fifth Series, Containing a Documentary History of the United States of America, from the Declaration of Independence, July 4, 1776, to the Definitive Treaty of Peace with Great Britain, September 3, 1783* (Washington, DC: M. St. Clair Clarke and Peter Force, 1848–1853), 1:682.

20. Journals of the Council of Safety of Maryland, January 1–March 20, 1777, *Maryland Archives*, 11:552–53.

21. E. James Ferguson, *The Power of the Purse: A History of American Public Finance, 1776–1790* (Chapel Hill: University of North Carolina Press, 1961), chap. 2; Ralph Volney Harlow, "Aspects of Revolutionary Finance, 1775–1783," *American Historical Review* 35 (1929): 46–68.

22. Richard Buel Jr., "Time: Friend or Foe of the American Revolution?" in *Reconsiderations on the Revolutionary War*, ed. Don Higginbotham (Westport, CT: Greenwood Press, 1978), 124–43. Buel, however, sees this "consent" and participation as primarily individual in nature. He argues that "the revolutionaries behaved from the start of the war" as if civic virtue and marketplace values "were perfectly reconcilable." Buel, "The Committee Movement of 1779 and the Formation of Public Authority in Revolutionary America," in *The Transformation of Early American History: Society, Authority, and Ideology*, ed. James A. Henretta, Michael Kammen, and Stanley N. Katz (New York: Knopf, 1991), 154. On continental money, see also Ben Baack, "Forging a Nation State: The Continental Congress and the Financing of the War of American Independence," *Economic History Review*, New Series 54 (2001): 639–56; Harlow, "Aspects of Revolutionary Finance"; Charles W. Calomiris, "Institutional Failure, Monetary Scarcity, and the Depreciation of the Continental," *Journal of Economic History* 48 (1988): 47–68.

23. Adam Smith, *An Inquiry into the Nature and Causes of the Wealth of Nations*, 2 vols., ed. R.H. Campbell and A.S. Skinner (Oxford: Clarendon Press, 1976), 1:266; *Journals of Each Provincial Congress of Massachusetts in 1774 and 1775 and of the Committee of Safety* (Boston: Dutton and Wentworth, 1838), 415–16, also 246–47. Rhode Island declared that anyone refusing the General Assembly's bills "ought to be held and esteemed as an enemy to its credit, reputation, and happiness." Harlow, "Aspects

of Revolutionary Finance," 55; "Vox Populi," *Boston Gazette*, August 14, 1775; Worthington Chauncey Ford, ed., *Journals of the Continental Congress, 1774–1789*, 34 vols. (Washington, DC: Government Printing Office, 1904–37), 4:49–50.

24. Rutledge to Robert Livingston, October 2, 1776, in *Letters of Members of the Continental Congress*, 8 vols., ed. Edmund C. Burnett (Washington, DC: Carnegie Institution of Washington, 1936), 2:113. A Tory paper derided the money: "WANTED, by a gentleman fond of curiosities, who is shortly going to England, a parcel of Congress Notes, with which he intends to paper some rooms." *New York Gazette*, October 28, 1775, in Moore, *Diary of the American Revolution*, 1:337. Harlow, "Aspects of Revolutionary Finance," 53–54, reviews statements by the state governments that attributed depreciation to the avarice of enemies to the cause (although he also considers those attributions irrational).

25. "In Committee of Inspection and Observation," Dunlap's *Pennsylvania Packet; or, The General Advertiser*, February 5, 1776; Ford, *Journals*, 4:49–50.

26. "North Carolina Council of Safety, July 11, 1776," in Force, *American Archives: Fifth Series*, 1:1363–64.

27. "Middletown (Connecticut) Committee, August 2, 1776," in Force, *American Archives: Fifth Series*, 1:732–33.

28. "Baltimore County Committee, August 19, 1776," in Force, *American Archives: Fifth Series*, 1:1056–57.

29. Harold B. Hancock, "County Committees and the Growth of Independence in the Three Lower Counties on the Delaware, 1765–1776," *Delaware History* 15 (1973): 287; *Pennsylvania Journal*, January 17, 1776.

30. Ralph V. Harlow, "Economic Conditions in Massachusetts during the American Revolution," *Publications of the Colonial Society of Massachusetts* 20 (1916–1919): 163–90.

31. "The Merchant Colton Documents," appendix in *The Longmeadow Centennial: Proceedings at the Centennial Celebration of the Incorporation of the Town of Longmeadow, 1883* (Longmeadow, MA, 1884), 213–20, 271–72; Smith, *After the Revolution*, chap. 1. On the many similar crowds from 1776–80, see Smith, "Food Rioters," 3–38.

32. *Boston Gazette*, September 9, 1776.

33. "Journal of the Proceedings of the Convention at Dracut, in November, 1776," *Collections of the New Hampshire Historical Society* 2 (1927): 64–65.

34. Royster, *Revolutionary People at War*, 127–28.

35. Petition to Col. Thomas Crafts, in *Massachusetts Archives*, 167:273.

36. Michael A. McDonnell, "Popular Mobilization and Political Culture in Revolutionary Virginia: The Failure of the Minutemen and the Revolution from Below," *Journal of American History* 85 (1998): 946–81; Albert H. Tillson Jr., *Gentry and Common Folk: Political Culture on a Virginia Frontier, 1740–1789* (Lexington: University Press of Kentucky, 1991); Tillson, "The Militia and Popular Political Culture in the Upper Valley of Virginia, 1740–1775," *Virginia Magazine of History and Biography* 94 (1983): 285–306; Richard Alan Ryerson, *The Revolution Is Now Begun: The Radical Committees of Philadelphia, 1765–1776* (Philadelphia: University of Pennsylvania Press, 1978); Ryerson, "Political Mobilization and the American Revolution: The Resistance Movement in Philadelphia, 1765 to 1776," *William and Mary Quarterly*, 3rd ser., 31 (1974): 565–88; E. Wayne Carp, "Early American Military History: A Review of Recent Work," *Virginia Magazine of History and Biography* 94 (1986): 259–84; Don Higginbotham, "The Early American Way of War: Reconnaissance and Appraisal," *William and Mary Quarterly*, 3rd ser., 44 (1987): 230–73.

37. Thomas Cushing to Robert Treat Paine, June 10, 1776, in *Robert Treat Paine Papers*, Massachusetts Historical Society, Boston.

38. *Boston Gazette*, December 23, 1776.

39. Charles J. Hoadly, ed., *The Public Records of the State of Connecticut*, 11 vols. (Hartford, CT: Press of the Case, Lockwood, and Brainard Co., 1894–1967), 1:62–63, 97–100.

40. Jonathan Trumbull to James Bowdoin, December 9, 1776, in *Massachusetts Archives*, 196:33.

41. Secondary works on price legislation and related regulations include Morris, *Government and Labor*, 92–135; Anne Bezanson, *Prices and Inflation During the American Revolution* (Philadelphia: University of Pennsylvania Press, 1951); Kenneth Scott, "Price Control in New England During the Revolution," *New England Quarterly* 19 (1946): 453–73; William B. Norton, "Paper Currency in Massachusetts during the Revolution," *New England Quarterly* 7 (1934): 43–69. Barbara Clark Smith, "The Politics of Price Control in Revolutionary Massachusetts" (PhD diss., Yale University, 1983). The laws of the New England states are at *Acts and Resolves, Public and Private, of the Province of Massachusetts Bay*, 21 vols. (Boston: Wright & Potter, 1869–1922), 5:583–89; Hoadly, *Public Records of Connecticut*, 1:62–63, 98–100; *Acts and Laws of the State of New Hampshire* (Exeter, NH: Published for the General Assembly, 1780), 69–72; John Russell Bartlett, ed., *Records of the State of Rhode Island and Providence Plantations*, 10 vols. (Providence, RI: Cooke, Jackson, 1856–1865), 8:85–89.

42. Bartlett, *Records of Rhode Island*, 8:89.

43. Convention of the Committees of Safety of Eighteen Towns in Essex County, *Continental Journal*, April 24, 1777.

44. Franklin P. Rice, "Worcester Town Records from 1753 to 1783," in *Collections of the Worcester Society of Antiquity* (Worcester, MA: Worcester Society of Antiquity, 1882), 4:284–88. Broadsides and pricelists include Newbury, Evans 15484; Ipswich, Evans 15375; Salem, Evans 15590; Marblehead, Evans 15386 (no copy extant); Wenham, Evans 15704. Walter A. Davis, comp., *The Old Records of the Town of Fitchburg, Massachusetts, 1764–1789*, 2 vols. (Fitchburg, MA: Fitchburg Historical Society, 1898), 1:139–45; Josiah Gilbert Holland, *History of Western Massachusetts*, 2 vols. (Springfield, MA: Samuel Bowles, 1855), 1:216–17, on the Northampton convention. Cf. James Russell Trumbull, *History of Northampton, Massachusetts, from its Founding in 1654*, 2 vols. (Northampton, MA: Press of the Gazette Printing Co., 1898–1902), who reports that thirty-three towns attended. For towns that recorded price ceilings in their records, see Donald G. Trayser, *Barnstable: Three Centuries of a Cape Cod Town* (Hyannis, MA: F.B. and F.P. Goss, 1939), 136–37; *Town Records of Dudley, Massachusetts* (Pawtucket, RI: Adam Sutcliffe, 1893), 181–83; *Old Town Records* (Town Clerk's Typed Copy, 1927), Weymouth Town Clerk's Office, 2:19–20; *Concord Town Records*, Concord Free Public Library, 4:464a–466a; *Concord Committee of Safety Records*, June 9, 1777, Concord Free Public Library; Reverend Edwin R. Hodgman, *History of the Town of Westford* (Lowell, MA: Morning Mail, 1883), 117.

45. Stephen Hopkins to President of the Massachusetts Council, January 1777, in *Massachusetts Archives*, 196:174.

46. Elbridge Gerry to Robert Treat Paine, February 14, 1777, in *Robert Treat Paine Papers*, vol. 2. A different opinion came from another correspondent of Paine's: "Any person, who chooses to evade the Law, may by means of privacy, Commissions, Gifts, & other Arts, steer clear of the Penalty, & that most people will have a Disposi-

tion thus to do I make not the least Doubt." William Baylies to Robert Treat Paine, March 6, 1777, ibid.

47. Congress had recommended laws to prevent monopoly of necessaries for both army and civilian markets at the end of October 1776. *Boston Gazette*, November 25, 1776.

48. "A Soldier," *Boston Gazette*, April 28, 1777; "Oppression: A Poem, or New-England's Lamentations on the dreadful Extortion & other Sins of the Times," broadside, Boston, 1777.

49. *Boston Gazette*, September 8, 1777.

50. Jonathan French, *A Practical Discourse Against Extortion* (Boston, 1777).

51. Abraham Ketelas, *Reflections on Extortion, Shewing the Nature, Malignity, and Fatal Tendency of That Sin* (Newbury-Port, 1778).

52. Quoted in Sarah Loring Bailey, *Historical Sketch of Andover, Massachusetts* (Boston: Houghton, Mifflin, 1880), 384–85.

53. Petition of Boston Tanners, in *Massachusetts Archives*, 182:161–62.

54. French, "Practical Discourse," 9–10.

55. Timothy Stone, "The Nature, and Evil, of Selfishness, Considered and Elustrated," (Norwich, CT: Green & Spooner, 1778), 26–27.

56. Nathaniel Whitaker, "An Antidote Against Toryism," in *The American Tory*, ed. Morton Borden and Penn Borden (Englewood Cliffs, NJ: Prentice-Hall, 1972), 69.

57. "A DIALOGUE between a *poor* Widow and an *honest* Farmer," *Boston Gazette*, December 8, 1777. The honest farmer admitted his goal was to lay up riches and make his sons gentlemen.

58. Anonymous, *The Downfall of Justice; and the Farmer Just Return'd from Meeting on Thanksgiving Day—a Play Lately Acted in Connecticut*, 2nd ed., John Carter Brown Library, Providence, RI.

59. Might this mean to say, "Jack he thrash[ed] . . ." to indicate that the farmer drove Jack to produce all this bounty?

60. Continental Congress broadside, April 11, 1777, in *Journals of the Continental Congress*, 9:957.

61. Morris, *Government and Labor*, 97–100. See, for example, Thomas Burke, "Abstract of Debates," February 12, 1777, in Burnett, *Letters*, 2:249; Samuel Adams to James Warren, February 1, 1777, in *The Warren-Adams Letters*, ed. Massachusetts Historical Society, 2 vols. (1917–1925; repr., New York: AMS Press, 1972), 1:286; John Adams to Abigail Adams, February 7, 1777, in Burnett, *Letters*, 2:237.

62. Adams elaborated his views about money in private correspondence, including letters to Abigail Adams. He recommended she read Lord Kames on coins. John Adams to Abigail Adams, April 6, 1777, in *Adams Family Correspondence*, 6 vols., ed. L.H. Butterfield (Cambridge, MA: Harvard University Press, 1963–1993), 2:201.

63. Benjamin Rush, "Diary," February 14, 1777, in Burnett, *Letters*, 2:252.

64. Rush's account of congressional debates does suggest that John Adams questioned "the wisdom, justice, and policy" of regulations proposed by the Providence convention. Yet the arguments Rush goes on to recount all spoke only to the wisdom and policy of the matter. James Witherspoon of New Jersey did worry that the regulations might be "unfair," but he was concerned that if states went about freezing the prices of farm products and imports *in their current proportions*, then farm interests—including his Jersey constituents—would suffer, for prices of imports had so far risen further and faster. Witherspoon was not suggesting that price regulations were necessarily or intrinsically unfair. Ibid., 2:250–52.

65. Harlow, "Aspects of Revolutionary Finance," 52–53, notes the general understanding of the causes of depreciation.

66. Richard Henry Lee, in Burnett, *Letters*, 2:251; Samuel Adams to unknown, Boston, January 10 1778, in *Writings of Samuel Adams*, 4 vols., ed. Harry Alonzo Cushing (New York: Octagon Books, 1968), 4:7.

67. Harlow, "Aspects of Revolutionary Finance," generally indicts Revolutionary leaders for naïveté for failing to approach finance as a purely financial—as opposed to political, social, or moral—matter. Buel, "Time," 130.

68. On the impact of such terms as "supply," "demand," and "price," see John Lie, "Embedding Polanyi's Market Society," *Sociological Perspectives* 34 (1991): 219–35. See also Stephen A. Marglin, *The Dismal Science: How Thinking Like an Economist Undermines Community* (Cambridge, MA: Harvard University Press, 2008).

69. See, for example, "Records of the Boston Committee of Correspondence, Safety, and Inspection, May to November 1776," *New England Historical and Genealogical Register* 30 (July 1876): 381–82; *New England Historical and Genealogical Register* 34 (January 1880): 17–18 and passim.

70. Adams, *First American Constitutions* (Jefferson quoted on p. 205); Marc W. Kruman, *Between Authority and Liberty: State Constitution Making in Revolutionary America* (Chapel Hill: University of North Carolina Press, 1997).

71. Gregory T. Knouff, *The Soldiers' Revolution: Pennsylvanians in Arms and the Forging of Early American Identity* (University Park: Pennsylvania State University Press, 2004); David Curtis Skaggs, "Maryland's Impulse Toward Social Revolution: 1750–1776," *Journal of American History* 54 (1968): 771–86.

72. Maryland Council to Baltimore Committee of Observation, December 1776, *Maryland Archives*, 12:526, 547–48, 560.

73. Concerns about committees had appeared as an argument for declaring independence in the spring of 1776, since independence would allow new provincial governments and prevent "the disorders which arise from the unlimited, undescribed, and sometimes arbitrary power of conventions, committees of safety, and committees of inspection." *Pennsylvania Evening Post*, April 20, 1776, in Moore, *Diary of the American Revolution*, 1:234.

74. Petition, May 29, 1776, in *Massachusetts Archives*, 181:50–51.

75. Robert J. Taylor, *Western Massachusetts in the Revolution* (Providence, RI: Brown University Press, 1954), 75–102. On courts in the eastern counties, Joseph Hawley to Robert Treat Paine, February 19, 1776; Thomas Cushing to Paine, February 27 and April 22, 1776, in *Robert Treat Paine Papers*; Stephen Patterson, *Political Parties in Revolutionary Massachusetts* (Madison: University of Wisconsin Press, 1973), 156–58.

76. Report of the Committee to Enquire into the Powers of the Committees of Correspondence, October 25, 1776, in *Massachusetts Archives*, 137:118. For an example of a New York committee seeking advice from provincial authority on how to enforce the Association, see "Tryon Committee to New-York Provincial Congress, August 12, 1775," in Force, *American Archives: Fourth Series*, 3:541.

77. Report to Enquire, 137:118.

78. "Speculator," *Boston Gazette*, September 23, 1776.

79. Harry A. Cushing, *History of the Transition from Provincial to Commonwealth Government in Massachusetts*, Studies in History, Economics, and Public Law, Columbia University, vol. 8, no. 1 (New York, 1896), 68–69, 71–72.

80. "Speculator," *Boston Gazette*, September 23, 1776. See also "Extract of a Letter on the Worcester Convention," *Boston Gazette*, December 30, 1776.

81. Distress from shortages throughout the maritime east can be traced in a series of petitions from various towns to the General Court in 1777. See *Massachusetts Archives*, 183:4, 57–59, 93, 106, 125, 131, 134, 258.

82. William H. Whitmore et al., eds. *Reports of the Record Commissioners of the City of Boston* 39 vols. (Boston: Rockwell & Churchill, 1876–1909), 18:260–61, 275–76 (hereafter *Boston Town Records*).

83. According to a report from fall 1776, "The committee forbear mentioning at present the names of some Persons hinted to them, who, by Engrosing and Forestalling, not only the Necessaries of Life, but many other Articles, are greatly injuring the Town." Should their names become public, they would surely be treated as Tories, "unworthy the Name of Friends to their Country." *Boston Town Records*, 18:249, 252–53.

84. Ibid., 18:260–61.

85. Ibid., 18:264–65.

86. Abigail Adams noted bakers' rationing of bread in a letter to John Adams, March 8, 1777, *Adams Family Correspondence*, 2:172. Her letters from Braintree over this period provide a window into mounting economic distress in the region.

87. Abigail Adams to John Adams, April 20, 21, 1777, *Adams Family Correspondence*, 2:217–218; Alfred F. Young, "Pope's Day, Tar and Feathers and Cornet Joyce, Jun: From Ritual to Rebellion in Boston, 1745–1775," *Bulletin of the Society for the Study of Labour History* 27 (1973): 27–39; Albert O. Matthews, "Joyce Junior," *Publications of the Colonial Society of Massachusetts* 8 (February 1903): 90–93; Matthews, "Joyce Junior Once More," *Publications of the Colonial Society of Massachusetts* 11 (April 1907): 280–94.

88. The suggestion is in "63 Persons," an anonymous lampoon of Boston Whigs, London, April 18, 1775. Massachusetts Historical Society, *Proceedings*, 2nd ser., 12 (1898): 139–42. If so, the descendant and namesake of the seventeenth-century founder of Massachusetts Bay Colony was playing the descendant and namesake of the seventeenth-century figure of Cornet George Joyce. Bostonians would have recognized the analogy and enjoyed the play.

89. Isaac Smith Sr. to John Adams, April 25, 1777, *Adams Family Correspondence*, 2:223.

90. Matthews, "Joyce Junior," 102–3.

91. *Boston Town Records*, 18:284–85.

92. Providence, RI, *Town Meeting Records*, June 16, 1777, Rhode Island Historical Society, Providence, RI, 71–73. The *Boston Gazette* reported the actions of other towns and their committees, such as Newburyport, in the *Gazette* of August 4, 1777.

93. *Boston Gazette*, June 16, 1777.

94. "Account of measures taken in the Boston shortage of 1777," July 5, 1783, *Robert Treat Paine Papers*.

95. Matthews, "Joyce Junior," 97–99; Abigail Adams to John Adams, April 21, 1777, in *Adams Family Correspondence*, 2:217.

96. Proclamation of the General Court, *Massachusetts Spy*, January 8, 1778.

97. James Warren reported that Tories were again engaged in town politics. James Warren to Samuel Adams, Boston, May 10, 1778, *Warren-Adams Letters*, 2:9–10.

98. *Independent Chronicle*, August 29, 1777.

99. *Continental Journal*, April 10, 1777.

100. Tertius Cato, *Independent Chronicle*, September 11, 1777.

101. Ibid.

102. Matthews, "Joyce Junior," 102–3.

103. Nathaniel Low, *An Almanac for the Year, 1778* (Boston).

104. William Shepard to Massachusetts Government, May 18, 1778, in *Massachusetts Archives*, 199:157.

105. On Pennsylvania after 1776, see Steven Rosswurm, *Arms, Country, and Class: The Philadelphia Militia and the Lower Sort During the American Revolution, 1775–1783* (New Brunswick, NJ: Rutgers University Press, 1987); Foner, *Tom Paine*; Robert Brunhouse, *The Counter-Revolution in Pennsylvania, 1776–1790* (New York: Octagon Books, 1971).

106. Charles Royster, "The Nature of Treason: Revolutionary Virtue, American Reactions to Benedict Arnold," *William and Mary Quarterly*, 3rd ser., 36 (1979): 163–93; Frederick D. Stone, "Philadelphia Society One Hundred Years Ago; or, The Reign of Continental Money," *Pennsylvania Magazine of History and Biography* 111 (1879): 361–92; J. Thomas Scharf and Thompson Westcott, *History of Philadelphia, 1609–1884*, 3 vols. (Philadelphia: L.H. Everts, 1884), 1:388–91: East, *Business Enterprise*, 126–48.

107. Brunhouse, *Counter-Revolution*, 68, 73; Hubertis Cummings, "Robert Morris and the Episode of the Polacre 'Victorious,'" *Pennsylvania Magazine of History and Biography* 70, no. 3 (1946): 239–57.

108. Foner, *Tom Paine*, 166–68; Brunhouse, *Counter-Revolution*, 70; *Boston Gazette*, June 14, 1779.

109. Foner, *Tom Paine*, 168–69; *Boston Gazette*, June 14, 1779.

110. On New York, Edward Countryman, "Consolidating Power in Revolutionary America: The Case of New York, 1775–1783," *Journal of Interdisciplinary History* 6 (1976): 661–62. Shortages in Massachusetts appear in petitions, in *Massachusetts Archives*, 184:312, 316. Concord, New Hampshire, convention to regulate prices, September 22, 1779, in *Massachusetts Archives*, 201:394. Portsmouth's price list, October 8, 1779, is in *Massachusetts Archives*, 201:346. Buel, "Committee Movement," 151–69; Ruth Bogin, "Petitioning and the New Moral Economy of Post-Revolutionary America," *William and Mary Quarterly*, 3rd ser., 45 (1988): 392–425; Smith, "Food Rioters," 3–38; Morris, *Government and Labor*, 107–19, surveys price regulations in 1779 and 1780.

111. Cummings, "Robert Morris," 244.

112. John K. Alexander, "The Fort Wilson Incident of 1779: A Case Study of the Revolutionary Crowd," *William and Mary Quarterly*, 3rd ser., 31 (1974): 589–612. On James Wilson, see Mark David Hall, *The Political and Legal Philosophy of James Wilson, 1742–1798* (Columbia: University of Missouri Press, 1997).

113. Ferguson, *Power of the Purse*, 46.

114. Paine to Joseph Reed, June 4, 1780, in *The Complete Writings of Thomas Paine*, ed. Philip S. Foner (New York: Citadel Press, 1945), 1186; Joyce Appleby, "The Social Origins of American Revolutionary Ideology," *Journal of American History* 64 (1978): 935–58.

115. Sung Bok Kim, "The Limits of Politicization in the American Revolution: The Experience of Westchester County, New York," *Journal of American History* 80 (1993): 868–89, raises the point that warfare, which politicized many Americans, also depoliticized many as it dragged on through the years, making some individuals less willing to sacrifice and catching many in the cross fire. The war might reinforce self-interest as well as discredit it.

5. The Freedoms They Lost

1. On changes in the Congress, see H. James Henderson, *Party Politics in the Continental Congress* (New York: McGraw-Hill, 1974), chap. 10–12.

2. This and the following paragraphs rely heavily on E. James Ferguson, *The Power of the Purse* (Chapel Hill: University of North Carolina Press, 1961), esp. chaps. 6–7. The quotations are on pp. 123 and 120.

3. "Robert Morris to the Governors of North Carolina, South Carolina, and Georgia," December 19, 1781, in *The Revolutionary Diplomatic Correspondence of the United States*, 6 vols., ed. Francis Wharton (Washington, DC: Government Printing Office, 1889), 5:58–59.

4. Ferguson, *Power of the Purse*, chap. 3. Morris himself wanted Congress to tax directly, despite the fact that it did not depend directly on the electorate, but the vast majority remained adamant on that point. On the end of paper bills, see ibid., 66–67.

5. Benjamin Franklin to Samuel Cooper, April 22, 1779, quoted in Ferguson, *Power of the Purse*, 48.

6. Thomas Paine quoted in Ferguson, *Power of the Purse*, 66. See also a broadside from Wilmington, Delaware, called "A Mournful Lamentation on the Untimely Death of Paper Money," 1781, mss broadsides, New York Public Library.

7. Ferguson, *Power of the Purse*, 124, 135–37.

8. Ibid., 39–40, 69, and passim.

9. Cotton Mather, *Fair Dealing between Debtor and Creditor* (Boston, 1716).

10. Ferguson, *Power of the Purse*, 151. In 1780, merchants for the first time formed voluntary associations to support Congress and its new policy, according to Robert A. East, *Business Enterprise in the American Revolutionary Era* (New York: AMS Press 1969), 208–9, 322–25.

11. Rush, writing as "Leonidas," *Pennsylvania Gazette*, July 17, 1782.

12. Ibid.

13. Treaty of Paris, Fourth and Fifth Articles, at http://avalon.law.yale.edu/18th_century/paris.asp (accessed February 5, 2009).

14. Wartime organizations vigilant toward Loyalists included the Free and Independent Whig Society of Observation of Boston, 1778–1780, which involved men who had long been active as Sons of Liberty; the Anti-Britannic Society of Charleston, which combined sailors' aid and anti-Tory activity; and Philadelphia's Whig Society of 1777, which watched "internal enemies." Eugene P. Link, *Democratic Republican Societies, 1790–1800* (New York: Columbia University Press, 1942), 27. On jurisdictional issues raised by the Treaty of Paris, see Lawrence C. Marshall, "Fighting the Words of the 11th Amendment," *Harvard Law Review* 102 (1989): 1356–59.

15. Robert M. Calhoon, "The Reintegration of the Loyalists and the Disaffected," in *The American Revolution: Its Character and Limits*, ed. Jack P. Greene, 51–74 (New York: New York University Press, 1987); Wallace Brown, *The Good Americans: The Loyalists in the American Revolution* (New York: William Morrow, 1969), 172–80; Robert M. Calhoon, Timothy M. Barnes, and George A. Rawlyk, eds., *Loyalists and Community in North America* (Westport, CT: Greenwood Press, 1994).

16. Lorett Treese, *The Storm Gathering: The Penn Family and the American Revolution* (University Park: The Pennsylvania State University Press, 1992), 185–200.

17. "Newtown Convention Instructions to Representative," July 29, 1783, *Pennsylvania Gazette*, August 6, 1783; Owen S. Ireland, "Bucks County," in *Beyond Philadelphia: The American Revolution in the American Hinterland*, ed. John B. Frantz and William Pencak (University Park: Pennsylvania State University Press, 1998), 43–44; Robert L. Brunhouse, *The Counter-Revolution in Pennsylvania, 1776–1790* (New York: Octagon Books, 1971), 140–47; "Meeting of Officers of Chester County Militia," *Pennsylvania Gazette*, August 6, 1783. Cf. Judge Burke, "Charge to the Grand Jury of Charleston, S.C," *Pennsylvania Gazette*, July 30, 1783.

18. Oscar Zeichner, "The Rehabilitation of Loyalists in Connecticut," *New England Quarterly* 11 (1938): 311–15, 321–22, 323–24; Catherine S. Crary, *The Price of Loyalty: Tory Writings from the Revolutionary Era* (New York: McGraw-Hill, 1973), 363.

19. There was a separate list of royal officials and country gentlemen to be banished as well, published in the *Boston Gazette*, September 1, 1783, according to Forrest McDonald and Ellen Shapiro McDonald, *Requiem: Variations on Eighteenth-Century Themes* (Lawrence: University of Kansas Press, 1988), 77–78. Jackson Turner Main, *Political Parties Before the Constitution* (Chapel Hill: University of North Carolina Press, 1973), 90–91; "Worcester's Resolutions regarding Absentees and Refugees, 1783," in James H. Stark, *The Loyalists of Massachusetts and the Other Side of the Revolution* (Boston: W.B. Clarke, 1910), 141; *Collection of Acts or Laws Passed in the State of Massachusetts Bay, Relative to the American Loyalists and Their Property* (London: John Stockdale, 1785).

20. "Governor of South Carolina Proclamation," *Pennsylvania Gazette*, June 9, 1784; "Extract of a Letter from Charlestown," *Pennsylvania Gazette*, June 9, 1784; Jerome J. Nadelhaft, *The Disorders of War: The Revolution in South Carolina* (Orono: University of Maine at Orono Press, 1981), 76–79, 92–104, and passim; Michael E. Stevens, "Legislative Privilege in Post-Revolutionary South Carolina," *William and Mary Quarterly*, 3rd ser., 46 (1989): 71–79. For cases in Virginia, see Isaac S. Harrell, *Loyalism in Virginia* (Durham, NC: Duke University Press, 1926), 137, 140–41, 143. For Georgia, see Robert S. Lambert, "The Confiscation of Property in Georgia, 1782–1786," *William and Mary Quarterly*, 3rd ser., 20 (1963): 80–94.

21. On the 1784 law, see Joseph S. Tiedemann, "Patriots, Loyalists, and Conflict Resolution in New York, 1783–1787," in Calhoon, Barnes, and Rawlyk, *Loyalists and Community in North America*, 80; John Cook, Dutchess County, September 1783, quotations in Daniel Parker Coke, *The Royal Commission on the Losses and Services of American Loyalists, 1783 to 1785* (New York: B. Franklin, 1971), xxvii. See also Crary, *Price of Loyalty*, 359–64; Jonathan C. Clark, "The Problem of Allegiance in Revolutionary Poughkeepsie," in *Saints and Revolutionaries: Essays in Early American History*, ed. David D. Hall, John M. Murrin, and Thad W. Tate (New York: W.W. Norton, 1984), 309; Edward Countryman, "Consolidating Power in Revolutionary America: The Case of New York, 1775–1783," *Journal of Interdisciplinary History* 6 (1976): 645–77.

22. Crary, *Price of Loyalty*, 364–65; Philip Ranlet, *The New York Loyalists* (Knoxville: University of Tennessee Press, 1986), 165–67, 171.

23. "Petition from Albemarle for Emission of Paper Money, Nov. 3, 1787," *William and Mary Quarterly*, 2nd ser., 2 (1922): 213.

24. On the many petitions in various states from Americans complaining of debt, see Ruth Bogin, "Petitioning and the New Moral Economy of Post-Revolutionary America," *William and Mary Quarterly*, 3rd ser., 45 (1988): 407–12. Regulating the

debts owed to Loyalists also figured in efforts to allow Tory return; see Zeichner, "Rehabilitation of Loyalists," 320n36.

25. "On Public Faith," in *American Museum, or Repository of Ancient and Modern Fugitive Pieces* (Philadelphia: Mathew Carey, 1787), 1:405–7.

26. Ibid., 1:408.

27. J. Witherspoon to Alexander Hamilton, October 1789, in *The Papers of Alexander Hamilton*, ed. Harold C. Syrett (New York: Columbia University Press, 1962), 5:465. Arguments on behalf of payment at face value include: "A Friend to the Community," in *American Museum*, 1:409–12; "Speech of a Member of the General Court of Massachusetts," in *American Museum*, 1:412–17; "On the Redemption of Public Securities," in *American Museum*, 1:417–19; "Extract General Assembly of Massachusetts to Constituents," in *American Museum*, 1:419–20.

28. Ferguson, *Power of the Purse*, 68: "Public opinion did not view contracts as sacred and tended to grade claims against government according to their real validity." "Petition from Albemarle," 213.

29. Ruth Bogin, *Abraham Clark and the Quest for Equality in the Revolutionary Era, 1774–1794* (Rutherford, NJ: Fairleigh Dickinson University Press, 1982), 33; Rowland Bertoff and John M. Murrin, "Feudalism, Communalism, and the Yeoman Freeholder: The American Revolution Considered as a Social Accident," in *Essays on the American Revolution*, ed. Stephen G. Kurtz and James H. Hutson, 256–88 (Chapel Hill: University of North Carolina Press, 1973); Stefan Bielinski, *Abraham Yates, Jr. and the New Political Order in Revolutionary New York* (Albany: New York State Bicentennial Commission, 1975).

30. Quoted in Bogin, *Abraham Clark*, 35.

31. Willi Paul Adams, *The First American Constitutions: Republican Ideology and the Making of the State Constitutions in the Revolutionary Era* (Chapel Hill: University of North Carolina Press, 1980), 201.

32. Bogin, *Abraham Clark*; Ruth Bogin, "New Jersey's True Policy: The Radical Republican Vision of Abraham Clark," *William and Mary Quarterly*, 3rd ser., 35 (1978): 100–109; *The True Policy of New-Jersey, Defined* (Elizabeth Town, NJ, 1784).

33. Bogin, *Abraham Clark*; Patrick T. Conley, "Rhode Island Constitutional Issues During the Early National Period," in *Federal Rhode Island: The Age of the China Trade, 1790–1820*, Rhode Island Forum Series, vol. 2, ed. Linda L. Levin (Providence, RI: Rhode Island Historical Society, 1978), 1–4; Frank Greene Bates, *Rhode Island and the Formation of the Union*, Columbia University Studies in History, Economics, and Public Law, vol. 10, no. 2 (New York: Macmillan, 1898); Daniel P. Jones, *The Economic and Social Transformation of Rural Rhode Island, 1780–1850* (Boston: Northeastern University Press, 1992), chaps. 1 and 2.

34. "Part of Judge Pendleton's Charge to the Grand Jurors of Gagetown, Cheraw, and Camden Districts," in *American Museum*, 1:483–84. On the breadth of disorder, and the concern with taxes and debt, see Woody Holton, *Unruly Americans and the Origins of the Constitution* (New York: Hill and Wang, 2007); Jean Butenhoff Lee, "Maryland's 'Dangerous Insurrection' of 1786," *Maryland History Magazine* 85 (Winter 1990): 329–44; Nadelhaft, *Disorders of War*, 104–71. Emphasizing the extent of the crisis is Terry Bouton, "A Road Closed: Rural Insurgency in Post-Independence Pennsylvania," *Journal of American History* 87 (2000): 855–65. In Virginia, Robert Smith asked pardon from death sentence on May 16, 1782. He had taken up arms with a group to protest heavy taxes, but being advised it was not proper, he had laid down arms. *Virginia Legislative Petitions: Bibliography, Calendar, and Abstracts from*

Original Sources 6 May 1776–21 June 1782, comp. Randolph W. Church (Richmond: Virginia State Library, 1984), 477. Also on opposition to taxes, see Robert A. Becker, *Revolution, Reform, and the Politics of American Taxation, 1763–1783* (Baton Rouge: Louisiana University Press, 1980).

35. John L. Brooke, "To the Quiet of the People: Revolutionary Settlement and Civil Unrest in Western Massachusetts, 1774–1789," *William and Mary Quarterly*, 3rd ser. 46 (1989): 425–62; Richard L. Bushman, "Massachusetts Farmers and the Revolution," in *Society, Freedom, and Conscience*, ed. Richard N. Jellison, 77–124 (New York: W.W. Norton, 1976); Leonard L. Richards, *Shays's Rebellion: The American Revolution's Final Battle* (Philadelphia: University of Pennsylvania Press, 2002); Robert A. Gross, "White Hats and Hemlocks: Daniel Shays and the Legacy of the Revolution," in *The Transforming Hand of the Revolution: Reconsidering the American Revolution as a Social Movement*, ed. Ronald Hoffman and Peter J. Albert, 286–345 (Charlottesville: University Press of Virginia, 1995); Alan Taylor, "Regulators and White Indians: The Agrarian Resistance in Post-Revolutionary New England," in *In Debt to Shays: The Bicentennial of an Agrarian Rebellion*, ed. Robert A. Gross, 145–60 (Charlottesville: University Press of Virginia, 1993), on conflicts in New Hampshire, 1786, and Maine, 1808; Richard L. Bushman, *King and People in Provincial Massachusetts* (Chapel Hill: University of North Carolina Press, 1992); John L. Brooke, *The Heart of the Commonwealth: Society and Political Culture in Worcester County, Massachusetts, 1713–1861* (New York: Cambridge University Press, 1989), 192–229.

36. Matthew Seccombe, "From Revolution to Republic: The Later Political Career of Samuel Adams, 1774–1803" (Ph.D. diss., Yale University, 1978), 223.

37. A Taunton mob against a sheriff's sale is described in Seth Paddleford to Robert Treat Paine, July 21, 1783, *Robert Treat Paine Papers*, Massachusetts Historical Society, Boston. See also Committee of Correspondence of Worcester to Joseph Hawley, February 21, 1783, ibid.; Van Beck Hall, *Politics Without Parties: Massachusetts, 1780–1791* (Pittsburgh: University of Pittsburgh Press, 1972); Elisha Douglass, *Rebels and Democrats: The Struggle for Equal Political Rights and Majority Rule During the American Revolution* (Chapel Hill: University of North Carolina Press, 1995), chap. 11.

38. Richard Buel Jr., "The Public Creditor Interest in Massachusetts Politics," in Gross, *In Debt to Shays*, 47–56, offers perspective on the court's decision.

39. Michael Lienesh, "Reinterpreting Rebellion: The Influence of Shays's Rebellions on American Political Thought," in Gross, *In Debt to Shays*, 161–84, explores the strikingly different perceptions of east and west. See also William Pencak, "'The Fine Theoretic Government of Massachusetts Is Prostrated to Earth': The Response to Shays's Rebellion Reconsidered," in Gross, *In Debt to Shays*, 121–44; Ronald P. Formisano, *For the People: American Populist Movements from the Revolution to the 1850s* (Chapel Hill: University of North Carolina Press, 2008), 24–27.

40. Shepard quoted in Richards, *Shays's Rebellion*, 33.

41. Historians have traced the way that many conservative men and public newspapers represented events, not as a "regulation" of economy and the courts by aggrieved farmers, but as a misguided uprising under the leadership of a veteran of the Revolution named Daniel Shays. Some historians accept the nomenclature of "Shays's Rebellion," while others dispute the characterization of events thereby implied. Such scholarly disagreements underscore for us the deeply incompatible "ideas and allegiances" held by different eighteenth-century Americans who might all qualify, in one view or another, as republicans, Patriots, and "real friends of their country."

Robert Gross, "The Uninvited Guest," in Gross, *In Debt to Shays*, 6. On the Federalist construction of events in the late 1780s, see Stephen E. Patterson, "The Federalist Reaction to Shays's Rebellion," in Gross, *In Debt to Shays*, 101–20.

42. To James Warren, October 17, 1778, in Henry Alonzo Cushing, coll. and ed., *The Writings of Samuel Adams*, 4 vols. (New York: G.P. Putnam's Sons, 1908), 4:75–77. Also see pp. 271–74 against Tories as likely to be "a dangerous Faction" if they return. Adams's continued opposition to return of exiles is in Seccombe, "From Revolution to Republic," 198.

43. Seccombe, "From Revolution to Republic," 181.

44. William Pencak, "Samuel Adams and Shays's Rebellion," *New England Quarterly* 62 (1989): 63–74, treats the issue of Adams's stand in 1787. See also Pauline Maier, "Coming to Terms with Samuel Adams," *American Historical Review* 81 (1976): 12–37, esp. 25–28.

45. Samuel Adams to Noah Webster, April 30, 1784, quoted in Pencak, "Samuel Adams and Shays's Rebellion," 66.

46. Gregory H. Nobles underscores the degree to which western farmers acted in the mode of prewar crowds, "Shays's Neighbors: The Contexts of Rebellion in Pelham, Massachusetts," in Gross, *In Debt to Shays*, 185–204. Cf. Pencak, "Fine Theoretic Government."

47. The phrase is from the Berkshire Constitutionalists' petition from 1776; Robert J. Taylor, *Western Massachusetts in the Revolution* (Providence, RI: Brown University Press, 1954), 87; Gordon S. Wood, *The Creation of the American Republic, 1776–1787* (New York: W.W. Norton, 1969), 306–43. Adams saw a similar threat in the assemblies of the Society of Cincinnati, which "convene expressly to deliberate & adopt Measures on great and National concerns proper only for the Cognizance of" elected congressional and state officials. Seccombe, "From Revolution to Republic," 206.

48. The quoted phrase is from "Speculator," *Boston Gazette*, September 23, 1776.

49. On the earlier conventions that worried Adams, see Taylor, *Western Massachusetts*, 107–23. Lois G. Schwoerer, "Locke, Lockean Ideas, and the Glorious Revolution," *Journal of the History of Ideas* 51 (1990): 535–36, discusses the problem of conventions and their claims to speak as the people in revolutionary times. Wood, *Creation of the American Republic*, 306–43; Bouton, "Road Closed," 855–87.

50. Francis Hopkinson, quoted in Bogin, *Abraham Clark*, 44–45.

51. Samuel Adams to Noah Webster, April 30, 1784, quoted in Pencak, "Samuel Adams and Shays's Rebellion," 66.

52. *American Museum*, 1:9. Horst Dippel identifies this quotation as by Benjamin Rush in Dippel, "The Changing Idea of Popular Sovereignty in Early American Constitutionalism," *Journal of the Early Republic* 16 (1996): 36.

53. Adams to the legislature of Massachusetts, January 16, 1795, quoted in Pencak, "Samuel Adams and Shays Rebellion," 67. On the Whiskey Rebels, see Bouton, "A Road Closed," 855–87.

54. This same premise, that voting was the central moment of consent in the new dispensation, led General Benjamin Lincoln, who had commanded troops to subdue western farmers, to oppose disenfranchising the insurgents. Taylor, *Western Massachusetts*, 163–64.

55. Rev. George Micklejohn, "A Sermon to Governor Tryon and His Troops" (1768), in *Some Eighteenth-Century Tracts Concerning North Carolina*, ed. William K. Boyd (Raleigh, NC: Edwards & Broughton, 1927), 408.

56. To both Massachusetts regulators and Pennsylvanians, "authorities seemed blindly bound to laws unresponsive to local conditions." G.S. Rowe, "Outlawry in Pennsylvania, 1782–1788, and the Achievement of an Independent Judiciary," *American Journal of Legal History* 20 (1976): 227–44. Nobles, "Shays's Neighbors," emphasizes the continuity between the Regulation and prewar practices. Circular letter, *Massachusetts Centinel*, September 13, 1786. Alan Taylor, "Regulators and White Indians," 149, notes the perception that regulators in Massachusetts and New Hampshire were "opposing a government of their own establishing."

57. Bruce Ackerman, "The Storrs Lectures: Discovering the Constitution," *Yale Law Review* 93 (1983–84): 1013–72. Ackerman here is treating the counter-majoritarian nature of judicial review; pertinent to us, however, is his distinction between normal and constitutional modes of politics. From the era of the 1780s, conventions became associated with the constitutional moment, when men gather in assemblies of some plausible legal standing but seek to ratify their proposals "by a procedure that *plainly departs* from pre-existing constitutional understandings."

58. Benjamin Rush, *An Enquiry into the Effects of Public Punishments* (Philadelphia, 1787). Quotations are on pp. 6 and 7. On this change, see Louis P. Masur, *Rites of Execution: Capital Punishment and the Transformation of American Culture, 1776–1865* (New York: Oxford University Press, 1989); Michael Meranze, *Laboratories of Virtue: Punishment, Revolution, and Authority in Philadelpha 1760–1835* (Chapel Hill: University of North Carolina Press, 1996). On the English experience, see Randall McGowan, "Civilizing Punishment: The End of the Public Execution in England," *Journal of British Studies* 33 (1994): 257–82.

59. Paul A. Gilje, *The Road to Mobocracy: Popular Disorders in New York City, 1763–1834* (Chapel Hill: University of North Carolina Press, 1987); Formisano, *For the People*. See also Frank Munger, "Suppression of Popular Gatherings in England, 1800–1830," *American Journal of Legal History* 25 (1981): 111–40.

60. Morton J. Horwitz, *The Transformation of American Law, 1780–1860* (Cambridge, MA: Harvard University Press, 1977); Gary C. Jacobsohn, "Citizen Participation in Policy-Making: The Role of the Jury," *Journal of Politics* 39 (1977): 73–96. On Jefferson and Hamilton as agreeing that juries could make law, see Justice Gary's dissenting opinion in *Sparf and Hansen v. United States*, 156 U.S. 51. See also William Nelson, *The Americanization of Common Law: The Impact of Legal Change in Massachusetts Society, 1760–1830* (Cambridge, MA: Harvard University Press, 1975).

61. Most notably, perhaps, shifts in courtrooms, punishments, and crowds occurred differently in Northern and Southern states in the nineteenth century, due to the institution of African American slavery and the practices of white supremacy that followed emancipation. See Richard D. Younger, "Southern Grand Juries on Slavery," *Journal of Negro History* 40 (1955): 166–78; David Grimsted, *American Mobbing, 1828–1861: Toward Civil War* (New York: Oxford University Press, 1998). On the distinctive impact of slavery on Southern development of a police, see Dennis C. Rousey, *Policing the Southern City: New Orleans, 1805–1889* (Baton Rouge: Louisiana University Press, 1997); Christopher Waldrep, *Roots of Disorder: Race and Criminal Justice in the American South, 1817–1880* (Urbana and Chicago: University of Illinois Press, 1998).

62. Alexis de Tocqueville, *Democracy in America*, 2 vols., ed. Phillips Bradley (New York: Random House, 1945), 1:291–97, 2:378–79. The quotation is on 1:293.

63. Theodore Sedgewick, 1803, quoted in Richard E. Ellis, *The Jeffersonian Crisis: Courts and Politics in the Young Republic* (New York: W.W. Norton, 1976), 190, 191;

Rowe, "Outlawry in Pennsylvania," 227–44. On the related question of the role of lawyers in the courtroom, see Benjamin Austin, *Observations on the Pernicious Practice of the Law* (Boston, 1787). Austin asked: "Shall we be content with the humble boon of making laws, but resign the prerogative of their execution into the hands of this 'order'?" *Pernicious Practice*, no. 2 (March 23, 1786): 7.

64. Frances Kahn Zemans, "Legal Mobilization: The Neglected Role of the Law in the Political System," *American Political Science Review* 77 (1983): 690–703, notes the absence of the court system from political scientists' analyses of political participation and suggests we view individual plaintiffs who initiate cases as, in aggregate, shaping the law.

65. Allen Steinberg, *The Transformation of Criminal Justice: Philadelphia, 1800–1880* (Chapel Hill: University of North Carolina Press, 1989); Roger Lane, *Policing the City: Boston, 1822–1885* (Cambridge, MA: Harvard University Press, 1967); Gilje, *Road to Mobocracy*, 275–82. A review of the history of the development of urban police departments is Eric Monkkonen, "From Cop History to Social History: The Significance of the Police in American History," *Journal of Social History* 15 (1982): 575–91. Jon Teaford, *The Unheralded Triumph: City Government in America, 1870–1900* (Baltimore: Johns Hopkins University Press, 1984), chap. 6. At the same time, the term "police" itself would shed many of its associations with the obligation to promote not only "safety" but "happiness" of a community. Christopher L. Tomlins, *Law, Labor, and Ideology in the Early American Republic* (Cambridge: Cambridge University Press, 1993), 47–51, treats this change. See also W.G. Carson, "Policing the Periphery: The Development of Scottish Policing 1795–1900," *Australian and New Zealand Journal of Criminology* 17 (1984): 207–32.

66. On voting, see Alexander Keyssar, *The Right to Vote: The Contested History of Democracy in the United States* (New York: Basic Books, 2000). On representation, see Rosemarie Zagarri, *The Politics of Size: Representation in the United States, 1776–1850* (Ithaca, NY: Cornell University Press, 1987).

67. Jürgen Habermas, *The Structural Transformation of the Public Sphere: An Inquiry into a Category of Bourgeois Society*, trans. Thomas Burger and Frederick Lawrence (Cambridge, MA: MIT Press, 1991); Michael Warner, *The Letters of the Republic: Publication and the Public Sphere in Eighteenth-Century America* (Cambridge, MA: Harvard University Press, 1990).

68. Gross, "Uninvited Guest," 22.

69. Jennifer Nedelsky, "Confining Democratic Politics: Anti-Federalists, Federalists, and the Constitution," *Harvard Law Review* 96 (1982): 344n11, emphasizes this paragraph. See also Nedelsky, "American Constitutionalism and the Paradox of Private Property," in *Constitutionalism and Democracy*, ed. John Elster and Rune Slagstad, 241–74 (Cambridge: Cambridge University Press, 1998).

70. Joyce Appleby, "The American Heritage: The Heirs and the Disinherited," *Journal of American History* 74 (1987), esp. 804–6; Holton, *Unruly Americans*. Edmund Randolph, "If a fair representation of the people is not secured, the injustice of the Govt. shall shake to its foundation." Randolph quoted in Peter H. Argersinger, "The Value of the Vote: Political Representation in the Gilded Age," *Journal of American History* 76 (1989): 59. A.V. Dicey, *Lectures on the Relationship between Law and Public Opinion in England During the Nineteenth Century* (London: MacMillan, 1905), suggested that the degree to which law followed public opinion was limited in the United States by constitutions.

71. Nedelsky, "Confining Democratic Politics," treats the conceptual division of law and politics in the era of the Marshall Court as a means to insulate some issues from democratic politics, esp. 352–60. Mary M. Schweitzer, "State-Issued Currency and the Ratification of the U.S. Constitution," *Journal of Economic History* 49 (1989): 311–22; Steven R. Boyd, "The Contract Clause and the Evolution of American Federalism, 1789–1815," *William and Mary Quarterly*, 3rd ser., 44 (1987): 529–48; Keyssar, *Right to Vote*.

72. On the exaltation of the yeoman farmer, the individual rather than the group or the community, following the Revolution, see Bertoff and Murrin, "Feudalism," 256–88.

Index